Marketing Communication

Marketing Communication

New Approaches, Technologies, and Styles

edited by
ALLAN J. KIMMEL

OXFORD
UNIVERSITY PRESS

OXFORD
UNIVERSITY PRESS

Great Clarendon Street, Oxford OX2 6DP

Oxford University Press is a department of the University of Oxford.
It furthers the University's objective of excellence in research, scholarship,
and education by publishing worldwide in

Oxford New York

Auckland Cape Town Dar es Salaam Hong Kong Karachi
Kuala Lumpur Madrid Melbourne Mexico City Nairobi
New Delhi Shanghai Taipei Toronto

With offices in

Argentina Austria Brazil Chile Czech Republic France Greece
Guatemala Hungary Italy Japan Poland Portugal Singapore
South Korea Switzerland Thailand Turkey Ukraine Vietnam

Oxford is a registered trade mark of Oxford University Press
in the UK and in certain other countries

Published in the United States
by Oxford University Press Inc., New York

British Library Cataloguing in Publication Data

Data available

Library of Congress Cataloging in Publication Data

Data available

Typeset by SPI Publisher Services, Pondicherry, India.
Printed in Great Britain
on acid-free paper by
Biddles Ltd, King's Lynn, Norfolk

ISBN 0-19-927694-3   978-0-19-927694-3
ISBN 0-19-927695-1 (pbk.)   978-0-19-927695-0 (pbk.)

In memory of James A. Fasanelli,
who taught me how to see.

Preface

This book represents one of the first attempts to provide a comprehensive overview and analysis of the rapidly changing world of marketing communication in the twenty-first century. The fourteen chapters that comprise this volume were written by some of the leading authorities in the field, resulting in a broad tableau of perspectives reflecting the insights and experiences of academics and practitioners from both sides of the Atlantic. It goes without saying that I owe a great debt of gratitude to each of the twenty-five contributors who agreed to participate in this project and I wish to convey to them my heartfelt thanks for a job well done.

With its timely and comprehensive focus on contemporary and evolving trends in marketing communication, it is hoped that this volume will be of interest to a diverse audience of academics, students, and professionals. Primarily intended as a supplemental reader for undergraduate, graduate, and MBA courses, I trust that the focus on emerging developments in the field will also be appealing to a broad range of researchers and marketing professionals.

AJK
Paris, France

Contents

List of Figures

List of Tables

List of Abbreviations

ACORN	A Classification of Residential Neighborhoods
CEO	chief executive officer
CRM	customer relationship management
CME	computer-mediated exchange
DoJ	Department of Justice
DTV	digital television
DRTV	direct response television
ELM	Elaboration Likelihood Model
EPOS	electronic point-of-sale
ESL	electronic shelf label
ESP	emotional selling proposition
FMCG	fast-moving consumer goods
GAM	global account management
GSM	Global System for Mobile Communication
GPS	global positioning system
GSR	galvanic skin response
GPRS	General Packet Radio Service
HIPAA	Health Insurance Probability and Accountability
IIT	Information Integration Theory
IOC	International Olympic Committee
IST	information systems and technology
IMC	integrated marketing communications
KMS	knowledge management systems
LCSP	Lead Client Service Partners
LED	light-emitting diode
MMS	multimedia message service
NAB	National Association of Broadcasters
PDA	personal digital assistant
PSA	personal shopping assistant

PVR	personal video recording
RFID	radio frequency identification
SCT	Social Cognitive Theory
SFA	Sales Force Automation
SMS	short message service
USP	unique selling proposition
VOIP	voice over Internet protocol
VOD	video on demand
WAP	Wireless Application Protocol
WHO	World Health Organization
WOM	word of mouth

Notes on Contributors

Eric Arnould is E. J. Faulkner Professor of Agribusiness and Marketing and Interim Director of Agribusiness Programs in the College of Business Administration at the University of Nebraska, Lincoln. He has taught at universities in North America, Europe, Australia, and New Zealand. He received his Ph.D. in Social Anthropology from the University of Arizona in 1982, and pursued postdoctoral work in marketing there. Continuing work begun during his doctoral research, he spent more than ten years working in economic development, conducting fieldwork in more than a dozen West and East African nations for governmental and nongovernmental organizations. Since 1990, he has been a full-time academic, teaching courses in consumer behavior, international marketing, and research employing qualitative data. His research investigates consumer ritual, inalienable wealth, postmodern motivation, magical consumption, service relationships, West African marketing channels, and the uses of qualitative data. His research appears in a variety of marketing and social science periodicals and books. He served for five years as an Associate Editor of the *Journal of Consumer Research*.

Janet Borgerson is Lecturer in the University of Exeter School of Business and Economics. She received her MA and Ph.D. in Philosophy from the University of Wisconsin, Madison, and completed postdoctoral work in existential phenomenology at Brown University. She has taught philosophy and management at the University of Wisconsin, University of Rhode Island, Stockholm University, and the Royal Institute of Technology, Stockholm. Her recent research has appeared in *European Journal of Marketing, Advances in Consumer Research, Consumption Markets & Culture, Journal of Consumer Affairs, Journal of Knowledge Management, Organization Studies, Gender Work & Organization, Feminist Theory, Radical Philosophy Review*, as well as in several edited books.

Douglas Brownlie is Professor of Marketing at the University of Stirling, UK. He has published and consulted widely on marketing management topics. His current research interests include the professionalization of marketing and visual culture.

Lars Thøger Christensen (Ph.D., Odense University) is Professor of Marketing Communications at The University of Southern Denmark, Odense. Previously he was research professor at The Copenhagen Business School where he established the CBS Center for Corporate Communication. He has published five books on marketing communications, corporate communications, organizational communications, and advertising. His research is published in *Organization Studies, European Journal of Marketing, Consumption, Markets and Culture, The New Handbook of Organizational Communication, The Handbook of Public Relations, Communication Yearbook*, and elsewhere.

Terry Daugherty (Ph.D., Michigan State University) is an Assistant Professor in the Department of Advertising at the University of Texas at Austin. His research focuses on investigating consumer behavior and strategic media management, and his work has appeared in the *Journal of Advertising, Journal of Consumer Psychology, Journal of Interactive Advertising, Journal of Interactive Marketing*, and in the forthcoming books *Online Consumer Psychology: Understanding and Influencing Consumer Behavior in the Virtual World* and *Advances in Electronic Marketing*, among others. Before joining the Department of Advertising, he held a Postdoctoral Fellowship with eLab in the Owen Graduate School of Management at Vanderbilt University and has worked in advertising media.

Matthew S. Eastin (Ph.D., Michigan State University) is an Assistant Professor in the School of Communication at the Ohio State University. His research focuses on social and psychological antecedents of current Internet behavior and outcomes. He has recently started to explore how users process peripheral information in online environments, the creation of cognitive scripts through virtual environments, and the relationships among consumer attitudes, self-efficacy, and e-service adoption. His research has appeared in numerous academic journals, including *Media Psychology, Journal of Broadcasting & Electronic Media, Computers in Human Behavior, Social Science Computer Review, Telematics and Informatics*, and the *Journal of Computer-Mediated Communication*.

Martin Evans joined Cardiff Business School in 2001. Prior to that he was Professor of Marketing at Bristol Business School. He also held professorial posts at the University of Glamorgan's Business School, where he was Marketing and Purchasing Subject Group Leader and Research and

Consultancy Coordinator, and the University of Portsmouth. In industry, he worked at Hawker Siddeley and has served as a consultant to a variety of organizations for over 25 years. He has held visiting professorships at HE Institutions in Holland, Denmark and Germany and holds several external examining posts for teaching and research degrees. He has published numerous articles and his current research projects include consumer reaction to direct and interactive marketing; interactive marketing and its social responsibility; C2C, an emerging eCommerce model; and contemporary targeting of families.

Chris Fill is Principal Lecturer in Marketing and Strategic Management at the University of Portsmouth, UK. His specialist area is Marketing Communications and his book *Marketing Communications: Engagement, Strategies and Practice, 4e* has become a standard university textbook for marketing communications courses. It is also the essential text for the Marketing Communications unit on the Diploma provided by Chartered Institute of Marketing. He has published widely in a number of academic marketing journals on topics reflecting his interest in corporate identity and integrated marketing communications. He was Course Director for the Portsmouth MBA for six years before his appointment as Director of Studies for the postgraduate marketing programs. He has been an External Advisor and Examiner for a number of UK Universities and has been Senior Examiner for the Chartered Institute of Marketing since 1997.

A. Fuat Fırat is Visiting Professor of Marketing at the University of Southern Denmark, Odense. His research interests cover areas such as macro consumer behavior and macromarketing, postmodern culture, transmodern marketing strategies, gender and consumption, marketing and development, and interorganizational relations. His has won the *Journal of Macromarketing* Charles Slater Award for best article (with coauthor N. Dholakia), and the *Journal of Consumer Research* best article award (with coauthor A. Venkatesh). He is Coeditor in Chief of the journal *Consumption, Markets & Culture*. His latest book is *Consuming People: From Political Economy to Theaters of Consumption*, coauthored by N. Dholakia.

James Fitchett is Reader in Marketing at the University of Leicester, UK. His research focuses on critical readings of consumer behavior drawing on social and cultural theory. He has written on a diverse range of consumption and marketing issues including consumerism and environmentalism, and tourism consumption. Current interests involve examining emerging ethical and moral considerations in marketplace behavior, and evaluating possible futures for mature, advanced consumer cultures.

Eamonn Galvin is a Principal in CompassBlue, a niche consulting business specializing in strategic marketing and ebusiness projects. He was previously a senior executive in GE Europe where he was responsible for eBusiness in Europe and Sales and Marketing Integration Leader for GE Life. He previously worked for ten years at Accenture, where he specialized in strategy projects. He holds an MBS degree from University College, Dublin and lectures at the MBA level on eBusiness. He has co-authored several books on marketing, including *Electronic Marketing: Theory and Practice for the 21st Century*, with John O'Connor and Martin Evans. His primary area of interest is developing multichannel strategies for companies.

Tom Gruen is Associate Professor of Marketing and e-Commerce at the University of Colorado, Colorado Springs. He obtained his Ph.D. in Marketing from Indiana University in 1997. His research interests pertain to the management of customer relationships, with particular emphases on membership relationships, peer-to-peer relationships, and supplier-retailer relationships in the fast-moving consumer-goods industry. His research has been published in many journals including *Harvard Business Review, Journal of Marketing, Journal of Retailing*, and *Journal of Business Research*.

H. David Hennessey (MBA, Clark University; Ph.D., New York University) is Professor of Marketing at Babson College. After working for American Can and Interpace, he joined Babson College in 1982. He has taught courses on global marketing, marketing strategy, and sales management strategy, and has written numerous articles and case studies. He coauthored the books *Global Account Management: Creating Value* (2003), *Global Marketing Strategies*, 6th edn. (2004), and *How to Write a Marketing Plan* (1986, 1990, and 1996). He has had executive and MBA teaching experience in a wide variety of programs at Babson College, Ashridge, IMD, Erasmus RSM, and Helsinki School of Economics and Business Administration, as well as in Costa Rica, France, Holland, Germany, Hong Kong, Switzerland, Finland, and Japan. He is past president and current member of the Board of Directors of the Sales and Marketing Executives of Boston.

Allan J. Kimmel is Professor of Marketing at ESCP-EAP, European School of Management, Paris, where he serves as director of the Marketing Major—English track. He is a returning Visiting Professor of Marketing at Université Paris IX-Dauphine, Paris and TEC de Monterrey, Mexico. He received an MA and Ph.D. in social psychology from Temple University. In addition to marketing communication, his research and writing interests focus on rumors, marketing ethics, and deception in consumer research. He has published extensively on these topics, including three books on research ethics, and articles in *American Psychologist, Psychology & Marketing*,

Journal of Applied Social Psychology, The Journal of Behavioral Finance, Business Horizons, Ethics & Behavior, and *European Advances in Consumer Research,* among others. His latest book is entitled *Rumors and Rumor Control: A Manager's Guide to Understanding and Combatting Rumors* (2004).

Maurice Lévy is the Chairman & Chief Executive Officer of the Publicis Groupe, one of the world's top international advertising and communications organizations. He joined Publicis in 1971, became Chairman in 1984, and has served as Group Chairman & CEO since 1988. One of the leading figures in the industry, he has successfully managed a multiyear program of international expansion that today assures Publicis' multinational clients of the broadest range of top advertising and communications services. He holds the distinctions of Commandeur of the French Légion d'Honneur and 'Commandeur' of the Ordre National du Mérite. He is a member of the Conseil Consultatif of the Banque de France, President of the Palais de Tokyo arts center, and is member of the Board of the Musée des Arts Décoratifs in Paris.

Tina M. Lowrey (Ph.D., University of Illinois) is Professor of Marketing at the University of Texas at San Antonio. She has published articles in the *Journal of Consumer Research, Journal of Consumer Psychology,* and *Journal of Advertising.* She has contributed chapters for *New Developments and Approaches in Consumer Behavior Research, Gift Giving: A Research Anthology,* and *Gender Issues and Consumer Behavior.* Her main research interests include psycholinguistic analyses of advertising, gift-giving, and ritual. She has presented numerous papers on these topics at various marketing and consumer behavior conferences and is a member of the *Psychology & Marketing* editorial board.

John A. McCarty currently teaches in the School of Business at The College of New Jersey in Ewing, New Jersey. Before taking this position, he taught at the University of Illinois at Urbana-Champaign, American University in Washington, DC, and George Mason University in Fairfax, Virginia. In the early 1980s, he was a research associate in the Chicago office of Needham Harper Worldwide (now DDB Chicago), an advertising agency. He has published in such journals as *Public Opinion Quarterly,* the *Journal of Advertising,* the *Journal of Public Policy & Marketing, Marketing Letters,* and the *Journal of Business Research.* He holds a Ph.D. in social psychology from the University of Illinois at Urbana-Champaign.

Albert M. Muñiz, Jr. is an Associate Professor of Marketing at DePaul University. His research interests are in the sociological aspects of consumer behavior and branding, and his teaching interests include consumer behavior, consumer culture and Internet marketing. He has published in the *Journal of Consumer Research* and the *Journal of Interactive Marketing*, and has been the recipient of a *Best Article in the Journal of Consumer Research* award. He received his MS and Ph.D. from the University of Illinois, Urbana-Champaign. Before coming to DePaul, he taught at the University of California at Berkeley.

John O'Connor is Chief Executive Officer of Deep-insight, a global leader in assessing customer relationship quality. He is also a Director of HotOrigin, an early-stage investment company based in Ireland, and previously was an Associate Partner in Accenture, where he specialized in CRM and financial services. He holds an engineering degree from Trinity College, Dublin and an MBA from the London Business School. He has co-authored several books on marketing, including *Electronic Marketing: Theory and Practice for the 21st Century*, with Eamonn Galvin and Martin Evans. His primary area of interest is customer retention in large, multinational B2B companies.

Dan O'Donoghue is Head of Strategic Planning of Publicis Worldwide. He began his career in marketing communication at Rowntree Mackintosh in 1968, joined Ogilvy & Mather in 1978, and CDP in 1981. He then joined Publicis London as Planning Director, becoming Planning Director in 1989 and Joint CEO in 1990. In 2002 he developed the 'holistic difference' approach now used throughout the Publicis network. He is a Fellow of the IPA, an honorary member of the Account Planning Group (APG), and a member of the Marketing Society, the Market Research Society, the ASA Council, and D&AD. He has contributed papers to ESOMAR, the MRS, Admap, the IPA and Media & Marketing Europe. In 1997 he wrote the media chapter of 'How to Plan Advertising' for the APG.

Thomas C. O'Guinn is Professor of Advertising and Business Administration and Professor of Sociology at the University of Illinois. He has published widely on advertising, branding and the sociology of consumption. He is particularly interested in brands and how their meaning is communicated and negotiated between marketers, consumers, and other interested publics. He argues that one of the greatest challenges facing contemporary managers is the reality of a consumer newly empowered by the ongoing revolution in mediated human communication. He has served on many editorial and advisory boards. He is an award-winning teacher whose academic work has received several honors and awards, including two *Best Article in the Journal of Consumer Research* awards. He is also the coauthor of a leading advertising and promotion textbook, *Advertising and Integrated Brand Communication*, 4th edn. He has served as a consultant to companies in the USA and Europe.

Michael A. J. Saren was appointed to Leicester University Management Centre as Professor of Marketing in 2004. Before this, he was Professor of Marketing at the University of Strathclyde. He is currently working on a number of research projects including investigation into subcultural consumption, branding, and identity. His other research interests cover the areas of the strategic marketing of technology, critical marketing, consumer culture, and marketing theory. In the past he has secured research funding from both public and private sectors including the EC, ICL, ESRC and SERC. In addition, he has acted as consultant to several companies, such as Westbury Homes, Lucas, Lawson Mardon, Vickers Oceanics and Dowty Communications. He has held external examinerships at over twenty-five universities in the UK and overseas and he was also a Special Advisor to RAE Panel Unit 43 on Relationship Marketing and Consumer Theory in 2001. His work has been published in many academic management journals in the UK, Europe, and the USA, including the *International Journal of Research in Marketing, Omega, British Journal of Management*, the *Association of Consumer Research and Industrial Marketing Management.*

Jonathan Schroeder is Chair of Marketing at the University of Exeter School of Business and Economics. He is also a Visiting Professor in Marketing Semiotics at Bocconi University in Milan. His research focuses on the production and consumption of images, and has been published widely in marketing, psychology, design, and law journals. His book, *Visual Consumption*, draws from art history, photography, and visual studies to develop an interdisciplinary, image-based approach to understanding consumer behavior. He has taught at the University of California, Berkeley, the University of Rhode Island, Novgorod State University, Russia, the Summer Exploration Program at Wellesley College, the Royal Institute of Technology, Stockholm and several executive management programs.

L. J. Shrum (Ph.D., University of Illinois) is Professor of Marketing at the University of Texas at San Antonio. His research investigates the psychological processes underlying media effects, particularly the role of media information in the construction of values, attitudes, and beliefs. This work has appeared in such journals as *Journal of Consumer Research, Human Communication Research, Journal of Advertising*, and *Public Opinion Quarterly*, as well as numerous edited books. He recently edited *The Psychology of Entertainment Media: Blurring the Lines Between Entertainment and Persuasion* (2004).

George Silverman, President of Market Navigation, Inc., is a recovered and reformed psychologist. His primary interests are in the psychology of marketing, decision-making, persuasion, and, particularly, word of mouth. He is the inventor of the telephone focus group, co-inventor of the peer word-of-mouth group (widely acknowledged to be the most powerful marketing method ever developed in the pharmaceutical industry), and has successfully used word-of-mouth techniques to accelerate purchase decisions for some of the most successful products ever introduced, including the VCR, the automatic teller machine, the Trac II razor, the NordicTrack, and many successful pharmaceutical products. He is a past Treasurer and Board member of the Qualitative Research Consultants Association (QRCA), and has been Chairman of its Professionalism Committee. His book, *The Secrets of Word of Mouth Marketing: How to Trigger Exponential Sales Through Runaway Word of Mouth* was published in 2001.

Elisabeth Tissier-Desbordes (Doctorat Université Paris IX Dauphine/ HEC) is Professor of Marketing at ESCP-EAP (Paris). She worked in some advertising agencies (Havas Conseil, Grey Advertising) prior to joining ESCP-EAP. Her research focuses on investigating consumer behavior and communications, nudity in advertising, men's consumption, renting, and hypermodernity. In addition to some marketing books, her research is published in *European Advances in Consumer Behavior, ACR Gender Conferences Proceedings, Décisions Marketing, Revue Française du Marketing, Revue Française de Gestion,* and *Journal of Consumer Services and Retailing.*

Introduction: Marketing Communication in the New Millennium

Allan J. Kimmel

If there is one constant certainty in the fluid and everchanging world of business and commerce, it is that communication represents an essential and vital aspect of the marketing process. As Kotler (2003) rightly pointed out in his classic marketing textbook, modern marketing requires more than the development of a good and useful product, which is attractively priced and made accessible to its target customers (the three 'Ps' of product, price, and place). It also requires that marketers communicate information about their products and services (the fourth 'P' of promotion).

Marketing communication (or the so-called 'promotional mix' consisting of advertising, sales promotion, personal selling, public relations, and direct marketing) represents a critical mediating process that links a company's offerings to its intended consumers. In recent years, the face of marketing communication has begun to develop into something much more complex and far-reaching than ever before, giving marketers an evolving and wider range of possible communication channels and technologies for getting messages across to their public and for stimulating desired responses from their target audiences. At the same time, audiences also have begun to change, in terms of demographics, lifestyle, consumer behavior, and the like, thereby requiring significant alterations in the nature of promotional messages delivered to them and the means by which they can be reached by those messages.

Among the most important changes that have confronted marketers in recent decades, both audiences and media have become more fragmented and should continue to become more so as we progress further into the twenty-first century. The range and variety of media have rapidly expanded—whereas marketing communicators once relied primarily on the more traditional above-the-line forms of communication, such as television, radio, print, and outdoor advertising, virtually 'anything goes' in the contemporary marketing environment. The choice of methods and channels for communicating to consumer and business audiences has expanded dramatically, such that significant portions of marketing budgets are now allocated to the creation of carefully targeted direct marketing efforts, public relations campaigns, sponsorships and event management, Internet advertising, product placement, and a growing arsenal of other creative and novel methods for message transmission.

In recent years, marketing messages have appeared in a variety of non-traditional contexts, including virtual advertising aired during live televised sporting events, underground parking garage billboards and coupon distribution, digital outdoor billboards, marketing messages imprinted on the sand by beach cleaners, 'pop-up' and 'pop-under' ads that appear when consumers visit certain websites, and the placement of ad stickers on everything from banana skins and gas pump handles to temporary tattoos on fashion models and professional athletes. These techniques have been introduced to counter the growing fear that traditional forms of marketing communication are no longer working as efficiently as they once did. Competition is so strong in the contemporary marketing environment that marketers are obliged to keep experimenting with different ways and means to direct their messages to increasingly jaded consumer audiences. If anything, marketing professionals expect the search for evermore novel means of communicating their products, services, and brands to continue well into the new millennium.

Further complicating communication decision making and adding to the ongoing challenges faced by marketers is the growing fragmentation of their target audiences. During previous decades, prime-time network television advertising represented a basic means for reaching a majority of the consuming public. Today, however, media usage habits and patterns have increasingly diversified with the advent of cable television programming, satellite reception, computers, mobile telephones, and other emerging technologies. With increasing communication channels now available to audiences, the ability for marketers to reach their targets has grown more complicated. For example, it has become much more difficult to reach young people who are increasingly tuning in to the Internet, their mp3 players, portable phones, and video games as opposed to more traditional forms of ad-financed media (Pfanner 2004). Additionally, different consumer audiences are emerging that have not previously been targeted by marketers (e.g. male consumers for traditionally feminine products, such as cosmetics; gay and lesbian consumers; affluent minorities; young children). These trends are forcing marketers to shift their communication efforts from an emphasis on traditional broadcasting media (as part of a market aggregation strategy aimed at reaching as many potential audience members as possible) to a more 'narrowcasting' approach for reaching specific, carefully delineated target audiences (consistent with market segmentation strategies). As target audiences become progressively more technology savvy, marketing communicators have begun to utilize more aggressive and unconventional strategies to reach them, with a greater reliance on interactive, mobile, and personalized tactics.

These changes in the nature of marketing technologies, media, and target audiences have given rise to a variety of emerging concerns and challenges for advertisers and other marketing communicators. The fact that the methods for communicating messages continue to expand means that today's consumers are bombarded with an ever growing number of marketing stimuli. According to some estimates, the average American is exposed to at least 3,000 marketing messages daily, ranging from television, radio, and billboard ads to logos on clothing and Internet banners (Johnson 2001). The number of promotional messages on television alone has increased more than 250 percent since the mid-1960s, from 2,600 advertisements per week to more than 6,000 per week by the late 1990s (Solomon 2001). As a result, the ability for any one promotional message to break through the clutter in order to capture attention, arouse interest, and have its intended effects has become exceedingly difficult. Moreover, as the number of marketing messages to which they are exposed continues to grow, consumers' ability (and desire) to differentiate among them has diminished. Marketers are well aware that a majority of messages are screened out altogether by their intended audiences. This screening process has become much easier for consumers with the development of technologies that allow them to avoid the intrusions of unwanted promotional messages (e.g. by 'zipping' or 'zapping' through recorded messages, installing Internet pop-up blockers on their computers, and the like).

Along with the growing tendency for target audiences to simply ignore the many marketing messages that are directed their way has been a rise in skepticism regarding the veracity and purpose of the messages that they do attend to, consistent with a growing trend among consumers to be less trusting of business enterprises than in the past. For example, according to a *USA Today*/CNN/Gallup survey, nearly 50 percent of adults surveyed said that corporations can be trusted only a little or not at all to look out for the interests of their employees as opposed to only 10 percent who think that corporations can be trusted a great deal in this regard (Armour 2002). The results of a widely cited, large-scale survey of American attitudes towards advertising revealed that while 44 percent of adult respondents claimed to like advertising in general, 52 percent believed that advertisements could not be trusted and 69 percent felt that they had been misled by advertising at least some of the time (Shavitt et al. 1998). A more recent survey of American attitudes, conducted by Yankelovich Partners, a leading marketing services consultancy firm, reported that 54 percent of survey respondents said they 'avoid buying products that overwhelm them with advertising and marketing', 60 percent said their opinion of advertising 'is much more negative than just a few years ago,' and 65 percent said they believed that they are 'constantly bombarded with too much' advertising (Greenspan 2004). As an indication of the extent to which many consumers now hold marketing efforts in disregard, another 33 percent of the Yankelovich survey participants said they would be 'willing to have a slightly lower standard of living to live in a society without marketing and advertising.' Similar findings regarding attitudes toward advertising have been reported among European consumers (e.g. Feick and Gierl 1996).

The rising levels of consumer distrust no doubt can be attributed to a variety of forces, including the prevalence of major scandals involving previously reputable companies (such as Enron, Worldcom, and Arthur Anderson) that have received extensive media coverage and have had widespread negative consequences for investors and employees; disapproval of multinational corporations and their aggressive marketing tactics; the prevalence of business scams, swindles, and unethical marketing practices; and the growing presence of large, anonymous companies (cf. Aditya 2001; Dery 1999; Klein 1999; Langenderfer and Shimp 2001; Schlosser 2001). In this context of growing consumer skepticism and the central role of image, greater attention has been directed to the ethical implications of marketing communications. This promises to continue as a major trend in the business environment during coming decades.

These developments have moved marketing communicators to create messages and develop campaigns that enhance the overall marketing objective of creating trusting relationships with target audiences. Emotional messages consistent with the so-called 'soft-sell approach,' oriented to the building of brand image, have increasingly taken the place of 'harder-sell' messages that provide objective reasons why the consumer should make a purchase. Further, marketers have begun to actively elicit the assistance of consumers themselves in the dissemination of positive word of mouth communications about products, services, and brands. Procter & Gamble (P&G), for example, utilized a *seeding* approach during the launching of its phenomenally successful teeth-whitening product, Whitestrips, turning early adopters into product evangelists by paying them for every positive referral they made to others within their social networks. According to P&G executives, the seeding method is just one example of the kind of one-to-one approach experts see as the holy grail of twenty-first century marketing communication ('P&G's Web Marketing' 2001). Taking this approach even further, BzzAgent, a Boston-based marketing agency, recruits consumer 'agents' who volunteer to participate in a buzz campaign for a client company. Once a company signs on, BzzAgent searches its database for agents who match the profile of target customers. Volunteers receive a sample product and a training manual describing buzz-creating strategies, which include talking about the product to friends, conversing with salespeople at retail outlets, and e-mailing influential people on the product's behalf. Similar developments are likely to continue in the future whereby consumer targets become active participants in the design and implementation of marketing communication efforts.

Overview and Objectives of the Book

The challenges that face marketing communicators have grown in complexity and promise to become even more formidable in coming decades, making this an exciting time to be involved in the marketing communication enterprise. However, if there is one certainty in predicting the future of marketing communication, as several of the contributors to this volume have adroitly pointed out, it is its unpredictability. Nonetheless, it *is* possible to provide a comprehensive and indepth panorama of the new and emerging trends in marketing communication, and that in a nutshell is what this book intends to do. This is accomplished with the viewpoints and specialized knowledge of several of the most prominent contemporary marketing experts from the USA and Europe, who draw on their own research and practical experience to provide an up-to-date perspective on the current and future states of the key areas of marketing communication.

This book covers a wide spectrum of topics related to new and emerging developments in marketing, with a specific focus placed on marketing communication activities. Current developments are placed in the context of what has come before, illustrating how contemporary approaches to marketing communication represent a natural outgrowth of technological advances, societal and business trends, and customer expectations and demands. Although there is little consensus about what the long-term future will bring in terms of marketing communication, it is clear that this integral area of marketing currently is in a state of flux and will continue to undergo significant changes in coming decades. Chapter contributors elucidate some of the key trends by focusing on developments in the marketing environment, changes in consumer behavior patterns, developments in media technology and the communications industry, and the changing face of the marketing function. Consistent with the evolving developments within the domain of marketing communication, the volume is divided into three major parts:

Part I. New Approaches to Marketing Communication
Part II. Developments in Marketing Communication Technologies
Part III. Rethinking Marketing Communication Styles

REFERENCES

Aditya, R. N. (2001). 'The Psychology of Deception in Marketing: A Conceptual Framework for Research and Practice', *Psychology & Marketing*, 18, 735–61.

Armour, S. (2002, February 5). *Year Brings Hard Lessons, Alters Priorities for Many.* Available: www.USAToday.com

Dery, M. (1999). *The Pyrotechnic Insanitarium: American Culture on the Brink.* New York: Grove.

Feick, L. and Gierl, H. (1996). 'Skepticism about Advertising: A Comparison of East and West German Consumers', *International Journal of Research in Marketing*, 13, 227–35.

Greenspan, R. (2004, April 23). *Consumers Becoming Marketing-resistant.* Available: www.clickz.com

Johnson, G. (2001, July 25). 'This Summer, It's Fast Pitch Everywhere'. *The International Herald Tribune*, p. 9.

Klein, N. (1999). *No Logo: Taking Aim at the Brand Bullies.* New York: Picador.

Kotler, P. (2003). *Marketing Management*, 11th edn. Upper Saddle River, NJ: Prentice-Hall.

Langenderfer, J. and Shimp, T. A. (2001). 'Consumer Vulnerability to Scams, Swindles, and Fraud: A New Theory of Visceral Influences on Persuasion', *Psychology & Marketing*, 18, 763–83.

P&G's Web Marketing Strategy Shows Its Bite. (2001, January 21). *Business Courier.* Available: www.cincinnati.bizjournals.com

Pfanner, E. (2004). On Advertising: On Sex, Life and, oh Yes, Swimsuits. *The International Herald Tribune*, (October 18) 9.

Schlosser, E. (2001). *Fast Food Nation.* Boston, MA: Houghton-Mifflin.

Shavitt, S., Lowrey, P., and Haefner, J. (1998). 'Public Attitudes Toward Advertising: More Favorable Than You Might Think', *Journal of Advertising Research*, 38, 7–22.

Solomon, M. R. (2001). *Consumer Behavior: Buying, Having, and Being*, 5th edn. Englewood Cliffs, NJ: Prentice-Hall.

I

....

NEW APPROACHES TO
MARKETING COMMUNICATION

'We live in interesting times.' – Maurice Lévy and Dan O'Donoghue probably could not have begun their essay, the first
chapter in our survey of new approaches to marketing communication, with a more appropriate quotation. To a large extent,
the veracity of that simple, much overused statement is what
perhaps has provided the greatest impetus for the development
of this volume. For most marketing communicators, it is clear
that the world in which they analyze (as academics) and ply
their trade (as practitioners) is changing at a pace that has never
before been witnessed, and that it no longer is possible for
marketers to maintain the status quo. Nonetheless, the fact
that these are interesting times can be a curse for marketers
who choose to persist with the tried and true, or an opportunity
for those who are quick to understand the necessity to adapt
their strategies and tactics and know-how to take the necessary
steps to succeed within the business world order of the twenty-
first century.

In order to respond most effectively and efficiently to a changing world, marketers must have a clear understanding and
accurate picture of the directions those changes are taking.
Such a picture cannot emerge without a consideration of
the evolving nature of businesses and consumers. With that
point in mind, the five chapters that comprise this first section
of the book are intended to do just that: to describe some
new approaches to marketing communication from the perspective of the contemporary and emerging business and social
environments.

In Chapter 1, Lévy and O'Donoghue discuss how in a rapidly changing world, all of the 'givens' in business and marketing have been virtually turned upside down, where consumers must now be thought of no longer as mere 'consumers' in a literal sense, but first and foremost as 'customers' with everchanging needs. This shift from consumer to customer has become more salient as consumers in industrialized nations have gained a stronger foothold in the marketplace. No longer the passive recipients of marketing messages, consumer targets have become more demanding, more jaded, and progressively more difficult to interest or incite to action. In fact, as the marketplace continues to evolve, Lévy and O'Donoghue argue that consumers/customers in many cases may be uncertain as to their needs. In order to cope with these emerging realities of the consumer marketplace, the authors argue for a *holistic approach* to communication that recognizes the full complexity of the consumer's relationship to the brand and marketers' relationship with the consumers they are selling to. According to Lévy and O'Donoghue, this approach will necessitate fundamental changes in the role of the advertising agency and in the nature of the advertising practitioner's responsibilities.

In Chapter 2, Eastin and Daugherty trace the developments in communication research over a seventy-year span that influenced and underlie our current theoretical understanding of how marketing communications work or do not work. They explain how the dominant mass communication approaches utilized by contemporary marketing communicators have been influenced and shaped by such research frameworks as the stimulus-response model, the uses and gratification paradigm, diffusion of innovation theory, and social cognitive theory. By placing current and emerging marketing communication practices within the context of historical developments in communication research, the authors provide a framework for a clearer understanding of the implications of ongoing trends in media consumption and technical advances in message delivery, thereby setting the stage for much of the discussion that follows in ensuing chapters.

Despite our growing appreciation of the impact of marketplace developments on consumer behavior, it is important to recognize that such insight does not guarantee greater acumen in our attempts to foretell the future. In Chapter 3, Fitchett argues that caution must be exercised in attempts to forecast the future even in the short term, while wearing the blinders of the present. Instead, he suggests that a credible imagining of future consumer societies can only emerge when we approach the future 'as a continuation of prior social trends and cultural dynamics.' That is, it is not enough to focus solely on potential technological advances in the communications industry and their likely impact on consumers, especially without considering the broad cultural and social developments that are likely to shape the needs and behaviors of future consumer markets. Nonetheless, in what he describes as a 'creative exercise,' Fitchett offers a fascinating glimpse at a future that is closer than we might have imagined.

In Chapter 4, Muñiz and O'Guinn further remind us that not all marketing communication is generated by or under the direct control of marketers. In their detailed analysis of brand communities—that is, loosely defined, nongeographically determined collectives of consumers who share deep commitments to particular brands—the authors provide insight into a fundamental force by which formal marketing communication campaigns can be boosted or undermined by the very persons they are intended to influence. According to Muñiz and O'Guinn, the power of such consumer communities to influence the efficacy of marketing campaigns has grown, and will continue to do so, with the emergence of the Internet and other technological advances that facilitate the development of cohesive social networks and the means by which individual members can communicate with one another. This emerging reality thus provides a challenge for marketing communicators who must tread a fine line in their attempts to find effective means for managing brand communities, without alienating their increasingly knowledgeable and wary targets. Some companies clearly are ahead of the curve on that score, in the sense of viewing brand community members as potential assets rather than threats, and by working with devoted brand users in mutual efforts to socially construct brands to the benefit of all concerned.

In Chapter 5, Hennessey surveys the developments and implications for marketing communicators of a dramatically expanded playing field. In his examination of the emerging global marketplace, he discusses ongoing trends in both consumer marketing and business-to-business (corporate and industrial) marketing in order to highlight the growing challenges facing marketers who are engaged in multicountry marketing efforts. Rather than offering a set of common guidelines for developing cross-national marketing communications, Hennessey suggests that companies must tailor their future campaigns to the specific demands of the situation through the appropriate integration of marketing communication tools, channels, and content, which can only be determined with an extensive understanding of varying cultural attitudes and behaviors.

1

New Trends in the Promotion of Companies and Brands to Stakeholders: A Holistic Approach

Maurice Lévy and Dan O'Donoghue

In the words of the Chinese curse, 'we live in interesting times.'

A consideration of what medical science is telling us reveals some startling possibilities. We are experiencing a world where the advances being made in genetics and in biotechnology are changing our perceptions of what is possible in life itself. The normal idea that most of us have lived with is that we are born, we grow up, we go to work, we have children, we retire, and then at some point, sadly we pass away. But now immortality is being dangled in front of us. Cloning of animals, even if it seems a bit unlikely, is making us think about new possibilities. The repairing of our bodies from diseases we previously could not cope with seems nearly attainable. Through cosmetic surgery we can transform our image or simply erase the effects of time. We are all not so sure about certainties anymore. Even retirement is drifting away. And before retirement it could be that we become the new 'teenagers' at fifty-five. The idea of teenagers invented after World War II is now old-fashioned. We now have a group of not quite workers, not quite retired—but, in the rich countries of the Western world, with money and influence. It is all a bit uncertain.

Then there is the vast discrepancy between the rich and the poor in the world. It is more difficult to grasp than ever before, because we now can see it in real time through the advances in technology and the development of the Internet. In some areas of the world people have everything they need, while elsewhere the provision of electricity or safe water represents a great advance. Why do people still have to suffer from droughts and floods in an age where we can photograph the surface of Mars to detect water? We are living in a divided world of rich and poor. If in most underdeveloped countries there are not enough resources to feed the people, the situation in the developed world is one of excessive supply.

RECENT DEVELOPMENTS IN MARKETING COMMUNICATION

The emergence of both enormous technological advances and excessive supply make the prediction of what will happen in the next few years to business in general and the communications business in particular both very easy and very difficult. Very easy because we know that things will *have* to adapt to the new opportunities and the fact that the customer is king. Very difficult because the things we have grown used to trusting appear to be changing so fast that we cannot understand them anymore, and the approaches that we thought were acceptable to consumers are now not so welcome.

Let us first consider the things people trust. There are two sorts of trust that people acquire: personal trust and abstract trust. *Personal trust* is where we trust someone or something because we 'know' it or them through experience. *Abstract trust* is where we place our trust in something because we intuitively recognize it. Abstract trust can be argued to be the basis of all development of commerce, given that one of the most widely known abstract symbols is money. Indeed, the spur to the original development of communication companies was the development of symbols of abstract trust that have become known as brands, rather than to be just media buyers. People trusted the brand and bought the product. That early period in the development of advertising in the middle of the nineteenth century was an era of invention during which the development of new communications methods, like the telegraph or radio, spread news at a much faster rate than people were used to. Since that era, we have developed sophisticated, multilayered, extended, and personalized brand communications. But we still have the same notion of creating symbols of trust at the heart of our job. Indeed, we recently worked to help in the creation of possibly the greatest new symbol of abstract trust in decades—the Euro. This project involved the creation of both local communication and multinational communication. The local work was intended to reassure people about the change from what they had known and trusted, whereas the objective of the multinational communication was to announce the new symbol of trust. In one sense, the Euro epitomizes the changing landscape of how people trust their abstract symbols and what needs these symbols or brands serve. The Euro is a physical expression of the European Union, which still has to gain the trust of some countries even in that community.

For those countries the issue is now slightly different in that the Euro exists and is a tangible entity, so some of the concerns about viability or ease of use have lessened as other worries have begun to take precedence. Thus, to some extent, the 'product' issues have diminished relative to the 'brand' issues of what the Euro stands for.

Much has changed in the way we communicate about brands. The development of the Internet and the World Wide Web has changed the needs of business, the approach to business, and the speed of business. To date, business has operated as if competitors were like runners in an Olympic Games race. Everyone had an equal chance, everyone did it their way, and usually the best performer won. So each company has tried to maximize its chances of winning in its own way, to suit its own culture. But the Internet has so speeded up the transmission of information around the world that as soon as a new approach to products, packaging, promotion, or communication appears, it can be copied by competitors and launched under their own brand elsewhere. The Internet and e-mail have made reaction times hundreds, if not thousands, of times faster. The competitive picture is now more akin to a boxing match. The competition is not only trying to win, but also is trying to ensure that you lose. It's the difference between local amateurs and the major leagues.

In most developed countries, consumers find themselves living in a world of oversupply. The business world has moved from a supply-and-demand economy, to a demand-and-supply economy. As Kash explained in his 2002 book *The New Law of Demand and Supply*, the emerging demand economy is increasingly complex, with an ever-increasing number of competitors who are coming at you in all shapes, sizes, and prices. So the first priority most business people have nowadays is the necessity to ensure that one's business is consumer focused. But the very words 'consumer focused' betray the problem for business. A 'consumer' is not merely a consumer any more. Being *customer-focused* or *consumer-friendly* is the fundamental challenge. That is, the key for most companies today is to treat those persons they previously considered as 'consumers' as real 'customers' instead, and to try to understand the *lives* of the people who consume their products—not doing more of what everyone in marketing has been doing for the past fifty years, which is focusing on targets and trying to persuade them to buy (Underhill 2000; Zaltman 2003).

This is a fundamental shift in the nature of business thinking. The main difference in being successful in the modern age is not to market products, but to sell experiences to customers. The modern marketplace is changing into something more akin to a fair, where people go to have fun and to be entertained by visiting their favorite stalls and by playing the games that they love. In a similar way, contemporary consumers want brands that are sympathetic to them, that lift their spirits, that promise (and deliver) a good time. For that is what consumers want more than ever—not products that simply fill a need state but those that make them happy to be in that need state. In the Western world people are concentrating more than ever on what works for them individually. People's relationships are being pressured by the need to be an individual as well as part of a family or a community. It is a revolution of what is possible. In any sort of revolution, forecasting is a dangerous business and developments often occur without warning. But some changes that are already with us are clearly fundamental.

One apparent certainty is that the mobile phone has become the dominant feature of how the world is being recreated. Text messaging is the fastest growing communication medium we have ever seen. In 1980, a phone conversation carried about one 'page' of information per minute by copper wire. Today a strand of optical fiber as thin as a human hair can transmit 90,000 volumes of an encyclopedia in one second. It is doubtful that we yet really appreciate what this ultimately will lead to. Indeed, the Internet is a fascinating medium but the mobile phone allows *you* to be the center of *your* universe. The convergence of phones, computers, cameras, television, and radio suggests that we are headed evermore quickly to an individualistic and increasingly nomadic world, where you can carry your world around with you, anywhere.

This technological convergence is creating a crisis in the way most of us view the world. Nearly all our societal values and traditions have their origins during the last revolution in the nineteenth century when modern industry was invented; however, the present notion of the family, the workweek, gender roles, religious attitudes, respect for authority, and loyalty to brands are all being put in a new light. Attempts to make sense of this new world are difficult because all the tried and tested models are being partially overturned. Although these models persist, they no longer sufficiently explain everything. In some ways this creates the most trouble. Should we trust our doctor or the Internet? Should we trust the head of state or the media?

So it appears that we are more and more unhappy, despite being better off both economically and technologically. Our emotions are constantly being put into an insecurity mode and we are constantly searching for personal improvement. Whether it be our mental or physical condition— everything is up for improvement. This is where brands can help and need to develop their offers.

Our needs for status, recognition, and emotional bonding are going unfulfilled in what postmodernists call 'a meltdown of society.' We have more information than ever before, but it makes us feel less secure. We are allowed to be more individualistic, but we belong less, which makes us lonely. The roles of the sexes have changed, but societies' traditions refuse to move as quickly and we are dazed and confused, with questions about whether to marry, to have children, to have cosmetic surgery, and so on.

Work seems to be taking up more and more of our time. Leisure is being consumed but is no longer being created. We do not feel fit for any purpose. The consumer is now an unhappy customer.

In her book *No Logo: Taking Aim At The Brand Bullies* Klein (2000) painted a convincing picture of why *brands are bad* and why *global brands are particularly bad*. Companies have become so intoxicated with brands and branding that they are no longer producers of *things* that are then branded, but simply brand companies that subcontract the messy production issues to the world at large—usually the Third World where costs are low. Brands are 'above' the production process and are the new symbols of abstract trust that, according to Klein, are becoming ever more influential. In her view, the young are becoming impatient with brands that seem to betray their trust in situations *they* see as unethical, even if companies do not. We can see all around us the growing demands that companies, or indeed industries like farming, should start behaving with more social and ethical responsibility. As companies seek a global scale, the social and ethical pressure on brands will grow (Drillech 1999). In some of the recent world conflicts, brands have even been targeted as a way to ultimately pressure governments. Pressure from the 2003 campaign by the Indian-based People's Health Movement to boycott brands like Pepsi, Coca-Cola, and Gillette was ultimately aimed at influencing American government policy on the Mideast. Because e-mail and the Internet facilitate a fast, global, cross-border information flow, Internet communities are being set up to monitor the activity of companies and to immediately inform opinion worldwide.

This same force—speed of information flow—is also creating an internal pressure within companies. Activities that are conducted in distant locales are now available in the head office overnight. Anomalies and mistakes are much easier to recognize and to correct. Companies are able to move best practice around more and more quickly and to improve their techniques by borrowing from other cultures (provided it is translated into English!). The main effect of both ethical pressure and internal speed of information flow is to raise corporate standards.

A NEW GLOBAL BRAND MARKETING APPROACH

The developments described above have moved companies to begin to think about global brand marketing from the point of view of starting from the similarities of consumers in different countries, rather than the cultural differences. Thus, the starting point for global brand thinking is to find segments across markets that are similar, and to try to 'own' those segments by delivering benefits to customers relevant to the segment and communicating to the segment in such a way as to lock out any competition. Business can no longer contemplate the old model of maximizing each product market; it has to consider maximizing the *brand as experienced* across markets. In order to do this, it has to have the company internally understand what the brand delivers as a total experience and why the chosen segment values this and, therefore, trusts the brand to deliver. Of course, companies are going to want to trade in the most profitable segments, so the race is on as to how best to define segments so that communications can effectively reach the most profitable ones. So the first trend of consequence for the promotion of brands is segmenting the market so as to use the segmentation to influence brand strategy and communication.

In the advertising profession, we are used to the notion of targeting demographic segments based on age, sex, and sociodemographics, but increasingly brands are defining attitude-driven segments, behavior-driven segments, and need-stage-driven segments. Whereas the use of demographic segmentation was easy to comprehend and implement, it has been unsuccessful in bringing sense to international brands. Segmenting by attitude, behavior, or need state enables a company to identify why certain brands are strong in some markets and weak in others. This also provides a way of explaining why and how local cultural influences affect brand share. The new marketing is about identifying the key demand segments, owning the segment, and winning back pricing power for the brand, because customers are willing to pay for something created specifically for them.

Once its segment is discovered the brand has to provide the benefits and communicate with the consumer in a way that keeps the brand constantly in the consumer's mind. But as many commentators have noted (e.g. Gladwell 2000; Levine et al. 2000; Morgan 1999) targeting the consumer will not get you anywhere anymore because the consumer has turned into a customer, and customers are more assertive of their own importance than consumers. At a simple level, simply calling your buyers 'customers,' rather than 'consumers,' implies that they have more standing in your eyes. This is a subtle but important change. Consumers are now in charge and companies will have to treat them with respect to gain their attention.

Rather like their clients, the approach taken by most advertising agencies to develop communication has to date been colored by an emphasis on supply rather than demand. In the contemporary marketing communication environment, agencies must supply the unexpected and they must supply surprise to their audiences. The main question the agency has to answer is, 'how can the creative work we supply get noticed?' The agency must affect potential customers so much that they will notice that the goods a client supplies are better than those offered by the competition.

Advertising professionals have traditionally concentrated on impact to gain better return on their investments. But nowadays customers increasingly remain resolutely unshaken, because they have too many things to mentally process. In an era where last week's impossibility becomes this week's mundane news, people are not sitting out there waiting for a 30-second television commercial, especially when that commercial tries to gain their attention in increasingly bizarre and surreal ways unrelated to anything having to do with the brand. Several recent studies have shown that the way people remember things differs depending on whether their brain is in active or passive mode, whether their emotions are aroused, and whether the brand message has any relevance for them (Carter 1998; Franzen and Bowman 2001; Heath 2001). In a demand-side model the key to owning the segment is to ensure that the brand message relevant to the segment *is the brief for all communications for the brand.* The 'brief' is a summary of the intended direction for brand communication; that is, the summary of how the advertiser views the competitive position that the brand should adopt with its customers. A demand-side model requires that we move *back* a stage in briefing so that the advertisement has the same brief as the package design and the sales promoter has the same brief as the customer relationship management (CRM) technician. The present 'supply' mentality means we brief each element as if to convert passive consumers. Each element of the communication is getting lost in its own special techniques and in things it can do particularly well—but without an overall *gestalt* for the customer.

As an alternative to the current approach, we propose a demand-side communication model that emphasizes what might be termed 'amazing relevance.' For this model, the starting point is the customer demand segment, with a consideration of the following sorts of questions:

- What does the customer seek from this brand?
- How do customers purchase the product?
- Why do they choose this brand and not a competitor's?
- What is their attitude to the sector?
- What is their need state?

Once defined, the brand relevance then forms the core of the brief. The next issue is how to connect this message with the customer at a point and time when the customer is likely to respond positively.

The communication job is not to dazzle or astonish one's customers, but to make one's brands amazingly relevant to them. Rather than someone we *test* our supply on, the customer must be thought of as being at the heart of the development process, the brand, and the communication strategy. Testing supply has its place, but it is increasingly a small place compared to connecting in the right place (Gordon 1999). This approach demands that we know *where* to talk to them before we decide *what* to say

to them. The important questions pertain to how, why, and when customers interact with the media in a particular sector, through which
channels, and which specific media. In short, the job is to *understand*,
not to *target*.

A demand-side model implies that it first is necessary to determine how
the customer interacts with the brand and the brand's communication
before the communication company supplies anything. The changes that
are occurring in the media and in how people use media mean that we
have to understand how to compete for customers' attention before we
define how to say what we want to say. In essence, this is a *holistic*
approach to communication—'holistic' because the process starts with
the relationship that a consumer has with all the many faces of a brand
and all the connections a brand can make with a customer, and builds on
that. This approach can also be considered holistic because it accepts the
different ways that media work and that the way one develops, for example, a press advertisement should be different from a TV advertisement—but all true to the brand segment relevance.

We will often need to use many different media channels to achieve a
good connection between the brand's message and the customer. Sometimes the traditional media work best, whereas at other times we have to
search for the nontraditional approach and build coherence across a
number of media channels. With a holistic approach, we look for media
solutions from the point of view of how the consumer uses media—not
which medium suits our supply; and this does not necessarily mean
classical media; it could just as well be a 30-second TV spot as a direct
marketing campaign, an in-store promotion, or a balloon on a beach.
Increasingly, we look to data on effectiveness to get clues about what
works, but we also can do connection studies to see how consumers say
they notice brands in the media that consumers themselves define as
important to the segment. This approach gives us a base for localism,
surely, but surprisingly can be equally compatible with globalization if
marketers are willing to be less monotheistic.

Historically, advertisers have tried to deliver communication to suit a
'supply-side' mentality. For example, an advertisement might be developed
that is then tested across four markets. We have taken a central supply and,
because we have involved the consumer in the decision, we felt justified.
Increasingly, pretesting will be standardized not because of a fear of failure
but to enable good ideas to be identified so they can be passed on to other
markets to be localized. We have always been unsure whether money saved
on producing one ad for everywhere was as effective as one idea for
everywhere made locally.

Our contention is that, increasingly, international brand communication
will be locally produced, but to a globally or regionally recognized demand
that is registered strongly in particular segments. This is just as important

for new brands as it is for existing brands. If this means the size of the demand varies between markets, so be it. It will mean that our media choices will be driven by local issues, but that our communication content will be driven by a clear and centralized brand thinking. When one market creates *amazingly relevant* communication then other markets will want to follow that lead because they will use the creative thinking and not be beholden to advertising technologies.

In our view, considerations related to culture are central to understanding why we are seeing so many problems with the notion of globalization. Culture is a difficult concept to be specific about, and we all have different cultural influences. It is a 'catch-all' word for a basket of influences. But whatever one's definition, it is easy to see that cultures are changing and developing. People have very few things to attach themselves to, and culture is undoubtedly what gives them roots.

We now can see the classic cultural unit of the country fragmenting into regions. Asturias, Brittany, Wales and Ireland share a Celtic melancholy and a Celtic dynamism. Countries also are becoming smaller and more numerous. Since 1990, twenty-five new countries have emerged. The latest, East Timor, has a smaller Gross Domestic Product (GDP) than the turnover of many companies. Yet we still value the culture that a country produces. Equally, clients are gaining in influence on the world scene in terms of the size of their franchise. Wal-Mart is now the biggest company in the world, slightly bigger in turnover than Turkey is in GDP.

What many people seem to be afraid of is that large global companies are going to be 'too strong' and threaten to squash localism. But is this necessary or even true? Understanding and fitting with local aspirations and culture do not seem to us to be at odds with globalization—if you are starting with the customers. Understanding *holistically* the customers' needs, wants, and connections to their media are the real concerns.

Our own professional experience has revealed that more and different cultures can help you to better understand your own culture. What we are really seeing is a whole new era in business thinking about brands and consumers and a gradual realization that there are people in all cultures who have strong similarities as people, and that brands, in a way, have to become inner-directed to people rather than outer-directed from companies.

It is progressively easier to see that strategy and the global concept of a brand are directed by the will of the company. But once a demand has been identified for a brand, the communication of that brand has to be directed by the reaction and relation to the customer locally. A brand will have entirely succeeded when consumers 'own' it in their minds. This is something most advertising professionals know instinctively. This is why consumers can recall commercial jingles from twenty years ago and sometimes for brands that have long since met their demise. A character-istic of this idea is that the old separations between theme and scheme, and between above- and below-the-line communication, are breaking down (see Chapter 8).

It may seem like heresy to suggest that a TV ad is the same as a website or that an outdoor poster is the equivalent of a direct mailing. The point is not that these vastly different craft skills can be done by anyone or that they affect people in the same way. The issue is that they all now must have the highest standards of creativity, because we cannot risk being dislodged from the consumer's mind by inconsistency, incoherence, or just by being second-rate. True creativity is when we have identified the segment, de-fined the brand relevance and, through understanding how the media channel works, provided communication whose relevance is so amazing that customers are strongly attracted to it and feel that they own it.

CONCLUDING REMARKS: FUTURE CHALLENGES

We stand on the threshold of a truly exciting time for the communication business but we need to face up to the challenges with a clear focus on what the demand is from the client's customers and not just what we can sell to clients. This holistic approach will then truly be greater than the sum of the communication parts.

What then does a holistic approach mean for the agency management and staff? First, the role and responsibilities of an agency chief executive officer (CEO) is quite radically changed. The role is no longer the manager of one creative resource but the manager of several different types of creative resource. Such a person needs to take a much wider view of what elements of a client's business he or she can contribute to. Crucially for our business, a holistic approach is a premium communication prod-uct because it considers all elements of a brand's connection with the consumer.

Second, the CEO also needs to take a much more proactive view on human resource management for the client service part of the agency as it exists today. The major impact of a holistic approach on the everyday activities of those working within the agency is on the client service and strategic planning resources, which require the learning of a completely new set of skills.

Because the role for strategic planning is becoming media channel focused and driven by effectiveness results for the brand on an increasingly shorter time scale, the agency's client service will be required to function as communication managers for clients across a much wider scope of com-munication deliverables and with a need to contribute to brand issues and business objectives. The CEO has to create a more client team-centric approach and less of a hierarchical and departmentally-focused management style.

A third key challenge is to cope with the need to play a role in ensuring that the increasingly international approach that client-centered brand management is following is compatible with a locally produced holistic communication program. With this in mind, the CEO locally has to be very active in ensuring that his or her team is cognizant with, and inspired by, the brand ambition of client headquarters. This is a more international 'animal' in agency management than the industry has hitherto been used to. It puts a particular onus on current center of creative excellence to be aware of the wider world and the increasing levels of sophistication and ambition that all the new technology is bringing. Just as an African team will one day win the soccer World Cup, how long before Croatia triumphs at Cannes?

Finally, a holistic approach demands that the manager of the agency of the future must take a very positive approach to financial transparency with the client. We live in a world consumed with 'reality,' and the financial reality behind holistic marketing is that one is offering a better communication product and requires higher resource levels to achieve it. The more astute clients have already seen this in many ways as they develop long-term relationships with agencies and are willing to pay more to get better results. The reality is that marketing communication professionals and their clients cannot afford to do anything less if they want to remain competitive and to prosper.

REFERENCES

Carter, R. (1998). *Mapping the Mind.* London: Weidenfeld & Nicolson.

Drillech, M. (1999). *Le boycott: Le cauchemar des enterprises . . . et des politiques.* Paris: Les Presses du Management.

Franzen, G. and Bouwman, M. (2001). *The Mental World of Brands: Mind, Memory and Brand Success.* Henley-on-Thames, UK: World Advertising Research Centre.

Gladwell, M. (2000). *The Tipping Point: How Little Things Can Make a Big Difference.* London: Little, Brown.

Gordon, W. (1999). *Good Thinking: A Guide to Qualitative Research.* Henley-on-Thames, UK: Admap Publications.

Heath, R. (2001). *The Hidden Power of Advertising: How Low Involvement Processing Influences the Way We Choose Brands.* Henley-on-Thames, UK: Admap Publications.

Kash, R. (2002). *The New Law of Demand and Supply: The Revolutionary New Demand Strategy for Faster Growth and Higher Profits.* New York: Random House.

Klein, N. (2000). *No Logo: Taking Aim at the Brand Bullies.* New York: Picador.

Levine, R., Locke, C., Searls, D., and Weinberger, D. (2000). *The Cluetrain Manifesto: The End of Business as Usual.* New York: Perseus Publishing.

Morgan, A. (1999). *Eating the Big Fish: How Challenger Brands Can Compete Against Brand Leaders.* New York: Wiley.

Underhill, P. (2000). *How We Buy: The Science of Shopping.* New York: Simon & Schuster.

Zaltman, G. (2003). *How Customers Think: Essential Insights into the Mind of the Market.* Boston, MA: Harvard Business School Press.

2

Past, Current, and Future Trends in Mass Communication Research

Matthew S. Eastin and Terry Daugherty

The construct of mass communication bridges many different disciplines. For example, advertising, journalism, broadcasting, and communication all function as components to mass communication. The current chapter outlines three key research frameworks that have influenced the dominant approaches being used today, discusses current trends and key research, and speculates about research directions yet to come. In doing so, this chapter focuses on how audience perception of media consumption has changed and the changes that marketing professionals have faced over the past fifty years. For example, the transformation of mass media, technological advancements in message delivery, and power shifts from the marketer to the media user have all made the art of marketing within the framework of mass media more complex in the contemporary media environment.

THE FOUNDATION OF MASS COMMUNICATION RESEARCH

Dating back to the 1920s, print, broadcast, and film were established media that had begun to work their way into our social system. However, while people were using newspapers on a daily basis and movie theater attendance was booming, little systematic empirical research was being conducted on media or the effects of consumption. Now, armed with new statistical advancements and methodologies, many researchers began to explore the effects of mass media. Of the research conducted at that time, the Payne Fund studies, which were designed to examine the relationship between movie attendance and children, had the most influential impact and greatly advanced the field of mass media research.

William Short, the executive director of the Motion Picture Research Council, asked university scholars in the disciplines of sociology and psychology to design a series of research projects examining the effect that movie attendance has on children. This research effort consisted of thirteen studies funded by a philanthropic organization known as the Payne Fund. In addition to a focus on the nature of the audience and film content, investigators used content analysis, survey methods, and experimental design to examine such topics as message content, information acquisition, attitude change, affect, health outcomes, general behavior, and moral judgments.

In defining the motion picture audience, Dale (1935a) found that school-aged children attended movies more than adults, boys comprised a greater percentage of the audience, and the average child went to the movies at least once a week. Turning to content, Dale (1935b) examined 1,500 movies produced between 1920 and 1930. Overall, the results tended to affirm early concerns over television content in that 75 percent of the films dealt with crime, sex, or love.

Testing 3,000 children and adults, Holaday and Stoddard (1933) examined recall of film content across seventeen motion pictures. Using a pretest-posttest design, the study revealed that factual recall of movie content was high and that film content generated ideas among children. Peterson and Thurstone (1933) supported these findings through experimental research and found that attitudes were influenced by movie exposure, with young children exposed to the same message displaying greater change persisting over a longer period of time. In another study, Dysinger and Ruckman (1933) examined the responses of children, adolescents, and adults to movie content using galvanic skin response (GSR), a physiological measure of arousal. Results indicated that while romantic and erotic content had no effect on children and adults, it had large effects on sixteen-year-old male and female viewers. Referring to these findings, the authors suggested that children were too young to be affected and that adults understand the fantasy component of theater content, but children of susceptible age have a great emotional response to sexual and dangerous content.

Other Payne Fund projects evaluated health and day-to-day behaviors. Health, defined generally by Renshaw et al. (1939) as individual sleep patterns, was found to deteriorate: sleep was disturbed by certain types of films, and it was believed that this could lead to other negative health outcomes. In an exploratory study of everyday behavior, college students reported imitating movie characters and content while experiencing increases in daydreaming and fantasy (Blumer 1933).

Although only briefly highlighted here, through the use of innovative research methods and great insight, the Payne Studies represented an initial effort to establish mass media research as a credible and rigorous scientific discipline and should always be recognized as a key point in mass communication research. Further, these empirically based studies laid the foundation for future mass media research by emphasizing cross-disciplinary collaboration in the study of attitude change, using content, behavioral modeling, social construction, and motivation research. With this in mind, the remainder of this chapter evaluates factors motivating media use and the subsequent outcomes from message exposure.

MEDIA CONSUMPTION

Beyond the Stimulus Response Model

With an increase in contemporary media, the 1930s brought a fast-changing media society. During this time, questions about mass media continued to proliferate around the effects on current culture, reasons for media use, and how people incorporate media in their daily life. Simply put, researchers at this time knew very little about how audiences decided what media to attend to when faced with many options.

Throughout the 1930s, social scientists were keenly interested in the impact of film; however, another contemporary medium was on the rise and reaching larger audiences on a daily basis—radio. The first systematic research conducted on radio sought to understand what role radio played in the lives of its audience (Lazarsfeld and Stanton 1944). From these early studies a new lens from which researchers could view mass audiences was developed. Rather than looking at the effects that media have on audiences, this new approach began to focus on how audiences use media.

In defining the audience as active, this new perspective challenged early theories, such as the 'magic bullet,' which considered mass audiences as relatively passive. The concept of a passive audience, defined as an audience thought to accept whatever information or content was presented, store it into memory, and then act upon it, was the dominant mode of thinking by media effects researchers. However, beginning in the early 1940s, researchers began to understand that people do actively seek media content, use what they need from the media, and experience different levels of satisfaction from their exposure. In one of the more famous and comprehensive projects, Herzog (1944) gathered basic information on audience characteristics and motivations of daytime serial listeners and nonlisteners, with findings demonstrating a strong inverse relationship among education and regular listening patterns.

In an attempt to understand the psychological reasoning for listening to daytime serials, Herzog identified emotional release and vicarious emotional experience, wishful thinking, and advice regarding how to deal with real-world situations as influences. Using survey methodology, this collective body of research demonstrated how an audience could be investigated outside the dominant stimulus-response theories by shifting the research question of what the media do to audiences to what audiences do with the media.

Over the next few decades this line of research became popularly known as the *uses and gratification* paradigm. During the period roughly spanning 1950 to the present, researchers turned to mass media audiences' newest outlet—television. Through countless research projects, it became increasingly apparent to media theorists that audiences made choices about their media consumption (Blumler 1979; Katz et al. 1974; Rubin 1984). According to Katz et al. (1974), the uses and gratifications perspective attempted to identify and explain the relationships between the social and psychological uses of media and the gratifications they provide by examining '(1) the social and psychological origins of (2) needs, which generate (3) expectations of (4) the mass media or other sources, which lead to (5) differential patterns of media exposure (or engagement in other activities), resulting in (6) need gratifications, (7) other consequences, perhaps mostly unintended ones' (1974: 20). More recently, Rubin (2002) extended this conceptualization to include (8) how motives affect attitudes and behaviors, (9) gratifications sought and obtained through specific media use, (10) how user background (i.e. socioeconomic status) affects social expectations of media, and (11) the method in which uses and gratifications data are collected.

Research utilizing the uses and gratifications paradigm has concentrated on user motivations and the belief that people build relationships with media based on their personalities, social status, personal relationships, and media access (Rubin 1984, 1993, 2002). Focusing specifically on one of today's most contemporary media environments, research on television viewing has examined motives such as information seeking, entertainment, parasocial interaction (i.e. the extent to which people use media in order to fulfill the basic human need for social interaction) (Cohen 2001, 2003), social maintenance, and passing time or habit (Conway and Rubin 1991; Ferguson and Perse 2000; Palmgreen and Rayburn 1979; Rubin 1981). Although the predictive power and measurement models of each motive have varied across studies, these constructs can be considered the core set of gratification motives for television use. Beyond television, these motives have also been instrumental in understanding new communication technologies that combine both mass and interpersonal communication, such as the Internet (Charney and Greenberg 2002; LaRose et al. 2001).

Prior uses and gratifications research on the Internet can be broadly conceptualized as 'computer-mediated engagement.' This research has developed a targeted approach to examining Internet use as a single unit of analysis. Similar to previous television use findings, researchers have established information seeking (Korgaonkar and Wolin 1999), entertainment (Charney and Greenberg 2002; Kaye 1998), and social development and maintenance (Papacharissi and Rubin 2000) as primary motives for Internet use.

While uses and gratification has been a dominant framework within the mass media research literature, other approaches, such as the diffusion of innovation model, have also had a major impact on our understanding of media consumption. The diffusion model developed out of a desire to understand how and why people adopt certain new innovations and not others. Drawing from the work of Everett Rogers, the following section briefly outlines some of the important components within the diffusion model that are particularly relevant to media scholars.

The Diffusion Model

Diffusion of innovations theory demonstrates the adoption of an innovation via communication channels across members of a social system over time. Rogers (1995) defined an *innovation* as an idea, practice, or object that is perceived as new and can be expressed in terms of knowledge, persuasion, or a decision to adopt. The basic nature of the diffusion process operates from the exchange of information about a new idea through communication channels, within a social system, and over a period of time. This information exchange can occur either through mass media channels or interpersonal social channels (Rogers 1995). One important element to consider when examining the diffusion of innovations theory is the decision process to adoption. Adopters typically pass through five stages (knowledge, persuasion, decision, implementation, and confirmation) as they learn about, form attitudes toward, and ultimately use an innovation (Rogers 1995). Similarly, the rate or speed in which an innovation is adopted is an equally important component of the diffusion of any innovation. This is generally measured by the length of time required for a certain percentage of members to adopt an innovation, with the majority of innovations following an S-shaped curve (Rogers 1995).

Since all innovations are not equal, the attributes of an innovation, as perceived by the user, affect its rate of adoption. Rogers (1995) revealed that from 49 percent to 87 percent of the variance in the rate of adoption of an innovation can be explained by five innovation attributes: (1) relative advantage, (2) compatibility, (3) complexity, (4) trialability, and (5) observability. While there are other factors that can influence the rate of adoption, the identification of these five represents the most prevalent attributes found throughout the literature.

1. *Relative advantage* is the degree to which an innovation is perceived as being better than the previous idea. Typically, this is often expressed in terms of economic profitability, low initial cost, decreased discomfort, social prestige, savings in time, or a reward (Rogers 1995).
2. *Compatibility* is the degree to which an innovation is perceived as consistent with existing values, experiences, and needs of adopters. The premise is that an idea that is more compatible with sociocultural values, ideas, and needs will likely be adopted faster.
3. *Complexity* is the degree to which an innovation is perceived to be difficult to understand and use. Generally, complexity is negatively related to the adoption rate of an innovation.
4. *Trialability* is the degree to which an innovation may be tested or experimented with on a limited basis. The premise behind this attribute is that the ability to try out an innovation before its adoption is positively related to the rate of adoption.
5. *Observability* is the degree to which the outcomes of an innovation are visible to others. Observability is likely to be positively related to an innovation's rate of adoption.

Additional variables linked to diffusion that have been investigated within the context of a more contemporary media environment are effectiveness, reliability, application, communality, and radicalness (Dearing et al. 1994). When specifically testing risky-innovations, Dearing et al. (1994) identified applicability and reliability as playing particularly key roles in the adoption process. Applying Dearing et al.'s concepts, Eastin (2002) examined the complex process of four e-commerce activities. In doing so, he identified risk, convenience, financial benefits, and self-efficacy as key diffusion attributes to e-commerce behavior. Further, research investigating technology such as computers has demonstrated great explanatory power using demographic variables (Rogers 1995) and attitudinal variables (LaRose and Akin 1992). Regardless, it is important to note that the explanatory power of demographics and attitudinal variables is dependent on the innovation itself; thus, when applying the diffusion model, analyses should always be accompanied by an evaluation of the innovation.

Numerous research projects utilizing the diffusion model have demonstrated how innovations spread among mass audiences. Further, in a time when convergence (regardless of the definition) is inevitable, the diffusion of innovation theory provides great insight into how media consumers will behave during the diffusion process of advanced and 'risky' media systems.

Marketing scholars hold a distinct methodological advantage within the diffusion of innovations theory (Rogers 1995). In many cases market research using the diffusion ideology is conducted as a joint venture with the product manufacturer. This relationship allows market researchers to observe and control the intervention strategies used to introduce a product into the marketplace. This type of field experiment is considered an 'especially powerful type of diffusion research design' (Rogers 1995: 86). However, rather than acting as a theory-building tool, such joint research ventures generally introduce a more practical understanding of the phenomenon due to the dominant role often assumed by the product manufacturer.

Current Research Trends

A recent series of research projects has redefined the uses and gratifications framework within Social Cognitive Theory (SCT) (LaRose and Eastin 2004, LaRose et al. 2001; Eastin and LaRose 2000). According to the investigators' interpretation, SCT, familiar to media scholars in its earlier incarnation as social learning theory (Bandura 1977), offers a theoretical explanation for the oft-observed empirical relationship between media gratifications and media usage. SCT, which posits reciprocal causation among individuals, their behavior, and their environment, represents a broad theory of human behavior that may be applied to media attendance and behavioral outcomes from media attendance such as recall or recognition performance. Within SCT, behavior is an observable act and the performance of behavior is determined in large part by the expected outcomes of behavior. These expectations are formed through our own direct experience with media or mediated by vicarious reinforcement observed through others.

The expected outcomes are organized around six basic types of incentives for human behavior: novel sensory, social, status, monetary, enjoyable activity, and self-reactive incentives (Bandura 1986). An analysis of these categories against Internet gratifications reveals that conventional uses and gratifications research underemphasized status and monetary incentives, which had significant positive correlations with new media use such as the Internet. Although there are some differences, the SCT incentive categories parallel conventional uses and gratifications dimensions (see LaRose et al. 2001 for details). Activity incentives, predicated on the desire to take part in enjoyable activities, correspond to the entertainment gratifications. Self-evaluative incentives, which involve attempts to regulate mood, parallel 'relieve boredom' gratifications. Novel sensory incentives include the search for novel information and are similar to information-seeking gratifications. Social incentives stemming from rewarding interactions with others correspond to social gratifications (for details see LaRose et al. 2001).

SCT also suggests new concepts that may extend our understanding of uses and gratifications and their impact on media behavior. Self-efficacy and self-regulation are particularly heuristic within the framework of electronic consumer behavior. Self-efficacy is the belief in one's capability to organize and execute a particular course of action (Bandura 1986). Self-efficacy is particularly relevant for novice Internet users who have not yet acquired the requisite skills to obtain useful information and deal with the discontents of life online, from viruses to balky home Internet connections. Self-efficacy directly relates to Internet usage, and also acts on usage indirectly, through expected outcomes (Eastin and LaRose 2000). In other words, as Internet users become more self-efficacious their expectations of obtaining specific outcomes (e.g. finding product information) also increases, and this reinforcing act encourages more usage. From an e-commerce perspective, self-efficacious Internet users should be less baffled by interactive features of e-commerce such as secure area warnings, and more likely to feel confident they can protect themselves against privacy and consumer credit problems.

Self-regulation examines the process by which people regulate their time and content exposure to media. Not surprisingly, there also is the chance that self-regulation will fail, subsequently increasing media consumption through habitual tendencies and deficient self-regulation (LaRose et al. 2003).

Although habit has been a consistent predictor of media consumption, recently it has been overlooked in mass communication research (cf. Stone and Stone 1990; Rosenstein and Grant 1997). Within SCT, habit is a failure of the self-monitoring function within self-regulation. Through repetition we become inattentive to the reasoning behind our media behavior and our mind no longer devotes attention resources to evaluating it, freeing itself for more important decisions. On the other hand, deficient self-regulation (defined as a state in which conscious self-control is diminished), has been proposed as an explanatory mechanism for Internet addictions or otherwise problematic Internet use (LaRose and Eastin 2004; LaRose et al. 2003). Applying this concept, LaRose and Eastin (2002) provide evidence that deficient self-regulation is an important factor in e-commerce and that unregulated buying exists online. Deficient self-regulation is potentially a more important determinant of online buying activity than either rational economic expectations about the cost and convenience of Internet shopping or the personal and economic characteristics of e-commerce consumers. Further, LaRose and Eastin (2002) revealed that self-efficacy is an important predictor of consumer behavior, suggesting that consumers must reach a certain level of comfort with the Internet before they actively engage in e-commerce. Taken together, unregulated online buying tendencies, expectations about e-commerce outcomes, and self-efficacy beliefs offer a compelling sociocognitive explanation for online buying.

Future research should continue to integrate literature from areas such as uses and gratifications, diffusion of innovations, and SCT in order to further understand mass audience use of new media. Further, research can apply this theoretical outline to content areas such as e-commerce to begin connecting fundamental cognitive components such as motives, engagement, and self-regulation to better understand advertising effectiveness, as reflected by click- through rates and online consumer behavior. Rather than using general models of media behavior on segmented audiences and media, researchers can begin to observe the complexity existing between media consumption and the everchanging users.

Understanding motivational and behavioral mechanisms only represents the first half of the equation. To this end, a primary goal of advertising is to persuade or influence another's state of mind in order to manipulate perceptions and behavioral outcomes. As discussed below, the motivational state from which an audience encounters a message can influence message perceptions, attention to the message, and message effectiveness. To assess these advancements and move from the individual state influences to the message, we next turn to past, current, and future research trends in the persuasion literature.

Dominant Themes in Persuasion (1950–2000)

Conceptually, persuasion is characterized as simply human communication designed to influence the beliefs and attitudes of others (Simons 1976: 21). As a paradigm, persuasion research is multidisciplinary, spanning across numerous academic fields, including advertising, communication, marketing, political science, and sociology, among others. Regardless of the perspective, the core focus of persuasion remains the intentional effort to influence another's mental state traditionally evaluated by cognitive, affective, and conative outcomes (O'Keefe 2002: 5). While an exhaustive account of this rich area of research is beyond the scope of this chapter, a general overview of the key areas applicable to mass communication and marketing will hopefully incite personal exploration of the subject.

One of the first 'classic' models of persuasion to receive widespread consideration was Lavidge and Steiner's (1961) hierarchy of effects. Although numerous variations of the model have emerged over the years, the basic principle remains that when presented with information, recipients progress in a linear fashion from a state of unawareness through stages of awareness, knowledge, attitude formation, intention and, ultimately, behavior. Like most of the persuasion research relative to marketing, work in this area was designed to explain how advertising is able to influence preference along each of these stages as consumers move toward a behavior outcome (i.e. purchase).

Krugman (1965) later questioned the notion that persuasive messages are capable of influencing attitudes and leading to overt behavior change without the message holding some form of personal relevance, characterized as involvement. He recognized that messages are sometimes followed by no detectable attitude change before a behavioral change, with attitude change potentially appearing after the behavioral change. Krugman asserted that in low-involvement situations we look for gradual shifts in perceptual structure, aided by repetition, activated by behavioral-choice situations, and followed at some point by attitude change. Undeniably, the construct of involvement has received extensive attention by marketing communication scholars, resulting in a diverse number of conceptual approaches (Andrews et al. 1992).

In exploring the relationship between persuasion and involvement, the majority of work has focused on situational manipulations designed to evoke alternate (high vs. low) levels of motivation (Laczniak et al. 1999). Specifically, high levels of motivation have been associated with cognitive thinking and verbal processing (Hansen 1981), whereas low levels have been linked to emotional or holistic styles of information processing (Brace et al. 2002). Motivation has consistently been shown to moderate the effects of elaboration to process persuasive messages by influencing perception. This effect is attributed to the belief that increasing motivation decreases the impact of nonessential message components on information processing, thereby leading attitude to have a greater impact on behavior intentions (MacKenzie and Spreng 1992).

Although early consumer research considered information processing primarily rational in nature, more recent work has acknowledged the limitations of this view to explore the experiential characteristics of behavior (Hoch and Loewenstein 1991; Holbrook and Hirschman 1982). Indeed, psychologists support the belief that we are served by a psychosomatic system involving both cognitive and emotional elements (LeDoux 1989; Zajonc 1980). Ultimately, influence from one system over the other in directing behavior is determined by the degree of motivation, availability of processing resources, and emotional involvement. For instance, when resources are high, consumer evaluations and judgments will primarily be based on the rational system, with cognition likely impacting behavior. When resources are low, evaluations and judgments will occur automatically, with emotion influencing behavior (Epstein 1994; Kisielius and Sternthal 1986; Petty and Cacioppo 1984).

One of the most widely recognized dual-process theories used in persuasion research is Petty and Cacioppo's (1981) Elaboration Likelihood Model (ELM). This model specifies conditions under which persuasion is mediated by messages and postulates that central and peripheral routes influence persuasion. Elaboration refers to the extent to which people process persuasive communication. For instance, when motivation is high, elaboration likelihood is said to be high and people are more likely to follow the central route of persuasion and be influenced by argument-based messages. When motivation is low, elaboration likelihood is likely to be low and people are more likely to be influenced by the peripheral factors of persuasion, such as source attractiveness and heuristic cues (Petty and Cacioppo 1981).

Two interrelated theories also widely used to explain how people process persuasive messages are the dual-coding model and the availability-valence hypothesis (Kisielius and Sternthal 1984, 1986). The fundamental assumption of the dual-coding model is that cognition consists largely of two independent, yet interconnected, systems specializing in either verbal or nonverbal information. In addition, words or text are received and stored in a sequential order in a verbal system while nonverbal (pictures) information is processed simultaneously in an imagery system. The result is that the mnemonic codes created from pictures are easier to remember than words when the task is simply recall rather than retrieval of a sequential order of information (Paivio 1986).

By contrast, the availability-valence hypothesis is intended to explain attitudinal judgments in terms of memory operation. This hypothesis is based on the principle that vivid imagery affects the extent to which consumers will engage in cognitive elaboration. The greater the cognitive elaboration of information the more available it is for attitudinal judgments (Kisielius and Sternthal 1986). The result is that persuasive messages using pictures, positive verbal copy, and instructions to imagine enhance memory associations, causing the information to be more salient.

Finally, Anderson's (1991) Information Integration Theory (IIT) states that all thought and behavior comes from multiple causes that interact with one another. A person's existing values and the information they receive will determine their responses, with integration of consistent meaning serving as an ongoing process by combining different parts into a whole (Anderson 1991). When applying this theory to persuasion, it is easy to understand that a message would produce a stronger influence if it is integrated throughout multiple sources of contact. Thus, in terms of persuasive communication all efforts should be integrated in order to ensure consistent meaning (Thorson and Moore 1996).

CURRENT AND FUTURE RESEARCH TRENDS IN MARKETING COMMUNICATION

Marketing professionals today are facing numerous changes within the field of mass communication that will continue to impact the creation and delivery of persuasive messages. One of the most dramatic has been the manner in which mass media have transformed during the past fifty years. First, society has shifted away from the oligopoly-dominated model prevalent in the early 1950s of only a few mass media sources. Second, advancements and increases in technology have changed the face of mass media forever. Third, the combination of a power shift from the media supplier to the media user, along with advances in technology, has resulted in mass media segmenting and fragmenting in order to effectively reach the public.

Media no longer represent the mass communication conduits that marketers conventionally relied upon for so many years. This change has occurred because traditional above-the-line media, such as television, radio, newspapers, and magazines, have splintered into targeting specific demographic segments. For instance, the once dominant medium of television has fragmented and lost its ability to truly reach a mass audience (see Chapter 6). Marketers must evaluate where to place persuasive messages across a multitude of choices ranging from network television, cable television, syndicated programming, or even pay-per-view content. Newspaper, radio, and magazines are no different, as there are now thousands of vehicles within each medium targeting special interests, regional areas, local communities, and global audiences. As a result, delivering persuasive messages using mass communication today requires researching the audience and strategically integrating marketing efforts. Mass communication is no longer just TV, magazines, and newspapers but encompasses a new gamut of alternatives such as the Internet and other forms of interactive media (Junu 1995). Thus, delivering consistent, integrated persuasive messages to mass audiences, throughout all marketing communications functions, is essential in order to break through the thousands of messages that consumers are exposed to daily.

Technological innovations have certainly played an important role in the transformation of mass communication. For instance, the emergence of the Internet and the subsequent information age has helped to create a new medium while altering existing media vehicles. A critical factor in the development of a new medium is that it must generally perform some additional function better than the existing media. For instance, newspapers were more effective than town criers because they provided a method of recording information; magazines developed because their quality of production and national news coverage was better than newspapers; radio emerged because it was more effective than magazines at delivering live and timely content; television was more effective than radio because it combined audio and video images; and the Internet is better than television because it combines all of these elements while adding the element of interactivity (Meeker 1997). In fact, it is the interactive nature of the Internet that offers marketers the possibility to form stronger relationships with people, providing a distinct advantage over traditional mass media (Upshaw 1995; see also Chapter 9).

Interactivity is a multidimensional construct often associated with the Internet and has been described as both the ability to communicate with people (person interactivity) and access information (machine interactivity) (Hoffman and Novak 1996). As a form of communication, interactivity is measured in terms of the level of responsiveness between users along a continuum ranging from one-way discourse to the reactive interaction of two-way communication (Rafaeli and Sudweeks 1997). Integrating variables such as telepresence, perceived skill, and experience, Hoffman and Novak (1996) emphasized that the Internet's potential as an efficient persuasive communication channel stems from a 'many-to-many communication medium,' where consumers are able to interact with and create content. Hence, consumers are able to experience a psychological state identified as *flow* because the medium creates a sense of interactivity and enjoyment that results in a loss of self-consciousness.

Mass communication scholars are just beginning to fully explore the persuasive implications of rich media. The concept of *media richness* is derived from research in multiple disciplines, which has long recognized that media vary in terms of information intensity (Daft and Lengel 1986). Steuer viewed this media characteristic as 'represented richness of a mediated environment as defined by its formal features; that is, the way in which an environment presents information to the senses' (Steuer 1992: 81). Media richness consists of two factors: (*a*) sensory breadth, which refers to the number of sensory dimensions simultaneously presented, and (*b*) sensory depth, which refers to the resolution within each of these perceptual channels. Breadth represents the ability of a medium to present information across the senses. Depth refers to the quality of information; that is, an image (or auditory stimulus) with greater depth is generally perceived as being of higher quality than one with less depth. This premise lies in the assumption that messages appealing to multiple perceptual systems are better perceived than those that call on single or fewer perceptual systems. Still, very little empirical evidence exists for measuring the impact of persuasive messages across multiple media designed to saturate sensory perception.

CONCLUSION

Future areas of research in mass communication pertaining to marketing will continue to build on the dominant themes and areas outlined within this chapter. Specifically, exploring further the persuasive effects of rich media is needed in order to fully understand the implications of creating a sense of presence. *Presence* (also known as *telepresence*) is the experience of 'being there' in a mediated environment and is generated from sensory input, mental processes, and past experiences assimilated together in a current state (Steuer 1992). All media and telecommunication systems generate a sense of being in another place by bringing the experience and objects closer to us, allowing us indirectly to meet and experience other objects, other people, and the experiences of others. The marketing implications are immediate for creating compelling experiences through media, using the illusion of presence as a form of persuasion capable of enhancing the value of information, actively engaging audiences, increasing message effectiveness, and ultimately establishing competitive advantages (Li et al. 2001, 2002, 2003).

Additionally, research suggests that the type of mass media could impact both cognitive and affective responses to marketing (Yoon 1991). For instance, Chaiken and Eagly (1983) contend that print advertising lends itself to cognition, whereas television is better suited for communicating affective messages. Chaudhuri and Buck (1995) further assert that electronic media encourage emotional communication because of the integration of sensory information. As a result, it is reasonable to contemplate that motivation toward a persuasive message can be initiated from a particular type of media. For instance, when consumers are exposed to television advertising, superficial processing begins at a low level of attention once the ad runs unless the volume is turned down or set turned off (Greenwald and Leavitt 1984). Although a number of consumers may experience comprehension or even high levels of elaboration from advertising via broadcast media, the level of meaningful cognitive impact for those consumers not interested at all will be greater than a less engaging and more passive medium such as print (Buchholz and Smith 1991). Additional research is needed to fully understand the implications of these persuasive effects.

Consistent with the previous discussion on motivation and self-efficacy, mass communication research will need to continue focusing on how and why people are engaging new media such as the Internet. Research has revealed that people use the Internet for social, information, and entertainment purposes, however, how these motivating factors influence short and long-term recall of products and product advertising is complex and relatively unknown. Additionally, people's confidence in relying on and using media is only beginning to be researched within the context of consumer behavior. The feeling of confidence in one's ability has been characterized as essential for any behavior to take place because this belief serves as a form of self-assurance (Dequech 2000). With regard to using mass media, self confidence in one's ability to successfully understand, navigate, and evaluate content should alleviate doubts when gathering information and ultimately correspond with heightened beliefs about issues and persuasive messages presented within the media. The beliefs formed reflect a person's perceived capability in using media to acquire information and accomplish tasks. Subsequently, as media confidence increases, attitudes toward the object of confidence-related beliefs should also increase (Ajzen and Sexton 1999).

Mass communication channels depend on forms of persuasive communication to offset expenses associated with delivering content, resulting in a symbiotic relationship between corporate sponsorship and the media. This relationship is built on trust, meaningful connections, and the transference of values through popular culture to the public (Monberg 1997). However, because of the previously noted changes within the mass media, reaching a mass audience using media is more difficult now than ever before. To combat these problems, another trend will continue to be the insertion of paid product placement in media content as a form of persuasion (Ebenkamp 2001; see Chapter 6). *Product placement* is a form of advertising and promotion in which products are placed in television shows, movies, or other entertainment content to generate visibility and obtain audience exposure. When brands are presented to consumers via product placement, the potential exists for positive associative connections to form. However, this connection does not occur directly because the focal purpose of media content is not about the placement of a brand. In traditional advertising, mass media audiences are consciously aware of information presented in the focal area of perception, yet when products are embedded in media content critics have begun to raise ethical questions regarding such practices (Gupta and Gould 1997).

The transformation of media has resulted in the greater need for consistent, integrated communication in order to deliver an effective message as efficiently as possible. This approach involves developing a consistent approach across mass communication vehicles, known as *integrated marketing communication*. Integrated marketing communications is the strategic approach that coordinates all marketing communications functions (advertising, sales promotion, public relations, direct marketing, etc.) in a consistent strategy for maximum impact (see Chapter 9).

Although this chapter has presented what the authors believe are substantial research areas that have affected mass media research over the past seventy years, it is important to note that several areas of substance were not included. Nonetheless, the body of literature covered in this chapter does provide key research developments and future research trends that many researchers can apply within and outside the scope of these topics.

REFERENCES

Anderson, N. H. (1991). *Contributions to Information Integration Theory*, Vol. I: *Cognition*. Hillsdale, NJ: Lawrence Erlbaum Associates.

Ajzen, I. and Sexton, J. (1999). 'Depth of Processing, Belief Congruence, and Attitude Behavior Correspondence', in S. Chaiken and Y. Trope (eds.), *Dual-Process Theories in Social Psychology*. New York: The Guilford Press, pp. 117–38.

Andrews, C. J., Akhter, S.H., Durvasula, S., and Muehling, D. (1992). 'The Effects of Advertising Distinctiveness and Message Content Involvement on Cognitive and Affective Responses to Advertising', *Journal of Current Issues and Research in Advertising*, 14, 45–58.

Bandura, A. (1977). *Social Learning Theory.* Englewood Cliffs, NJ: Prentice-Hall.

—— (1986). *Social Foundations of Thought and Action: A Social Cognitive Theory.* Englewood Cliffs, NJ: Prentice-Hall.

Blumer, H. (1933). *The Movies and Conduct.* New York: Macmillan.

Blumler, J. (1979). 'The Role of Theory in Uses and Gratifications Studies', *Communication Research*, 6, 9–36.

Brace, I., Edwards, L., and Nancarrow, C. (2002). 'I Hear You Knocking...Can Advertising Reach Everybody in the Target Audience?', *International Journal of Marketing Research*, 44, 193–247.

Buchholz, L. M. and Smith, R. (1991). 'The Role of Consumer Involvement in Determining Cognitive Response to Broadcast Advertising', *Journal of Advertising*, 20, 4–17.

Chaiken, S. and Eagly, A. (1983). 'Communication modality as a determinant of persuasion: The role of communicator salience', *Journal of Personality and Social Psychology*, 45, 241–56.

Charney, T. and Greenberg, B. (2002). 'Uses and Gratifications of the Internet', in C. Lin and D. Atkin (eds.), *Communication, Technology and Society: New Media Adoption and Uses.* Hampton Press.

Chaudhuri, A. and Buck, R. (1995). 'Media Differences in Rational and Emotional Responses to Advertising', *Journal of Broadcasting & Electronic Media*, 39, 109–25.

Conway, J. and Rubin, A. (1991). 'Psychological Predictors of Television Viewing Motivation', *Communication Research*, 4, 443–63.

Daft, R.L. and Lengel, R.H. (1986). 'Organizational Information Requirements, Media Richness and Structural Design', *Management Science*, 32, 554–71.

Dale, E. (1935a). *Children's Attendance at Motion Pictures.* New York: Macmillan.

—— (1935b). *The Content of Motion Pictures.* New York: Macmillan.

Dearing, J., Meyer, G., and Kazmierczak, J. (1994). 'Portraying the New: Communication Between University Innovators and Potential Users', *Science Communication*, 16, 11–42.

Dequech, D. (2000). 'Confidence and Action: A Comment on Barbalet', *Journal of Socio-Economics*, 29, 503–16.

Dysinger, W.S. and Ruckman, C.A. (1933). *The Emotional Responses of Children to the Motion Picture Situation.* New York: Macmillan.

Eastin, M. S. (2002). 'Diffusion of E-commerce: An Analysis of the Adoption of Four E-commerce Activities', *Telematics and Informatics*, 19(3), 251–67.

—— and LaRose, R. L. (2000). 'Internet Self-efficacy and the Psychology of the Digital Divide', *Journal of Computer Mediated Communication*, 6, Available: http://www.ascusc.org/jcmc/vol6/issue1/eastin.html

Ebenkamp, B. (2001). 'Return to Peyton Place', *Brandweek*, 42, 10–18.

Epstein, S. (1994). 'Integration of the Cognitive and the Psychodynamic Unconscious', *American Psychologist*, 49, 709–24.

Ferguson, D. A. and Perse, E. M. (2000). 'The World Wide Web as a Functional Alternative to Television', *Journal of Broadcasting & Electronic Media*, 44, 155–74.

Greenwald, A. G. and Leavitt, C. (1984). 'Audience Involvement in Advertising: Four Levels', *Journal of Consumer Research*, 11, 581–92.

Gupta, P.B. and Gould, S.J. (1997). 'Consumers' Perceptions of the Ethics and Acceptability of Product Placement in Movies: Product Category and Individual Differences', *Journal of Current Issues and Research in Advertising*, 19, 37–50.

Hansen, F. (1981). 'Hemispheral Lateralisation: Implications for Understanding Consumer Behavior', *Journal of Consumer Research*, 8, 23–36.

Herzog, H. (1944). 'What Do We Really Know about Daytime Serial Listeners?' in P. Lazarsfeld and F. Stanton (eds.), *Radio Research 1942–1943*. New York: Duel, Sloan and Pierce, pp. 3–33.

Hoch, S.J. and Loewenstein, G.F. (1991). 'Time-inconsistent Preferences and Consumer Self-control', *Journal of Consumer Research*, 17, 492–507.

Hoffman, D.L. and Novak, T.P. (1996). 'Marketing in Hypermedia Computer-based Environments: Conceptual Foundations', *Journal of Marketing*, 60, 50–68.

Holaday, P.W. and Stoddard, G.D. (1933). *Getting Ideas From the Movies*. New York: Macmillan.

Holbrook, M.B. and Hirschman, E.C. (1982). 'The Experiential Aspects of Consumption: Consumer Fantasies, Feelings, and Fun', *Journal of Consumer Research*, 9, 132–40.

Junu, K. (1995). 'Media Buying & Planning; Strategy Regains Prominence with Planners; Price Is Right Mentality Losing to Choosing Best Reach', *Advertising Age*, 28 (July), S10.

Katz, E., Blumler, J., and Gurevitch, M. (1974). 'Utilization of Mass Communications by the Individual', in J. Blumler and E. Katz (eds.), *The Uses of Mass Communications: Current Perspectives on Gratifications Research*. Beverly Hills, CA: Sage, pp. 19–32.

Kaye, B. K. (1998). 'Uses and Gratifications of the World Wide Web: From Couch Potato to Web Potato', *New Jersey Journal of Communication*, 6, 21–40.

Kisielius, J. and Sternthal, B. (1984). 'Detecting and Explaining Vividness Effects in Attitudinal Judgments', *Journal of Marketing Research*, 21, 54–64.

—— and —— (1986). Examining the Vividness Controversy: An Availability-Valence Interpretation', *Journal of Consumer Research*, 12, 418–31.

Korgaonkar, P. and Wolin, L. (1999). 'A Multivariate Analysis of Web Usage', *Journal of Advertising Research*, 39, 53–68.

Krugman, H.E. (1965). 'The Impact of Television Advertising: Learning Without Involvement', *Public Opinion Quarterly*, 29, 349–56.

Laczniak, R.N., Kempf, D.S., and Muehling, D.D. (1999). 'Advertising Message Involvement: The Role of Enduring and Situational Factors', *Journal of Current Issues and Research in Advertising*, 21, 51–61.

LaRose, R. and Atkin, D. (1992). 'Adiotext and the Reinvention of the Telephone as a Mass Medium', *Journalism Quarterly*, 69, 413–21.

—— and Eastin, M.S. (2004). 'A Social Cognitive Explanation of Internet Usage: Toward a New Theory of Media Attendance', *Journal of Broadcasting & Electronic Media*, 48 (3).

—— and —— (2002). 'Is On-line Buying Out of Control? Electronic Commerce and Consumer Self-regulation', *Journal of Broadcasting & Electronic Media*, 46 (4), 549–64.

Larose, R., Lin, C. A., and Eastin, M. S. (2003). 'Unregulated Internet Usage: Addiction, Habit, or Deficient Self-regulation?' *Media Psychology*, 5, 225–53.

—— Mastro, D. A., and Eastin, M. S. (2001). 'Understanding Internet Usage: A Social Cognitive Approach to Uses and Gratifications', *Social Science Computer Review*, 19, 395–413.

Lavidge, R. and Steiner, G. (1961). 'A Model for Predictive Measurements of Advertising Effectiveness', *Journal of Marketing*, 25, 59–62.

Lazarsfeld, P.F. and Stanton, F.N. (1944). *Radio Research 1942–1943*. New York: Duel, Sloan and Pierce.

LeDoux, J. E. (1989). 'Cognitive-Emotional Interactions in the Brain', *Cognition and Emotion*, 3, 267–89.

Li, H., Daugherty, T. and Biocca, F. (2001). 'Characteristics of Virtual Experience in E-commerce: A Protocol Analysis', *Journal of Interactive Marketing*, 15, 13–30.

—— —— and —— (2002). 'Impact of 3-D Advertising on Product Knowledge, Brand Attitude, and Purchase Intention: The Mediating Role of Presence', *Journal of Advertising*, 31, 43–58.

—— —— and —— (2003). 'The Role of Virtual Experience in Consumer Learning', *Journal of Consumer Psychology*, 13, 395–405.

Lin, C. (1999). 'Online-Service Adoption Likelihood', *Journal of Advertising Research*, 39, 79–89.

MacKenzie, S.B. and Spreng, R.A. (1992). 'How does Motivation Moderate the Impact of Central and Peripheral Processing on Brand Attitudes and Intentions?', *Journal of Consumer Research*, 18, 519–29.

Meeker, M. (1997). *The Internet Advertising Report*. New York, NY: HarperBusiness.

Monberg, J. (1997). ' "You Will": Social Implications of Advanced Marketing Technologies', *Ethics & Behavior*, 7, 229–38.

O'Keefe, D.J. (2002). *Persuasion Theory and Research*. Thousand Oaks, CA: Sage.

Paivio, A. (1986). *Mental Representations: A Dual Coding Approach*. New York: Oxford University Press.

Palmgreen, P. and Rayburn, J. (1979). 'Uses and Gratifications and Exposure to Public Television: a Discrepancy Method', *Communication Research*, 6, 155–79.

Papacharissi, Z. and Rubin, A. M. (2000). 'Predictors of Internet Usage', *Journal of Broadcasting and Electronic Media*, 44, 175–96.

Peterson, R.C. and Thurston, L.L. (1933). *Motion Pictures and the Social Attitude of Children*. New York: Macmillan.

Petty, R. E. and Cacioppo, J. T. (1981). *Attitudes and Persuasion: Classic and Contemporary Approaches*. Dubuque, IA: William C. Brown.

—— and —— (1984). 'The Effects of Involvement on Response to Argument Quantity and Quality: Central and Peripheral Routes to Persuasion', *Journal of Personality and Social Psychology*, 46, 69–81.

Rafaeli, S. and Sudweeks, F. (1997). 'Networked Interactivity', *Journal of Computer-Mediated Communication*, 2. Available: http://www.ascusc.org/jcmc/vol2/issue4/rafaeli.sudweeks.html

Renshaw, S., Miller, V., and Marquis, D.P. (1939). *Children's Sleep*. New York: Macmillan.

Rogers, E. M. (1995). *Diffusion of Innovations*, 4th edn. New York: Free Press.

Rosenstein, A. W. and Grant, A.E. (1997). 'Reconceptualizing the Role of Habit: A New Model of Television Audience Activity', *Journal Of Broadcasting and Electronic Media*, 41, 324–44.

Rubin, A. (2002). 'The Uses and Gratifications Perspective of Media Effects', in J. Bryant and D. Zillmann (eds.), *Media Effects: Advances in Theory and Research*, pp. 525–48.

—— (1993). 'Audience Activity and Media Use', *Communication Monographs*, 60, 98–103.

—— (1984). 'Ritualized and Instrumental Television Viewing Patterns and Motivations', *Journal of Communication*, 34, 67–77.

—— (1981). 'An Examination of Television Viewing Motivations', *Communication Research*, 8, 141–65.

Simons, H.W. (1976). *Persuasion: Understanding, Practice and Analysis*. Reading, MA: Addison-Wesley.

Steuer, J. (1992). 'Defining Virtual Reality: Dimensions Determining Telepresence', *Journal of Communication*, 42, 73–93.

Stone, G. and Stone, D. (1990). 'Lurking in the Literature: Another Look at Media Use Habits', *Mass Communications Review*, 17, 25–33.

Thorson, E. and Moore, J. (1996). *Integrated Communication: Synergy of Persuasive Voices*. Mahwah, NJ: Lawrence Erlbaum Associates.

Upshaw, L. (1995). 'The Keys to Building Cyberbrands', *Advertising Age*, (May 29).

Yoon, C. (1991). *Tears, Cheers, and Fears: The Role of Emotion in Advertising*. Cambridge, MA.: Marketing Science Institute.

Zajonc, R. B. (1980). 'Feeling and Thinking: Preferences Needed no Inferences', *American Psychologist*, 35, 151–75.

3

The Twenty-First-Century Consumer Society

James Fitchett

The main objective of this chapter is to critically evaluate some of the prospects for the twenty-first-century consumer society. As the discussion progresses a number of possible future scenarios are introduced and evaluated. The goal is not to present a coherent series of projections of the future that could be used, for example, as part of some sort of planning process. Interesting and captivating as these often are, the chapter instead emphasizes the fictional and constructed nature of futuristic accounts of consumer society. The future is both unknowable and unavoidable. Despite this obvious truism, marketers and business professionals have a peculiar and definite interest in the future. We might say that the ability to accurately predict future trends in consumer behavior or to foresee the next generation of new product developments constitutes the modern elixir of management. The desire to know the likelihood of future market trends represents an attempt to manage the risks associated with uncertainty. Having considered the marketing perils associated with uncertainty, I then briefly examine some of the more inspiring attempts at imagining possible marketing futures by drawing on a range of sources.

One of the recurrent problems with many futuristic accounts of consumer society is that beneath the creativity of potentials we often find deeply engrained tropes of the present. Thus, for example, imagining a future of high-speed data transfer is probably best understood as a manifestation of present-day frustrations with slow download times and poor interconnectivity rather than a rational analysis of possible technological developments. To overcome this pitfall, I argue that a more sensitive and credible forecast for twenty-first-century consumer society can only be constructed by seeing the future as a continuation of prior social trends and cultural dynamics. Throughout the twentieth century, consumer society gradually colonized global culture but it did not progress haphazardly and chaotically. Consumer culture emerged as both a reaction to and a consequence of broader social conditions that it in turn shaped and modified. Although specific features and characteristics of the future might be difficult to predict, I suggest that its overall general structure can at least in part be mapped by first identifying and then logically progressing from identifiable underlying social trends. This analysis allows us to evaluate various prospects for the twenty-first-century consumer society and to consider some of the possible responses that may have to be faced by marketing organizations.

THE UNCERTAIN FUTURE

Some characteristics of consumer society in the twenty-first century can and have been forecasted. For example, demographic data can be used to identify trends in population dynamics to show that in developed economies people are living longer than ever before. The United Nations predicts that by 2050 one-third of the population in the developed world will be over sixty years of age (United Nations 2004). Statistics on family size and birth rates, when combined with data on global population movement, indicate with some certainty that as well as having aging populations, developed economies are likely to become more ethnically diverse. Thus, it is likely that consumer societies of mid-twenty-first century developed economies are likely to be very different from the youth-orientated, ethnically homogeneous consumer societies of the mid-twentieth century.

Taking a more global perspective, it is estimated that by 2030 the urban population is likely to reach 5 billion, whereas the rural population is expected to decline (United Nations 2004). Population growth is expected to be particularly rapid in the urban areas of less developed regions. In fact the United Nations anticipates that almost all the growth in the world's total population between 2000 and 2030 is expected to be absorbed by the urban areas of less well developed regions. Given that historical research has linked the emergence of consumer societies in the USA and Europe with urbanization, these demographics suggest that the establishment of consumer societies elsewhere in the world is virtually inevitable.

These sorts of demographic estimates are powerful indicators of the shape, proportion, and size of future consumer societies. However, other types of forecasts pertaining to what consumers might be like in future decades are less straightforward. There are so many potential influences on consumers that it is probably realistic to conclude that their behavior is for all intents and purposes unpredictable or, to use Gabriel and Lang's

(1995) phrase, *unmanageable*. Decades of dedicated consumer behavior research have shown that the motives of consumers are often inscrutable. Their most trivial actions can mean volumes or their most extraordinary conduct may depend upon the seemingly insignificant. In the absence of any substantial evidence to support the contrary, all that we can really be reasonably certain about twenty-first-century consumers is that they are likely to continue to be as unpredictable as their twentieth-century forebears.

Nonetheless, the fact that the future is largely unknowable has not discouraged theorists, visionaries, fiction writers, and forecasters from trying to second-guess what life at some future time might be like. From a marketing communications and consumer behavior perspective, one of the most interesting and relevant discourses of futurism is the science fiction genre, especially its cinematic variation (Fitchett and Fitchett 2001). We need only recall futuristic movies such as *Blade Runner*, the *Back to the Future* trilogy, and *2001: A Space Odyssey* to appreciate the significance that marketing technologies such as brands, product innovations, and changing consumer lifestyles could have on both the near and the distant future.

A simple analysis of futuristic cinema reveals that film directors often use marketing concepts and marketing symbols to visualize their fantasy productions. The incorporation of these market signifiers not only enables futuristic fantasies to appear more 'realistic' to the viewing audience but also implies that most of us, whether scriptwriters, directors, or viewers, have a deep subconscious expectation that marketing technologies will have a significant presence in the societies of the near future. Perhaps the dismal, dark, metropolitan future of *Blade Runner* would be somehow less believable without the neon Coca-Cola signs that permeate the Los Angeles landscape of 2030. When 1968 cinema audiences first watched the PAN-AM passenger shuttle waltz towards the revolving Hilton space station in *2001: A Space Odyssey*, the brave new world of moon vacations and space tourism no doubt appeared but a generation away. Although this may seem wildly unrealistic today, it must have seemed reasonably likely to a society in the midst of exploring increasingly exotic opportunities for intercontinental travel and tourism for the first time.

Of course, history now shows that PAN-AM never made it to 2001, collapsing into bankruptcy a decade earlier. To contemporary viewers, this brand must seem as fantastic as the plot of the film in which it appeared. However, the significance of this example is not that we have yet to make vacations to the moon a reality but that brands that appear permanent and unshakeable are in actuality vulnerable to future uncertainties. As we analyze consumer society in the first decade of the twenty-first century it is equally hard for us to conceive of a world without Coca-Cola, McDonald's, Microsoft, or any of the other highly visible global brands that retain a high profile in today's consumer imagination. The PAN-AM space shuttle reminds us that the long-term future survival of even the most successful and secure brands is far from guaranteed. During the 1950s, cultural theorist and semiotician Roland Barthes (1972) wrote that although one can conceive of very ancient myths, there are no eternal ones. One might also say that although we can conceive of very old and very powerful brands, neither age nor power guarantees their future. Thus, like the consumer, the future—and the future of brands—is unpredictable.

Total Retinal Marketing?

In 1999, film director Stephen Spielberg prepared for his science fiction movie, *Minority Report* by gathering together what he referred to as 'some of the best minds in technology, environment, crime fighting, medicine, health and social services, transportation, and computer technology' (*Minority Report* 2002). These individuals participated in a three-day think tank to come up with ideas and concepts about society in the middle of the twenty-first century. *Minority Report* was released in 2002 and, in addition to a captivating plot and a dynamic story line, the film contained some fantastic futuristic marketing and communication concepts. As Tom Cruise's character, John Anderton, leaps aboard a metro train to escape the law enforcement officers pursuing him he crouches down opposite a fellow passenger reading the newspaper *USA Today*. As he attempts to escape, we see live headlines rushing across the front page in real time, until suddenly Cruise's face appears as breaking news.

Earlier in the film Cruise is shown sitting at home in front of his holographic projector watching home movies. As he scans the recordings he reaches out casually and lifts a packet of breakfast cereal and takes a mouthful straight from the carton. All over the packaging cartoon characters dance around to a playful jingle. In a later scene, Cruise escapes to what appears to be the entrance to a mall. Retinal sensors in the surrounding walkways instantly read his identity and project personalized advertisements onto video advertising panels as he walks by. In another scene, we see Cruise's character passing by a Guinness beer advertisement replete with Irish dancing tunes calling out to him: 'Hey John Anderton you could use a Guinness right now.' As a vision of total relationship marketing, the video monitor at the entrance to The Gap asks the character how he got on with the items he purchased during his last visit.

In a special commentary included with the 2002 special DVD release of the film (Minority Report 2002) Spielberg commented on the marketing communication environment he envisions for the future: 'Everything will be identified. Advertisers will target you. A billboard will read your eyes at a great distance of 200 yards and directly project both sound and visual imagery.'

Technology, Spielberg and his think tank predict, will eventually allow marketers to fill our very field of vision with persuasive slogans, captivating images, and precise offers that will appeal directly to our personal desires, wants, shopping histories, and credit ratings at the exact moment when they are likely to have lasting effect.

The Love of Technology

Like the majority of futuristic accounts of the twenty-first century, *Minority Report* reserves a special place for technology and its potential consequences on everyday life. More optimistic futurists consider technology to offer potentially positive outcomes and solutions to contemporary ills. For example, technological innovations in energy generation might eventually help overcome global dependence on fossil fuels, or faster data links might enable us to communicate more quickly. Others envision a more dismal, even sinister role for future technology resulting in the infringement of civil rights, further exploitation of scarce resources, and perhaps new and more complex forms of crime. But care needs to be taken when considering the potential consequences and impact of technology. As Jacoby (1999) cautioned, we need to bear in mind that technology does not represent a coherent vision of the future but only the means of shaping possible futures.

When we become engrossed in futuristic fantasies about technology, whether positive or negative, there is a potential to get carried away with imagined gadgets, mechanisms, and consumer products. By definition, a futuristic technological project is a fiction about which we can only be subjective. Only once the project is turned into objects and institutions can it be assessed objectively (Latour 1996). A more considered evaluation of futuristic technological wonders often brings the fantasy crashing down into reality. We need to accept that although technology will inevitably change the consumer landscape to a considerable extent, it is other, more complex social, economic, and geodemographic factors that may be of more general consequence. To illustrate this point, let us briefly indulge in a little futuristic fantasy of our own by considering the potential of Spielberg's imagined marketing communications technologies, using existing concepts and data from consumer behavior and communications research.

In our future hypothetical scenario, by the middle of the twenty-first-century marketers will be able to collect personal identity information via retinal scanning as consumers wander through a shopping area. It will then be possible to beam individually customized holographic advertisements directly into the consumers' visual and aural vicinity. It is worth noting that some of the technological advances necessary for these types of marketing communications techniques to be achieved are already being developed. These include technological advances that allow the capture and storage of biometric data such as fingerprints and facial and retinal recognition, as well as positioning and targeting technologies for transmitting location-based services.

As consumers pass a billboard for the new *Lexus* automobile, for example, it could ask whether they would like to schedule a test drive. An insurance company could remind consumers that their car insurance is due for renewal as they pass by the broker's office, describing enticing offers and discounts to encourage new policy sign-ups. Consider walking down an aisle in a grocery store and having the packaging calling out to you. Brands you had purchased previously could ask: 'How did you like me? Didn't I tell you I could get your clothes whiter than white? Now you've tried me once, why not have another pack, half price?' Competitors' brands might then begin calling out rival claims and making counteroffers. Walking by the sodas the latest pop idol might step out from the display and seductively ask: 'Why not try Pepsi for a change, I guarantee you'll prefer the taste or your money back.' At the confectionary stand cartoon characters from TV franchises might dance along with children while sensual and voluptuous images promoting a new range of chocolate are targeted to parents. One could even envisage picking up a packet of cookies in one aisle only to be reminded in another aisle by a holographic celebrity dentist that you really should buy some extra dental care products if you intend to include that type of food in your diet.

Although the potential appears vast for such futuristic technology, a more considered evaluation raises a number of more sobering prospects. First, although technologies such as these may change the way marketers seek to communicate, the basic marketing principles being applied in the scenario have not changed from those already commonplace. The principles of sales promotion, consumer behavior, and direct marketing are consistent with those that have been applied for decades. The efficiency and effectiveness of contemporary marketing techniques may improve with future technological advances such as these, assuming that it becomes feasible to realize them, but they would only be expected to be effective so long as consumer behavior norms and communication expectations remained largely unchanged. The scenario only determines the impact of a specific technology and fails to account for other possible changes.

For instance, retail formats like malls and self-service hypermarkets are relatively recent phenomena. By 2050 these retail formats could become largely defunct, having been replaced by more interactive, automated purchasing methods. Many of the products we consume today, such as packaged breakfast cereal, have a relatively recent history. For example, Kellogg's Frosties date back only to the 1950s. A recent marketing intelligence report revealed that European consumer needs in the 'cold ready to eat' market are evolving and moving towards portable, out-of-home formats (Mintel 2004). This trend has forced manufacturers to begin to consider new product launches in the snack and convenience markets in order to compensate for the deterioration of in-home breakfast meal occasions. Although it might become possible by mid-century to have live animated characters dancing around on a corn flakes packet, the consumer demand for such products and associated technologies may have long since passed.

It is possible to offer a number of other qualified suppositions about consumer reactions to the sort of futuristic marketing communication technology described above. When the new and advanced technology is first introduced, we might expect marketing and management consultants to proclaim that a revolution is taking place that will change the nature of marketing forever. As with the *fin de siecle* e-commerce discourse of the late 1990s (De Cock et al. 2005), such claims are likely to exaggerate the potential of the technology and its viable applications. Anticapitalist protestors could join forces with other protest groups to criticize the infringements the technology has on human rights and individual privacy. Marketers could respond to these protests by asserting that such methods are in principle no different to a public announcement or a personal recommendation from a sales representative. More protectionist governments then might impose restrictions on the use of the technology, banning its use for products aimed at children, for example, whereas more free-market cultures might call upon the industry to continue to regulate itself by amending and updating codes of practice. One could also anticipate the odd health scare in which the potential long-term problems associated with retinal damage are raised, with the predictable response of industry scientists who would make every effort to maintain public confidence.

Additional sociostructural considerations finally bring us to consider some potential problems linked to consumer behavior that futuristic marketing communications such as these could entail. Like junk mail today, consumers likely would complain about the increasing bombardment of marketing-related images. We could expect consumers to quickly develop a capacity to ignore, filter out, distort, and disregard many of the received messages, much as they now do with television and print advertising (Joacimsthaler and Aaker 1997). The technology would certainly appeal to a basic consumer desire to feel unique and special, and in this regard walking down a street with billboards and shop windows calling out with personalized messages might be relatively favorably received. This is likely to be all the more relevant if the predicted rise in 'the new individualism' among consumers is realized (Wilmott and Nelson 2003).

Our brief exercise in an imagined future has made clear that in order to produce an informed assessment of the possible future characteristics and forms of consumer society it is necessary to examine a broad set of underlying sociostructural dynamics. For example, we need to do more than simply expect new data technologies to replace CDs and DVDs, just as they themselves replaced magnetic tape, gramophone records, and wax cylinder recordings. Instead, we need to question whether the consumer mass market for recorded music might go into decline or mutate into a format that is completely different from the present market structure. Although new products, technologies, and brands certainly will emerge to replace those currently available, an analysis of these innovations does not by itself constitute the basis of a credible forecast. To understand the twenty-first-century consumer society we need to look beyond supposed incremental advances in technology or fantasies that are thinly obscured reactions to present-day realities. We need to imagine a broad range of social dynamics and to consider their impact on anticipated marketing practices.

MAPPING THE PROGRESS OF CONSUMER SOCIETY INTO THE TWENTY-FIRST CENTURY

In order to develop a qualified projection for the twenty-first-century consumer society let us begin with a basic conceptual framework that charts the dynamics of consumption over the last century or so in three stages. Drawing on generally accepted histories (Bocock 1993; Fraser 1981; McKendrick et al. 1982), this framework summarizes three periods or eras describing the development of consumer society as a gradual, sequential, and emulative process. This outline is not meant to provide a complete narrative for consumption but rather a basis from which to understand some of possible structures of twenty-first-century consumer society, as well as explaining present-day reactions to some of these prospects. Of course, any linear, progressive, and sequential mapping of the history of consumer society is open to debate and criticism (Agnew 1993). From the viewpoint of the present, the past is open to continual reinterpretation. This scheme is an attempt to conceptualize future trends in consumption as a continuation of ongoing social and economic dynamics.

Each of the three eras shown in Table 3.1 is structured around three dimensions. The first dimension, *the realm of consumption*, defines the areas, regions or social contexts in which consumption can be understood as an emerging and dominant cultural order. The second dimension describes the prevailing characteristics of consumption within this realm in terms of the *archetypal consumer* and the *site of consumption*. The

Table 3.1. Three eras in the development of consumer society

Era	The realm of consumption	The characteristics of consumption		The dangers of consumption
		Archetypal sites of consumption	Archetypal consumers	
1850s–1920s	Bourgeois consumer society	Department store, the metropolitan cityscape	Women, the 'flaneur'	Social decay and diversion from reason and social progress
1930s–1980s	Mass Western consumer culture	Mall and Hypermarket	Youth culture	Moral degradation and the loss of 'traditional' values
1990s–	Emerging global consumption	Global media, Cyberspace	Non-Western elites/the 'international' consumer	Ecological decay and the loss of environment

archetypal consumer in any given period can be understood as a prevailing collective idea that organizes and defines common perceptions about the consumer. This dimension is broadly consistent with what Ritzer (1999) referred to as the *cathedrals of consumption* and their archetypal occupants. The third dimension captures the dominant fears and concerns over the *dangers of consumption*.

The history of consumer society reveals that as consumption values have colonized greater and greater aspects of social life, a corresponding intellectual and moral discourse has emerged warning of the potential negative consequences that this new wave of consumerism is likely to have. As one would expect, these warnings have tended to originate from the interests of the elites that had previously enjoyed a monopoly on consumption values. Thus, establishment criticism of consumption in Europe and the USA at the turn of the twentieth century drew upon a discourse of aristocratic superiority to define arguments regarding the socially degenerative effects that consumerism might have if left to bourgeois society (Horowitz 1985). Half a century later these same middle-class interests, which had once been the target of criticism themselves, voiced comparable concerns about the dangers of a mass consumer society. It is interesting to contrast these different 'warning discourses' that have been enlisted in each generation of consumer ideology from the perspective that they illustrate dynamic and future trends.

Nineteenth-Century Bourgeois Consumer Society

At the turn of the twentieth century, what were to become consumer cultural values gradually expanded beyond the realm of upper social elites and aristocratic society. These values flourished in the newly emerging metropolitan culture of Europe and the eastern region of the USA, finding particular expression among the new wealth of a confident, nouveaux riche middle class (Horowitz 1985; Veblen 1995). The site of consumption during this era is best characterized by the emergence of the department store in major metropolitan centers (Williams 1982), with women and the *flaneur* (a self-indulgent, aimless wanderer or 'man about town'), constituting the corresponding archetypal consumers for the period (Benjamin 1999). Laermans' (1993: 98) described this era as follows:

The immense and rapid success of the early department stores not only resulted from their roles as leisure and 'taste centers' for middle-class women. The vast appetite for status symbols of the new middle class of professionals and employees was actually fostered by their particular conditions of living. A major portion of the *petite bourgeoisie* lived in steadily growing cities of the nineteenth centuries. The people living in these cities had to invent new ways of living, new habits, new forms of social interaction.

During this period several influential commentators and theorists turned their attention to the potential consequences of consumer society, envisioning the future of the twentieth century as a time when the seeds of consumption currently being planted by upper middle-class values would blossom into full-scale consumer cultures. Victorian commentators such as Wayland and Thoreau viewed emerging middle-class consumption as self-indulgent and socially degenerative (Horowitz 1985). The main concern—that is, the main *danger of consumption,*—during this period was understood principally in terms of the moral degeneration that was likely to occur if groups in society that were morally ill-equipped to resist the lure of increased consumption opportunities gained full status as consumers.

In 1899, Veblen famously condemned the conspicuous consumption that he saw engulfing middle-class sensibilities and traditional values. Once released from a life totally dominated by work, it was feared that the self-indulgent lower classes would be prone to satisfying lower senses and that this in turn would create a society of decadence. In the same vein, it was argued that once released from a life dominated and controlled by the domestic sphere, middle-class women would be prone to the tyrannies of irrational desire and related hysterias. It is both interesting and relevant to note that the groups considered most vulnerable to new consumption opportunities in Victorian society also posed the greatest threat to upper middle-class patriarchy. It is not coincidental that an increasingly influential lower middle-class or petit bourgeois stood to gain most from the opportunities offered by social change and were also the subject of most condemnation with regard to the emerging consumer society.

Twentieth-Century Mass Western Consumer Culture

Throughout the first half of the twentieth century, middle-class consumer culture gradually gave way to an emerging mass consumer society. Middle-class preserves were increasingly under threat from a newly confident working class for whom consumer society was to become evermore accessible. This shift from bourgeois to mass consumer society occurred first in the USA, followed by Western Europe. By the end of the 1960s mass consumer cultures were well established throughout the developed economies of the world. The site of consumption during this era is best characterized by the emergence of the shopping mall and the supermarket. These mass retail formats were designed to meet the needs and demands of an emerging mass consumer culture in which the working classes began to develop a coherent brand consciousness. The archetypal consumers of this era were the young (or so-called 'youth culture'). Mass consumption, made possible by postwar affluence and advances in mass production, provided the necessary conditions by which a new popular culture consciousness could emerge.

The main danger of consumption during this era related to general fears over social decay and a disintegration and eventual breakdown of traditional values of respect, social obedience, and social coherence. The youth consumer culture tended to be described at that time as replete with drug abuse, sexual libertinage, and a general anarchy against established tradition and authority (Nava 1992). One need only consider the immense social, medical, and technological changes that characterized the mass consumer societies of the developed West to appreciate the revolutionary significance of consumption and market structures during this period. As early as the 1930s, newly emerging mass technologies, such as radio, helped define an increasingly commercialized culture in which the boundaries between commodity and noncommodity were becoming blurred (Lavin 1995). By the 1960s, mass popular culture had evolved into a form almost wholly consistent with a commodity discourse. By this time, the 'culture industries,' to use Adorno's (1991) phrase, whether in terms of fashion, popular music, or other proto-lifestyle movements were well advanced for this baby boom generation.

Early Twenty-First-Century Elite Global Consumption

Although the previous era of Western consumer culture was characterized by mass consumption, it is important to recognize that it remained restricted to certain parts of the world defined mainly by geopolitical and economic ideology. Just as the working classes of Europe and the USA had once been excluded from participating in bourgeois consumer society at the turn of the twentieth century, so too the global mass popu-lation remains largely excluded from 'developed' mass consumer society at the turn of the twenty-first century. Economic (under)development and the legacy of communism are among the primary reasons for this state of affairs. The current era of consumption therefore is best understood as a transition period, which might best be termed *emerging global consump-tion*. Consumer cultures are apparent among the elite social classes in China and India, and it is reasonable to expect that what is currently seen as an elite preserve will become a mass global phenomenon in the near future. For example, by 2002 there were over 10 million private cars in China and some forecasts suggest that this will increase by fifteen times to over 150 million by 2015 (Gardner et al. 2004).

The characteristics of consumption corresponding to the era of emer-ging global consumption are more fragmented and less tangible than in previous eras. Developments in information communication technologies might suggest that this consumption era is virtual and web-based, but although this may be part of the explanation, it certainly is not all of it. The era of emerging global consumption is perhaps best thought of in a more intangible way, as a combination of mass media, branding, and image. The corresponding archetypal consumer also is difficult to concep-tualize. The archetype is best defined in opposition; that is, as non-Western and to a certain extent either nonmodern or postmodern. One of the reasons why it becomes difficult to conceptualize contemporary consumer society is because it has transcended the social in a strict sense of the term (Baudrillard 1983). Likewise, the danger of consumption lies beyond cat-egories of class, gender, and demographics, which are no longer suffi-ciently robust for conservative forces to use as a basis of criticism. Global consumer culture has evolved its own corresponding global discourse for the danger of consumption, best understood as ecological or environmen-tal destruction. The future prospect of a globalized consumption and the likely establishment of mass consumer cultures across the developing world have raised concerns among a diverse range of interests, from academics to policymakers.

Although many aspects of these arguments are sound, this general critique of consumerism needs to be understood as the latest phase in an ongoing process by which consumer opportunities are opened up and made available to a greater diversity of groups and cultures. Many writers have focused on the unsustainable character of modern consumption (Gardner et al. 2004). It is argued that the twenty-first century will be characterized by ever-increasing resource exploitation together with a general worsening of the already poor status of the natural environment. This will include ecological and social problems associated with global warming, a shrinking biodiversity leading to mass extinction of many species, increasing strains on natural resources such as clean water and air, and health problems and diseases caused by pollution. This bleak forecast of the future is premised on an assumption that consumption and the actions of consumers lie at the root of many current ecological and social problems (see McMurty 1998). Moreover, although current levels of consumption are deemed to be unsustainable, the prospect of citizens from the world's developing economies seeking modern consumer lifestyles for themselves is seen as doubly alarming. Critics question whether the environment can sustain consumer societies in the developing world, and what can or should be done now to prevent developing populations from aspiring to and achieving consumer lifestyles and a standard of living equivalent to that currently enjoyed by the consumers in affluent developed economies.

The simple framework depicted in Table 3.1 suggests that this general environmental critique can be located as part of a long tradition. The problem of the future of consumer society has always been written from the perspective of those who have recently benefited most from the opportunities of consumer society but nevertheless perceive a time in the near future when exclusive access to these benefits is likely to cease. The Western intellectual movement to establish a clear correlative association between the emergence of consumer societies in other parts of the world with an environmental protectionist campaign can be interpreted as but the latest phase in this tradition. This does not mean that environmental concerns are not in many cases legitimate or well founded, but that alongside the scientific reasoning exists a corresponding ideological principle.

Forecasting the Mid-Twenty-First-Century Consumer Society

The consumer society framework provides a clear and consistent indication with regard to the nature of the emerging twenty-first-century: It suggests that most of the radical, transformational, and progressive movements that are likely to influence the twenty-first-century consumer societies will probably take place outside of traditional North American or Western European social contexts. As this transformational framework implies, emerging consumer cultures will continue to adopt and incorporate values and technologies from established consumer cultures, which in turn will mutate into new and discrete forms and trends. However, we must eventually anticipate a turning point whereby the sites that were characterized by consumption in the twentieth century will come to follow innovations and advances that emerge in new twenty-first-century consumer cultures.

Although it is also reasonable to expect that consumer cultures will remain an established part of Western societies, this framework suggests that the innovations and changes will emerge elsewhere. Indeed, there is some evidence to suggest that the fascination with the ideology of consumption already is being questioned in many of the social groups that have lived with mass consumption the longest. The problems associated with materialism and the paradoxes of luxury in Western societies have become the focus of considerable debate among academics and social critics (Frank 1999; Hamilton 2004; Shankar and Fitchett 2002). Theorists have begun to consider the possibilities of a postmaterialistic society and, in so doing, have begun to challenge the status of consumption in everyday life.

Modern marketing practices are themselves products of the twentieth-century mass consumption era (Fullerton 1988). They were developed to meet the emerging social and economic realities of postwar North American markets, before being transposed onto a corresponding Western European model (Usunier 2000). Attempts to universalize these principles for an international or global marketing context are probably short-sighted and we must also seriously consider the possibility that these techniques and concepts, which continue to remain at the core of marketing science, may themselves eventually be consigned to the history of the twentieth century. For over a decade, a growing number of academics have begun to question the basis and value of many core marketing principles and have brought into question the credibility of the dominant historical account of the development of marketing and the continuing relevance of marketing concepts (see Brown 1995). We need to acknowledge that not only will the most revolutionary and transformational aspects of twenty-first-century consumer society take place outside of the developed Western world, but the concepts, theories, and models that are applied to understand these changes may evolve elsewhere as well.

NEWS FROM NOWHERE

The preceding discussion argues that questions about the future of consumer society are fundamentally social and ideological in character. Forces that are expected to shape the future, such as technology, ecology, democracy, and the global market are best understood within a contemporary set of dominant social expectations and values. Attempts to predict, manage, or plan for consumer society can in one sense be thought of as exercises in utopianism in that they create idealized projections about the future through the use of imagined scenarios or social thought experiments. In order to conclude this discussion, the remainder of this chapter reviews some of the many attempts to outline and imagine the twenty-first-century consumer society. Before considering specific utopian consumer society narratives, it is worth considering some of the contexts and conventions on which utopian writings rely. Utopian writings are just as much part of the social discourse and social institutions as any other means of representation and, in this respect, utopian writing from any one historical period reveals much about the dominant powers, ideologies, and forces prevalent at that time.

The questions for us to consider here are what are the dominant utopias of today and where are they to be found? One response to these questions was suggested by Jacoby (1999), who argued that Western culture has abandoned its utopian tradition and this has led to a social order without any real vision or progressive agenda. His nihilistic thesis portrays a twenty-first century in which politics, lacking any coherent ideology, are reduced to mere administration. Lacking any coherent purpose, culture is reduced to mere spectacle in this view. In one sense, Jacoby is correct in arguing that the intellectual, or ideological, tradition that emerged during the nineteenth century and ultimately dominated the first half of the twentieth century is no longer a primary social force (Bauman 1992). But in another sense, Jacoby fails to appreciate that the dominant interests in any given social structure typically write utopian narratives. It is not that twenty-first-century consumer society no longer has utopias, but rather that they are written elsewhere. In a culture that is increasingly defined and organized by discourses of globalization, free markets, and corporate power we should no longer search for utopians among academics and novelists. This may have been appropriate in the previous periods when these interests maintained a dominant social position. Instead, attention should be focused on those groups or classes that embody contemporary inspirational and utopian ideals. In my view, these can readily be found among the publications of management consultants, think tanks, and commercial research projects. Popular management books often adopt a strong utopian flavor (Rhodes 2004). To illustrate some of the utopian potentials evident in modern management writing, I briefly consider below three different narratives that offer clear and well-developed ideas to help forecast aspects of the twenty-first-century consumer society.

Feather's 'Future Consumer'

Frank Feather (2000), a former strategic planner for three of the world's leading banks, offers a vision of the future where current marketing practices have been revolutionized. His forecast, titled *Future Consumer.com: The Webolution of Shopping to 2010*, focuses on the imagined changes that will result from new technologies such as the Internet, e-commerce, and m-commerce. In his view, by 2010, home shopping in virtual community environments will have largely replaced the conventional retail format.

Eagerly anticipated technologies are expected to change almost every aspect of the consumer experience. Consider the following prediction (Feather 2000: 49):

WebPhones will replace cash, checks, debit cards and credit cards in paying for products and services of all kinds. Diners in restaurants and cafeterias will simply point their WebPhone at the waiter's portable WebPhone-Reader to zap money into the eatery's bank account.

Feather anticipates a consumer society in which all personal identity information and other data will be stored in a digitally compatible manner and that with the integration of various biotechnologies (such as retinal scanning) this will make market transactions quicker, more efficient, and more secure. In this twenty-first-century consumer society the home, leisure, and work environments are expected to be integrated into a vast stream of interactive data, thereby creating a borderless, real-time utopia unconstrained by all forces that do not directly attend to consumer desires and demands.

The assertive and optimistic view of the future in Feather's utopian account now probably appears somewhat naive to many readers who witnessed the crash and subsequent disenchantment associated with the new economy during 2002. But we should not discount the real power that e-commerce-based utopian writing had on markets at the time (De Cock et al. 2005). Feather was not alone in making these kinds of predictions; indeed, similar utopian conceptions appeared in academia and the mass media from the mid-1990s to the early 2000s. With the benefit of hindsight it is easy to discredit and discount the utopian ambitions of earlier decades; nonetheless, when one looks back at the e-commerce phenomenon the major disappointment is not that predictions were too bold but rather that they were not bold enough. Although able to conceptualize wonderful new technologies and their anticipated social consequences, management experts were unable to imagine anything other than mundane commercial applications, such as new ways of buying groceries or paying for a meal.

Wilmott and Nelson's 'Complicated Lives'

Perhaps a more credible attempt to consider a broader, more socially grounded future consumer society was offered by Wilmott and Nelson (2003) in their book, *Complicated Lives: Sophisticated Consumers, Intricate Lifestyles, Simple Solutions*. The authors are affiliated with the British-based Future Foundation think tank, and their book draws upon extensive research conducted for a large retail bank. Wilson and Nelson envision the future of consumer society as largely fragmented, dislocated, and highly pressured. In their view, an increasingly individualized society will place less emphasis on gender, class, and age categories, resulting in a more complex, even chaotic, consumer culture. Greater choice, increasing affluence, and a market dominated by products delivering rewarding experiences will emerge alongside barriers of cultural capital and informal networks.

As with much management utopianism, technology is expected to play a defining role in the lifestyles and consumer behavior of the future, although the authors acknowledge some of the downsides that these developments could have. From a utopian or futurist perspective, perhaps one problem with *Complicated Lives* is its acute sense of realism. In a sense, Wilmott and Nelson do not offer a credible prediction for twenty-first-century consumer society but rather an empirical description of the very near present.

Although their predictions have much to say about the very near future it is less informative about more medium- to long-term prospects. We might, for instance, reflect on the eventual adult attitudes and reactions of the current generation of children growing up in the context of the complicated lives of their parents. Perhaps this mid-twenty-first-century generation will revive and romanticize less complicated lifestyles, or reassert class or gender boundaries. If such trends were to emerge, they would be expected to have a considerable impact on the shape and form of consumer society.

Baldock's 'Destination Z'

In *Destination Z: The History of the Future*, consultant Robert Baldock (1999) presents his own exercise into the utopian imagination through a strategic scenario-planning perspective. Like the other two approaches described above, Baldock emphasizes new information technologies, increasingly demanding customers, changing global demographics, and the rising power of branding as the key forces shaping the twenty-first-century consumer society. Unlike Feather's e-commerce based *web-olution*, Baldock acknowledges that there is a considerable margin of error in any prediction of future events and presents not one but five alternative possible futures. Four of the scenarios follow from a conventional strategic planning model and present different combinations of various consumer and organizational characteristics. For example, in one scenario Baldock considers a future of highly specialized firms delivering standardized products and services to otherwise passive consumers. In another he envisions a future of highly integrated corporate conglomerates servicing extremely demanding customers. For the purposes of this discussion, however, it is his 'Thunderstrike scenario' that is the most utopian in nature. Having stuck faithfully to the conventions of managerialism to explain the other four strategic planning alternatives, Baldock allows his imagination (and anxiety) to run freely in discussing the Thunderstrike future as a twenty-first century in which much of the world is at war. Conflicts rage between countries on the Indian subcontinent as well as across the Far East, and far right nationalism and fundamentalism have become the political mainstay elsewhere. The global economy will descend into chaos and barter trade and black markets will become the predominant structures of exchange. Fear of terrorism and crime will become the key drivers and security products and services will provide the only major growth market.

The three futuristic visions described above present very different views of the coming century and the likely characteristics of consumer society. In certain respects each of the accounts can be expected to contain elements that may come to pass, whereas other aspects will remain hypothetical management fantasies. As suggested, one of the disappointing aspects of the contemporary managerial utopianism is their lack of imagination. Many of the key factors and conditions of change envisioned in scenarios for the future are to some extent evident in the present and are simply reported in a more extreme or logically derived form. One of the weaknesses of this new managerial utopianism is that the futures that they imagine are often poorly composed, quickly outmoded, and ultimately discredited. This brings into question their value in forming accurate social forecasts for the twenty-first-century consumer society.

Perhaps a more radical exercise in the future of consumption would attempt to imagine a society vastly different from that of today. Rather than fantasizing about supposed new gadgets and technologies, or overestimating and forecasting supposed current trends, it might be worthwhile to consider the possibility of social change beyond present-day parameters. For instance, we might contemplate mid-twenty-first-century Western societies as postmaterialistic and nonconsumer orientated. Alternatively, ethnic, cultural, and racial integration may result in fragmented, dispersed consumer societies existing alongside other types of social orders in common, shared spaces. It is also worth considering those groups that are likely to be excluded or may choose to exclude themselves from consumer society norms and what some of the consequences of this exclusion are likely to be.

CONCLUSION

Many of the issues discussed in this chapter are primarily concerned with macro factors. Future trends in consumption have been discussed in terms of broad social and cultural changes as well as potential technological advances. Transferring these wide-ranging debates down to the level of specific marketing activities such as considering how marketing communications strategy might be approached in the future, or how the communications industry will adapt to new market trends, is not straightforward. The discussion nevertheless helps to provide some ideas about the shape and form that marketing communication practices might take in the next century. First, in order for any type of prediction to be useful it must be broad in focus. An assessment of the future viability of the use of print media in marketing communications, for example, needs to take into account many different types of factors. Technological advances in printing and data transfer must be assessed alongside forecasts for the future markets for magazines, newspapers, and other print outlets. Likewise, assessments about the future of in-store merchandising and sales promotion require some consideration of the future of retail formats, as well as how power in distribution channels might adapt and change.

Second, it is necessary to assess likely market trends in particular societies and to evaluate the role that communications may have in light of these assessments. For example, Western models of brand management and consumer behavior might need to be revised or even rewritten in order for communications strategies to be successfully developed for consumer societies expected to be important in the coming decades. Finally, it is important to acknowledge and accept that because specific predictions for consumer society are uncertain, the future role of marketing communications is equally unknowable. This requires all forecasts concerning the future of marketing communications to be understood as creative and imaginative exercises rather than indications of trends that are likely to come to pass. Acknowledging the utopian, even fictional, quality of forecasts should not detract from their utility and value but rather prepare marketers with the necessary outlook to approach communications decisions with adaptability and flexibility.

REFERENCES

Adorno, T.W. (1991). *The Culture Industry: Selected Essays on Mass Culture*. London: Routledge.

Agnew, J.C. (1993). 'Coming Up for Air: Consumer Culture in Historical Perspective,' in J. Brewer, and R. Porter (eds.), *Consumption and world of goods*. London: Routledge, pp. 19–39.

Baldock, R. (1999). *Destination Z: A History of the Future*. Chichester, UK: Wiley.

Barthes, R. (1972). *Mythologies*. New York: Hill and Wang.

Baudrillard, J. (1983). *In the Shadow of the Silent Majorities*. New York: Semiotext(e).

Bauman, Z. (1992). 'Legislators and Interpreters: Culture as an Ideology of Intellectuals,' in Z. Bauman (ed.), *Intimations of Postmodernity*. London: Routledge.

Benjamin, W. (1999). *The Arcades Project*. Cambridge, MA: Harvard University Press.

Bocock, R. (1993). *Consumption*. London: Routledge.

Brown, S. (1995). 'Life Begins at 40? Further Thoughts on Marketing's "Mid-life Crisis",' *Marketing Intelligence & Planning*, 13 (1), 4–17.

De Cock, C., Fitchett, J.A., and Volkmann, C. (2005). 'Making History of e-Commerce: Print Advertising and the New Economy,' *British Journal of Management*, 16, 37–50.

Feather, F. (2000). *Future consumer.com: The Webolution of Shopping to 2010*. Toronto: Warwick GP.

Frank, R.H. (1999). *Luxury Fever: Money and Happiness in an Era of Excess*. Princeton, NJ: Princeton University Press.

Fitchett, J.A. and Fitchett, D.A. (2001). 'Drowned Giants: Science Fiction and Consumption Utopias,' in M. Parker, M. Higgins, G. Lightfoot, and W. Smith (eds.), *Science Fiction and Organization*. London: Routledge, pp. 90–101.

Fraser, W.H. (1981). *The Coming of the Mass Market: 1850–1914*. Hamden: Archon Press.

Fullerton, R. A. (1988). 'How Modern is Modern Marketing? Marketing's Evolution and the Myth of the "Production Era",' *Journal of Marketing*, 52 (1), 108–26.

Gabriel, Y. and Lang, T. (1995). *The Unmanageable Consumer*. London: Sage.

Gardner, G., Assadourian, E., and Sarin, R. (2004). 'The State of Consumption Today,' in B. Halweil, and L. Mastney (eds.), *State of the World 2004: The Consumer Society*. New York: Worldwatch Institute & Norton.

Hamilton, C. (2004). *Growth Fetish*. London: Pluto Press.

Horowitz, D. (1985). *The Morality of Spending: Attitudes Towards the Consumer Society in America, 1875–1940*. Baltimore, MD: The Johns Hopkins University Press.

Jacoby, R. (1999). *The End of Utopia: Politics and Culture in an Age of Apathy*. New York: Basic Books.

Joachimsthaler, E. and Aaker, D.A. (1997). 'Building Brands Without Mass Media,' *Harvard Business Review* (January-February), 39–50.

Latour, B. (1996). *Aramis, or the Love of Technology*. Cambridge, MA: Harvard University Press.

Laermans, R. (1993). 'Learning to Consume: Early Department Stores and the Shaping of Modern Consumer Culture (1860–1914),' *Theory, Culture and Society*, 10, 79–112.

Lavin, M. (1995). 'Creating Consumers in the 1930s: Ima Philips and the Radio Soap Opera,' *Journal of Consumer Research*, 22, 75–99.

McKendrick, N., Brewer, J., and Plumb, J.H. (1982). *The Birth of a Consumer Society*. Bloomington: Indiana University Press.

McMurty, J. (1998). *Unequal Freedoms: The Global Market as an Ethical System*. West Hartford: Kumarian Press.

Minority Report (2002). 2 DVD set. Twentieth Century Fox.

Mintel (2004). *Breakfast Cereals, UK: February 2004*. Mintel International Group.

Nava, M. (1992). *Changing Cultures: Feminism, Youth and Consumerism*. London: Sage.

Rhodes, C. (2004). 'Utopia in Popular Management Writing and the Music of Bruce Springsteen: Do You Believe in the Promised Land?,' *Consumption, Markets and Culture*, 7(1), 1–21.

Ritzer, G. (1999). *Enchanting a Disenchanted World: Revolutionizing the Means of Consumption*. London: Pine Forge Press.

Shankar, A. and Fitchett, J.A. (2002). 'Having, Being and Consumption,' *Journal of Marketing Management*, 18 (5/6), 501–16.

United Nations (2004). *World Population in 2300: Proceedings of the United Nations Expert Meeting on World Population in 2300*. New York: United Nations.

Usunier, J.C. (2000). *Marketing Across Cultures*. London: FT Prentice-Hall.

Veblen, T. (1995). *The Theory of the Leisure Class: An Economic Study of Institutions*. London: Penguin.

Williams, H. (1982). *Dream Worlds: Mass Consumption in Late Nineteenth-century France*. Berkeley, CA: University of California Press.

Wilmott, M. and Nelson, W. (2003). *Complicated Lives: Sophisticated Consumers, Intricate Lifestyles, Simple Solutions*. London: The Future Foundation and Wiley.

4

Marketing Communications in a World of Consumption and Brand Communities

Albert M. Muñiz, Jr. and Thomas C. O'Guinn

Marketing communication has been seriously undertheorized for decades, but the ongoing telecommunications revolution has finally made it inescapably obvious that the field needs a much better model of marketing communications. The reasons for this state of affairs are many, but prominent among them are the intellectual insularity of the marketing field and the lack of any meaningful sociological tradition (or even awareness) that could be brought to bear on the study of a metaphenomenon that is inherently social. In addition, there is the small matter of reality: mediated communication itself has changed. Strategies and tactics considered marginal and radical just ten years ago have become the standard practice of many traditional marketers. Marketing theory has not kept up, and now the gap between theory and real world practice is more of a chasm. Because medium is inseparable from message (McLuhan 1965; Ong 1982), a major recasting of marketing communication models is essential.

This chasm should not be bridged by merely aping industry heuristics and tales of best practice. Scholars should not cede their role as crafters of theory, nor take theory entirely to ground. Understanding how the essential meets the new is critical knowledge, practical, and ostensibly the academic's métier. We believe that a major problem with contemporary marketing communication theory is its singular obsession with the isolated individual mind (also known as 'information processor'), and an outdated and impoverished view of human mediated communication and consumption. In this chapter we attempt to begin to address this critical need. This chapter is about marketing communication in the era of connected consumers, and more specifically about a particular form of social connectivity: the brand community.

We must employ the obvious in our theory: brands are important to the citizens of consumer societies. This reality must have a stronger presence in consumer communication theory. Consumers don't just buy brands; they display them, use them as social markers, and talk about them (Ritson and Elliot 1999). Through this talk and other marketplace forces and behaviors, brands take their shape, becoming something negotiated in the space between marketer and consumer. In fact, brands are meaningless outside a notion of social construction and mediated communication. Unfortunately, marketing scholarship has been very slow to catch on to this reality, and has not advanced consumer communication theory significantly beyond what it appropriated as its basic communication model close to forty years ago. We hope to remedy this.

Today, everything from vehicles (Volkswagen), to computers (Macintosh), to soft drinks has a dedicated consumer base (generally small in numbers, but not in communicative properties) that interacts with other consumers. Through their interactions, members of these consumer communities enact consumption practices, influence product development, interpret the meaning of the brand (to users and nonusers alike), and otherwise fold within what used to be the corporate marketing agenda. They become part of the brand-building process. These consumers are drawn together by a common interest in, and commitment to, the brand and a social desire to bond with like-minded others. New modes of computer-mediated communication facilitate and favor communal communication, and thus influence both community and brand.

In order to develop these ideas, in this chapter we draw upon several years of research conducted by both authors on brand community and communication (Muñiz and Hamer 2001; Muñiz and O'Guinn 2001; Muñiz and O'Guinn 1995; Muñiz et al. in press; Muñiz and Schau 2005; O'Guinn and Muñiz 2004; O'Guinn and Muñiz 2000; Schau and Muñiz 2002). Our effort is organized in the following way: We first offer some critical exemplars, many with touch-points to communication theory. These exemplars focus on consumer communication that is communal, computer mediated, and brand centered. We then present a basic model of contemporary marketing communication. This model reflects the active and prominent role of consumers in the creation of brand meaning.

BRANDS AND BRAND COMMUNITIES

To fully appreciate the extent of social change as it relates to branding and marketing, some historical background is necessary. As anthropologists, sociologists, historians, rhetoricians, literary theorists, and many others well know, things and the meanings associated with things have always mattered to people. The human record consists of no place where materiality, social construction, and meaning were strangers (Schudson 1984). There are no purely utilitarian things (O'Guinn and Muñiz in press; Schudson 1984), and this certainly includes brands. Brands are particularly marked things, their power being *derived* from their social marking and meaning.

In the late nineteenth century, brands began to gain prominence in society. Between 1875 and 1900, thousands of newly branded products emerged. Through the early efforts of Procter & Gamble (P&G), Coca-Cola, Budweiser, and others, brands replaced previously 'unmarked' commodities (i.e. soap, soft-drinks, beer) and enabled the growth of modern market economies. By turning commodities into brands, critical demand inelasticities and resultant market share growth were achieved. Brands were invented by the thousands, the modern advertising industry was born, and mass magazines flourished. When this era began, relatively few things were branded. Today, virtually everything is branded, from universities to water to soil. One of the obvious hallmarks of the twentieth century was the rise of the brand in human existence and human consciousness.

A few years ago we became interested in brand communities (Muñiz and O'Guinn 1995). To us and a handful of others (Cova 1997; Fischer et al. 1996; Fournier 1998; Maffesoli 1996; Schouten and McAlexander 1995), it seemed obvious that some form of community surrounded brands. We were confident that this had been going on for quite some time, but were equally convinced that it was accelerating in the new communication environment. At first, we had a difficult time convincing some academics that what we were observing was community, but at no time did we have any difficulty convincing brand managers or marketing professionals. For example, shortly after our initial involvement in the idea of brand communities, a senior P&G marketing executive informed us that not only do communities form around big brands (such as Tide), but that P&G was very interested in managing the process. Clearly, professionals were ahead of the academic marketing community in acknowledging and addressing this new reality. What we were observing *was* community, and community has turned out to be very critical in the new communication era. Brand communities are now widely recognized as key actors in the new communications epoch. But what is a brand community?

Brand communities are nongeographically bound collectives of brand admirers who, through their ability to aggregate and communicate at very little cost, assert themselves as important marketplace collectives. Brand communities are similar to other forms of community, but have their own unique market logic and expressions. They possess three key community characteristics: (*a*) consciousness of kind, (*b*) rituals and traditions, and (*c*) community responsibility (Muñiz and O'Guinn 2001). The ways in which these community markers are manifest greatly impacts several aspects of marketing communication. We briefly consider these three characteristics below before exploring the relevance of brand communities to marketing communications.

Consciousness of kind refers to the collective sense of identity experienced by members of the brand community. Members feel an important connection to the brand, as well as a connection to one another. They feel like they know each other, even if they have never met. Members also frequently note a critical demarcation between users of their brand and users of other brands. They feel there is some important quality that sets them apart from 'the others' and makes them similar to one another. Our research has shown considerable evidence of consciousness of kind in a variety of brand communities in several different product categories (Muñiz and O'Guinn 2001; Schau and Muñiz 2002). These complex connections greatly affect the meaning and social construction of the brand.

Brand communities are also host to a variety of *traditions and ritualized exchanges* that serve to reify the culture of the community, including celebrating the history of the brand, sharing brand stories and myths, ritualistic communications and utterances, special lexicon, and the communal appropriation of marketing communications. The textual nature of the Web provides an excellent forum in which members share their knowledge of the brand's origins, often replete with illustrations and photographs. It is in the expression of these rituals and traditions that these communities most powerfully and effectively challenge the marketer's supremacy in creating brand meaning.

The third aspect of brand community is *moral responsibility*, which refers to a shared commitment to the brand, the community, and other individual members of the community. Moral responsibility is what produces collective action and motivates the provision of assistance to other members. Members work to help the brand, or at least their vision of it, and others who share the same appreciation. Members will help one another with repairs, modifications, and technical assistance. Responsibility also manifests via an apostolic function; that is, members of brand communities generally think that new members (but only appropriate new members) should be recruited to keep the community alive. This is seen as a group moral duty. Here again, the impact on the brand is obvious: the brand is promoted, supported, and made easier to use at no cost to, but also beyond the control of, the marketer.

COMMUNITY COMMUNICATION PROCESSES

Brand communities are participants in the brand's larger social construction and play an important role in the brand's meaning. Electronic communication has facilitated a rapid growth in the number, size, and power of brand communities. Groups whose members rarely achieved critical mass (and power) due to their dispersed nature can now bring force to bear on the marketer. While not all brands are as purely communal (e.g. Apple Computer) as others, all brands are socially situated and all brands have communal aspects. This results in an increase in consumer power for all brands. This power may be to the benefit of the marketer, as when community members help one another solve problems with the brand, thus increasing the value derived from the brand at no additional cost to the marketer. However, consumer strength may manifest in ways less beneficial to the marketer. Members of a brand community may decide, with conviction and strength of number, that the marketer is wrong and actually try to drown out the marketer's voice by talking back. They may reject the actions of the marketer and endeavor to impede them. Community members may feel that the marketer does not care about them or the brand and may make their displeasure known to existing and prospective buyers alike. In the following, we explore several relevant processes by which brand communities can impact marketing communications.

Communal Interpretation of Brand Advertising

Members of brand communities tend to have very well-developed ideas concerning the brand to which they are committed. This includes notions of what the brand means and what directions this meaning should take in the future. Many feel they understand the true essence of the brand better than the marketer does. As a result, they can be quite opinionated about branding and marketing efforts, spending a great deal of time analyzing and critiquing marketing communication in community forums. Ads for the brand are interpreted collectively by the community, with special attention directed to the degree to which the brand as presented in the ads corresponds to the brand as experienced by members. When the ads map onto the brand as understood by the community, the themes in the ads are embraced, celebrated, and elaborated upon (in stories and personal webspace). When the ads are at odds with the community's conceptualization of the brand, the ads are likely to be rejected as members endeavor to create their own meanings for the brand (Brown et al. 2003; Muñiz and O'Guinn 2001).

As an example, consider the nascent community centered on the Pontiac Vibe, a multipurpose vehicle introduced by General Motors in the USA in 2002. After only three model years, Vibe aficionados had developed some strong and well-developed ideas of what is appropriate for the brand. Some strongly rejected changes to the car's appearance for the 2005 model year. Members of the Vibe brand community frequently discussed ads for the Vibe, sometimes subjecting televised ads to close, shot-by-shot scrutiny. Consider the following comments, in which a participant in a Vibe brand community Internet forum took issue with what he considered a less than optimal execution:

They've been running a 'stealth' Vibe commercial in central Indiana. I'm paraphrasing, because I can't type or write fast enough when the commercial comes on to get the full transcript, but here goes: A man is talking to a couple. 'Variable Valve Timing … high performance …' yada-yada-yada Obviously it's a reference to the VVT-i/VVTL-i engines available to Pontiac buyers ONLY in the Vibe. Then another man approaches the three of them and asks the couple if he can help them. 'No, we're already being helped by this man' they reply. The (real) salesman says, 'He doesn't work here!' And the voice-over goes on about a great financing or leasing deal on a Grand Am! No actual mention of the Vibe models, features, or financing. What the h-e-l-l is GM thinking???

Such comments reflect a concern that the manufacturer is doing a poor job of promoting and developing a strong and unique meaning for the brand. These concerns are then communally explored, where they can be reacted to by current and prospective brand users alike.

The need for a strong and unique brand meaning is a powerful one. It is frequently reflected in the community quest for legitimacy. This occurs on two fronts: First, the community wants to ensure that the brand is sincere and accurate in the depiction of its meaning. Second, the community wants to make sure that particular brand users are legitimate and 'appropriate' for the brand (Muñiz and O'Guinn 2001). These understandings are often normative and possessive in nature. Through the added weight of Internet brand-talk, consumers come to form very clear opinions about who should and should not use the brand. Advertising and marketing efforts for the brand will then be judged by members of the community on these dimensions. Long-time members may resent new consumer segments being courted by the marketer, particularly if they fear these new consumers will be attracted to the brand for the wrong reasons.

A powerful example of this can be seen in the Volkswagen (VW) brand community (Brown et al. 2003; Muñiz et al. in press). Many long-time members of the VW community resent VW's continued move upmarket and these sentiments frequently emerge in discussions of VW's advertising. Consider the following message from a VW Usenet newsgroup discussion of ads for the VW Passat, a midsize car targeted to an affluent market segment.

[These ads] stink outloud. Obviously, they reflect VWoA's [Volkswagen of America] attempt to take their cars upmarket, and in the process have lost any of the flair and humor which has been a trademark of their ads for years. I personally think it is an extension of how VW has lost it's way and is going to end up alienating the very people they need to touch to buy their cars.

Many resent the new drivers being attracted to VW as well, labeling them 'yuppies' or 'white preppy clients.'

The relevance of such brand community member tendencies is obvious. Content authored by members of the brand community is routinely consumed by users whose connection to the brand is less communal and by prospective users as well. A new buyer may conduct an Internet search on VW and immediately be put into contact with a vision of VW (and VW drivers) that is at odds with the vision management intended. Because the information created by the community is as easily accessible as that created by the marketer, the brand community becomes just as important a player in the marketing communication process.

Consumer Stories and Narratives

Much brand community talk is in the form of stories about personal experiences and the experiences of others. These stories are often transmitted at dealerships, random encounters, and on Internet forums. Communities recreate their histories, values, and meanings through communal stories, and brand communities are no different. These stories, which are frequently retold, are often well-written and replete with collages of images of the product (Brown et al. 2003; Muñiz and O'Guinn 2001; Schau and Muñiz 2003).

Consider the story-telling culture of the Miata brand community. The Miata is a compact sports car produced by Mazda. Members of the Miata brand community like to share stories of ideal consumption experiences with the Miatas they own. Typically, these stories involve a beautiful day in which the windows can be rolled down and the top can be taken off. Such experiences have been termed 'perfect Miata drives' and are a frequently recurring theme in the Miata community Internet forums. A perfect Miata drive involves a deserted, sometimes hilly, frequently winding road, with breathtaking scenery. The following comments from a Miata Internet forum were posted under the heading 'Seattle area twisties':

There are good, short roads to the south off the Maple Valley Hwy—Jones Rd, Green Valley Rd, the west (steep) end of Lake Holm Rd, Tiger Mountain Rd, Lake Francis Rd, Auburn/Black Diamond Rd. The Issaquah/Fall City Rd is terrific. All of these have relatively high mailbox coefficients, unfortunately. There are also some unbelievable, twisty, tree-lined, two-lane highways up north around Mt. Baker State

Park. I don't recall the names or specific locations right now but some of them are very sparsely populated and little traveled. Chuckanut Drive is both exciting and beautiful. Lake Washington Blvd west (south of I-520) is slow but has a few great hairpins.

There is even a website devoted to this phenomenon (miatadrives.com), featuring detailed descriptions and maps. In this way, the community continually creates the perfect brand consumption experience. These ideals typically are influenced by the advertising for the brand, but are communally scripted. Their potential to influence the consumption experience and the meaning of the brand is great.

Consumer story-telling is not limited to manufactured goods. Consumers also like to tell stories about services, such as those experienced while traveling or on vacation. Several consumption-oriented websites offer consumers a chance to post their reviews of products and services as well (e.g. consumerreview.com; epinions.com; rateitall.com). Stories are often included with these reviews in order to justify or explain a rating of a product or service. These stories are probably easier for other consumers to appreciate, embrace, and pass along than are numerical ratings. Obviously, stories add to the value of the brand for both the consumers who tell these stories and those who read them. They may also make the brand attractive to those who are only just starting to consider a purchase. We have seen several instances in which prospective buyers have followed these conversations before buying the brand. Some consumers even appeal to different brand communities for experiences and advice before making a purchase in a product category. Once again, the brand community is approximating the marketer's role in the brand communication process.

Rumor

A closely related narrative phenomenon is rumor. Much content in brand communities takes the form of rumor (Kimmel 2004; Muñiz et al. in press). The history of the brand and personal stories centered on the brand are often transmitted via communal rumor. Rumors can be distinguished from story-telling in that the experiences tend not to be personal but refer to an unknown other entity (e.g. 'someone my friend knows') or organization, and are often prefaced with 'I heard' or 'I saw somewhere.' As such, they allow for the expression of properties and attributes that might not be true, but what the community *wants* to be true or fears may be true. Rumors play an important role in the consumer construction of the brand.

Cultural capital and issues of credibility loom large in brand communities. Brand communities tend to be structured, with complex hierarchies. The contribution of a new and valuable piece of communal brand talk carries status. The search for new information, such as modifications the manufacturer intends to make to the product or new line entries, can be intensely competitive (Muñiz et al. in press). As a result, consumers sometimes share brand-related information from nonreputable sources. Such utterances are particularly relevant in the Internet age as they may be afforded the same credibility as official information owing to its referability (Schindler and Bickart 2002). Speculation becomes accepted as fact and the information becomes part of the brand's communally accepted legacy. The multimedia nature of the Web provides an excellent forum in which members can share their knowledge of the brand's origins, often replete with illustrations, photographs, and video.

Looking again at the Pontiac Vibe brand community, one can find several instances of rumor pertaining to a variety of brands relating to several dimensions of car ownership: possible modifications in design and styling of the brand, long-term performance and reliability, and safety. For example, brand community members posting on a Vibe Internet forum discussed issues relating to wiring and radios, speculating on possible consequences of replacing a factory radio with an aftermarket radio:

at one point I had my radio removed, completely disconnected, and the door chime still worked. I remember reading about some of the early wiring adapters people were using to put aftermarket radios in these cars, and they had wires to run to the stock radio. Even with the aftermarket radio in the dash, some folks had the stock unit buried somewhere still marginally connected. That was unnecessary. There was even a rumor that the airbags wouldn't work if you replaced the stock radio, as well as rumors that if you disconnected power to the stock radio, you would need to go back to the dealer to get it reprogrammed. I am glad the vibe radios do not include any of those 'features.'

The focal brand for this thread was a competing vehicle (Mitsubishi Eclipse). In this way, members participated in the process of collectively constructing additional reasons to believe that the Vibe was superior to a competing make of car. They actively conceived and publicly rehearsed reasons not to switch to other brands, and the value of the Vibe was socially constructed relative to the Eclipse. Such a communally constructed vision then becomes available to any consumer of the brand.

Consumer-Created Ads

Members of brand communities sometimes endeavor to create something that explicitly looks like an ad and uses the conventions of advertising. In this age of advertising-savvy consumers, it is not entirely surprising that some brand community members believe in the power of advertising to create strong and unique meanings. What is striking, however, is the sophistication with which they may create such artifacts.

A good illustration of this tendency can be found in the brand community for the Apple Newton. The Apple Newton was a personal digital assistant (PDA) introduced in 1993. The Newton never did particularly well in the marketplace, but it did inspire a strong grassroots brand community. This community has persisted even since Apple abandoned the product in 1998. It continues to develop new software and accessories for the Newton, provides parts sources and technical support, and advertises the brand to various audiences (Muñiz and Schau 2005). Members take advertising themes and conventions from a variety of sources to create their own personal Newton ads. The following example from a Newton brand community website mimics Apple's ads for another product, the Apple Powerbook laptop computer. Powerbook ads from the late 1990s featured testimonial data from different Powerbook users, including why they bought a Powerbook and how they used it.

Name: John
Occupation: Student
Newton: MP 110 (right now), getting an MP 2100 soon
Why I bought a Newton: I saw the MP 110 in a pawn shop, and thought it looked cool. It was also cheap. =) I was thinking about a Palm, but the Newton is a lot better than the Palms I've seen. I then read about the MP2100, and started drooling. Luckily, I found a friend of mine who hasn't used his in forever, and bought it off of him. =)
What I love about the Newton: I love the laptop abilities in a smaller package. I will love the ability to use Ethernet. What I dislike: Steve Jobs. =) No, I think Apple was stupid for canceling them. I'd like a smaller form factor, and I wish there were more device drivers. I wish the interconnect port was more available. =)
Carrying case: The Apple Leather one for my 110.
Strangest place I've ever used my Newton: None yet. =) I'm planning on doing an externship to Great Britain next year, and I'll probably take my MP2100 along.
What's on my Newton: Mystic 8 Ball, SoloDX, and whatever the Othello for OS1.3 is (I can't remember the name).

Several Newton users have contributed their own versions of this ad, many of which are complex and with multiple pages of text, to a popular Newton brand community website. Similarly, several professional-looking, user-created ads have circulated among the Volkswagen brand community and there are Web pages for the Saab brand community that also look like advertisements for the brand (Muñiz and O'Guinn 2001; Schau and Muñiz 2002).

Brand community members also engage in a competitive brand community process called *oppositional brand loyalty* (Muñiz and Hamer 2001; Muñiz and O'Guinn 2001). Oppositional brand loyalty is a process in which community members derive an important aspect of their community experience, as well as an important component of the meaning of the brand, from their opposition to competing brands. Thus, many Apple brand community members are not just fans of Apple, they are sworn enemies of Windows. In a similar way, Coke community members stand in opposition to Pepsi, and so on. Many statements evincing oppositional brand loyalty read like passionate comparison advertising, as is apparent in the following from a user-created Coke website that bills itself as the 'Coke Army':

This establishment is for the good of the people. It represents all which is true and right. Our mission: destroy Pepsi. Our weapon: Coca-Cola Classic. Yes! Why destroy Pepsi you may ask? Well, because it's the evil soft drink!

Such content encourages loyalty to the brand, but is largely out of the control of the marketer. It also blurs the already fuzzy lines between marketer-created and consumer-created marketing communication content. Given the increasingly sophisticated creations of consumers in this regard, marketers not only face increasing clutter from competing brands, they also face an increasing amount of clutter, as well as potentially conflicting branding messages, from consumers. The content created by the brand community has become as easily accessible as that created by the marketer and is beginning to approach the level of professionalism as well.

AntiBrand Community Communication

Consumer-created websites do not always pertain to the consumer's favorite brands. Sometimes brands are the center of community attention and action for what members believe the brands have done *wrong*. These sites represent a phenomenon that we have termed *antibrand community* (Aron and Muñiz 2002). The difference between this phenomenon and oppositional brand loyalty is that members of antibrand communities are not necessarily loyal to the competing brand; rather, they appear united primarily in their dislike of a particular brand. Many of these sites have loyal and active followings and appear to have the same three community markers as the brand communities we have encountered (Aron and Muñiz 2002). More importantly, they are just as sophisticated in their efforts to create alternative brand meanings, mimicking advertising and branding conventions for the brands that they target (France and Muller 1999). At the time of this writing, such sites existed for dozens of brands, including Best Buy (bestbuysux.org), Ford (fordreallysucks.com), Pac Bell (mikeandmabell.com), Pontiac (mypointacsucks.com), Starbucks (starbucked.com), United Airlines (untied.com), and Windows (ihatewindowsxp.com).

In addition to organized antibrand community sites, several other complaint sites exist, including thecomplaintstation.com, complaints.com, complaintbook.com, and complain.com. These sites allow consumers to air grievances about any particular company. The impact these sites have is subject to much debate and organizations vary wildly in how they choose to respond to them. Some companies choose to ignore such sites, while others work diligently to record and correct the problems that lead to the creation of the site. United Airlines, target of one of the largest antibrand community sites, Untied, takes the threat posed by such sites very seriously and tracks the site to identify issues that need to be addressed (France and Muller 1999). Similarly, Dunkin' Donuts recognized the potential to capture valuable information from an attack site targeting their brand and worked with contributors to a Dunkin' Donuts attack site to resolve the complaints they had posted (Warner et al. 1999). Nevertheless, all of these sites represent yet another source of the socially constructed brand meaning that impacts the marketing communication process.

MARKETING'S RESPONSE

Recognizing many of the opportunities and challenges presented by brand and consumption communities, many marketers have attempted to devise appropriate response strategies and tactics. Often, these strategies further blur the lines between consumer and marketer generated content. For example, a campaign for the Ford Sportka, which depicts the car killing a curious cat, was *intended* to look like a user-created ad so that it would be spread via e-mail. In fact, it spread quite rapidly, but it also generated controversy. The negative impact of this controversy was increased when the ad was attributed to Ford and its ad agency, rather than a Sportka user (Brier 2004). In the following section, we describe some strategies by which marketing has attempted to manage the influence of brand communities on the marketing communication process.

Pseudo-Grassroots Marketing Communications

Marketing practitioners have long recognized the value of consumer word of mouth (WOM) and several strategies have recently been developed to create it (see Chapter 10). These strategies go by many names: astroturf, buzz marketing, grassroots marketing, viral marketing, and word-of-mouse. Through them, marketers attempt to create a buzz around their product that does not look like active marketing communication. Much of this buzz is intended to mimic brand and consumption community discourse. Indeed, in some instances, marketers attempt to infiltrate an existing brand community with an agent who will promote their product under the guise of a community member, further reinforcing the powerful role of these communities in marketing communications. Engineered WOM approaches have been employed to promote a variety of brands, including American Express, Burger King and Honda (Brier 2004), BMW, Mercedes and Renault (White 2004), and Kraft, Pantene, Pringles and Toyota (Wells 2004). The interaction of such contrived WOM, consumption, and brand communities, and the interconnected world of the Internet create significant challenges for marketers who utilize such approaches.

Another New Coke. When the Coca-Cola Company launched Vanilla Coke in 2002, it was the first new flavor from Coke in over fifteen years. Coke wanted a marketing campaign that would get consumers, including those in Coke's brand community, talking. To achieve this, their introductory marketing campaign included a fictitious narrative component. Coke created a web-site called the VC Lounge. It featured a marketer-fabricated account of the historical origins of Vanilla Coke. The story told of a rogue researcher at Coke who anonymously received a sample of the original Vanilla Coke and managed to crack the formula. According to the story, the researcher then began selling his version of Vanilla Coke at a soda fountain and its sales were so great that it got the attention of Coke management and prompted them to 'officially' launch the flavor. The web-site presented the story as an illicit insider's account and included several components common to corporate rumor: secret labs, stolen formulas, and promises of 'the real story.' Consider the following excerpt, quoted on BadAds.org:

You've probably heard that Coke is launching a new flavor—Vanilla Coke. What you haven't heard is the REAL story behind this product, and why Coke HAD to launch the product when they did. There's a long story behind why I'm building this website and you can find it all out here. What you do need to know is that the new launch of Vanilla Coke is shrouded in controversy and Coke is trying really hard to keep the real story under wraps.

The entire approach was explicitly designed to mimic consumer WOM and rumor in order to create a folklore around the brand that members of the Coke brand community could share and build upon ('Coca-Cola Creates' 2002). A message board on the VC Lounge website encouraged consumers to discuss the story and its details and offered a tool where visitors could e-mail their friends a link to the site.

Illustrating that the dangers inherent in this approach are the same as those associated with all rumors, Coke quickly lost control and the plan backfired. Many consumers were immediately suspicious of the story offered on the website and several of the messages posted on the VC Lounge forum expressed skepticism (BadAds.org 2002). This skepticism turned to anger as consumers were able to quickly learn of the true origins of the website from a host of other online sources, including trade publications where Coke had discussed the strategy. The approach angered a lot of consumers, including members of Coke's brand community. Eventually, after becoming an undesirable part of Coke lore, the site was taken down.

The VC Lounge example illustrates a basic peril of using a contrived grassroots strategy: consumers can become very vocal when they learn they are being misled. In this interconnected world, it is now easier for consumers to find out when this is happening and it is easier for them to share their displeasure. These risks are even greater in brand communities where, as noted before, issues of legitimacy, sincerity, and cultural capital loom large. Brand community members are strongly motivated to identify and chase out marketer agents posing as members in order to keep their community pure. In some of the communities we've examined, members will apply the term 'shill' to anyone whose enthusiasm for a product or service is suspect.

Managing Brand Community and Marketing Communications

The Swedish car manufacturer, Saab, has done an excellent job of managing the marketing communication process with the Saab brand community. Saab works with members of the community who produce important community publications, giving some access to the company president to provide comments and feedback on behalf of the community (Cook 2003). Saab also sponsors an annual Saab owner's convention, which plays heavily on notions of brand history and legacy. By working with community information sources, Saab can gain awareness of, and to some degree affect, what information is being relayed to and by the community. By sponsoring community events, Saab makes it less likely that the Saab brand community will develop an adversarial relationship with the manufacturer.

Jeep has also been successful in interacting with and supporting its brand community. Several years ago, Jeep decided to leverage its brand community by organizing jamborees, weekend-long events where Jeep drivers get together and bond while having off-road adventures in their vehicles. Participants in these jamborees often emerge with a strong sense of community, even among those who felt little connection to their fellow brand users beforehand (McAlexander et al. 2002). Jeep understands that drivers who feel a sense of community through the brand are more likely to generate positive WOM. They become what Jeep officials refer to as 'ambassadors of the brand' (Christian 1997), becoming apostolic in their desire to attract others to the brand.

CONSUMER COMMUNICATION RECONSIDERED AND RECAST

Today, most academic marketing models of communication look very much like they did more than three decades ago. They are ill-equipped to deal with the social nature of communication, and appear largely unaware of recent advances in communication theory. To be fair, we should note that this problem is far more acute in the USA than in Europe, where the sociological imagination has more than survived in the marketing literature. (There are notable exceptions in the USA; see, e.g. Ward and Reingen 1990; Wallendorf and Arnould 1991.)

American marketing research flirted with the sociological communications tradition from the late 1950s to the early 1970s. During the mid-1950s, communication scholars and the nascent field of marketing became rightfully interested in the two-step flow hypothesis (Katz and Lazarsfeld 1955) and in tracking down the so-called 'generalized opinion leader,' a person who was thought to be broadly influential in all market matters (Robertson 1971). These ideas came on the heels of, and in reaction to, several stunning failures in mass persuasion and advertising (including the Ford Edsel launch), that had been based on asocial models of consumer psychology, which emphasized individual messages affecting individual consumers.

The two-step model of communication (see Fig. 4.1) posited that rather than flowing directly from the media to consumers, information (and influence) was more socially mediated. Influence flowed first to opinion leaders, who then had disproportionate influence on other individual consumers. Opinion leaders were presumed to interpret and then retransmit formal marketing messages to other consumers to great effect. This model pointed to something very important and seemingly obvious: that mass communication (including advertising) is a socially stratified process, and that there are systematic inequalities in information possession, access, flow, retransmission, and interpretation that result in significant differences in adoption, influence, and consumer response. It also pointed to the folly of trying to separate consumer communication from consumer behavior. If that fact was not clear then, it certainly is now.

Reasonable attention was paid to the notion of opinion leaders and social stratification of influence for about a decade. Marketing practitioners became completely convinced that this process was entirely real and important. The academic marketing discipline shortly thereafter turned its attention, training, and politics to acquiring legitimacy by adopting the laboratory methods of American social psychologists. Marketing diffusion research was ceded to mathematical modelers who have had considerable success at predicting diffusion rates, while keeping the behavioral 'why' question off the table. The academic marketing wisdom

Two-step flow

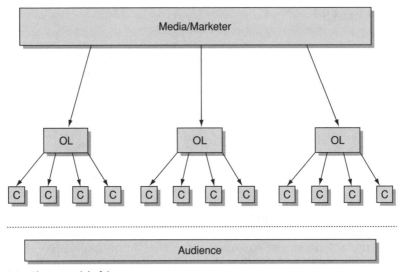

Fig. 4.1. Classic model of the communication process
Source: Katz, E. and Lazarsfeld, P. (1955).

(on the behavioral side of the field) came to be, that efficiently manipulating and tracking WOM communication was impractical due to methodological limitations. As a result, the American marketing academic field lost touch with virtually all things sociological, particularly human communication. What remained was a socially challenged consumer information-processing model, unequipped theoretically or methodologically to meaningfully study human communication in human ecology.

Online brand and consumption communities may finally force marketers to recognize the reality of consumer-to-consumer communication, and its ability to affect significant influence on the marketer, in rapid order and with the power of social mass. Before the advent of computer-mediated connectivity, the opportunity for consumers to easily connect directly to a multitude of like-minded people from around the world was fairly limited. As a result, marketing communications were, to a greater extent, under the control of the marketer. The advent of consumer-controlled interactive electronic media has changed all that. Consumers can now congregate virtually and asynchronously to exchange complex notions of brand meanings and the details of their consumption practices and beliefs. Now, individually and within groups, consumers can exert considerable influence on how the brand is represented in the marketplace. Firms are faced with the challenge of integrating these consumers into the marketing process.

A Social Model of Brand Creation and Brand Communication

As an alternative to prior marketing models of communication, we present below a social model of brand creation and communication, which emphasizes both explicitly and implicitly that communication is a social process.

Production

This component of the model reflects the fact that brands are not made by marketers. Rather, brands can be understood as plastic vessels of meaning, which are cocreated by several key publics: consumers, marketers, advertising professionals, governments, lobbyists, NGOs, shareholders, the press, media, regulators, and so on. All of these stakeholders are also communication agents—they communicate with each other to varying degrees, through various paths, and with varying effects. To speak of the creation of brand meaning isolated from communication is pointless. Whether the marketing relationship is marketer-to-consumer, consumer-to-consumer, or consumer-to-marketer, none of these parties are socially isolated single actors; rather, they are socially immersed institutional agents, institutions, and social aggregations.

As an example, consider the marketer and the consumer. Marketers are *organizations* that collaboratively produce brands through social processes. They *imagine* their consumers, the users of their brands. Typically, they do not directly interact with more than a tiny fraction of their users, and very rarely in naturalistic environments; instead, they imagine legions of them. Their imagination is guided by survey research, focus groups, concept testing, sales data, previous experience, etc. The acquired data are themselves provided by social organizations with political and economic agendas, and structural facets that allow certain views of the consumer's reality, but which have blind spots as well. These data collectively represent an idea of the user, a representation, but not the user themselves. The user is thus 'constructed' by various forms of research and indirect experience. Brand histories are replete with competing visions of who (and what) the consumer is.

In his 1993 book, *For God, Country and Coca-Cola*, Tom Pedergrast revealed that even the world's most popular brand is itself a product of constantly competing personalities, palace intrigue, serendipity, political allegiances, and social dynamics, all hinging on an imagined consumer. And that is before a single bottle ever leaves the plant, or a single Coke ad is produced. Thus, even at the market's most proximal locus of control, brand meaning is anything but simple and overly determined. That brand meaning is still anything but simple, even within the marketing organization, should be clear from the Vanilla Coke example presented earlier. Even in a highly contrived dyadic moment, brand meaning is negotiated. When one adds consumers, public policy institutions, and shareholders to the mix, complication is exponential. Multiple actors negotiate and accommodate the meaning of brands.

Reception

When the consumer's domain is brought into the equation (the right side of Fig. 4.2) it is quite obvious that the marketer's meaning of the brand is hardly accepted without question. Consumers react, talk back, make the brand their own, and add their own meanings to the brand. As suggested by the model, they also negotiate. Recall the discussions by Vibe and VW owners concerning the ads for those brands or of Coke drinkers to the Vanilla Coke campaign. Reception is an active and discursive social process, and not a simple 'cognitive response.' Consumers compare their reactions with each other and use them in creative and even playful ways (Ritson and Elliot 1999). Their reactions are affected, among other things, by their past history, their idea of what the advertisers and company representatives are like, and the perceived intent of marketing efforts.

Accommodation and Negotiation

To accommodate is to accept to some degree some other party's preferred meaning. To negotiate is to work toward an agreed upon meaning between interested parties. Human communication involves both of these processes. In other words, meaning is not just delivered—consumers talk to each other, imagine each other, and observe each other. This plays out in reactions to ad campaigns, to net-brand-talk of all sorts, and ultimately to

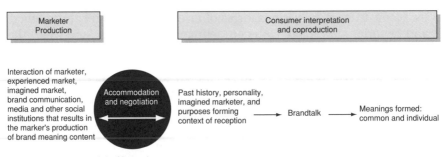

Fig. 4.2. Social model of brand creation
Source: Adapted from Anderson, J.A. and T.P. Meyer (1989). *Mediated Communication: A Social Interaction Perspective*, Newbury Park, CA: Sage.

active acceptance, rejection, or reinvention of the brand. Marketers do the same: they talk to consumers and listen back. They advance their preferred meaning, while accommodating the other. This is communication's essential dynamic.

Sometimes, aspects of market meaning are accepted by consumers, and thus the marketer is 'accommodated,' as when brand community members put ads on their websites and respectfully acknowledge, repeat, and celebrate them. At other times, the marketer's meaning is partially accepted, but the consumer contributes as well. Some aspects of brand meaning are accepted (i.e. accommodated), while other aspects remain contested and open for negotiation. Recall the stories of Miata drivers that drew heavily from Miata ads. Marketer-created meaning (in the form of ads) was being accommodated and combined with user-created content (stories of the perfect consumption experience) in order to negotiate the meaning of the Miata brand. On the other hand, the marketer's meaning may be rejected, and the consumer may put something else in its place entirely; recall the Newton users and VW and Saab drivers who created their own ads. The community created its own content to reinforce the meaning that the *members of the community* had attached to the brand.

Marketers learn something about how the accommodation and negotiation process is playing out for their brand through marketing research. Focus groups and brand community tracking data can then influence what marketers say in subsequent communications. Recall how Saab monitors and supports its brand community or how Dunkin' Donuts followed postings on its antibrand community 'gripe site' for *precisely these reasons.* Such companies observe the reactions of the community and respond appropriately, adjusting their marketing communications to accommodate and negotiate brand meaning. As this process moves along, there is a fluid and dynamic discourse.

Consider this social model of brand creation with the brand community operating somewhat like the 1950s concept of 'opinion leaders.' Fig. 4.3 shows the brand community as a computer-mediated analog of the opinion leader or market maven (Feick and Price 1987), operating between marketer and other consumers. While brand communities may be small in terms of absolute numbers, their influence is not. Consumers frequently solicit feedback from brand communities before making a purchase. The somewhat fluid aggregations of vested consumers that are brand communities function as communication agents. They are consulted by other consumers and by the marketer in what is increasingly becoming a population of considerable marketing surveillance. Unlike the 1950s, we are no longer hampered by the methodological obstacles and we can now observe and even model these networks in real time. These aggregations tend to leave much electronic and textual residue, which provides unobtrusively obtained data for the marketer.

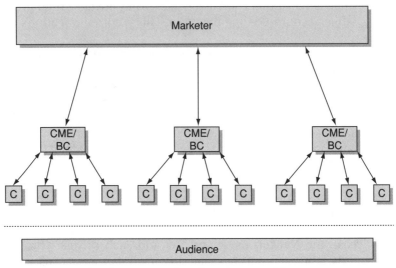

Fig. 4.3. Computer-mediated environment/brand community model

The Computer Mediated Environment/Brand Community model depicted in Fig. 4.3 is also recursive. Interested parties constantly imagine, anticipate, react, assume, and create communication and, in doing so, the brand. Marketers who interact with their communities can then incorporate these understandings into subsequent branding efforts.

CONCLUSION

'The mass-marketing model is dead. This is the future,' declared P & G's global marketing head when asked about his company's peer-to-peer marketing efforts (cf. Wells 2004: 84). Significant changes in contemporary society float on a true sea-change in mediated human communication, and brands are among the most affected. Brands are social creations, creations of communication, and this reality has never been more important. In this chapter we have argued that marketing communicators must significantly rethink their views of brands, brand communication, and their obsession with the individual consumer. To be truly sociological, one must meaningfully consider milieu.

Brands are currently comingling with, or substantially emulating, the form and function of traditional social institutions. Our central thesis is that social forces, some of them nearly a century in the making, have only recently met at a critical juncture—the brand. In this new marketing context, to not consider a socially embedded consumer, connected instantaneously and virtually at no cost to other socially embedded consumers, is unrealistic and unwise. These processes existed long before there was an Internet or World Wide Web, whether marketing academics understood that or not (although many practitioners did). But now that these new communication technologies exist, offering consumers fantastically greater power in the social construction process, it would indeed be foolish to conceive of communication as simple linearly delivered meaning. Now, connected nodes of consumers who can communicate at virtually no cost, and who can find each other almost effortlessly, are obvious and powerful cocreators of brand meaning. It is time to recognize that consumers have significant power in the social construction of brands, and that this power will only grow in the years to come. It is time to see brands as more than summed attitudes floating in preference factor space, rather as bundles of meaning, where accommodation and negotiation between marketer and consumer is on-going and radically different than it was in the past.

Entities like brand communities matter because they look and behave like other forms of community. These are socially embedded and entrenched entities. Community is an essential human phenomenon, and it can be leveraged. Leveraged or not, brand managers will have to deal with such social forces. Social aggregations of empowered consumers are not going away; on the contrary, they will continue to grow, providing marketing communicators with heretofore unknown research and marketing opportunities. But, it requires new thinking, and conceptualizations. The old will not do.

Brand community is just one example of the sociological nature of contemporary branding and brand communication. There are many more. Even if one does not accept what is widely considered axiomatic and obvious, that nonmodal individuals are often important change agents, one must still acknowledge that even modal users of a brand are active participants in the social construction of that brand. Communication has to be part of brand theory, and the individual actor reunited with social reality.

REFERENCES

Aron, D. and Muñiz, A. M., Jr. (2002). *Firing Back: Antecedents and Desired Outcomes of Consumer-created Brand Hate Sites*. Paper presented at the 105th annual convention of the American Psychological Association, Chicago, IL., July.

BadAds.org. (2002, July). Chokin' on Coke. Available: www.badads.org

Brier, N. R. (2004). 'Buzz Giant Poster Boy,' *American Demographics, (June),* 10–16.

Brown, S., Kozinets, R. V., and Sherry, J. F., Jr. (2003). 'Teaching Old Brands New Tricks: Retro Branding and the Revival of Brand Meaning,' *Journal of Marketing,* 67, 19–33.

Christian, N. M. (1997). 'One Weekend, 52 Jeeps, a Chance to Bond,' *Wall Street Journal,* (May 23), B1.

Coca-Cola Creates 'Myth' Online to Help Sell Vanilla Flavor. (2002). *Sun-Sentinel,* (July 12), D1.

Cook, B. (2003). Membership Has Its Privileges. *Brand Channel.com.* Available: *http://www.brandchannel.com*

Cova, B. (1997). 'Community and Consumption: Towards a Definition of the Linking Value of Product or Services,' *European Journal of Marketing,* 31 (Fall/Winter), 297–316.

Feick, L. F. and Price, L. L. (1987). 'The Market Maven: A Diffuser of Marketplace Innovation,' *Journal of Marketing,* 51 (January), 83–97.

Fischer, E., Bristor, J., and Gainer, B. (1996). 'Creating or Escaping Community? An Exploratory Study of Internet Consumers' Behaviors,' in K. Corfman and J. Lynch (eds.), *Advances in Consumer Research,* 23, 178–82. Provo, UT: Association for Consumer Research.

Fournier, S. (1998). 'Customers and Their Brands: Developing Relationship Theory in Consumer Research', *Journal of Consumer Research,* 24 (March), 343–73.

France, M. and Muller, J. (1999). 'A Site for Soreheads,' *Business Week,* 36 (May), 86–9.

Katz, E. and Lazarsfeld, P. (1955). *Personal Influence,* Glencoe, IL: Free Press.

Kimmel, A. J. (2004). *Rumors and Rumor Control: A Manager's Guide to Understanding and Combatting Rumors.* Mahwah, NJ: Lawrence Erlbaum Associates.

Maffesoli, M. (1996). *The Time of the Tribes: The Decline of Individualism in Mass Society.* Thousand Oaks, CA: Sage.

McAlexander, J. H., Schouten, J. W., and Koening, H. F. (2002). 'Building Brand Community', *Journal of Marketing,* 66 (January), 38–54.

McLuhan, M. (1965). *Understanding Mass Media: The Extensions of Man.* New York: McGraw-Hill.

Muñiz, A. M, Jr. and Hamer, L. O. (2001). 'Us versus Them: Oppositional Brand Loyalty and the Cola Wars', in M. C. Gilly and J. Meyers-Levy (eds.), *Advances in Consumer Research,* 28, 355–61. Provo, Utah: Association for Consumer Research.

—— and O'Guinn, T. C. (2001). 'Brand community,' *Journal of Consumer Research,* 27 (March), 412–31.

—— and —— (1995). *Brand Community and the Sociology of Brands.* Paper presented at the Association for Consumer Research Annual Conference, Minneapolis, MN., October.

—— and Schau, H. J. (2005). 'Religiosity in the Abandoned Apple Newton Brand Community,' *Journal of Consumer Research,* 31 (March), in press.

—— O'Guinn, T. C., and Fine, G. A. 'Rumor in Brand Community,' in D. Hantula (ed), *Advances in Theory & Methodology in Social & Organizational Psychology: A Tribute to Ralph Rosnow.* Mahwah, NJ: Lawrence Erlbaum Associates, in press.

O'Guinn, T. C. and Muñiz, A. M., Jr. 'Communal Consumption and the Brand,' in D. G. Mick and S. Ratneshwar (eds.), *Inside Consumption: Frontiers of Research on Consumer Motives, Goals, and Desires.* New York: Routledge, in press.

—— and —— (2004). *The Polit-brand and Blows Against the Empire.* Paper presented at the Association for Consumer Research Annual Conference, Toronto, Ontario, October.

—— and —— (2000). *Correlates of Brand Communal Affiliation Strength in High Technology Products.* Paper presented at the Association for Consumer Research Annual Conference, Salt Lake City, UT, October.

Ong, W. J. (1982). *Orality and Literacy.* London: Routledge.

Ritson, M. and Elliott, R. (1999). 'The Social Uses of Advertising: An Ethnographic Study of Adolescent Advertising Audiences,' *Journal of Consumer Research,* 26 (June), 260–77.

Robertson, T. S. (1971). *Innovative Behavior and Communication.* New York: Holt, Rinehart and Winston.

Schau, H. J. and Muñiz, A. M., Jr. (2003). 'Brand Communities and Personal Identities: Negotiations in Cyberspace', in S. M. Broniarczyk and Nakamoto (eds.), *Advances in Consumer Research.* Provo, UT: Association for Consumer Research, 29, 344–9.

Schindler, R.M. and Bickart, B. (2002). 'Published "Word of Mouth:" Referable Consumer-generated Information on the Internet,' in P. Haugtvedt, K. Machleit, and R. Yalch (eds.), *Online Consumer Psychology: Understanding and Influencing Consumer Behavior in the Virtual World,* pp. 45–72. Hillsdale, NJ: Lawrence Erlbaum Associates.

Schouten, J. W. and McAlexander, J. (1995). 'Subcultures of Consumption: An Ethnography of the New Bikers,' *Journal of Consumer Research,* 22 (June), 43–61.

Schudson, M. (1984). *Advertising, The Uneasy Persuasion,* New York: Basic Books, 129–46.

Wallendorf, M. and Arnould, E. J. (1991). 'We Gather Together: Consumption Rituals of Thanksgiving Day,' *Journal of Consumer Research,* 18 (June), 13–31.

Ward, J. C. and Reingen, P. H. (1990). 'Sociocognitive Analysis of Group Decision Making Among Consumers,' *Journal of Consumer Research,* 17 (December), 245–62.

Warner, F., Ball, J. and Anders, G. (1999). 'Holes in the Net: Can the Big Guys Rule the Web?,' *Wall Street Journal,* (August 30), A1.

Wells, M. (2004). Kid Nabbing. *Forbes,* 173 (February), 84–9.

White, E. (2004). 'Renault Gets Hip with Minivan Ads,' *Wall Street Journal,* August 26, B2.

5

Marketing Communications Trends in the Emerging Global Marketplace

H. David Hennessey

Managing the communications process for a single market is no easy task. However, the task is even more difficult for global marketers, who must communicate to prospective customers in many markets. In the process, they struggle with different cultures, habits, and languages. This chapter describes the marketing communications trends in the emerging global marketplace, focusing on marketing communications in multiple countries. It examines the opportunities and challenges of global advertising, personal selling, and global account management. New methods of sales promotion are discussed, and the effects of new communications media, such as the Internet and the World Wide Web, satellite TV, online advertising channels, cable TV, and mobile devices on global marketing operations are explored. In short, this chapter highlights emerging trends in marketing communications for global marketers in both business-to-consumer and business-to-business contexts.

GLOBAL ADVERTISING

Global advertising, which uses common positioning with common ads, can be an important part of a multicountry marketing program (Jeannet and Hennessey 2004). However, the volume of communications directed simultaneously toward targets in multiple countries is actually small. The majority of advertising activity still tends to be directed toward one country at a time. Despite the 'local' nature of global advertising, it is important to recognize that the initial input, in terms of either the product idea or the basic communications strategy, will often originate in another country.

Consequently, although there is a local aspect to most global advertising, there is also a global country-to-country aspect to consider, which can offer significant synergies across countries. Two important questions must be answered in global advertising: (*a*) How much of a local versus a global emphasis should there be? (*b*) What should be the nature and content of the advertising itself?

The diversity of views and approaches to global advertising can be described with two examples. Coca-Cola and Kleenex, both very successful brands and companies, have chosen diametrically different approaches and strategies for their global advertising. Kimberly-Clark spent a considerable amount of time in the past to develop commercials that fit many countries for its Kleenex brand campaign 'Thank Goodness for Kleenex' ('Global Kleenex' 2000). Involving many parties from different countries, Kimberly-Clark spent months creating many spots to serve many markets. In its recent approach, Kimberly-Clark invited a small team of executives to collaborate with its agency in order to create a single spot (visuals) to be used in all markets. For example, one of the advertisements had Kleenex come to the rescue of a father sharing a tender moment with his son, who had a runny nose. The resulting commercials outperformed existing ads in tests in the USA and in Europe.

The Coca-Cola Company, which has considerable experience making commercials for its leading Coke brand, produced just one global ad to go with the 1998 football World Cup. For the 2002 version of the World Cup, the company reused a reedited version of the earlier ad, but decided to augment it with some twenty-five commercials tailored to individual markets ('Coke's Local' 2002). Although the company still pursues a strategy of leveraging its marketing skills globally, the company believes that producing a single perfect global ad working in many markets may take an inordinate amount of time and resources to produce. Thus, Kimberly-Clark has moved from a local approach to a global approach, while Coca-Cola has gone from a global approach to a more local campaign.

No other aspect of global marketing has received as much attention as advertising. Many mistakes have been made in translating advertising copy from one language into another. Most of these mistakes occurred in the 1960s. Today, most companies and advertising agencies have reached a level of sophistication that reduces the chance of translation error. This does not mean that language is not a factor to consider in today's global communications strategy. However, the industry has moved from a primary concern regarding translation to concerns about ways to more efficiently use creativity and promotion resources across multiple countries, as illustrated by Kimberly-Clark.

A second cause of global advertising mistakes has been the neglect of cultural attitudes of consumers in different countries. Benetton, the Italian clothing manufacturer and retailer with operations throughout the world, was one example of a company that ran into cultural problems with its advertising. The company launched a global campaign under the theme 'United Colors of Benetton,' which had won awards in Europe. The ads had started innocently in 1983 featuring models of different races in Benetton clothes with the images intended to promote racial harmony and world peace. When the ads became increasingly controversial, such as an ad in 1992 showing an AIDS patient moments before death, a newborn baby with umbilical cord still attached, or prison inmates sentenced to death, relatives of depicted victims or other offended groups began to sue the company. In its most recent campaign, Benetton went out of its way to be less controversial by featuring models in colorful knitwear ('About Face' 2001).

In another case, Nike found that its flame logo on shoes offended Islamic followers. The flame was alleged to be similar to the Arabic symbol for Allah, whereas in Islam the feet are seen as unclean. Nike has now withdrawn the use of the flame symbol (Stewart-Allen 1998).

Challenges of the Language Barrier

Translation blunders that plagued global advertising in the past were the result of literal translations performed outside the target country. The translators, not always in contact with the culture of the target country, were unable to judge the actual meaning of the translated copy for the target audience. The faulty translation could not be checked by the executives involved because they were from a different culture and did not possess the necessary language skills.

Today, most companies avoid the use of faulty translations through the involvement of local nationals or language experts. Typically, global marketers have translations checked by either a local advertising agency, their own local subsidiary, or an independent distributor located in the target country. Because global firms are active in a large number of countries, which requires the use of many languages, today's global marketers must find an organizational solution to eliminate translation errors.

In the European Union (EU), many official languages are spoken. As a result, more and more advertising puts a special emphasis on communicating visually rather than through the various languages. Graphics are used more effectively in print media, too ('Picture Puzzle' 2001). Satellite TV channels have discovered that not everyone in Europe speaks English well enough to understand English commercials and that, if given a chance, most people like to watch programs in their own language. Sky Television and Super Channel, the two pan-European satellite television stations, moved to trilingual program services, and rather than offer pan-European programs, operators of satellite channels in Europe have also moved toward multiregional programming. There are economies-of-scale benefits if a campaign can be run across a number of countries with a multilanguage approach. The economies of scale are derived from only needing to create the advertising concept once and only shooting the commercial once rather than for each individual country. For example, Pepsi ran a multilanguage consumer promotion in nine countries on Pepsi products, which offered exclusive Spice Girl prizes, with a menu of redemption options tailored to the market needs and legal requirements of each country (Stewart-Allen 1999).

Adjusting to a local language can require changes in the product name or positioning. For example, Coca-Cola was first rendered as *Ke-kou-ke-la* in Chinese, which meant 'bite the wax tadpole' or 'female horse stuffed with wax,' depending on the dialect. After the problem was discovered, Coke researched 40,000 Chinese characters and found *Ko-kou-ko-le* a close phonetic for Coca-Cola, meaning 'happiness in the mouth,' which is used in China today ('Getting Lost' 1998).

Challenges of the Cultural Barrier

When global marketers fail because of misinterpretation of the local culture, they usually do so because they advocated an action inconsistent with the local culture or because they chose an appeal inconsistent with the motivational pattern of the target culture. Advocating the purchase of a product whose use is inconsistent with the local culture will result in failure, even if the appeal itself does not violate that culture per se. Similarly, companies can also fail if the appeal or message employed is inconsistent with the local culture, even if the action promoted is not. Consequently, a foreign company entering a new market has to be aware of both cultural aspects: the product's use and the message employed.

Sara Lee, the US-based global firm that owns such lingerie brands as Playtex, Cacharel, and Wonderbra, faced intensive opposition to a series of billboards in Mexico. The company launched a global Wonderbra campaign that featured a Czech model posing in the bra on all of its outdoor advertising. In Mexican cities, citizens protested the ads as offensive and, pressured by the public, the company redesigned its billboards; for Mexico, the model wore a suit. Sara Lee learned that in some countries it had to change the visual of the global campaign on a case-by-case basis ('Mexico Cover-up' 1996).

To ensure that a message is in line with the existing cultural beliefs of the target market, companies can use resources similar to those used to overcome the translation barriers. Local subsidiary personnel or local distributors can judge the cultural content of the message. Advertising agencies with local offices also are helpful. Global marketers cannot possibly know enough about all cultures to assess the appropriateness of appeals.

Sometimes, global companies have to use advertising to overcome expressed cultural biases or attitudes that can be harmful to their business. McDonald's, which is the largest restaurant chain in France with some 800 outlets and sales of 1.5 billion euros, found itself in the midst of a controversy aimed at globalizing forces. The company resorted to a full-fledged advertising campaign in France emphasizing its local roots and the use of French supplies and foods, such as beef, to prepare its hamburgers in an effort to reduce cultural bias ('Hey Why' 1999).

The Impact of Regulations on Global Advertising

Although there are numerous situations in which different customer needs require tailor-made advertising campaigns, in many instances the particular regulations of a country can prevent firms from using standardized approaches, even when they would appear desirable. In countries such as Malaysia, regulations are a direct outgrowth of changing political circumstances. Following the influence of Islam in many parts of the world, Malaysia, a country with a large Muslim population, outlawed ads showing women in sleeveless dresses and pictures showing underarms. Given the strict rules in Malaysia governing the production and screening of commercials, Unilever found it best to film its Lipton Yellow Label Tea commercial in Malaysia. Using local talent and internationally acceptable scenery, Unilever was able to shoot three versions of the commercial on the same storyline for fifteen European and Asian countries at a substantial savings over doing local commercials in each market (Bani 1999).

Advertising for cigarettes and tobacco products is under strict regulation in many countries. Members of the World Health Organization (WHO) are negotiating a treaty that will establish global regulations on cigarette advertising; limits will be set as to where smoking will be allowed, and cigarette taxation will be raised in all countries (Williams 1999). Brazil, home to some 30 million smokers, has even surpassed Europe with its regulations against advertising for cigarettes. The country instituted one of the most comprehensive bans on tobacco advertising, gradually forbidding advertising everywhere except the counters where cigarettes are sold. Furthermore, Brazil adopted a ban on terms such as 'light' or 'mild' from cigarette packs ahead of a similar, recently enacted ban in the European Union ('Smoking Offensive' 2002).

The EU is debating a series of rulings that could have a great impact on advertising in Europe. The discussions involve efforts toward both greater harmonization and the extent of regulation. Greater harmonization is generally viewed as desirable throughout Europe and potentially would result in uniform regulations for advertising. This would greatly enhance the potential for pan-European marketing campaigns and bring greater advertising efficiency.

Self-regulation plays a major role in advertising, with watchdogs established in many countries who will call on any advertiser who violates established local norms. In France, a recent issue concerned advertising portrayals of women and the depiction of the human body. Europe's leading fashion houses were singled out for portraying women in a degrading way. But the self-regulation is specifically directed at firms that use advertising agencies. Those that produce ads in-house are often considered outside the pressure of voluntary regulations. Benetton of Italy refused to withdraw an ad showing a young woman in a suggestive pose ('Clampdown on "Porno Chic"' 2001).

Other regulations companies may encounter involve the production of advertising material. Some countries require all advertising, particularly on television and radio, to be produced locally. As a result, it has become a real challenge for global advertisers to find campaigns that can be used in as many countries as possible to save on production costs. However, such campaigns are possible only if a marketer has sufficient input from the very beginning on the applicable legislation so as to take all regulations into account.

Selecting a Global Advertising Theme: Standardization versus Customization

For marketers with products sold in many countries, the basic decision tends to center on the appropriate level of standardization for the advertising theme and its creative execution. As a result of early failures by inexperienced companies that employed a totally standardized approach, some companies shifted to the other extreme by allowing each country to design its own campaign.

Advantages of Standardizing Global Advertising

Because *creative* talent is scarce, a single effort to develop a campaign will likely produce better results than forty or fifty separate efforts. This particularly applies to countries for which the marketing or advertising experience is limited. A second advantage centers on the economics of a global campaign. To develop an individual campaign in many countries creates costs for creativity, photographs, layouts, and the production of television and cinema commercials. In a standardized approach, these production costs can be reduced and more funds can be spent on purchasing space in the media. In addition, the fewer messages to be produced can be created with higher production budgets, thus increasing communication effectiveness. A third reason for a standardized approach is found in global brand names. Many companies market products under a single brand name in several countries within the same region. With the substantial amount of international travel occurring today and the considerable overlap in media across national borders, companies are interested in creating a single image to avoid any confusion caused through local campaigns that may be in conflict with each other.

The following examples illustrate how a global advertising campaign can be used in many markets. Patek Philippe, the prestigious watchmaker, has supported its brand with a global print and TV campaign using the theme 'You never actually own a Patek Philippe. You merely look after it for the next generation.' The campaign has been successful in many markets, including the USA, Europe, China, Japan, Singapore, and Taiwan ('Patek Philippe' 1999).

Procter & Gamble (P&G) launched Pringles potato chips in the 1970s and existed for fifteen years without any significant penetration in the global salty-snack market, dominated by Frito-Lay. However, between 1995 and 1999, P&G doubled the sales of Pringles to $1 billion. Now one of P&G's top three global brands, Pringles are in over forty countries. P&G attributes the global success of Pringles to a uniform package, product, and advertising message aimed at young children and teens. The message used around the world is 'once you pop, you can't stop.' Although P&G allows some local tactical differences market to market, including some flavor variations, the bulk of the advertising and merchandising is global (Pollack 1999).

When Warner Lambert Co. was revitalizing the image of Chiclets gum, advertisements in the past were created on a country-by-country basis with no central theme. Research had shown that Chiclets faced low visibility in many countries. The new positioning campaign was targeted to the eighteen- to twenty-four-year-old consumer. The commercial, shot in the sand dunes of northern Brazil, included a desert shack occupied by a young man and a monkey. By rattling a Chiclets box they summoned an international audience ranging from Japanese geishas to English schoolboys. The tag line in English was 'Chiclets make cool things happen.' By using the ad worldwide, Warner Lambert was able to maximize the impact of its advertising expenditures ('Chiclets Tries New Language' 1993).

Requirements for Standardized Campaigns

For a company to launch a worldwide standardized campaign, some requirements first have to be met with regard to the product name, packaging, competitive situation, and consumer attitudes. The need for a standardized brand name or trademark is viewed by many companies as a prerequisite to a standardized campaign. Not only should the name always be written in identical format, but it should be pronounced identically. Trademarks or corporate logos can also help in achieving greater standardization of corporate campaigns. Well-known logos such as Kodak's, Sony's, and General Electric's are used the world over. The power of a company's brand name has a considerable influence on whether the company can use a standardized campaign.

When Whirlpool acquired the Philips business in 1991 following an earlier joint venture, the firm became the world's largest appliance maker, overtaking Electrolux of Sweden. Since Whirlpool was largely unknown to European consumers, the company undertook a pan-European advertising campaign over several years. The advertising was the result of some exhaustive testing of housewives in the UK, France, Spain, and Austria. Whirlpool maintained its share of the European market by focusing most of its advertising efforts on promoting the Whirlpool brand name at the expense of some locally acquired brands, such as Bauknecht for Germany ('The New Europe' 1998). Following eight years of success in Europe, Whirlpool adapted the campaign, consisting of four 30-second TV spots and one 60-second brand treatment TV spot, to the USA. The campaign's feature of the 'spirit of the all-powerful female,' made even more powerful with Whirlpool products by her side, tested well in focus groups consisting of North American women. The campaign was extended to Latin America as well and ran in more than forty countries ('Whirlpool Asks Commerce' 2000). This campaign was successful in many markets because the purchasing criteria and the purchase motivation of women were sufficiently similar.

To aid the prospective customer in identifying the advertised product with the actual one placed in retail stores, consumer products manufacturers in particular aim at packages that are standardized in appearance. Despite differences in sizes, these packages carry the same design in terms of color, layout, and name. Nonstandardized packages cannot be featured in a standardized campaign. Naturally, this concern is of interest to consumer products companies because the package has to double both as a protective and as a promotional device.

GLOBAL BRANDING

Global branding received a considerable amount of attention in the 1980s and is now considered one of the most controversial topics in global marketing. The debate was triggered by Levitt (1983a,b), who asserted that markets are becoming increasingly alike worldwide and that the trend is toward a global approach to marketing. The fervent advocates of global branding argue that consumer tastes, needs, and purchasing patterns are converging. This can be supported by the converging trends in demographics across many countries. At the forefront of these trends has been the decline of the nuclear family, both in North America and in many countries around the globe. In most countries, more women have entered the workforce. Divorce trends have similarly increased in North America, Europe, and other developed countries. These trends have changed the role of women in society almost everywhere. Standards of living have risen in many countries, and differences among nations have been reduced. In addition to these demographic trends, common media such as films, television, the Internet, and music are creating cultural convergence as well. These developments are said to reduce cultural barriers among countries, and such barriers are expected to diminish even further through satellite television networks covering many countries with identical programs.

Global branding usually signifies that the same product name, product logo, packaging, product composition, and product positioning would be used across the globe, supported by a single advertising campaign. Many marketing executives remain skeptical about the value of global advertising campaigns; however, global campaigns do appear to work if the target market is relatively narrowly defined. For example, Sprite is a brand owned by the Coca-Cola Company. Central to the brand's global advertising strategy is the fact that the meaning of Sprite as a brand—what it stands for in the eyes of consumers—is exactly the same globally. Many Sprite ads are run worldwide unchanged, while others are tailored locally. All share the same basic theme of self-reliance and trusting one's instincts. The company found that despite cultural differences in different markets around the world, there was strong global similarity among teenagers no matter which country was involved. Thus, the entire global campaign was built on the apparently universal teenage sentiment toward soft drinks and similar products, and toward what Sprite 'symbolizes' ('Sprite is Riding' 1996). Whereas Sprite was an American campaign exported around the world, Fanta, another Coca-Cola brand, has its strength in overseas markets. As a leading global soft drink brand, Fanta launched a campaign building on overseas market positions and emphasizing Fanta as a fashion statement ('Coca-Cola Touts Overseas Strength' 1996).

The Coca-Cola Company had moved its main brand, Coke, from a global campaign with few ads to a more regional or locally driven campaign that was built around the understanding that the product was basically consumed in many different local communities. As a result, Coca-Cola was moving towards more local control and approaches at a time when many other companies, as well as some of its own other brands, moved towards global campaigns. To compensate, Coca-Cola created an advisory council with its lead agency, Interpublic Group, whose subsidiary McCann-

Erickson has worked on the Coke account since 1942 and creates ads in some 89 countries. Interpublic's role is to develop, refine, and focus strategies to ensure relevant and consistent messages around the world are being used by the ten agencies that work on the Coke account in more than 200 countries ('Coke Brands IPG' 2000).

TECHNOLOGY AND THE EMERGENCE OF NEW COMMUNICATION CHANNELS

New technologies have opened new opportunities to communicate with potential customers. For example, both satellite TV and mobile telephones can now be used to communicate with consumers and businesses.

Satellite Television

Satellite television channels are not subject to government regulations and have revolutionized television in many parts of the world. The impact of satellite television channels is especially great in Europe. The leader in this field of privately owned satellite channels is Sky Channel, which is owned by Rupert Murdoch. In 1993, Murdoch, who controls vast media interests in many countries, purchased the Star Satellite System, serving millions of people from Egypt to Mongolia. The Star System relies heavily on advertising revenue. The Murdoch group currently is eyeing expansion in Asia. Through its News Corp, the company produces three Chinese-language news and entertainment channels from studios in Hong Kong that can reach most of Asia. Similar to the other twenty-one foreign broadcasters sending signals into China, the programs are supposed to be seen only in hotels rated 3 stars and above, in housing complexes attracting international residents, and in offices. But Phoenix TV, which is the station sending the signals, can be obtained by many privately installed satellite dishes across China and in upmarket local housing complexes ('Phoenix Rising' 2001).

One of the most successful global satellite TV ventures is the MTV Network. This music channel, launched in 1981 in the USA, by 1999 reached 285 million households in more than sixty countries. Its MTV Mandarin has an audience of 44 million households, and MTV Southeast Asia accounts for another 23 million ('Global Media' 1999). MTV Networks International, the music channel and its sister operations VH1 and Nickelodeon, reach 1 billion people in 18 different languages in 164 countries. Eighty percent of all MTV viewers live outside the USA. Although the design and structure of the broadcast is similar, the music is adapted to the local requirements.

The network, owned by the US company Viacom, is highly profitable. With a reach that is twice that of CNN, it has become a truly global media channel of value to global companies ('MTV's World' 2001).

For satellite-shown commercials to be effective, companies have to be able to profit from a global brand name and a uniform logo. Also, language remains a problem. English is the common language of the majority of satellite channels; however, there is a trend toward local language satellites. Satellite channels are now available in several other European languages, such as German, French, and Swedish.

Cable Television

In the more densely populated countries of Europe, cable TV networks have been installed with considerable implications for global marketers. In Europe, close to 84 million out of 148 million TV homes are connectable to cable. Some 49 million of those subscribe to cable today. Some countries, such as Germany, The Netherlands, Belgium, and Switzerland are fully cabled, whereas Italy and Greece have very little cable installed ('Cable in Europe' 2000). Access to cable networks eventually drives access to broadband and Internet, which also impact on the global companies' ability to reach large audiences cost effectively.

Mobile Devices

The growth of mobile handheld devices with Internet capabilities is opening a new market for delivering entertainment, information, and advertising. Nokia, the largest manufacturer of mobile devices, has had discussions with both AOL and News Corporation about providing content for these devices ('Nokia in "Exploratory Talks"' 2000). The new use of mobile devices provides potential global advertising opportunities.

The emergence of multiple media and advertising channels on a global scale is both a commercial and technical challenge for global companies. Increasingly, companies are beginning to create entire global campaigns across multiple platforms, or so-called 'cross-platform packages.' When Toyota relaunched its leading Camry model in 2002 with the intent of repositioning it from an older woman's car to a younger man's car, the company teamed up with AOL Time Warner to buy a bundle of advertisements in magazines, cable-TV channels, and websites. Time Warner, which is owned by Time, Inc., proposed to let Toyota sponsor an entire issue of *Time Magazine* written around a theme of 'Music Goes Global'. Time Warner's sister publications (e.g. *People*) published concurrent articles about global music and accepted advertising from Toyota. This practice of linking editorial content with advertising had not been a standard practice at Time, Inc. In addition, Toyota sponsored music shows on CNN and TNT cable channels in order to support the repositioning of the Camry ('AOL Lands Toyota' 2001).

Future technologies will offer new communications options with global marketing potential. With more and more consumers having cellphones, personal digital assistants (PDAs), internet access and e-mail, companies may be able to develop new communication channels directly to consumers. As cable TV, hard wire telephone, cellular telephone, and electric companies battle to provide internet access, telephone services, and television access, there will be more options to communicate with consumers. The set-top box on televisions may offer additional two-way communication options as well as services to manage home security, lighting, heating, and more. It is important for global marketers to be on the lookout for these potential communication opportunities.

Personal Selling

Personal selling takes place whenever a customer is met in person by a representative of the marketing company. When doing business globally, companies must meet customers from different countries. These customers may be accustomed to different business customs and may speak a different language. That is why personal selling in an individual context is extremely complex and requires special skills on the part of the salesperson.

There is a difference between global selling and local selling. When a company's sales force travels across countries and meets directly with clients abroad, it is practicing *global selling*. This type of selling requires an ability to manage across several cultures. Much more often, however, companies engage in *local selling*—they organize and staff a local sales force made up of local nationals to do the selling in only one country. Managing and operating a local sales force involves different problems from those encountered by managing multicountry salespersons. To serve global companies, many firms have adopted global account management systems.

Global Account Management

Traditionally, account management has been performed on a country-by-country basis (Hennessey and Jeannet 2003). This practice invariably led to a country-specific sales force, which was typical even for large global firms. Over the last few years, an emerging trend has seen companies organize their sales force into global account teams. The global team services a customer globally in all the customer's locations around the world. Global account teams may comprise members in different parts of the world, all serving segments of a global account and coordinated through a global account management (GAM) structure.

The trend toward GAM is rooted in ever-increasing global purchasing logic among large global customers, like GM, Toyota, Siemens, IBM, Unilever, and many others. Companies that purchase similar components, raw materials, or services in many parts of the world realize that by combining the purchasing function and managing it more centrally, they can obtain substantial savings. Companies are scanning the global market for the best buy, and in the process they want to deal with the best source that can serve their global needs.

The system of GAM is practiced widely in the professional service sectors. Globally active banks like Citibank have maintained global account structures for years. Likewise, advertising agencies offer global clients GAM with seamless coordination across many countries (Jeannet and Lanning 2001). The world's leading accounting firms, such as Deloitte Touche Tohmatsu, have long-standing traditions of leading their engagements for international clients from one single place. At Deloitte, the system of lead client service partners (LCSPs) is well developed. For example, the LCSP is empowered to direct a global audit engagement for a large multinational account across all countries where the work must be performed (Jeannet and Collins 1993).

GAM is greatly enhanced by sophisticated information technology. With members of the team dispersed around the globe, it becomes essential to coordinate all actions meticulously. The development and rapid spread of such tools as video conferencing, electronic mail, and groupware applications have greatly extended the reach of a management team beyond the typical one-location office. Many customers who are ambitious to do business across the world but who prefer to deal with fewer suppliers will demand this new sales approach more and more. Many of the national selling organizations now maintained by international firms will inevitably be transferred, or transformed, into smaller, but globally acting, account teams.

Global Trade Fairs

Participation in global trade fairs has become an important aspect of marketing industrial products abroad. Trade fairs are ideal for exposing new customers and potential distributors to a company's product range and have been used extensively by both newcomers and established firms. In the USA, business-to-business customers can be reached through a wide range of media, such as specialized magazines with a particular industry focus or a focused trade fair such as an annual toy show. In many other countries, the markets are too small to allow for the publication of a trade magazine in only one country. As a result, prospective customers usually attend global or regional trade fairs on a regular basis.

Trade fairs also offer companies a chance to meet with prospective customers in an informal atmosphere. For a company that is new to a certain market and does not yet have any established contacts, participation in a trade fair may be the only way to reach potential customers. There are an estimated 600 major international trade shows in 70 countries every year. The Hanover Fair is considered the largest industrial fair in the world. With over 7,100 exhibitors in engineering and technology from over 70 countries, the fair attracts 330,000 visitors ('Welcome to Europe's Biggest' 1998). Other large general fairs include the Canton Fair in China and the Milan Fair in Italy.

Specialized trade fairs concentrate on a certain segment of the industry or user group. Such fairs usually attract limited participation in terms of both exhibitors and visitors, and may not take place every year. One of the leading specialized fairs is the Achema for the chemical industry in Germany, which is held every three years. The HomeTech Trade Fair in Cologne is a leading German trade fair for the household appliance industry. HomeTech Cologne 2004 had a total of 1,323 exhibitors from 53 countries who presented their products to 25,000 international trade visitors. The high percentage of exhibitors from abroad (74 percent) is a clear indicator of HomeTech Cologne's importance for the trade in Germany and around the world ('Final Report' 2004).

Global exhibiting may require additional planning compared with domestic shows. First, planning should begin twelve to eighteen months in advance because international shipping may involve delays. Second, show attendance should be checked, as it is common for many shows to allow the public to visit; marketers therefore may want to plan a separate private area for viable prospects. Third, at many global shows, customers expect to see the chief executive officer (CEO) and senior management. Finally, local distributors, consultants, or sales representatives are typically engaged to help with the logistics and bridge to the local culture.

OTHER FORMS OF MARKETING COMMUNICATION

To this point, our discussion has concentrated on advertising and personal selling as key elements of the communications mix. However, various other forms of marketing communications play a key role in global marketing. Usually combined under the generic title of *global sales promotions*, they may include such elements as in-store retail promotions and coupons. Many of these tools are consumer goods oriented and are used less often in industrial goods marketing. In this section, our focus turns to sales promotion activities, including sports promotions and sponsorships.

Sales Promotion

Sales promotion has a largely local focus. Although some forms of promotions, such as coupons, gifts, and various types of reduced-price labels are in use in most countries, strict government regulations and different retailing practices tend to limit the options for global firms.

In the USA, coupons are the leading form of sales promotion ('Do Coupons Make Cents?' 2003). Consumers typically bring product coupons to the retail store and obtain a reduced price for the product. Second in importance are refund offers. Consumers who send a proof of purchase to the manufacturer receive a refund in the form of a check. Also used, but less frequently, are money-off labels or factory-bonus packs, which induce customers to buy large quantities because of the price incentive.

Couponing varies significantly from country to country. Coupon distribution is popular and growing in Italy, whereas it is declining in the UK and Spain. Couponing is in its infancy in Japan, with restrictions on newspaper coupons lifted in 1991, and is becoming more accepted in Germany, Holland, Switzerland, and Greece. The European Commission is working toward a policy of allowing pan-European sales promotion as long as the practices are legal in the country of origin, thereby requiring each country to mutually recognize the laws of the other countries (Murphy 1999). The new EU regulations will harmonize sales promotion activities across the EU and likely will significantly increase the use of sales promotion ('Removing Restrictions' 2002).

In most overseas markets, price reductions in the store are usually the most important promotional tool, followed by reductions to the trade, such as wholesalers and retailers. Also of importance in some countries are free goods, double-pack promotions, and in-store displays.

Most countries have restrictions on some forms of promotions. Frequently regulated are any games of chance, but games in which some type of skill is required are usually allowed. For example, Belgium and France do not allow games of chance, while Sweden allows competition requiring some skill. When reductions are made available, they often are not allowed to exceed a certain percentage of the product's purchase price. Because global firms will encounter a series of regulations and restrictions on promotions that differ among countries, there is little opportunity to standardize sales promotion techniques across many markets. This has caused most companies to make sales promotions the responsibility of local managers, who are expected to understand the local preferences and restrictions. Also, sales promotion can be influenced by local culture. A study of consumer attitudes regarding sales promotion found significant differences between Taiwan, Thailand, and Malaysia. The Taiwanese consumer preferred coupons over sweepstakes and had a low fear of embarrassment when using coupons. The Malaysians and Thais preferred sweepstakes over coupons, and although they were generally price conscious, this did not influence their sales promotion attitudes (Huff and Alden 1998).

Sports Promotion and Sponsoring

With major sports events increasingly being covered by the mass media, the commercial value of these events has increased tremendously over the last decade. Large sports events, such as the Olympics or world championships in specific sports, can no longer exist without funding by companies, which do this either through advertising or through different types of sponsorships.

In the USA, companies have for some time purchased TV advertising space for such regularly broadcasted sporting events as baseball, basketball, and American football. Gillette is one company that regularly uses sponsorship of the baseball World Series to introduce new products. This is just another extension of the company's media strategy to air television and radio commercials at times when its prime target group can be found in large numbers watching TV or listening to the radio.

About two-thirds of the television rights revenue for the Olympic Games comes from the USA market. The cost of purchasing the rights to broadcast the Olympics on television in the USA continues to escalate. NBC acquired the TV rights for the USA in a long-term contract with the International Olympic Committee (IOC) through the 2008 Olympic Games for a total of $2.3 billion. For the 2008 games, NBC agreed to pay $894 million and 50 percent of the advertising revenue. The typical 30-second television spot has increased from $380,000 for the 1996 Atlanta games to $445,000 for the 2000 games and to an expected $608,000 for the 2008 games ('NBC, IOC Chase' 1995). Similarly, the rights to broadcast the Olympics elsewhere were sold to the European Broadcasting Union, which covers Europe, North Africa, and the Mideast, through the 2008 games for a reported $1.44 billion ('Murdoch Loses Bidding' 1996). About half of the broadcast revenues flow to the host city for the games, with the other half going to the International Olympic Committee for its activities.

To circumvent restrictions on commercial television during sports programs, companies have purchased space for signs along the stadiums or the arenas where sports events take place. When the event is broadcast on television, the cameras automatically include the signs as part of the regular coverage. Also, sporting events have begun to offer advertisers the option of providing virtual advertising on TV telecasts of the games. For example, BMW ran virtual advertisements on Brazilian and Argentine football matches with the BMW logo on the playing pitch as well as sending virtual vehicles across the field (Greenburg 2003).

Coca-Cola already is gearing up for the Summer Olympic Games to be held in China in 2008. Given that China has moved from purchasing just 4 million cases of Coke to absorbing 450 million cases in 2001, Coca-Cola is interested in using sponsorships to increase its volume in what now represents its sixth important market ('Cashing in on World Cup' 2002). Coca-Cola also sponsors many other sports events, such as the European and world football championships, and the Tour de France, the famous multi-stage bicycle race.

To take advantage of global sports events, a company should have a logo or brand name that is worth exposing to a global audience. It is not surprising to find that the most common sponsors are companies producing consumer goods with a global appeal, such as soft-drink manufacturers, consumer electronics producers, and film companies. To purchase sign space, a firm must take into consideration the popularity of certain sports. Few sports have global appeal. Soccer is the number one spectator sport in much of the world. MasterCard International has renewed its official sponsorship of the World Cup football games, held in 2002 in Japan and South Korea. Between 1999 and 2002, MasterCard sponsored 400 championship matches, with a cumulative television audience of 50 billion people ('Mastercard Renews Commitments' 2002). By contrast, baseball and American football have little appeal in Europe and parts of Asia and Africa. Many other sports also have only local or regional character, which requires a company to know its market and the interests of its target audience very well.

Korean global firms have used sports sponsorship abroad extensively. Typically, Korean firms have underwritten individual teams overseas. Samsung currently is sponsoring ten sports teams or events in Eastern Europe, eight in Latin America, and two each in Asia and the Mideast. Among the Samsung-sponsored teams are twelve foreign football teams, which the company plans to invite to Korea for a Samsung tournament. Other Korean firms also are active; for example, Hyundai supports eastern European and African football teams, and the LG Group has been very active in sponsoring local sports teams (Chaebol 1997). These Korean firms consider sports sponsorship a cost-effective way to boost their brand or company recognition in emerging or untapped markets.

As part of its aggressive plan to raise its profits in sports sponsorship, the American firm Nike has moved beyond the sponsorship of individual superstars to sponsor entire teams. In 1997, for a sum of $200 million, Nike obtained sole sponsorship of the Brazilian national teams at all levels for ten years, including football world championships and Olympic Games ('Nike Learns the Flipside' 2000). Nike capped its deal with the largest known sponsoring deal in sports history. Under a contract that began in 2002, Nike will pay Manchester United, one of the world's leading football clubs, $450 million over a thirteen-year period. In addition, the company will take over the clubs' retail stores and pass on one-half of all profits from merchandise sales. With football the most popular sport worldwide, Nike aims to increase its competitiveness against major rivals like Reebok and Adidas.

Many will remember the pictures of winning race car drivers with all the various corporation names or logos on their uniforms. Although these promotions once tended to be mostly related to sports products, sponsors increasingly have no relationship to the sports. Sponsoring a team for competition in the sixteen Grand Prix races all over the world is estimated to cost about $45 to $60 million for one year. The main sponsor is expected to carry up to two-thirds of the cost and gets to paint the cars in its colors with its logo. Major sponsors for Grand Prix races have included tobacco companies (Marlboro, Camel, John Player, Gitanes/Loto) and other consumer goods firms (Benetton). The WHO's Framework Convention on Tobacco Control, a new treaty which is awaiting adoption by WHO countries, would eliminate all tobacco advertising, promotion and sponsorship. Once adopted, this would eliminate tobacco company sponsorships ('Nicotine Addition' 2004).

Through the intensive coverage of sports in the news media all over the world, many companies continue to use the sponsorship of sporting events as an important element in their global communications programs. Successful companies have to track the interest of various countries in the many types of sports and to exhibit both flexibility and ingenuity in the selection of available events or participants. In many parts of the world, sports sponsorship may continue to be the only available way to reach large numbers of prospective customers.

GLOBAL MARKETING VIA INTERNET AND WORLD WIDE WEB

The emergence of the commercial use of the Internet, along with the rapid expansion of World Wide Web applications, has been one of the most recent important developments affecting global marketing. In 2001, ACNielsen estimated that there were 429 million people worldwide with Internet access, with 59 percent outside North America ('429 Million People' 2001). The Internet offers companies an entirely new vehicle to communicate and interact with current and potential customers.

The availability of Internet technology is of particular importance to global marketers. Firms are able to eliminate the time and distance gaps that hinder many international dealings, using the most interactive of all direct marketing tools. A company anywhere in the world can establish a website on the Internet and be instantly available to potential customers from anywhere in the world. This immediate availability, of great importance to all firms, gives a particularly valuable opportunity to smaller firms that lack established international sales channels.

The potential power of the Internet is demonstrated by both large- and small-sized companies. The Dutch chemicals group DSM announced in early 2000 that within three years 100 percent of their purchases and 50 percent of their sales would be via the Internet. DSM planned to increase its Internet-based dealings with customers and suppliers ('DSM Set to Expand' 2000). Also, the company is trading through ChemConnect, an Internet exchange for chemicals in which DSM has equity ownership.

The Internet is also moving ahead in areas such as Latin America. Business-to-business marketing was expected to increase to $67 billion by 2004, compared to 2000 revenue of only $3.6 billion for all forms of e-commerce. The leading country was Brazil with some 3.9 million Internet users, accounting for about 40 percent of the Latin American potential. Together with Mexico and Argentina, these three countries represented 65 percent of the 9.9 million Latin American users. Usage of the Internet was expected to further increase with the penetration of personal computer ownership in Latin America ('Study Examines E-Commerce' 2000).

Online Advertising Channels

Not to be underestimated is the global reach of Internet properties that are available for electronic forms of advertising, such as banner ads used in connection with websites. Measured in terms of reach of the Internet population, the leading websites entering the twenty-first century were Microsoft Sites, AOL Network, Google, and Yahoo, each covering between 50 to 60 percent of the global Internet user population ('Top 10 Digital' 2000). Because these sites are used by a global population, they act as global media allowing advertisers to reach a global audience.

Online advertising has already reached about 5 percent of total US advertising expenditures, but accounts for only 1 percent in the next eight largest global markets. The American market is larger because it reaches a global audience through global websites properties. With some 50 percent of Internet users from outside the USA, websites with global content are of great value to advertisers ('Going Global' 2002).

The impact of the Internet on global marketing will be pervasive. Small and large companies alike will be able to reach customers across the world almost instantly, and vice versa. Answers to questions transmitted via e-mail will arrive in seconds. Small firms that previously had little chance to reach into global markets will be able to do so. Electronic commerce will bring global competition to small or domestic firms, which will suddenly see their markets invaded. The result will be pressures on prices where margins are high. The ultimate winner may be the world's large number of consumers, who will suddenly have an astonishing array of purchasing options.

CONCLUSION

Marketing communication has changed significantly over the past five years within the emerging global marketplace. It likely will continue to change with advertisers looking for new channels to communicate with their potential customers beyond traditional print advertising, TV advertising and direct mail. New technologies such as the cell phone and the Internet are making it easier and less expensive to communicate directly with consumers. We can expect that there will continue to be new communication options available to savvy global marketers.

REFERENCES

About Face (2001). *Forbes,* (March), 178.

AOL Lands Toyota for Multimedia Pact (2001). *Wall Street Journal,* (August 28), B7.

Bani, E. (1999). Lipton Shoots Its Latest Commercial in Malaysia. *Business Times (Malaysia),* (June 9), 15.

Cable In Europe: Prospects for Development and Profitability. (2000). *IDATE Newsletter,* 26: 1.

Cashing in on the World Cup (2002). *Far Eastern Economic Review,* (June 6), 43.

Chaebol Takes a Sporting Chance, Raises Spending on Advertising (1997). *Nikkei Weekly,* (January 27), 26.

Chiclets Tries New Language (1993). *Advertising Age International,* (April 19), I–1.

Clampdown on 'Porno-Chic' Ads is Pushed by French Authorities (2001). *The Wall Street Journal,* (October 25), B4.

Coca-Cola Touts Overseas Strength for Fanta Brand (1996, November 4). Available: AdAge.com

Coke Brands IPG as Global Ad Strategist (2000, December 4). Available: AdAge.com

Coke's Local World Cup Tactics (2002) *Marketing,* (May 30), 15.

Do Coupons Make Cents? (2003). *Incentive,* (May), 19.

DSM Set to Expand Web-based Dealings (2000). *Financial Times,* (February 24), 17.

Final Report: Sharply Focused Trade-Fair Concept a Success (2004, June 28). Available: http://www.hometech-cologne.com

429 Million People are on the Net Worldwide (2001). *Direct Marketing*, (September), 18.

Getting Lost in the Translation (1998). *Computer Dealers News*, (April 6), 56.

Global Kleenex Effort Breaks K-C Boundaries. (2000). *Advertising Age*, (April 10), 3.

Global Media (1999). *Advertising Age International*, (February 8), 23.

Going Global With Banner Ads (2002, July 16). Available: www.sun.com

Greenburg, Karl. (2003). BMW's goal: 'Score with Soccer Pitch,' *Brandweek*, (May 12), 9.

Hennessey, H. D. and Jeannet, J. P. (2003). *Global Account Management: Creating Value*. London: Wiley.

Hey, Why Do You Think We Call Them "French Fries"? (1999). *Wall Street Journal Europe*, (December 9), 1.

Huff, L. C. and Alden, D. L. (1998). 'An Investigation of Consumer Response to Sales Promotion in Developing Markets,' *Journal of Advertising Research*, (May–June), 47–57.

Jeannet, J. P. and Hennessey, H. D. (2004). *Global Marketing Strategies, 6th edn*. Boston, MA: Houghton Mifflin.

—— and Collins, R. (1993). *Deloitte Touche Tohmatsu International Europe Case*. Lausanne: IMD.

—— and Lanning, M. (2001). *Euro RSCG: Global Brand Management in Advertising Case*. Lausanne: IMD.

Levitt, T. (1983*a*). 'The Globalization of Markets,' *Harvard Business Review*, (May–June), 92.

—— (1983*b*). *The Marketing Imagination*. New York: Free Press.

MasterCard Renews Commitments with FICA World Cup Through 2002 (1999). *Comline Pacific Research Consulting*, (March 19), 1–2.

Mexico Forces a Wonderbra Cover-Up (1996). *Financial Times*, (August 19), 4.

MTV's World (2001). *Business Week*, (February 18), 81.

Murdoch Loses Bidding for Olympic Television Rights (1996). *Financial Times*, (January 31), 1.

Murphy, D. (1999). 'Sales Promotion: Cross-border Conflicts,' *Marketing*, (February 11), 30.

NBC, IOC Chase Long-Term Deals (1995). *Advertising Age*, (December 18), 3.

Nicotine Addiction; Survey finds Americans want US to sign global tobacco treaty (2004). *Drug Week*, (June 11), 425.

Nike Learns the Flipside of Associating with Success (2000). *Marketing Week (London)*, (November 30), 37.

Nokia in 'Exploratory Talks' with News Corp. about Internet Tie-Up (2000). *Financial Times*, (February 2), 13.

Patek Philippe: Tradition Anyone? (1999). *Advertising Age International*, (January 11), 9.

Phoenix Rising (2001). *Newsweek*, (November 12), 46.

Pollack, J. (1999). 'Pringles Wins Worldwide With One Message,' *Ad Age International*, (January 11), 14.

Removing Restrictions on Sales Promotion (2002). *European Business Journal*, 54.

Smoking Offensive: Brazil's Strict Measures Open Unlikely Front in War on Cigarettes (2002). *Wall Street Journal*, (January 15), A1.

Sprite Is Riding Global Ad Effort to No. 4 Status (1996). *Advertising Age*, (November 18), 30.

Stewart-Allen, A. L. (1998). 'Cultural Quandaries Can Lead to Misnomers,' *Marketing News*, (November 23), 9.

—— (1999). 'Cross-border Conflicts of European Sales Promotions,' *Marketing News*, (April 26), 10.

Study Examines E-Commerce/Internet Use in Latin America (2001). *Direct Marketing*, (April), 9.

The New Europe: Whirlpool's European Sales Short-Circuit (1998). *Asian Wall Street Journal*, (April 15), 1.

The Picture Puzzle: Advertising's New Visual Language (2001). *Communications Arts*, (December), 240.

Top 10 Digital Properties (2000). *Ad Age Global*, (November), 5.

Welcome to Europe's Biggest Industrial Fair: Hannover Messe 1998 (1998). *Modern Materials Handling*, (March), E3.

Whirlpool Asks Commerce to 'Just Imagine' (2000). *Twice*, (May 15), 38.

Williams, F. (1999). Curbs on Tobacco: WHO to Launch Talks on Treaty. *Financial Times*, (October 26), 6.

II

DEVELOPMENTS IN MARKETING
COMMUNICATION
TECHNOLOGIES

When it comes to emerging developments in technology, for
marketing communicators, there is no doubt that the future is
now. Although the Internet may be the first relatively new technological advancement to spring to mind when one considers
the contemporary marketer's growing arsenal of high-tech tools
for reaching target audiences, a simple trip to the local supermarket can effectively highlight some of the significant changes
that the marketing landscape has undergone in recent years. For
example, one's shopping cart might be equipped with a video
screen to inform about store promotions and new products,
with a map of the store layout appearing from time to time to
point out their shelf locations. Infrared beams emanating from
various store areas could activate videos that highlight products
and brands as the consumer approaches them. Store signage,
consisting of electronic scrolling information, might be bilin-
gual, especially if the store is located in a multicultural neighborhood and the retailer is striving to establish a strong bond
with local ethnic groups.

Continuing our tour of the supermarket, additional details
about a product might be available immediately by pushing a
button next to the product on the shelf in order to hear a
recorded voice providing product information, perhaps along
with some serving suggestions. Shoppers might be approached
by a salesperson who is wearing an interactive computer screen
embedded within the store uniform, which can be used to

display what the product looks like in action, deliver money-saving coupons, engage shoppers in competitive contests or games, or file immediate feedback or recommendations from consumers for store improvement. One's grocery items might be tagged with radio frequency identifiers, thereby dramatically speeding up the checkout process while at the same time alerting supermarket staff that some of the products need to be restocked. These and many other new communication techniques are not on the horizon—they are already here.

The five chapters in this section provide a comprehensive assessment of the many new and emerging technologies for carrying out marketing communication campaigns, as well as a detailed consideration of the challenges these developments entail. Technological advances can facilitate marketing objectives (e.g. by providing interactive media for better responding to consumer concerns), but they also pose growing threats to the success of promotional efforts (e.g. by making it easier for consumers to screen out marketing messages). The new (and potentially new) marketing tools that draw from these technological advances also raise important ethical questions, in terms of customer privacy, data protection, and unwanted intrusions into everyday life.

With all the attention devoted to emerging technologies, it is important to bear in mind that television continues to represent a primary medium of choice for advertisers around the world, and likely will continue to serve as such for many years to come. However, where once television was considered an essential medium for broadcasting messages to wide audiences, marketers have gradually come to view television in terms of its potential for reaching individually targeted and more narrowly defined audiences (so-called 'narrowcasting') in an increasingly interactive fashion. These issues are covered in detail by Lowrey, Shrum, and McCarty in Chapter 6. Importantly, the authors emphasize how the blending of commercial and noncommercial programming content (e.g. in the form of product placements) has become a rapidly growing trend that is likely to ultimately change the face of advertising on television as we have come to know it. Because of the advent of technologies making it easier than ever for viewers to intentionally avoid marketing messages (from remote control devices that enable viewers to channel surf without leaving their seats to hard drive television devices that record everything but the ads), product integration may indeed represent a solution that consumers and marketers alike can accept. The authors consider several potential innovative solutions to the various problems currently faced by the television advertising industry, especially with regard to rising levels of advertising clutter.

In Chapter 7, European marketing practitioners O'Connor, Galvin, and Evans emphasize that contemporary and future marketing communication in the form of *electronic marketing* is 'not just about the Internet.' The authors clarify this point by highlighting a wide range of other electronic tools and techniques that are currently (or soon-to-be) available to marketing communicators, and argue that the customer database is critical to the success of these new approaches. O'Connor and his colleagues describe the impact of electronic technologies on marketing communication through the explication of five key messages, which are essential for marketers to understand if their campaigns are to meet with success in the twenty-first century.

Fill extends the discussion of recent developments in technology in Chapter 8 by focusing on the influence of information systems and technology (IST) on below-the-line marketing (i.e. nonadvertising) communication approaches, such as sales promotion, public relations, personal selling, and direct marketing. The author clarifies the sometimes blurry distinction between above- and below-the-line tools and then provides numerous examples of emergent technologies for each of the nonadvertising marketing communication approaches, including short message services (SMS; also known as 'texting'), multimedia message services (MMS), mobile commerce, wireless networking, data mining and visualization tools, smart devices, and newly-emerging types of loyalty programs. Fill also considers the central role of customer data management, particularly in terms of the potential impact of technological advances on the development of customer relationships.

One of the key messages that emerges from the discussion of new technologies in Chapters 7 and 8 is that these developments alone do not guarantee that a marketing communication campaign will meet with success. According to Fill, 'technology is an enabler, whereas management's ability and willingness to engage with new technology is the key determinant of successful marketing communication efforts.' The two chapters also caution that the flipside to the benefits that can be accrued through the appropriate application of technology is a range of security-related issues (such as those linked to invasions of privacy, fraud, and data protection), and emphasize that security will continue to represent one of the basic information technology priorities for businesses in the years to come.

In Chapter 9, American marketing professor Thomas W. Gruen tackles the important notion of *integrated marketing communications* (IMC) within the context of a discussion of the important functions of the company website. IMC is the well-known idea that emerged during the second half of the twentieth century emphasizing the necessity for a promotional campaign to be unified and consistent with all of the company's other marketing efforts, including the development of the product or service offering, pricing, distribution, and so on. This concept continues to be followed today by many companies in order to effectively achieve marketing objectives. Gruen expands the IMC concept by arguing that electronic marketing and the Internet can play an essential integrative role for marketing campaigns, and offers several examples of how company websites have been used to integrate the communications of various organizational functions.

Our survey of new technologies concludes with a look at what is no doubt the oldest technology for accomplishing marketing communication—word of mouth (WOM). In Chapter 10, Silverman explains the various forms that interpersonal marketing communication can take in the digital age and emphasizes how, in the current era of rapid change and high-tech developments, WOM and its utility for satisfying marketing goals might be more powerful than ever. In fact, the author boldly proclaims that, in his view, 'word of mouth is more powerful than all of the other marketing methods in this book *put together*' [his emphasis]. Of course, the tricky part about using WOM as a marketing communication technology is that much of it is not directly (or even indirectly) under the control of marketers. Silverman presents ideas for how a WOM campaign can be developed and identifies several proven strategies for harnessing WOM in order to achieve various beneficial marketing outcomes.

6

The Future of Television Advertising

Tina M. Lowrey, L. J. Shrum, and John A. McCarty

> The camera focuses on 'Bud' Miller, CEO of Ford Motors. Bud has been kidnapped by ZANNA, a terrorist organization that will use the ransom money to finance a membership drive. Although he's been captive for weeks, Bud has been able to conceal his tiny Cingular cellphone from his captors, allowing him to stay in contact with Ford headquarters. This is particularly important given the new ad campaign being created by Saatchi and Saatchi to showcase the newest model of Ford Explorer. Bud knows he is crazy not to reveal his whereabouts, but his captors are relatively benevolent (keeping him well-supplied with Pepsi and Snickers bars, because, as his captors say, 'That's what Americans eat, isn't it?') and he just can't afford any delays in the start of the ad campaign...
>
> Scene from the new television show, *All My Cars*

Perhaps we exaggerate when we suggest that the above vignette describes the future of television advertising, an environment in which the lines between entertainment and promotion have not just been blurred, but have been almost completely removed. Yet, as we detail in this chapter, the above scenario is not all that far-fetched. With so many technological innovations emerging that challenge the traditional method of delivering entertainment, many question the viability of television commercials as we know them. This is true not only in the trade press, but also in academe (cf. Baker 2003; Rust and Oliver 1994). Advertisers are experimenting with a wide array of solutions, many of which have been around since the advent of television broadcasting, to address their concerns over the dwindling commercial audience. However, there are also industry voices claiming that many are exaggerating the picture.

How to approach the task of commenting on the future of television advertising? The task is daunting if for no other reason than its ambiguity.

What do we mean by 'the future,' by 'television,' and by 'advertising'? With respect to the future, we have greatly restricted the time horizon, and have focused primarily on the very near future, roughly comprising the next five to ten years. Although it is possible to imagine what the far future holds (e.g. personalized ads sent directly to brain-embedded chips, bypassing conscious processing), the unpredictability of technology, advertisers, and consumers themselves makes accurate forecasting a low-probability endeavor. With respect to television, we consider the medium as it is currently used, but also consider a future that includes interactive television. With respect to advertising, we liberally include any type of paid promotion that appears within or between programming. Thus, this definition not only includes traditional commercials, but also promotional practices such as product placement, product immersion, sponsorships, or any combination of these.

Given our near-term focus, the objective is to outline the current major trends, examine them in-depth to assess their likelihood of contribution to significant future change in the industry, and to offer observations about what is likely to occur over the next decade to commercial television. One important limitation that should be acknowledged is that our assessment and critique emphasizes American television advertising. This is primarily because American television developed as a commercial enterprise and advertising has always been the major source of revenue for the industry in the USA. Although advertising is definitely a part of the television landscape in European countries, state-owned and noncommercial stations have been a major force in Europe for many years. In many European countries, these stations garner a significant share of the viewing audience. Furthermore, television in Europe is more heavily regulated than it is in the USA. Therefore, America tends to be the extreme example of both the problems and the potential solutions that likely will inform the future of television advertising.

CURRENT TRENDS

There are several trends causing both excitement and consternation in the industry. A recent review of selected trade publications (including *Advertising Age, Mediaweek, TelevisionWeek, and The New York Times*) offers a wide array of concerns. Despite different terminologies for related concepts, these can be loosely categorized into three major areas, the first and foremost of which is technological innovation and its implications. Of particular concern are the consequences of deep penetration of personal video recorders (PVRs) and video-on-demand (VOD). These devices allow viewers to avoid ads within and between recorded noncommercial programs with remarkable ease, and much of the concern in the industry pertains to how to deal with this presumably inevitable loss of ad viewership. At the same time, advertisers are excited about the prospect of interactive television, which should allow for customized and direct contact with the viewer.

The second issue is in many ways a response to these technologies: the trend toward product placement, or, more broadly, product integration. Product integration involves weaving the product into the 'fabric' of the program, usually through a combination of such techniques as product placement and immersion, blurring the lines between entertainment and promotion (Shrum 2004). Given that many industry analysts believe that technology that allows viewers to avoid ads surely means that viewers will do so, these alternative tactics are an outcome of strategies to reach viewers through the programs themselves.

The third area of concern revolves around the issue of ad clutter. Over the years, two trends have clearly emerged, particularly in the USA: (a) more television time devoted to ads and (b) shorter ads. These two trends translate into a huge leap in the number of ads shown in any given time period. Industry professionals worry about two consequences of clutter: less ad effectiveness due to cognitive overload and loss of viewers due to their annoyance with the barrage of ads.

In the following sections, we address in more detail each of these issues and attempt to provide a balanced perspective on the current state of practice. As previously noted, the continued success and viability of television advertising has been questioned time and again, particularly when the discussion focuses on the effects of new technologies. Of course, this is to be expected: new technologies often spawn apocalyptic visions regardless of the domain, and provide substantial material for science fiction writers (see Chapter 3). Moreover, it can be very exciting to think about a brave new world in which technology has fundamentally changed the way we live. Yet two points are often overlooked. With respect to the end-user (i.e. the viewer), old habits are often difficult to break, so the diffusion of technologies and their correspondent effects usually take much longer than is predicted. With respect to the producer (i.e. the advertiser or network), it again is the case that old habits are hard to break, so the 'tried-and-true' methods typically have remarkable staying power in spite of predicted revolutions in business practice. Nevertheless, when faced with real and imminent threats, businesses often prove eager to adopt new methods for dealing with change. For these reasons, it is important to assess the proper weight to be assigned to particular threats.

Technological Innovation

The greatest area of concern for the industry involves technologies that allow for greater viewer control over ad exposure. Whether they take the form of VOD, PVRs, or interactive television, their threat to traditional viewing habits is fairly clear. VOD refers to the ability of networks to provide programming to individuals at any time, rather than at a specific scheduled time for a mass audience. PVRs are devices that allow individuals to easily record programming and avoid undesirable elements (such as ads). Interactive television will allow viewers to interact directly with producers to influence specific aspects of programs.

VOD's threat pertains to its ability to provide easy access to alternative programming such as movies. Networks worry that such greatly expanded program choice, and particularly *commercial-free* program choice, will siphon away viewers from their own advertising-supported programming. The threat of the PVR is in its ability to easily avoid traditional ads. PVRs allow users to record a program in digital format, store the information on a hard drive, and play back the program at the users' convenience. Moreover, this playback can occur in real time such that the user can pause a 'live' event and start playing it again without missing any programming. Most important from the network and advertiser perspective, PVRs allow for very quick and efficient skipping through recorded segments such as ads. It is estimated that the household penetration of PVRs will be over 20 percent in the USA, France, Germany, and Great Britain by 2007 (Greenspan 2003) and that worldwide shipments of PVRs will be over 30 million units by 2007 (In-Stat/MDR 2004).

It seems clear that these new technologies have the very real potential to change the way we view television. Research indicates that 70 percent of PVR users report skipping ads (Baron 2003). Additionally, a viewer can give a program (such as a sporting match) an hour head start, then tune in and fast-forward through uninteresting parts (e.g. lulls in the match). However, the new technologies also allow advertisers to adapt to their advantage. For example, interactive television, which will allow viewers to interact with the show, request information, and even change endings, will also allow advertisers to provide very targeted, customized ads to individual viewers. This type of technology should greatly enhance the efficiency of ads and media buys.

Product Integration

Product integration is the tactic that advertisers have adopted to combat the ad-zapping possibilities of new technologies. It essentially involves weaving the brand into the programming. The logic of many advertisers is that they want to become 'zap-proof,' and one of the ways of accomplishing this is to get out of stand-alone ad insertions and into the program itself. It should be noted that the extent of the practices discussed in this section vary dramatically across countries. Most of this discussion draws from what is happening in the USA; product integration has traditionally been severely restricted in many European countries.

Product placement

One of the well-known forms of integration is product placement, which involves having the brand visible in a scene, such as a Viking range in a kitchen or a character drinking Coca-Cola. Until recently, product placements tended to be more prevalent in films than in television, if for no other reason than regulation: placement within films is largely unregulated, whereas regulatory agencies in the USA and the European Union (EU) have restrictions regarding paid placements for television programming. Of course, films typically appear later as televised movies, and advertisers are developing clever ways of getting around the 'paid' aspect of placements. In particular, complex barter arrangements may be used in which actual cash does not change hands, but the advertiser supplies a free location for filming (e.g. a department store), free products for the production crew (e.g. cars, computers), joint promotions of the film or program, and so forth (McCarty 2004). Although the amounts 'paid' by the advertiser may seem minimal compared to the cost of advertising, they are often crucial for program production. In many cases, it may mean the difference in being able to produce a particular program.

Recent content analyses provide a glimpse of current practice and future potential. For example, in a study that assessed the top three American networks (ABC, NBC, and CBS), fifteen branded products appeared in the average 30-minute program, of which approximately 40 percent were negotiated product placements (Avery and Ferraro 2003). Although the presence of product placements revealed in this study was significant, there is clearly potential for additional placements (by either increasing the number of branded appearances in a program or increasing the percentage that are negotiated placements).

With respect to product placement in Europe, the EU as a whole and individual European countries have enacted much stricter limitations compared with those in the USA. Generally, a product is allowed to be in a scene only to the extent that it is essential to the story. However, the restrictions are difficult to enforce, and the practice appears to be evident in numerous countries in Europe (Freys 1993). Over the last decade, there have been suggestions made by many to legalize the practice (Cowen

2003), motivated to some extent by the presumed diminishing impact of traditional advertising.

The possibilities for an expanded presence for product placements have spawned a cottage industry of firms that specialize in brokering such placements. Placement brokers contract with companies interested in having their products placed in films and television programs, arrange for a network or film company to supply them with scripts in progress, read through the scripts to determine points in which it would be reasonable to show their client's product, and then negotiate for placement (Ganguzza 2002). The negotiation may involve varying levels of influence on the nature of the script. At the simplest level, it may involve something as innocuous as a mention in a script of a desktop computer being used, and the placement broker merely asking whether it could specifically be an Apple computer. However, the broker's client may be in the process of rolling out a new laptop, and thus the broker may ask if the script could be altered such that the desktop computer becomes the new Apple laptop. Still more influence on the script process might occur if no computer is specifically called for, but could be easily integrated into the scene, and thus the broker negotiates the inclusion of the product category into the program.

The extent to which the product placement process intrudes on the creative vision of writer and producer can vary substantially. Although many placement brokers are adamant that they do not want to inhibit creativity in an effort to promote their clients' products, and in fact suggest that to do so would actually hurt the industry (Ganguzza 2002), it is also clear that it is in the client's best interest (and therefore the broker's) to do whatever is possible to secure the placement, and it may be difficult for a producer running overbudget to turn down some sort of financial incentive. Indeed, some placement brokers are becoming so sophisticated that they get input from producers, writers, and advertisers as to how their client's product could be integrated into a script in a creative way (Whitney 2003).

Product immersion

It is one thing for a brand to appear as a placement in the background of a scene, but quite another for it to be an integral part of the storyline. Clearly, within certain constraints of realism, the impact of being an integral part of the story plot should be substantial. Product immersion refers to this process of weaving a brand into the forefront of a story rather than into its background. Thus, for example, ABC has incorporated Revlon into one of its soap opera plots, and it has been reported that NBC will integrate a new Avon cosmetic line into three episodes of its soap opera *Passions* ('Product Placement' 2003).

Placement-friendly program development

Given the phenomenal success of product placement (McCarty 2004) and the consequent eagerness of advertisers to reap additional benefits, it has not escaped the notice of networks and program producers that certain types of programs may be particularly conducive to product placement. However, it is important that there is a 'fit' between the program and the product being placed within it.

   Product placements have become part and parcel of such reality shows as *Survivor*. In this case, it is natural to focus on a beverage if the contestant is suffering from extreme thirst. A reality show called *The Bar* on Scandinavian television uses furniture supplied by the Swedish furniture manufacturer IKEA (Marsh 2001). But why stop there? It is a logical step to develop a program in which the products themselves are a major focus. In ABC's *Extreme Makeover: Home Edition*, which is sponsored by Sears and includes frequent placements of their tools and appliances, a team of designers and workmen race to completely renovate a house in just a few days. In Discovery Channel's *No Opportunity Wasted*, contestants are challenged to 'live in the moment' and attempt to fulfill a dream, such as being a rock star. Mastercard sponsors the show because they believe that the challenge theme of the program is consistent with their brand identity (Stanley 2004). Contestants are given $3000 credit on Mastercard for their attempt to fulfill their dream. Another example is *Queer Eye for the Straight Guy*, a reality program in which five gay men give a heterosexual man a fashion and lifestyle make-over (hair, clothes, home decoration, food and wine, etc.). Clearly, this is an ideal show for a variety of product categories to be promoted, and many of the placements on *Queer Eye* have resulted in phenomenal sales increases (Song 2003). In general, reality shows are an excellent venue for product promotion and these kinds of shows have become popular in several countries. For example, versions of the Dutch program *Big Brother* have found success in the UK, the USA, Italy, France, and Spain (Riding 2001).

Client-developed programming

Although it has not yet happened in the current television environment, the next logical step in developing product integration opportunities is for brands to create the programs themselves. Assuming the programs are in fact popular, it is a win-win situation for networks and advertisers. The networks avoid the expense of costly program production, and the advertisers avoid the time-consuming process of negotiating the quantity and quality of placements. At one time, Ford was rumored to be creating a prime-time drama in which Ford cars and trucks were shown prominently throughout the program. This creative endeavor is similar to the series of films that BMW created and offered via the Internet in which their cars were not only featured prominently, but were in fact intended to be the stars of the show. Time will tell whether such practices will make their way to television. Regulation will also affect the extent to which this may happen. The 'Television Without Frontiers' directive of the EU states that advertisers and program sponsors cannot influence the editorial content or scheduling of the programs (Aubry 2000). Therefore, it is unlikely that such collaboration will make its way to European television in the near future. In the USA, such production by advertisers may also be avoided, as it is reminiscent of problems in the early days of television, when such influence over programming by advertisers led to quiz show scandals.

Program sponsorship

Also increasingly popular as a promotional strategy are sponsorships, which refer to situations where the advertiser pays all or some of the production costs of the program, such as a televised sporting event. In the USA, the sponsors receive frequent mention (e.g. 'Brought to you by....'), often purchase a significant portion of the advertising for that program, and now receive product placements in the package. Sponsorship in European countries is generally more restricted. For example, regulations in the UK restrict what can be said in the sponsorship credit and when the credit can appear in the program. However, there is evidence that some of these restrictions have begun to relax in recent years (Carter 2004).

As previously noted, Sears has sponsored a reality home improvement program that prominently features their products. Another example is *Pepsi Smash*, a summer live music series in which Pepsi is the primary sponsor. In exchange for sponsorship, Pepsi contributed significantly to the production costs, is mentioned prominently throughout the broadcast, and receives numerous product placements (Bachman and Flass 2003).

It is interesting to note that the concept of sponsorship is not at all new. In fact, many early American programs were sponsored by single advertisers. Examples from the 1950s include *Goodyear TV Playhouse* and *Kraft Television Theater*. These shows were controlled by a single sponsor and the ad agencies acted as producers and fought for control of programming. There was a tendency for commercial messages to be blended into the programming of the shows (Fox 1984). This practice was stopped primarily due to the quiz show scandals of the 1950s, which revealed that the contests were in fact rigged, and thus the supposed 'reality' nature of the programming was actually scripted. Ironically, some of the same charges have been leveled against today's reality television programs (Soriano 2001).

The common thread underlying all of the different types of product integration is that the advertiser is as much partner as client with the networks in the production process (Consoli 2003). Whereas advertisers once were solely given consideration in terms of placements within programs and the avoidance of programs whose content might reflect negatively on the advertisers, the advertisers now have much more input into the actual programs, which are increasingly becoming showcases for the brands that are placed within them.

Advertising Clutter

Advertising clutter refers to the proliferation of advertising that produces excessive competition for viewer attention, to the point that individual messages lose impact and viewers abandon the ads (via fast-forwarding, changing channels, quitting viewing, etc.). Two particular trends in television advertising practice in the USA contribute to this clutter: (*a*) the increase in the number of ad minutes per program hour and (*b*) the use of shorter commercials (e.g. 10- and 15-second ads). These two trends have produced an environment in which the viewer is bombarded with a constant stream of rapid-fire ads, and industry analysts rightly worry that viewers will become alienated.

To truly understand current trends in ad proliferation, it is necessary to view current practice within its historical context. In the 1950s, the standard length of American commercials was 60 seconds and the networks did not sell advertising in smaller units, although the practice of 'piggybacking' (i.e. ads for two unrelated products presented in the same 60-second commercial slot) began around 1956 (Martilla and Thompson 1966). In the early 1970s, the networks finally recognized the interest in shorter ads and began to sell 30-second spots ('*Advertising Age's* History' 2004). The 30-second spot became the norm during the 1970s, with a majority of spots being 30 seconds in length from the early 1970s until today (Cobb-Walgren 1990). In the mid-1980s, 15-second spots became relatively common. In 2002, the majority of spots were 15 or 30 seconds, and only 6 percent were 60 seconds in length (Television Bureau of Advertising 2004).

More striking is the increase over time in total ad minutes. In the early 1960s, the National Association of Broadcasters (NAB) revised their code to limit the number of commercials per hour, the number of minutes of commercial time per hour, and the number of products advertised in a commercial (Campbell 1999). However, piggybacking of ads continued throughout the mid-1960s, and it was estimated that up to 25 percent of 60-second ads were piggybacks (Martilla and Thompson 1966). Although more 30-second spots were being sold in the 1970s, the amount of commercial time per hour remained fairly constant, given that the NAB code dictated the amount of time that could be devoted to nonprogramming time.

In 1982 the US Department of Justice (DoJ) brought an antitrust lawsuit against NAB. The DoJ took the position that limiting the length and the number of commercials per hour effectively constrained the supply of ad time, artificially increasing the price of time to advertisers, thereby violating federal antitrust laws (Campbell 1999). Because of this lawsuit, the NAB ceased enforcing the code, effectively allowing networks and local stations to sell more advertising time per hour. From slightly over five minutes of advertising per hour for prime time programming in 1986, prime time advertising time per hour began to rise in the mid-1980s (Kent 1995). Note that American 'prime time' occurs between eight and eleven p.m. on the East and West coasts, and between seven and ten p.m. in the central region of the country. Fig. 6.1 shows the ad minutes per prime time hour from 1992 to 2001. As the graph illustrates, ad minutes have increased from just under 10 minutes per hour in 1992 to slightly over 12 in 2001, a 140 percent increase from the 1986 levels and a 24 percent increase in just the last ten years.

Other day parts have an even greater number of ad minutes, and these have also increased over recent years. Table 6.1 shows the number of minutes of ad time in 1992 and 2001 for the various day parts. All day parts except local news have shown a clear increase since 1992. Note also that these figures are based only on the major broadcast networks. On many cable channels in the USA, ad minutes per hour can run well over 20 minutes, even during prime time.

According to a study from PhaseOne Communications, the total break time for prime time has increased over the past decade (Misdom 2004). Total break time includes commercials, sponsorship announcements, promotions, teasers, and public service announcements. The average time for these messages during the three hours of prime time increased from 38.7 minutes in 1991 to 52.7 minutes in 2003 (roughly, an increase from 13 to 17.5 minutes per hour), as shown in Table 6.2. The average length of breaks has also increased over that same period of time, resulting in the total number of breaks declining during prime time (see Table 6.2).

These numbers suggest a startling amount of advertising during a given hour of American programming. Contrast this with the early days of television, when there were typically four commercial breaks lasting two minutes each per hour, and today's viewers are treated to twice as many ads (and, of course, much less programming content). Given that the majority of spots are now 30 seconds in length (rather than the minute-long commercials of the past), with some 15-second spots thrown in for good measure, one can appreciate the information overload consumers no doubt experience as a result. Additionally, the fact that adver-

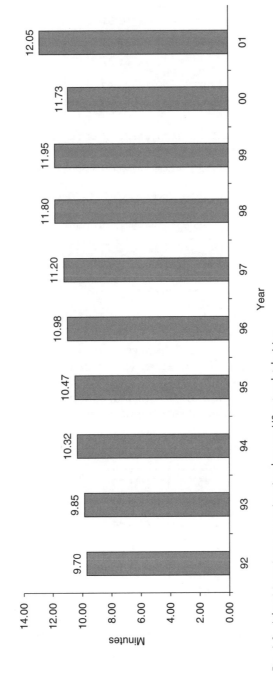

Fig. 6.1. Advertising minutes per prime time hour on US network television
Source: American Association of Advertising Agencies and Association of National Advertisers, Inc.

Table 6.1. Minutes of advertising time per hour for day parts, network television, USA (1992, 2001)

Day part	1992	2001	Percent change
Network news	14.12	15.67	11.0
Local news	13.80	13.87	0.5
Early morning	13.82	14.93	8.0
Daytime	14.80	17.23	16.4
Late night	13.93	15.85	13.8

Source: American Association of Advertising Agencies and Association of National Advertisers, Inc.

Table 6.2. Analysis of commercial break time, network television, USA, for total 3 hours of prime time

	1991	1998	2000	2003
Total break time	38.73	47.64	49.94	52.72
Average break length	1.77	2.17	2.95	3.16
Total number of breaks	22.33	22.00	17.00	17.00

Source: Misdom (2004), PhaseOne Communications.

tisers currently produce fewer commercials (Ephron 2003) suggests that viewers end up watching the same ads repeatedly. Even very creative spots are likely to wear on viewers if they see them several times per hour.

At present, clutter is not as much of a problem in Europe, compared to the USA. Table 6.3 shows the average minutes of advertising per hour for four countries in Europe and the USA for four different years. For each of the countries, the amount of advertising of the major stations or networks is

Table 6.3. Average number of minutes of advertising per hour (Average of top networks in each country)

	1996	1999	2001	2003
UK[a]	7.00	7.00	7.00	7.00
France[b]	4.79	5.84	4.19	4.96
Germany[c]	7.33	8.72	6.49	8.40
Italy[d]	7.63	9.62	7.24	9.61
US[e]	13.63	14.72	14.97	N/A

[a]Average of stations ITV, Channel 4, Channel 5, and GMTV. [b]Average of stations TF1, France 2, France 3, and M6. [c]Average of stations RTL, RTL 2, SAT.1, and PRO 7. [d]Average of stations Canale 5, Italia 1, and Rete 4. [e]Average of networks ABC, CBS, NBC, and Fox. Note that these numbers differ from Fig. 6.1 because they include all day parts (Fig. 6.1 is prime time only).
Source: European data from ZenithOptimedia, Western Europe Market & MediaFact, 1996–2003; US data from American Association of Advertising Agencies and Association of National Advertisers, Inc.

averaged. The average minutes of advertising per hour in each of the European countries is below ten minutes for all four years. The amount of advertising in the UK is consistent, averaging the maximum amount allowed for each of the years. For the other European countries, no clear trend in the amount of advertising is apparent. By contrast, there is a trend toward more minutes of advertising per hour in the USA across the same years.

POTENTIAL SOLUTIONS TO THE CURRENT INDUSTRY CRISIS

In the previous section, we detailed trends that are developing in the relations among advertisers, networks, and viewers. Although the short-term future of some of these trends seems self-evident, it is unclear they will last for a significantly long time. Moreover, the longevity of each of the trends (technology, product integration, and clutter) is dependent on the viability and longevity of the others. In fact, it is difficult to overemphasize the irony of this interdependency: growing dissatisfaction with advertising due to excessive clutter fuels demand from viewers for technologies that will allow them to bypass the source of dissatisfaction, which in turn fuels demand from advertisers and networks to develop technologies and promotional practices that will allow them to bypass viewers' efforts to bypass that dissatisfaction. In the following sections we assess the longevity potential of each trend. We also make predictions and suggestions about what each trend, or its consequences, will or should look like in the near future.

Technology

As noted earlier, the PVR has prompted a number of pronouncements that television ads are heading toward a quick death. The popularity of PVRs is very high among those who have them. One study found that 23 percent of PVR owners indicated they avoided all commercials and more than 20 percent indicated they no longer watch 'live' television but instead only watch via their PVR (Chunovic 2002). However, assessing the success of technological innovations can be tricky. Indeed, the penetration of PVRs appears to be only about 4.5 million units worldwide as of the end of 2003 (In-Stat/MDR 2004). Such low penetration may result from an enthusiastic but small market of consumers who are willing to change their viewing habits, or it may result from the inability of PVR manufacturers to intensively produce and distribute their product.

In addition, legal issues surrounding the use of recording devices such as PVRs are far from clear. Some legal opinions have even suggested that fast-forwarding through ads is illegal (Felten 2003), and networks sued one PVR provider (now bankrupt) for its inclusion of an option allowing viewers to automatically skip ads. Thus, just as with videocassette recorders and audiocassettes, the affected industry tends to mount legal barriers to the penetration of the technology. However, in most cases, these barriers serve to only slow the diffusion of technology.

Product Integration

At the time of this writing, the use of product integration, in all its various forms, is widespread in the USA. The logic underlying its use is that if it is the case that viewers are annoyed with advertising (both in terms of quality and quantity), skipping ads when they can and ignoring them when they cannot, advertisers can circumvent this practice by getting their products into the program. This logic has some immediate, short-term appeal, but unfortunately tends to break down upon closer scrutiny. The problem lies in how the practice is executed, the extent of the integration of the product into the program, and how viewers react to the practices. Each of these has ramifications for understanding the potential effectiveness of product integration.

The level of product integration has important implications for the viability of the practice. The industry thinking seems to be that more intrusiveness equates with more effectiveness. Presumably, the industry also feels that being noticed a *lot* is a key to placement effectiveness, although there is an understanding that as a placement becomes more intrusive and overt, it needs to be seamless so that it does not register with viewers as an outright product plug. This notion is also starting to influence the measurement of placements. iTVX has launched new software that evaluates how integrated the brand is into the scene, how clearly visible the logo is, and how seamless the placement is. The software combines these assessments with how many times the episode has run to assess overall impact in terms of monetary value (Sherman 2003).

The notion of intrusiveness presents a paradox of sorts for marketers (Ephron 2003). Even though intrusiveness may in fact increase awareness and recall of placed brands, the intrusiveness may also entail a different type of mental processing. Friestad and Wright (1994) addressed this notion in their *persuasion knowledge model*. In their view, consumers have a schema regarding marketers' persuasion attempts. When consumers are confronted with what they believe to be a marketing attempt, they process the information differently than if they did not recognize the attempt as persuasive: they scrutinize it more carefully, argue with the message, and effectively change the meaning of the message (McCarty 2004). To the extent that the placement is more noticeable, it is more likely to be recognized as a persuasion attempt. However, most marketers also seem to believe that unless the product is noticed, it cannot have an effect, in terms of either increased awareness or more favorable product attitudes. In other words, 'If you notice, it's bad. But if you don't, it's worthless' (Ephron 2003: 20).

Recent scientific research on how people process information contradicts this view, however. Research in cognitive and social psychology clearly shows that learning, preference formation, and persuasion can occur outside of conscious awareness (see Erdelyi and Zizak 2004; Zajonc 1980). Moreover, not only can information be stored outside of awareness, it can be retrieved outside of awareness as well (Jacoby 1984; Schacter 1987). It is possible that product placements can avoid being overtly noticed by viewers—and thus avoid activating consumers' persuasion schemas—and still have the types of effects that marketers desire. Of course, it is one thing to show support for these processes in the lab and quite another to show effects in the field. Still, as Law and Braun-LaTour (2004) noted, *new* methods should be developed for measuring the effects of product placements that operate at a low level of awareness. Current methods are inadequate precisely because they assume that even if the encoding of information into memory is not conscious, it should still be possible to consciously retrieve those memories. Thus, methods need to be developed to ascertain the effect of both nonconscious encoding and nonconscious retrieval.

This discussion clearly implies that less overt placements may actually have the greatest long-term effects, particularly on more complex processes like attitude change. But how does a product get mentioned and handled 'covertly?' In addition, what are the implications of the overt versus covert distinction on more integrated practices such as product immersion and integrated sponsorships? Clearly, the entire premise of these practices is their overt nature. In our view, the answer to these questions lies in the notion of *fit*; that is, the extent to which the product placement fits with the plot and scene structure. The notion of fit is important because it focuses on not simply whether a placement is noticed, but *how* a placement is noticed. A product placement may be a relatively seamless one in which a logo, product mention, or product use makes sense, both in terms of the plot and the filming. For example, viewers will likely tire (if they haven't already) of the constant, overt logo or brand name placements in which an actor awkwardly drinks a beverage so the brand name is never obscured, or the camera lingers on the grill of a car just a little longer than seems normal so that the logo registers more deeply. Such devices can annoy viewers because they interrupt the feeling of 'transportation' into the program, and they may also activate processing effects that serve to raise defenses against persuasion (Friestad and Wright 1994). In addition, the process of transportation, in which the viewer feels transported into the program or film itself, has been shown to increase the persuasive power of fiction (Green et al. 2004), and thus interrupting such transportation actually works against the goals of the placement.

The same notions of fit and seamlessness are equally applicable to practices such as product immersion and integrated sponsorships. For example, viewers have become accustomed to the close link between sponsorships and sports (see Chapter 5). Not only are many sporting events sponsored (e.g. the Nokia Sugar bowl for American college football), but logos appear on golf bags, shirts, and caps, and brand names are widely apparent at NASCAR races. Thus, it may not have caused that much viewer disruption or annoyance when the American network Fox Sports entered into sponsorship agreements with various beer and automobile makers, allowing their products and logos to be prominently displayed and mentioned in programs like *The Best Damn Sports Show Period* (Linnett 2003). Similarly, reality programs such as *Queer Eye*, in which the focus on particular products is an important part of the plot, make for a relatively seamless fit between the placement and the entertainment value of the program.

Despite these examples, it remains unclear whether advertisers and networks can hold the line on excessive proliferation of these practices to avoid such an oversaturation of product integration that viewers cannot escape noticing. Networks clearly are very enamored of the reality genre of programming, for at least two reasons: (*a*) the programs are relatively inexpensive to produce and (*b*) they provide ready-made vehicles for placement, which generates more money on top of the normal revenue for the traditional ads. However, even if these programs remain popular with many viewers, excessive reality programming reduces the viewing options for people who do not like them, making it likely they will turn to entertainment other than television.

Ad Clutter

Ad clutter is perhaps the most potentially vexing problem that advertisers and networks face. Clutter results from too many ads competing for the viewer's attention, thereby reducing the effect of any particular ad. However, the solution to the problem of clutter would require some decisions that may prove to be too difficult for networks and advertisers; networks would have to reduce the amount of ad time they sell and advertisers would have to make longer ads.

Despite the difficulty of these decisions, we argue that they are precisely ones that networks and advertisers should make. The current state of advertising will surely be untenable as technology provides viewers with more options. Not only will viewers likely leave traditional television programming, but also the excessive clutter will reduce the effectiveness of ads. Persuasion is a complex process that takes time. Viewers must not only be induced to attend to the ad, but to also elaborate upon it in their minds. This capability is surely absent in the 10- and 15-second ads and it is unclear whether 30-second ads do it particularly well either.

Nonetheless, there is some evidence that advertisers and networks may be willing to make some of the required changes. Some marketers are developing longer commercials that more resemble the programs themselves in that the focus is as much (if not more) on the story as on the product. These so-called 'advertainments' are short stories that use sponsorship and relatively minimal product placement. For example, the American sports network ESPN helped Sears create a short, six-minute program called *The Scout*. The program is shown in 90-second segments on ESPN's *SportsCenter*. ESPN also has plans for another short film to be sponsored by Miller Brewing (Ives 2004). These efforts resemble the innovative short films that were created by BMW and offered via the Internet, but with fewer and less overt placements.

These efforts appear to be an innovative attempt to address the clutter issue. But one important issue still remains: Do these advertisements take the place of ads or the place of programming? Clearly, to address clutter, it must be the former. However, a concern is that rather than replacing the current, overexposed ads, they will replace programming, thereby reducing the value of the entertainment program that induced viewers to watch television in the first place.

CONCLUSION

Our purpose in this chapter was to assess the current state of television advertising with a particular eye toward trends over the next decade. Although this time horizon is very conservative, it seems somewhat pointless to speculate on what advertising will look like twenty or thirty years from now when all of this depends on precisely how advertisers and networks address their near-term problems. For example, much of what has spurred a near panic in the industry is the threat of technologies such as PVRs. Yet the appeal of this technology is almost solely a result of the current state of television advertising (such as ad clutter and program alterations). It may well be that if advertisers and networks addressed the customer dissatisfaction issue, by making programs more appealing (i.e. with fewer ad minutes, and thus longer shows) and ads more appealing, then the desire to aggressively seek out these new technologies might lessen.

Unfortunately, this is not likely to be the case. Advertisers seem to think that consumers do not like television advertising. If not simply wrong, that notion may be a gross overstatement in that consumer attitudes are more positive than commonly believed (Shavitt et al. 1998). Commercials are some of the most talked-about, most-remembered, and hence, we would argue, most effective marketing phenomena. In the USA, programs devoted exclusively to ads are common (e.g. *The World's Funniest Commercials*), Super Bowl advertising is discussed frequently on news programs both before and after the game, and many viewers even indicate they watch the Super Bowl just to see the ads.

What consumers do not like is *bad* advertising (and too much of it). Yet advertisers seem reluctant, if not unwilling, to squarely address this issue. Instead, advertisers assume that in order to get viewers to watch ads, they must be tricked into doing so. As Kalter (2003: 18), CEO of Doner Advertising recently argued, advertisers are 'treating consumers as wild animals that must be trapped inside an advertising "environment," ' and 'the underlying message is one of hostility, distrust and disrespect.' We wholeheartedly concur with this view.

So what is the future of television advertising? Does the opening vignette paint an accurate picture of the viewer landscape to come? Although such a scenario may come to pass, we doubt that it has a prolonged future. Once complete saturation is reached, viewers will likely be sufficiently repelled that they will turn to other sources of media entirely. Perhaps they might even return to print.

REFERENCES

Advertising Age's History of TV Advertising (2004, March 6). Available: www.adage. com

Aubry, P. (2000). The 'Television Without Frontiers' Directive, Cornerstone of the European Broadcasting Policy. Available: http://www.obs.coe.int

Avery, R. J., and Ferraro, R. (2003). 'Versimilitude or Advertising? Brand Appearances on Prime-Time Television,' *Journal of Consumer Affairs*, 34, 217–44.

Bachman, K., and Flass, R. (2003). 'Viacom, Tribune and Pepsi Test Cross-media Strategy,' *Mediaweek*, (February 3), 10.

Baker, S. (2003). 'My Son, the Ad-zapper: Will TiVo Be the Death of Commercials? If Jack is any Indication . . .' *BusinessWeek*, (November 10), 76.

Baron, R. (2003). 'DVR Threat Real, Growing,' *TelevisionWeek*, (October 20), 11.

Campbell, A. J. (1999). 'Self-regulation and the Media,' *Federal Communications Law Journal*, 51 (3), 711–52.

Carter, M. (2004). 'A Word from Our Sponsors . . . Again,' *Marketing*, (May 12), 42–3.

Chunovic, L. (2002). 'The PVR Revolution: Mere Myth or Nightmare to Come?' *Electronic Media*, (November 18), 8.

Cobb-Walgren, C. J. (1990). 'The Changing Commercial Climate,' *Current Issues and Research in Advertising*, 13, 343–68.

Consoli, J. (2003). 'Nets Eye New Ways to Spice Up Summer: More Advertiser Involvement Seen as Key to Financing Fresh Programming,' *Mediaweek*, (July 28), 4.

Cowen, M. (2003). 'Beyond the Break,' *Campaign*, (November 7), 28.

Erdelyi, M. H., and Zizak, D. M. (2004). 'Beyond Gizmo Subliminality,' in L. J. Shrum (ed.), *The Psychology of Entertainment Media: Blurring the Lines Between Entertainment and Persuasion*, Mahwah, NJ: Lawrence Erlbaum, pp. 13–43.

Ephron, E. (2003). 'The Paradox of Product Placement,' *Mediaweek*, (June 2), 20.

Felten, E. W. (2003). Freedom to Tinker: Aimster Loses. Available: http://www.freedom-to-tinker.com

Fox, S. (1984). *The Mirror Makers: A History of American Advertising and its Creators*. New York: William Morrow and Company, Inc.

Freys, A. (1993). 'Naming Names,' *Managing Intellectual Property*, 33, 25–8.

Friestad, M., and Wright, P. (1994). 'The Persuasion Knowledge Model: How People Cope with Persuasion Attempts,' *Journal of Consumer Research*, 22, 62–74.

Ganguzza, P. (2002). *Integrating Programming and Promotion: How it Works in Practice*. Paper presented at the annual Advertising and Consumer Psychology conference, New York, May.

Green, M. C., Garst, J., and Brock, T. C. (2004). 'The Power of Fiction: Determinants and Boundaries,' in L. J. Shrum (ed.), *The Psychology of Entertainment Media: Blurring the Lines Between Entertainment and Persuasion*, Mahwah, NJ: Lawrence Erlbaum, pp. 161–76.

Greenspan, R. (2003). Remote Power: Can PVRs Kill TV Spots? Available: http://www.internetnews.com

In-Stat/MDR (2004). *Personal Video Recorders : Worldwide Unit Shipment Forecasts*.

Ives, N. (2004). Commercials have Expanded into Short Films with the Story as the Focus Rather than the Product. *New York Times*, (April 21), C6.

Jacoby, L. L. (1984). 'Incidental versus Intentional Retrieval: Remembering and Awareness as Separate Issues,' in L. R. Squire and N. Butters (eds.), *Neuropsychology of Memory*, New York: Guilford Press, pp. 145–56.

Kalter, A. (2003). Unnecessary Force. *Adweek*, (June 30), 18.

Kent, R. J. (1995). 'Competitive Clutter in Network Television Advertising: Current Levels and Advertiser Responses,' *Journal of Advertising Research*, 35, 49–57.

Law, S., and Braun-LaTour, K. A. (2004). 'Product Placements: How to Measure their Impact,' in L. J. Shrum (ed.), *The Psychology of Entertainment Media: Blurring the Lines Between Entertainment and Persuasion*, Mahwah, NJ: Lawrence Erlbaum, pp. 63–78.

Linnett, R. (2003). 'Fox Sports Specialty: Product "Immersion," ' *Advertising Age*, (January 30), 3–4.

Marsh, H. (2001). 'Does Reality TV Deliver for Advertisers?' *Marketing*, (May 24) 18–19.

Martilla, J. A., and Thompson, D. L. (1966). 'The Perceived Effects of Piggyback Television Commercials,' *Journal of Marketing Research*, 3, 365–71.

McCarty, J. A. (2004). 'Product Placement: The Nature of the Practice and Potential Avenues of Inquiry,' in L. J. Shrum (ed.), *The Psychology of Entertainment Media: Blurring the Lines Between Entertainment and Persuasion*, Mahwah, NJ: Lawrence Erlbaum, pp. 45–61.

Misdom, L. (2004). *Advertising Environment Study 2003/2004*. PhaseOne Communications.

Product Placement Is a Slippery Slope (2003). *Television Week*, (October 6), 8.

Riding, A. (2001). 'Reality TV in France: A Smash Hit with Dialectics,' *The New York Times*, (May 22), E2.

Rust, R. T., and Oliver, R. W. (1994). 'The Death of Advertising,' *Journal of Advertising*, 23, 71–7.

Schacter, D. L. (1987). 'Implicit Memory: History and Current Status,' *Journal of Experimental Psychology: Learning, Memory, and Cognition*, 13, 501–18.

Shavitt, S., Lowrey, P., and Haefner, J. (1998). 'Public Attitudes Toward Advertising: More Favorable Than You Might Think,' *Journal of Advertising Research*, 38, 7–22.

Sherman, J. (2003). 'New Software Fine-tunes Product Placement Values,' *TelevisionWeek*, (September 15), 10.

Shrum, L. J. (2004). *The Psychology of Entertainment Media: Blurring the Lines Between Entertainment and Persuasion*. Mahwah, NJ: Lawrence Erlbaum.

Song, S. (2003). 'Queer Eye, Straight Plugs,' *Time*, (August 18), 20.

Soriano, C. (2001, February 7). 'CBS, Tribe Speak Out on Lawsuit,' *USA TODAY*, Available: http://www.usatoday.com

Stanley, T. (2004). 'A Kinder, Gentler Reality TV Unfolds,' *Advertising Age*, (May 31), S12.

Television Bureau of Advertising (2004). Network Television Commercial Activity by Length of Commercial. Available: http://www.tvb.org

Whitney, D. (2003). 'Integrating the Brand,' *TelevisionWeek*, (March 31), 17.

Zajonc, R. B. (1980). 'Feeling and Thinking: Preferences Need no Inferences,' *American Psychologist*, 35, 151–75.

ZenithOptimedia, *Western Europe Market & MediaFact, 1996–2003*.

7

Electronic Marketing and Marketing Communications: The Role of Technology

John O'Connor, Eamonn Galvin, and Martin Evans

Commerce and marketing are changing, as distribution channels, services, and even payments are becoming more technology oriented and 'virtualized.' This growth of new technologies is part of a wider 'electronification' of marketing, which is called *electronic marketing*. This migration has occurred in the context of wider societal changes such as increasing customer sophistication and individualism, and the increasing globalization of markets.

Electronic marketing is having a dramatic impact on marketing communications. The most obvious technology is the Internet, but others include short message service (SMS) messaging, digital television, and new consumer innovations such as television hard discs. These technologies provide both opportunities and challenges for marketing communicators. The growth of SMS and its newer multimedia version, multimedia message service (MMS), for example, provide an opportunity to target marketing communications at a younger generation, while hardware that stores television programs on hard discs threatens traditional television advertising because it allows consumers to remove advertising (see Chapter 6). These changing technologies have a powerful role to play in marketing communications; however, the real paradigm shift in marketing communications has less to do with the arrival of new technologies, such as interactive TV and SMS/MMS marketing, than the way in which existing technology can be used by marketing managers to a deeper improve the marketing communication process. For many companies, the customer database still represents a huge opportunity for improving marketing communications.

So how does electronic marketing impact the way we deliver marketing communications? In order to address this question, we have chosen to organize this chapter around five messages that we believe today's marketers need to understand if they are to deliver marketing communications effectively in the twenty-first century.

MESSAGE 1: ELECTRONIC MARKETING AND MARKETING COMMUNICATIONS REQUIRE A MODIFIED MARKETING MODEL

The growth of new technologies and applications requires new marketing frameworks and models. We argue that such new models should be developed based on the tried and tested frameworks of the past, along with a recognition of the changes driven by new technology. Below, we consider some of the drivers of a new model and propose a modified model that takes account of the 'electronification' of marketing that is occurring today.

Increasingly, the electronic age is putting more power in the hands of the buyer than the seller. It empowers the buyer with information and allows consumers to decide for themselves what, where, and when they should buy. For example, car insurance is routinely purchased over the telephone, after ringing around to find the best price. Car buyers can check and compare car prices over the Internet before they enter the showroom. With Internet auctions, buyers set the price, not the sellers. In the USA, many patients search for advice about their medical symptoms on websites such as WebMD (*www.webmd.com*) before they go to see their family doctor—a feature that shifts the balance of power significantly away from the doctor and into the hands of the patient. In turn, marketing communicators need to recognize these developments and customize communications to segments and individuals, as opposed to a 'one-size-fits-all' communications strategy.

Promotional and marketing communication activities are also becoming more targeted as a result of more, and better, information. Customer segmentation is moving into a new information-rich era based on behavior rather than traditional demographic methods. Distribution channels are multiplying and intermediaries are coming under increasing threat as manufacturers market their products directly to the customer. Companies are being forced to adapt their marketing and communication models in order to create an effective response to these changes. Technology and the greater availability of data are increasingly driving changes in the organization–customer interaction. In short, 'traditional marketing' is giving way to 'electronic marketing', and a series of new marketing methods and tools

Table 7.1. Traditional versus electronic marketing

Marketing area	Traditional marketing	Electronic marketing	New marketing methods and tools
Pricing	Seller-driven	Buyer-driven	Internet/Digital TV
Segmentation	Demographic	Biographic	Customer database
Advertising	Broadcast	Interactive	Internet/Digital TV
Promotions	Mass	Tailored	Customer database
Sales management	Data with sales department	Shared data	Marketing information systems
Distribution channels	Intermediaries	Direct	Multichannel
Customer ownership	Company	Network	Alliances
Product	Constrained	Buyer-driven	Marketing information systems

are being deployed by marketing executives. Some of these changes are summarized in Table 7.1.

Electronic marketing involves the effective use of technology in all its forms, including new software applications and new hardware like mobile phones. It is not just about the Internet; in fact, the most important piece of technology in electronic marketing is probably the customer database. In the discussion that follows, we expand on this idea to illustrate how Internet marketing is only one component of electronic marketing's impact on marketing communication.

In our recent book, *Electronic Marketing: Theory and Practice for the 21st Century* (O'Connor et al. 2004), we proposed a framework for electronic marketing, which is summarized in Fig. 7.1 below.

The framework depicted in Fig. 7.1 is built around a customer relationship management (CRM) concept, and shows how technology can be used to support marketing efforts in all areas of interaction with the customer. This framework has implications for the way marketers structure marketing communications and the key points include:

- using new technology to get to know the customer more intimately than marketers have in the past;
- managing the relationship with the customer through more effective use of customer information and customer database technology;
- developing the customer offering, using technology and the Internet to enhance the product, price, place, and promotion elements of the offering; and
- delivering the offering to the customer, again using technology and the Internet to support effective sales and service delivery.

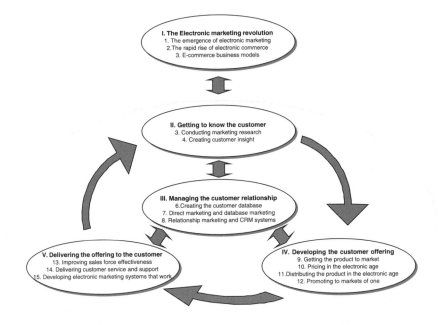

Fig. 7.1. Framework for electronic marketing

The key point to remember is that technology is only an enabler. It only provides a series of tools that must still be deployed by marketing communicators. Ours is not a radically different framework to those employed in 'traditional marketing'; rather, it is an extension that uses technology to supplement existing marketing methods.

MESSAGE 2: THE MARKETING DATABASE IS STILL AT THE CENTER OF MARKETING COMMUNICATIONS

For our second message, we propose that 'electronic marketing' is based more on the sensible use of a marketing database than on the Internet. In other words, electronic marketing is not just Internet marketing, and marketing communications in the twenty-first century is not simply reliant on Internet-based communications.

Our proposition is that the customer database is probably the most important application of information technology (IT) in marketing communications—more important than newer technologies such as the Internet, e-mail, SMS, or MMS. A marketing database with high quality data on customers and prospects will remain at the heart of excellent marketing communications for many years to come. Given that an effective marketing communication strategy requires customers to be grouped into sensible target segments, let us begin the discussion with an examination of recent improvements that have taken place in customer segmentation.

Good customer segmentation requires individualized data on customers and prospects. One of the more significant events in moving from general customer profiles to more individual profiles has been the availability of census information and the development of *geodemographic analysis* from it. More than two decades ago, forty financial, educational, family, and employment variables from the 1981 British census were analyzed and the emerging clusters of households led to the creation of thirty-nine neighborhood types, which comprised the first geodemographic system in the UK, called ACORN (A Classification of Residential Neighborhoods). This was a significant improvement to the leading alternative segmentation approach at the time, social grade, which classified the population into just six groups on the basis of a single variable (occupation of the chief income earner in the household). Whereas these early profiles typically were based on sample surveys of approximately 1,000 persons, the British marketing industry now has computerized access to census data on 56 million people (Dugmore and Moy 2004).

In other countries similar segmentation systems exist, and various geodemographic companies now operate throughout Europe, such as Experian, which offers its MOSAIC brand. At the time of writing, Experian was developing its MOSAIC geodemographic product for China and this represents a major development in consumer segmentation in one of the fastest growing economies in the world. The marketing company Claritas has a system called MicroVision that uses census data to assign all of America's consumer households into one of fifty segments based on their postal zip codes.

Even with the availability of valid geodemographic information, marketing managers still face the problem that the smallest neighborhood unit that a system like ACORN can define consists of about 150 households. The problem with this limitation is that two customers in the same segment (or even next-door neighbors) are likely to have different tastes, attitudes, and purchasing behavior. In addition, reliance on data from a national census that is carried out once every ten years has been seen as a drawback to the traditional geodemographic segmentation approach. Newer *micro-segmentation approaches* include psychographics, the use of transactional data, and biographics.

The main recent development in lifestyle research and segmentation is the 'lifestyle survey approach,' developed by companies such as Experian, which uses a series of survey questions to identify particular lifestyle traits of consumers so that they can be grouped into defined targetable segments. Some questions are developed by specific companies; for example, a car insurance company might sponsor a question asking for the month in which the car insurance is renewed. Because these surveys are not anonymous, the data typically are stored in a database by name and address of respondent. Thus, it is possible that before a respondent's renewal date, he or she will receive direct mailings soliciting defection to the sponsoring company.

During the 1990s, the increasing use of these new micro-segmentation methods sparked a fierce 'geodemographic versus lifestyle' debate (Evans 2003; Sleight 1997). It is now widely accepted that the combination of both approaches offers a more complete solution. For example, Lifestyles from CACI (*www.caci.co.uk*) and PRIZM from Claritas (*www.claritas.com*) are among a number of targeting systems that combine the individual details of lifestyle data with the solid foundation of census information and the statistical reliability of market research to give more targeted marketing information.

Advances in IT also have enabled marketers in recent years to gather large amounts of data on customer behavior, sometimes referred to as *transactional data*, which can be used to segment customers based on such variables as product usage, repeat purchasing rates, and purchasing patterns. The increasing use of electronic point-of-sale (EPOS) information is providing companies with detailed information on individual customers. By the end of 2002, the British supermarket chain Tesco had identified 100,000 different segments based on purchasing behavior, each of which was targeted differently. By knowing what individual consumers buy, the retailer could target them with relevant offers, with the consumer saving money in the process.

In addition to psychographics and transactional data, a third micro-segmentation approach that has emerged in recent years is *biographics*. With transactional data now at the heart of many databases, overlaid with a multitude of profile data, we appear to be moving into the era of bio-graphics—the fusion of profile and transaction data. Indeed, the ability to match names, addresses, purchasing behavior, and lifestyles all together onto a single database allows companies to build a model of someone's life. By linking a number of different databases, companies are beginning to match individual customer data to credit history, actual purchasing behavior, media usage, and frequency and monetary value of purchases.

One of the cornerstones of integrated marketing communications is having data available to all members of the organization who might have contact with current or potential customers (see Chapter 9). In this context, it is worth mentioning the concept of *tacit data* (Kreiner 2002). This is a somewhat intangible approach, which is more 'affectively' based on items such as expertise, 'gut feeling,' subjective insights, and intuitions. For example, tacit data include the reactions of an individual customer during a telephone contact, which can be recorded by the customer service representative who receives the call. This is important because such information can be useful if shared across all members of the organization who might be in contact with the customer concerned. Consider the case in which experience suggests that a customer is a bit grumpy on Monday mornings. There have been examples of (surely innocent) errors occurring, such as when a direct mailing includes a tacit data field with an unintended personal notation (e.g. the phrase 'pain in the neck!' following the salutation 'Dear Mr. Jones'). Such negligent abuse of database knowledge is not frequent, but is clearly unacceptable. It also is an example of how electronic communication vehicles can enhance or destroy relationships between salespeople and customers.

It also is important for new marketing approaches to not only adopt statistically rigorous data mining and testing approaches, but also to complement them with insightful understanding of customers and markets via more traditional market research. To be effective, marketing should not focus exclusively on transactions with customers but rather it should move toward greater understanding of customers in order to identify and target those with whom there are more likely to be mutually satisfying relationships. It is not always appropriate to base everything on data-informed marketing analysis. As Reed (2004: 23) argued, 'it is all very well predicting customers' next moves by their buying habits, but if you do not understand what motivates them the marketing potential is limited. That is why combining behavioral data and attitudinal data is essential.'

MESSAGE 3: NEW TECHNOLOGIES CAN IMPROVE COMMUNICATION WITH CUSTOMERS

The synergy of insightful data and new interactive media is leading to new business models. Data (or rather the appropriate analysis of it) can identify relevant and well-defined targets for marketing communications and we now see a variety of existing and emerging technologies for more effectively targeting such communications. We explore this theme below under the following four headings:

- The evolution of interactive marketing media
- Loyalty programs
- Trends in direct marketing
- Other marketing technology developments

The Evolution of Interactive Marketing Media

A major contemporary trend is for communications media to facilitate two-way, not just passive one-way, interaction between organizations and customers. Also, media such as telephony, the Internet, and interactive

TV, if used correctly, can lead to the enhancement of relationships between organizations and their customers. Traditional communications like television advertising are essentially 'push' based, where the advertiser creates a message and broadcasts it to the widest possible audience. However, television and radio suffer from one key drawback—because they are based on analogue (as opposed to digital) technology, they are broadcast media and do not allow any form of interactivity between the broadcaster and audience members. Newer applications, such as interactive television and the Internet, have the advantages of interactivity as well as being more focused by targeting specific customers. Interactivity requires greater bandwidth and different technology, both of which can only be provided by digital media. As Table 7.2 shows, digital media do not automatically provide interactivity, only the potential for interactive services.

Digital television (DTV) is an improved way of transmitting television pictures that compresses the digital signal and can fit five channels into the frequency bandwidth currently used by a single conventional station. Digital signals are compressed at the transmission site before being decoded by the television. DTV signals are delivered by satellite, cable, or terrestrial (the latter being received by an ordinary aerial). Since early 1996, the DTV market in the European Union (EU) has enjoyed a rapid growth in subscribers, with the number of digital households rising from only two million at the end of 1997 to over 18 million in 2000. From a marketing communication perspective, some of the more interesting developments in digital television are the interactive services that are being promised to consumers, which will eventually provide services such as home shopping, home banking, games, e-mail, and other e-commerce services. Digital television allows greater targeting of specific market segments in light of a dramatic increase in the number of television

Table 7.2. Interactive services

	Broadcast	**Interactive**
Digital media	Digital television Digital radio Digital teletext	Digital television Videotext Digital radio Digital teletext Internet SMS/MMS
Analogue media	Television Teletext Radio	N/A

channels available to consumers. With more channels and greater choice, audiences have become increasingly fragmented and smaller. The good news for advertisers is that this allows them to be more focused on target-ing specific audiences by regional, ethnic, or social differences. However, advertisers are less enthusiastic about products like personal video records (PVRs), which allow viewers to skip commercial breaks.

Another related area of dramatic growth has been *direct response television* (DRTV) advertising, where customers respond directly to a specified tele-phone number or address. The explosion in the number of television chan-nels allows stations to offer more specifically defined audiences to advertisers. Direct response television advertising has also altered the direct marketer's perception of television campaigns. Traditional television adver-tising is difficult to measure, whereas the number of calls to the DRTV toll-free phone number provides an immediately measurable result of advertis-ing effectiveness. There are different direct response television formats, including the *infomercial*—the long, sometimes tacky, low-budget program designed to exhibit products in the manner of an in-store demonstration. There also is the more sophisticated direct response commercial that exists only to generate phone calls. Using clever targeting, the traditional direct response advertisement can sidestep the expensive prime-time slots with placement around low-interest programs, thereby making it easier to mo-tivate the viewer to call. Within minutes of screening, the telephone lines typically begin to ring.

Another useful communication channel is *teletext*, where pages of text information are transmitted with television broadcasts to domestic televi-sion sets. In the UK, the BBC offers Ceefax and ITV offers Teletext UK. Although a TV advertisement usually only lasts one minute or less and does not convey much detailed information, the teletext service can provide additional detail. In some situations, TV and print ads refer the customer to the teletext service for more information. The advantage of teletext is that consumers can access it whenever they want and can control the speed with which they receive information.

While teletext is effective when customers know what they are looking for, the initial prompt to look for additional information must be provided by traditional TV and print advertising. In the future, digital teletext will offer a faster, more comprehensive service than its analogue rival. In time, the graphics and 'look and feel' of digital teletext will change, and may eventually look similar in format to the Internet. There are a number of advantages to digital teletext as it has greater interactivity and can support enhanced graphics and animation, including photographs and video clips.

A more interactive development is *videotext*, which is a two-way system for transmitting text or graphics across a telephone network for display on a television screen or personal computer. Examples of videotext services in Europe include Prestel in the UK and Teletel in France. In general, videotext has been less successful as a vehicle for marketing promotion when compared with technologies such as the Internet, which provide a faster, more reliable service.

Digital radio brings listeners CD-quality sound, more channels, and inter-activity via small screen displays. However, it does not have the same obvious benefits associated with digital television. At the time of this writing, only a handful of radio stations were granted digital licenses by the UK's Radio Authority. Most commentators believe that it will take up to fifteen years before digital radio overtakes analogue in the consumer marketplace.

Another rapidly developing communication channel is the mobile phone. There are more mobile phones in the world than personal computers and most of these are capable of receiving SMS text messages. Until recently, the *New York Times* and the *Los Angeles Times* faxed several page summaries of the day's top news stories to companies in Japan and Russia. Today, dissemination and syndication is conducted electronically with updates delivered using Internet and SMS technology. In the UK, Sky News offered its customers SMS updates on the war in Iraq during March and April 2003. In the future, wireless marketing will become more sophis-ticated and interactive, allowing personalized one-on-one conversations with a target audience. A 2002 UK survey of its members by the Direct Marketing Association (DMA 2002) found that:

- 60 percent of respondents were running e-mail marketing campaigns;
- 16 percent of marketers running such campaigns were using e-mail marketing more than direct mail;
- 30 percent elected to use e-mail marketing rather than telemarketing; and
- 55 percent were using e-mail marketing more than SMS.

With the arrival of newer generation mobile handsets, a new marketing medium is beginning to open up through the use of MMS technology. MMS is basically an upgrade of text messaging that allows pictures and images to be sent via mobile phone. Mobile telecommunications com-panies like Vodafone have a vested interest in the promotion of SMS and MMS technologies for marketing purposes as it drives up the traffic on their networks.

Loyalty Programs

Information technology is becoming a vital component in developing customer loyalty. In addition to consumers benefiting from cheaper shop-ping (in the sense of 'customer-specific pricing' rather than scattershot discounts) loyalty programs can also potentially provide the retailer with a great deal of information about individual customers. This information can be used in targeting customers with offers via direct marketing mechanisms, at point-of-sale or later in-home. For example, the large UK retailer Tesco has shifted the emphasis of its £30m advertising and marketing budget from above-the-line expenditure on advertising to direct marketing. It is using its loyalty card, the Tesco Clubcard, to drive its marketing and gather data on its customers in order to target them more carefully.

Trends in Direct Marketing

Direct mail's share of promotional expenditure has increased steadily over the years. For example, the average household in the Netherlands received 102 pieces of direct mail in 2003, a four-fold increase over the past twenty years (Schober International 2004). There is strong evidence that people react well to material that is directly relevant to them and that the key to successful direct mail advertising is very close analysis of the target audience. The ability to target customers closely is dependent on building an accurate database with sufficient information to identify key customer groups. As Evans et al. (1996: 259) described it:

The sooner marketers move to using direct mail in response to customers' requests, rather than 'cold' prospecting, the better it will be for all concerned. Marketers will be able to target more accurately and more effectively, and consumers will see a phenomenal reduction in unsolicited direct mail. This will lead to more true 'relationships' between marketer and consumer and will probably significantly alleviate privacy concerns among consumers and legislators, and will clearly be beneficial for the industry.

It is instructive to look back at the changes that have taken place in recent years in the way marketers use direct marketing methods to communicate with their target audiences. Fig. 7.2 provides a breakdown of direct marketing expenditure by media type, showing the continued rise of electronic forms of direct marketing, particularly telemarketing and new media, at the expense of more traditional forms of direct marketing such as direct response advertising in magazines, national press and regional press.

Today, the most widely-used forms of direct marketing in the UK are telemarketing and direct mail which, according to the DMA (DMA 2002), accounted for half of the £11 billion spent on direct marketing during 2001. Given that direct response television, radio, and press typically require listeners and readers to contact the advertiser by telephone or the Internet, these figures show the increasingly important role that such new media have in direct marketing, even if the actual expenditure on new media is still relatively low in overall terms. The DMA agreed, pointing to an increasing combination of new and old direct marketing techniques.

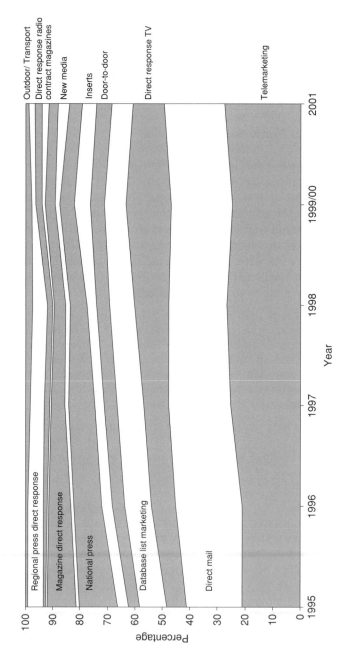

Fig. 7.2. Direct marketing expenditures in the UK by media type
Source: Direct Marketing Association (2002).

The Internet is continuing to develop as an advertising medium. By the end of the 1990s, most major organizations had migrated a portion of their advertising spending to the Internet and almost all had established a Web presence. Nearly all companies have 'brochureware' on their websites that is useful in advertising a company's range of products and services but is not a particularly effective form of advertising on its own, as it requires the potential buyer to search the Internet or the website for the product description. This medium is giving way to advertising on other people's websites using banner advertising, the ubiquitous rectangular advertisements that are either always present, or pop up, on a website. A more effective approach to banner advertising recognizes that Internet traffic is concentrated around a relatively small number of 'destination sites' such as high-content websites like Amazon.com, search engines like Google, or Web portals such as Yahoo. These sites are particularly attractive to advertisers seeking a wide audience for their products. Yahoo has more than 200 million users, 60 percent of whom are outside the US (*www.yahoo.com 2004*).

Although *Internet search advertising* is a relatively new business, it was already worth around $1 billion in 2002 and growing fast. *Pay-for-placement* is a sponsored search approach that involves putting a small number of paid-for links in a separate section at the top of a search page. Because they are highly targeted, such commercial messages generally get click-through rates of 12 to 17 percent, according to Yahoo (*www.yahoo.com 2004*). Conversion rates like these are highly attractive when compared with the banner advertising market, and advertisers pay a minimum fee for each click. Another form of Internet search advertising is *paid inclusion* where advertisers pay to have their websites 'crawled' by an Internet search engine such as Google, Lycos, or Alta Vista, so that the sponsoring company's information is included in the regular search results, rather than in a separate advertising section. Companies that provide this service, such as Look-Smart, which feeds websites such as MSN, advise advertisers how to write their listings in a way that gives them the best chance of showing up prominently in a search. Paid inclusion is somewhat controversial because the companies providing the service alone understand how the algorithms inside their search engine 'black boxes' work. The controversy surrounding paid inclusion has begun to divide the search business. Google, the industry's leading search company, has rejected the idea, claiming it will destroy the integrity of Internet searches, although Yahoo planned to launch its own service.

According to the consultancy firm eMarketer (*www.emarketer.com*), Internet advertising revenues in the USA fell from a peak of $8 billion in 2000 to $6 billion in 2002. Despite this decline, Internet advertising spending subsequently began to increase again, albeit at much lower growth rates than in the late-1990s. Leading the charge were the global motor manufacturers and fast moving consumer goods (FMCG) companies, attracted by the fact that in the USA alone, there are more than 120 million active Web users.

The Internet can also be seen as an important mechanism in conjunction with other advertising formats. Most companies now combine the Internet with traditional forms of advertising. There is an increasing propensity for companies to include their Internet addresses alongside other forms of advertising—on posters, magazine advertisements, and even in television commercials. Many companies have taken the concept one step further: Joe Boxer (*www.joeboxer.com*), a manufacturer of men's underwear, and EasyJet (*www.easyjet.com*), the low-cost airline carrier, have emblazoned their Web addresses clearly on products themselves—boxer shorts and aircraft.

Other Marketing Technology Developments

Improvements in printing and binding technology, in particular digital printing, are making it easier and more cost-effective to customize magazines for selected target audiences. Advertisers can use these customized editions to selectively target advertising messages. This allows for the production of several different magazine editions, each addressing the needs of different constituencies. Direct response advertising in newspapers and magazines present the direct marketer with a cost-effective means of generating response from relatively large audiences. In addition, the fragmentation of these media means that direct marketers can use them to reach more tightly defined audiences than was previously possible.

Technology now allows advertising to be targeted to individual stores on large and small screens, an approach that can be very effective. For example, a video advertisement for baked beans at a store entrance is likely to have a higher impact on the purchase decision than a commercial seen the previous night on television. Place-based (so-called 'point-of-purchase') promotions are important, as research by Block and Morwitz (1999) revealed that unplanned purchases (i.e. items not prewritten on a shopping list) are common and that consumers can be persuaded to buy at the point of sale. According to Inman and Winer (1999), almost 60 percent of household supermarket purchases are unplanned and the result of in-store decisions.

The movie *Minority Report* demonstrated real-time recognition of customers as they entered a store or even just walked around a shopping mall. Recognition was gained via automatic retina identification, and on this basis customer transactional and profile records were accessed and relevant promotional offers were immediately delivered. This might have been futuristic at the time of the film's 2002 release, but the technology is certainly available and, as many countries move swiftly toward biometric recognition technology for identification card schemes, it is likely to be extended into the marketing arena. A London department store and a casino already have introduced biometric recognition (via facial recognition software) so that their 'special' customers can be recognized as they enter and then quickly greeted personally by a manager (Steiner 2002).

Outdoor electronic displays also are becoming more sophisticated. Recent developments have enabled light-emitting diode (LED) screens to produce a true red, green, and blue, which means that they can reproduce color as faithfully as television and cinema. LED video billboards are perhaps the most spectacular formats of outdoor display advertising. Outdoor communications also are becoming more interactive. One of the first of this genre was applied by the lingerie brand Pretty Polly. The Adshel poster asked for the 'pressing' of a button under the model's bust and this then revealed information about the range of underwear (Beer 2002). More recently, the marketing company Adwalker launched a 'wearable' poster that 'combines the visual impact of television and traditional outdoor media, the responsiveness of direct marketing, the accessibility of press and radio and the interactivity of sales promotion.' In effect, it is an electronic sandwich board—a wearable computer with a flat panel screen that can be strapped to a marketing representative's chest and used to interact with consumers in the street. It is too early to say whether this technology application is anything more than a novelty, but it does hold out the promise of more targeted marketing messages in locations such as music festivals and concerts, sporting events, product launches, in-store promotions, trade shows, shopping centers, and sponsored events.

Over the last twenty-five years, sales promotions have become an increasingly important element of the marketing mix. In the USA, the ratio of advertising to promotion was 60:40 in 1977; by 1987, this ratio was reversed. In the past, promotions served to jump-start sales and rarely involved the use of technology. Many campaigns were aimed at a broad audience, with little differentiation made on the basis of a customer's past activity or behavior. Customer databases were rarely used, as they tended to be out-of-date or inaccurate. Using IT, marketers can now use sales transaction data to create offers aimed at changing customer behavior. The resulting promotions are more effective because they relate directly to the customer's preferences and lifestyles. Major opportunities exist in marketing to customers when they are about to make a purchase and are most susceptible to a marketing message. This is sometimes called 'just-in-time marketing' and examples include point-of-purchase coupons tailored to the buying preferences of the customer. Indeed, as Peattie and Peattie (2003: 458–484) suggested, 'it is in sales promotions that many of the most exciting marriages of technology and creativity are occurring.'

MESSAGE 4. ELECTRONIC MARKETING REQUIRES NEW SKILLS AND WAYS OF TRANSFERRING KNOWLEDGE WITHIN AN ORGANIZATION

So far, our primary focus has been placed on the role of technology in marketing communications. However, there is an important caveat that must be added regarding the role of technology in marketing: implementing the technology is easier said than done. This message must be understood by all marketing executives, including those involved in marketing communications.

CRM is an example of technology-enabled marketing that has had a somewhat inauspicious track record, with many projects failing and practitioners turning away from CRM tools. Technology might have fuelled these projects but a more strategic and organization-wide role can lead to improved interactions between their stakeholders. It also is becoming generally recognized that new marketing skills are required.

Based on an interview of leading American marketing practitioners, Carson (1999) concluded that analytical skills and statistics topped the list of areas in which practitioners' education was lacking. Carson also found that businesses are demanding more accountability than ever before, making it essential for marketers to 'know how to do the numbers and prove their financial contribution to the bottom line' (Carson 1999: 481). In research conducted for the Chartered Institute of Marketing (2001) to explore the impact of IT on both marketing and marketers, some significant gaps were discovered in marketers' skills:

Marketers should develop IT/new technology skills—(maybe via 'junior mentors'—younger people who are 'IT savvy' and who can educate their senior colleagues). We cannot influence the development and usage of IT within companies unless we know something about it.

Marketing academics must consider the implications of these findings for their own course design and delivery. As marketing is increasingly driven by marketing databases and strives to achieve a degree of personalized and interactive CRM, marketing students would benefit from being able to deal with customer modeling and database analysis.

Related to skill development is how to maintain marketing and customer knowledge in an organization. Many companies underestimate the knowledge that is held within their companies. The speed at which knowledge is shared has become a key differentiating factor between the excellent organizations and the mediocre ones. Technologies such as intranets and extranets, and tools such as knowledge repositories, groupware applications, and knowledge-management systems, can play a central role in the way information is disseminated throughout an organization. *Knowledge repositories* are designed to manage external knowledge and comprise, in essence, electronic libraries that consist of a series of database tools and indexing systems. However, the most important component of a repository is arguably not the technology but the 'librarian' function that must be put in place to manage the repository.

Groupware provides rich content and interactivity using presentations, discussion databases, and shared audio or video files. Examples of groupware include Banyan's *BeyondMail*, Fujitsu's *Teamware*, Novell's *Groupwise*, and the most popular and best-selling groupware product of all, *Lotus Notes* from IBM.

Knowledge management systems (KMS) are programs such as expert systems and intelligent agents that allow nonexperts to make decisions comparable to those of experts, typically by accessing information held in knowledge repositories. Many customer service centers employ KMS to allow relatively untrained agents to trouble-shoot customer problems. Compaq's European technical customer services center in Dublin, Ireland employs such a system to help answer a variety of complex technical questions that customers have about Compaq products. The duties of the call center agents include the creation of 'solutions' to common technical problems that customers have with different products. The solutions can be accessed by any member of the product team when a customer calls. Compaq's KMS is very sophisticated: reuse rates of the solutions are constantly monitored to ensure high-quality solutions are entered into the database, and the solution sets are used as the basis for training and monitoring technical capabilities of team members.

Depres and Chauvel (2000) demonstrated how information can be transferred from the individual across groups, such as the marketing communications function, as well as to other marketing and nonmarketing functions in the organization. They have developed a useful model for knowledge management (see Fig. 7.3). On the left hand vertical axis, the model recognizes how knowledge is created at the different levels of organization, group, and individual. The horizontal axis defines the key steps for creating knowledge management, ranging from capturing knowledge to ultimately using the knowledge to transform and innovate. The model maps how useful applications like benchmarking and data warehousing fit into knowledge management.

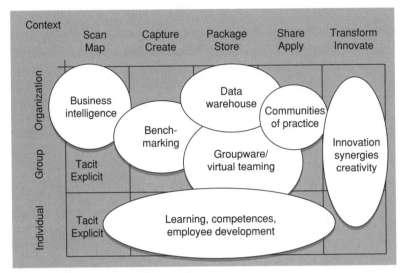

Fig. 7.3. Knowledge management framework
Source: Depres and Chauvel (2000).

MESSAGE 5. COMPANIES NEED TO ADDRESS THE INCREASINGLY COMPLEX ISSUES OF DATA PRIVACY AND DATA PROTECTION

Technology has brought unprecedented power and information into the hands of the marketing community. However, the marketing communications function in any organization is also obliged not to abuse this power. This obligation is increasingly becoming a legal requirement in most countries. The 1998 EU directive on data protection obliges all member states to update their data protection legislation to allow the processing of personal data only where the individuals concerned have given their consent or where, for legal or contractual reasons, this processing is deemed to be necessary (e.g. consumer credit legislation requires financial institutions to ask certain questions of any individual applying for a loan). Personal data processing is given a much wider definition in the directive than in most existing data protection legislation in operation throughout Europe. Individuals also have the right to object to being targeted by direct marketing activities. The directive also lets EU citizens sue organizations that misuse personal data. As EU member countries enact their own national laws in accordance with the directive, the protection afforded to the individual is likely to increase, as will customers' understanding of their rights to privacy. These changes will pose particular issues for the holders and users of customer information, particularly where direct marketing activities are concerned.

Whereas companies operating in the EU must comply with the sweeping Data Protection Directive, American companies are governed by a patchwork of legislation covering specific sectors, such as financial services, health, and telecommunications; however, this situation is also changing as the USA moves towards adopting more stringent data privacy regulations for the online world. The Health Insurance Portability and Accountability Act (HIPAA), effective in the USA since 2003, was developed in response to growing concerns about the privacy of personal health information in the information age.

The increasing use of spam (i.e. junk e-mail) and unsolicited direct mail and telephonic messages has begun to hasten calls for additional legislation. As more unsolicited e-mails for products like Viagra, Xanax, and consumer loans arrive in consumers' electronic mailboxes each day, attitudes toward electronic marketing communications in general have become more negative. Consumers are increasingly asked in communications with companies to choose whether or not they wish to receive additional marketing material from companies. This is called 'opting-in.' But even when consumers decide to 'opt-in,' the situation is not always straightforward, as is illustrated in the following example. In a follow-up to the movie *Minority Report*, Twentieth Century Fox used an audio clip of the film in an outbound message to mobile phones. This clip, complete with heavy breathing, was sent to individuals who had opted-in to receive information about films. However, several people complained to the Advertising Standards Association, claiming that it caused offense, fear, and distress. The complaint was upheld, but the company has said it will continue to use this approach because those individuals had 'opted-in' (Rosser 2003).

CONCLUSION

As Fig. 7.4 illustrates, there is an increasing trend toward data-informed interaction between customers and organizations, and between organizations. Nonetheless, we have concerns about a purely 'data-driven' paradigm. If data are used tactically in a mechanistic way to drive targeting within marketing campaigns, then we feel marketers are in danger of reinforcing customer perceptions of 'junk' targeting in much the same way as many direct marketing companies developed such a bad reputation for junk mail. Although the technology is different, receiving an inappropriately targeted SMS message is no doubt just as annoying for a customer as receiving a piece of junk mail. If, however, data can lead to a deeper understanding of customers, then the resulting knowledge can be used to inform more effective interactions. This is not merely between organizations and

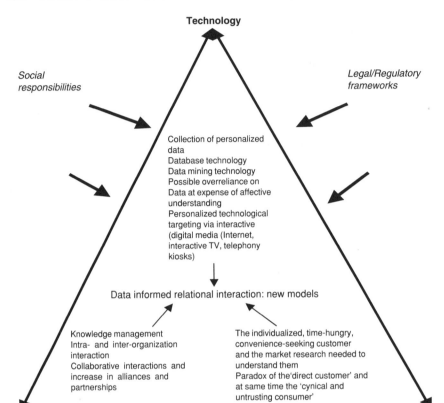

Fig. 7.4. Pyramidal model of relationship interactions
Source: Evans et al. (2004).

customers, but increasingly with suppliers and partners and requires so-phisticated and effective management of data across these parties in order for knowledge and insight to be used strategically and tactically.

Technology is having a significant impact on the way companies deliver marketing communications. However, it is important that the new changes are marketing and customer-driven and not solely technology-driven. Perhaps the most important conclusion is that while technology allows us to do different things, its real benefit is to allow us to do the same things better, or more efficiently. Successful marketers are not blinded by technology or the Internet. Rather, they use it wisely to get the basic things right—to create good products, focus on the customer, and generate a profit.

REFERENCES

Beer, R. (2002). 'MCBD Creates Interactive Poster in First Campaign for Pretty Polly,' *Campaign*, (November 1), 8.

Block, L. G. and Morwitz, V. G. (1999). 'Shopping Lists As an External Memory Aid for Grocery Shopping: Influences On List Writing and List Fulfillment,' *Journal of Consumer Psychology*, 8(4), 343–76.

Carson, C.D. (1999). *What it Takes and Where to Get It*. Working paper, University of North Carolina.

Chartered Institute of Marketing. (2001, October). *The Impact of E-business on Marketing and Marketers*. Cookham: CIM. Available at www.cim.co.uk.

Depres, C. and Chauvel, D. (2000). 'How to Map Knowledge Management,' in D.A. Marchand, T.H. Davenport, and T. Dickson (eds.), *Mastering Information Management*, London: Financial Times/Prentice Hall, pp. 170–76.

DMA. (2002). *Census of the Direct Marketing Association 2001–2*. (*www.dma.org.uk*)

Dugmore, K. and Moy, C. (2004). *A Guide to the 2001 Census: Essential Information for Gaining Business Advantage*. London: The Stationery Office.

Evans, M. (2003). 'Market Segmentation,' in M. Baker (ed), *The Marketing Book*, (5th edn.), Oxford: Butterworth-Heinemann, pp. 246–83.

—— O'Malley, L. and Patterson, M. (1996). 'Direct Mail and Consumer Response: an Empirical Study of Consumer Experiences of Direct Mail,' *Journal of Database Marketing*, 3, 250–62.

Inman, J. and Winer, R. (1999). *Where the Rubber Meets the Road: a Model of In-store Consumer Decision Making*. Marketing Science Institute. Working Paper. 1998.

Kreiner, K. (2002). 'Tacit Knowledge Management: the Role of Artifacts,' *Journal of Knowledge Management*, 6(2).

O'Connor, J., Galvin, E., and Evans, M. (2004). *Electronic Marketing: Theory and Practice for the 21st Century*. Harlow, UK: Prentice-Hall.

Peattie, K. and Peattie, S. (2003). 'Sales Promotion,' in M. Baker (ed), *The Marketing Book*. Oxford: Butterworth-Heinemann.

Reed, D. (2004). 'Marrying Data,' *Precision Marketing*, (April 16), 23–26.

Rosser, M. (2003). '20th Century to Persist with Voicemail Ads,' *Precision Marketing*, (February 14), 1.

Schober International Website. (2004). Available: www.schober-international.com

Sleight, P. (1997). *Targeting Customers—How to Use Geodemographic and Lifestyle Data in your Business*, 3rd edn. Henley-on-Thames, UK: World Advertising Research Center.

Steiner, R. (2002). 'Watch Out, Big Spenders, Big Brother is Watching You,' *Sunday Times*, Business section, (August 11), 1.

8

Recent Developments in Below-the-Line Marketing Communications

Chris Fill

The rapid growth and development of technology over the past two decades has had an enormous impact on the form and nature of the marketing communications used by organizations. Originally, mass communications, predominantly advertising, represented the only realistic way of reaching large audiences in a cost-effective manner. Advances in information systems and technology (IST) have enabled new channels and communication tools to be developed, which in turn has stimulated the design of alternative, more targeted, and personalized communication opportunities. Two main forms of communication can be identified: (*a*) advertising (which uses paid-for media) and (*b*) all other tools (which do not use paid-for media).

The primary goal of this chapter is to consider the current and future impact of IST on this second group of marketing communication tools, which have become known as 'below-the-line' communications. Space limits the range and scope of the technology and its various applications that can be considered here. Secondary goals are to consider their influence on the relationships between organizations and their customers, and the emergence and practice of integrated marketing communications.

In order to achieve these goals, this chapter is structured in the following way. It starts by exploring the concept of the 'line' and how the marketing communications mix evolved around it. The subsequent sections examine the nature of the main below-the-line tools and the impact of technology on different aspects of below-the-line tools. The chapter concludes with a consideration of some of the leading IST developments and their influence on below-the-line marketing applications, communication strategies, and marketing relationships.

THE CONCEPT OF THE 'LINE' IN MARKETING COMMUNICATIONS

For many years advertising represented the central method of marketing communication for many consumer-oriented organizations. Clients outsourced the management of their advertising campaigns to specialist or full-service agencies. These agencies were remunerated indirectly through a commission system which was geared to the value of their clients' media spending. Traditionally, this was worth 15 percent, but in practice this figure was often discounted to reflect competitive and market pressures. The key element here is the notion of commission and this became known as the 'line.' Marketing communications that utilized paid-for media generated a commission and were said to be 'above-the-line.' All other forms of marketing communications were remunerated by other methods, primarily fees and payment-by-results systems. Not surprisingly, these became known as 'below-the-line' communications. Direct response activities can incorporate an element of media-based communications and this hybrid form of communication is sometimes referred to as 'through-the-line.'

This demarcation based around the 'line' has become a defused, and increasingly marginalized, form of terminology. One reason for this is the impact of IST on reducing the reliance on advertising and increasing the potency and attractiveness of sales promotions, public relations, direct marketing, and personal selling. Other reasons include the increased emphasis on integrated marketing communications (IMC) and media neutral planning, which purport to harmonize the delivery of marketing communication messages and incorporate a greater proportion or balance of the other communication tools.

In recent years there has been an increased focus on marketing relationships, suggesting that any potential barrier to the development of mutually rewarding (i.e. trusting) relationships, should be discouraged. As commission-based systems are a potential source of acrimony, they can serve as a negative factor in relationships. In addition, a move towards greater managerial objectivity and accountability in communication budgets also puts pressure on the viability and appropriateness of the commission-based system. (See Said 1999 for a further discussion.)

THE DEVELOPMENT OF BELOW-THE-LINE COMMUNICATIONS

Although below-the-line marketing communications comprise an increasingly wide range of approaches, the core tools are sales promotion, public relations, personal selling, and direct marketing. In fact, a variety of other communication methods are derived from these primary tools, including sponsorship, events, field marketing, in-store and merchandizing activities, product placement, lobbying, customer magazines, conferences, facility visits, websites, and exhibitions. Their contribution to an overall campaign can be significant, but typically they are used to support and supplement the primary methods. They can offer depth and character in order to avoid clutter, can provide points of communication distinctiveness, and can overcome general promotional noise.

Below-the-line communications are used by organizations to play a particular role within campaigns and to achieve specific overall tasks. These roles and tasks are not mutually exclusive; indeed, they are best used in conjunction with advertising activities, as advocated by proponents of IMCs. However, traditionally, the above- and below-the-line approaches have each played a distinctive role that becomes apparent when one considers some major developments in the history and evolution of advertising.

The core capability of advertising is its ability to help build brands. However, its role in brand building has changed over the years, and through change has encouraged the growth of other tools. Initially, brands developed through advertising worked by leading audiences through various sequential processes and stages of readiness to buy. Advertising was used to develop first an audience's awareness of a brand's existence and availability, then to provide product feature-based information, and then to persuade audiences to prefer one particular brand before enticing them into purchase. The strength of this persuasion process was partly based on the attraction of the benefits that ownership conferred (Jones 1995; McGuire 1978; Strong 1925). In addition, the potency of this process of brand development was built on the notion that a brand had a unique selling proposition (USP), meaning a single point of functional differentiation. Indeed, the vast majority of brands did have functional advantages up until the early 1980s and advertising's task was to present these to audiences and persuade them to act, preferably by making a purchase. However, developing technologies, the ability to copy products and get them to market quickly, and increasing opportunities to exploit growing markets resulted in the erosion of USPs to the extent that they became invalid points of differentiation and negated advertising's primary role.

An alternative idea concerning the role of advertising suggests that it serves to reinforce previous purchase behavior by reminding customers of the value of their purchases (Ehrenberg 1974). Rather than acting as a tool of persuasion based on a single USP, the focus has become one developed though the use of emotional selling propositions (ESPs). For example, Jones (1998) argued that advertising can have a strong short-term persuasive impact on sales, but agrees that the medium- to long-term impact of advertising is based on reinforcement principles. The power of the USP to enable advertising to achieve sales has been eroded and advertising's role has moved to more of an emphasis on developing brand values based on emotion and imagery. The creation of brand values based on emotion and ESPs is a sound approach except that this form of advertising does not always provide customers with a motivation or explicit reason to buy (a so-called 'call to action'). It is in this context that sales promotions and direct marketing have increased in significance and impact within the reconfigured promotional mix.

BELOW-THE-LINE TOOLS

Below-the-line marketing communication tools emerged as an important counterbalance to advertising because they are capable of delivering the call to action. With the exception of public relations, all have the capacity to induce a behavioral response. For example, sales promotions are often used tactically to provide added value, the aim being to accelerate customer behavior by bringing forward sales that might otherwise have been made at some point in the future. The use of price reductions, sampling, coupons, premiums, competitions and sweepstakes, bonus packs, refunds, and rebates are all designed to affect customer behavior. This may be in the form of converting or switching users of competitive products, creating trial use of newly introduced products, or encouraging existing customers to increase their usage of a product. In addition, sales promotions provide a means of gathering market and individual customer information. This ability to add value and to bring forward expected sales is very important when organizations are orientated to short-term financial performance.

Personal selling is an interpersonal below-the-line communication tool that involves face-to-face interaction. The immediacy and inherent flexibility of this form of communication enables participants to inform, persuade, or remind an individual or group to take appropriate actions. However, the degree of control that an organization might have over the consistency and accuracy of messages delivered through personal selling can be of concern. This is because the salesperson is free at the point of contact to deliver a message other than that intended (Lloyd 1997). This need not be deliberate information deviance but may be induced through the immediacy of the sales context and an urge to provide a suitable level of customer service. Indeed, many different messages can be delivered by a single salesperson. Some of these messages may enhance the prospect of the salesperson's objectives being reached (e.g. making the sale), or they may retard the process and thus incur more time and costs.

Of all below-the-line tools, *public relations* has the widest sphere of activity as it seeks to influence the thoughts and actions of a range of stakeholders, not just customers. The increasing use of public relations, and in particular publicity, is a reflection of the high credibility attached to this form of communication. As with personal selling, a potential weakness is poor message control. Of all the various methods and forms of public relations, event management and lobbying have the greatest potential to influence behavior. Publicity, media relations, and sponsorship-related activities affect individuals cognitively rather than advance the purchase sequence.

In contrast to below-the-line tools *direct marketing* attempts to build a one-to-one relationship with each customer. This can be achieved by communicating on a direct and personal basis. The increased use of direct marketing by organizations over the past ten years has been significant as it signals a shift in focus away from mass communication and towards personalized communications. In some ways, the development of direct marketing is a response to some of the cost and effectiveness weaknesses associated with the other tools, most notably advertising.

The use of direct mail, telemarketing, and the fast-developing area of interactive communications, such as the Internet, are indicative of significant developments in technology. Direct marketing applications have made it possible for organizations to reach individual customers, personalize messages, exert a high level of control over the delivery of such messages, and present real opportunities for an ongoing dialog to be achieved.

In addition to these primary tools, exhibitions (especially in business-to-business markets) and field marketing (particularly in-store and merchandizing activities) are prominent and effective offline ways of stimulating customer behavior. In-store activities involve window displays, posters, signs, information cards, and counter and check-out displays. Merchandizing is concerned with floor and wall racks, end of aisle bins, and the specific, optimal presentation and display of merchandise, all designed to attract attention and prompt purchase behavior.

Below-the-line tools share a number of characteristics but an overriding strength is their capacity to stimulate action and to bring about behavioral responses in target audiences. Does this mean that the use of these tools impairs the development of brands? In some cases this might be the case, particularly if they are used heavily in markets where high involvement predominates in consumers' behavior. High involvement is characterized by the careful and considered purchase behavior of products and services that are bought relatively infrequently. In these circumstances, where the utility or status associated with ownership is very important, the continued presence and association of sales promotions may dilute the value of the brand. For example, most luxury fragrance brands are only available through particular retail outlets and the overuse of sales promotions is avoided because they may distract consumers from a luxury to an everyday perception. However, brand development in many consumer markets is often undertaken through the sole use of below-the-line tools, simply because there are insufficient financial resources to use advertising (Riezebos 2003). This is where the integrated school of thought has a strong argument in that below-the-line tools can complement and assist the development of brands and at the same time reduce costs and a dependence on advertising.

The transition from transactional to a relationship marketing orientation has yet to be completed, but the move appears to be irreversible and an inevitable development, at least over the medium term. There are three main distinguishing characteristics of relationship marketing (Christopher et al. 2002). The first is the adoption of a strategy based on the recognition that all actions should seek to maximize the lifetime value of a customer. This is calculated by discounting the flow of future net profits associated with a specific customer. This approach recognizes that not all customers represent the same level of profitability and that decisions are required to target specific customer groups and to decline business with others. The second characteristic is the recognition that marketing actions need to be addressed to multiple markets, not just customer markets. This is because other domains, such as those associated with regulating marketing activities or members of the marketing channel, can influence an organization's ability to win or retain profitable customers. The third characteristic is the recognition that marketing is a cross-functional activity and not merely the preserve and responsibility of a marketing department. Organizations have internal as well as external markets to serve.

The practice of relationship marketing is geared to four main phases: (a) customer acquisition, (b) development, (c) retention, and (d) decline, each of which can vary in intensity, duration, and magnitude (Bruhn 2003). Of these, most attention is now given to the retention phase to the extent that some argue it should be an element integrated into an organization's strategic marketing plans (Ahmad and Buttle 2001). However, it also is argued that customer retention alone is insufficient because some long-lasting customer relationships are not always profitable, even though customers themselves are perfectly satisfied (Grönroos 1994). The potential for a long-lasting relationship can only be realized when both the economic and emotional imperatives of both parties attain an approximate and acceptable level of symmetry. Thus, if relationship marketing focuses on customer retention, then a key task is to manage customer behavior. The role of marketing communications in this context is to encourage and reinforce behavior, to convey trust, and build commitment in order to encourage increased purchase frequency, cross buying, and product experimentation. In other words, there is a strong complementary aspect with the tasks of below-the-line communication tools.

CURRENT TECHNOLOGICAL INFLUENCES
ON BELOW-THE-LINE COMMUNICATIONS

The development of *customer relationship management (CRM) systems* has been regarded as a critical component of relationship marketing. Despite questionable levels of success, such systems also became the aspiration of many companies (Stone 2003). The purpose of a CRM system is to enable organizations to track all types of customer interactions in order to better manage their customer relationships. Although tracking is important, it is the analysis of customer activity data that can provide organizations with a competitive insight into the profile and relationship potential of different customers. Christopher et al. (2002: 16) crystallized the valuable role of CRM when they suggested that it is the unification of 'the potential of Information Technology and Relationship Marketing to deliver profitable, long-term relationships.' In order for this unification to work, customer data must be recorded, analyzed, and actively managed.

The Database

At the heart of the various technological advances, and CRM systems in particular, lies the database and the processes by which data are managed. The use of current, reliable customer data to drive marketing communications enables relationships to move from monolog to dialog and from passive to interactive. Data management is therefore a key factor in the way organizations communicate and manage their brands in order to achieve their marketing goals. Indeed, technology is empowering interactivity and creating new opportunities for customer contact and brand enrichment. In order to harness technology and channel it to the benefit of the brand, it is important that data are accurate and managed efficiently.

Data can be kept current and reliable through two main methods. One is to use data quality management software (DMQ) in-house and the other is to outsource the task to a data-processing bureau. Suppression processes are used to 'clean' the data by removing records relating to those who have requested that they be removed from such lists, those who have died, and those who have simply relocated. Enhancement processes enable new data to be added, often by matching against profiling and lifestyle templates. The pressure to use clean and high quality data is increasing for organizations. This is partly because consumers develop negative perceptions of, and are increasingly prepared to challenge, organizations that misuse their personal information, perhaps by boycotting brands. Organizations that are prepared to keep clean data are more likely to exhibit a strong customer orientation and with it a propensity for sharing information to which consumers are more likely to respond.

Data mining and visualization tools enable trends within data to be identified, key customer profiles to be highlighted, customer behavior to be scrutinized and compared, and market opportunities and compatible strategies to be developed, implemented, and monitored. It is in these aspects of campaign management that database technology can assist and enhance marketing communications. Whatever marketing communications strategy is followed, a sound database can be used to integrate and coordinate activities. Without a database, organizations tend to run a few large and widely dispersed campaigns, which might be referred to as 'spray and pray.' With a database and sound marketing management, many smaller, more narrowly targeted campaigns can be run simultaneously across multiple channels.

Although the role of the database and the development of data ware-housing techniques have evolved in order to support the goal of customer retention, technology has simultaneously developed innovative methods of communication. Some of these are explored in the following sections.

Direct Marketing

There are a number of reasons why the development of direct marketing, and direct response marketing in particular, has been particularly dramatic over the recent past. Here again the impact of IST has been significant. For example, technology has reduced the time necessary to develop direct marketing materials. It has increased the processing power associated with list management and lowered the costs per contact, also known as the relative costs. Further, IST has significantly altered the way organizations segment markets and target individuals, as well as having improved the methodologies and techniques used to evaluate direct marketing campaigns. Above all else, technology has improved the communication devices necessary for the delivery of direct marketing campaigns. Both the offline and digital aspects of direct mail, telemarketing, e-mail, and viral communications (in the sense of one user passing a message to another and increasing the distribution and reach of the message) have helped transform the spectrum of direct marketing, for example, by improving the accuracy of the marketing communication messages delivered and the sheer numbers of consumers reached.

Newly Emergent Delivery Mechanisms

Short Message Services

As O'Connor et al. described in Chapter 7, the use of short message services (SMS), or 'texting,' has grown considerably in recent years and is an important aspect of both informal customer-to-customer and formal organization-to-customer communications. SMS has been central to both customer acquisition as well as retention strategies and, because of low costs and a high level of control, the text-based format is likely to continue as a pivotal aspect of many below-the-line activities. It is used increasingly to prompt awareness of sales promotions, such as announcing special offers, and reflects the increasing ubiquity of contemporary mobile communications.

Some would argue that marketers have been slow to capitalize on the potential of SMS, with 2001 marking the start of significant penetration. Text volumes in the UK were considered to be around 20 billion in 2003 and these were expected to rise to approximately 23 billion by 2004 (Short 2004). Wireless Application Protocol (WAP) Mobile Internet page impressions were expected to grow from 8 billion to 13 billion during the same period. This does not take into account the slow, but increasing use of MMS picture and instant messaging.

Doyle (2003) suggests that the growth of SMS is due to several reasons. The primary one is that the Global System for Mobile Communication (GSM) enables users to cross geographic boundaries, as it is now a standard protocol. Another reason is that SMS is a nonintrusive but timely way to deliver information. For example, users can receive text messages notifying them of new voice mail messages or special offers. As users become more comfortable with SMS, other simple applications are emerging, including games, e-mail notification, and information-delivery services, such as sports and stock market updates. SMS communications have a number of advantages compared to traditional media-based communications, which make them attractive to users and organizations. These are considered under the so-called '3Cs framework': the level of communication effectiveness, cost, and marketing-management control (Fill 2002).

- *Communication effectiveness.* Delivery by mobile phone enables short-text messages to be sent directly to an individual, at virtually any time and at any location, so that messages can be read at the user's convenience. Messages can be adapted to individual preferences and circumstances (i.e. location) and they can invite dialogue.
- *Cost.* The relative costs of SMS communications are just a fraction of more traditional media delivery systems. Even the absolute costs are

substantially lower because sending text messages from a mobile phone does not require additional software or hardware.

- *Control.* Because of the ability to target a specific audience, management's control over the message content and timing of the delivery is high. However, an additional feature of SMS is the opportunity to encourage 'message forwarding' to other individuals or groups. Under these circumstances control is reduced as the atmosphere of the message forwarded cannot be influenced and is user specific.

An example of SMS being used to drive action, literally, is the London Taxi Point scheme. Anyone wishing to book a London cab can now use SMS by entering a four-digit code from a Taxi Point sign. The code represents the customer's precise location. Using global positioning systems (GPS) technology, the system identifies the nearest available participant cab, which then delivers a confirmatory booking SMS and an alert when it arrives at the taxi point. The advantage of this new system is that, unlike other technologies, a precise point location is used rather than a general base station that can cover several buildings. It is this form of application (e.g. using GPS-enabled SMS) that will empower retailers and manufacturers to make increasing use of mobile technology in the future. For example, marketers will increasingly have opportunities to reach consumers while they are shopping, with rich content in terms of incentives and information that is pertinent to their contextual needs.

These types of benefits are attracting marketing professionals to consider SMS for more complex services. However, marketers also need to consider the potential concerns of consumers, most notably privacy. Just as with e-mail, there is the potential for unwanted messages (i.e. spam), which will inevitably continue to increase as SMS becomes more widespread. Given that most consumers pay for SMS functionality, marketers should realize that invading personal privacy greatly reduces the potential value and effectiveness of SMS.

Multimedia Messaging Services

The development from simple text-based services to multimedia facilities with data channels capable of handling larger, more complex messages, was an inevitable result of advances in technology. An example of a multimedia message service (MMS) application is apparent at the international hair salon chain, Toni and Guy. This company has developed an MMS that seeks to add value for consumers through mobility, content, interaction, and a call to action. Pictures of potential new hairstyles can be downloaded from the Toni and Guy website to a mobile phone. These can then be shared with friends and family, as well as a salon stylist, through the mobile phone and without the need to print paper copies. This use of technology simulates the traditional form of in-store sampling and can substitute for magazine advertisements designed to develop brand values and demonstrate flair and innovativeness. Under MMS, the process is driven and managed by the consumer, costs are borne by the consumer (e.g. fee per hairstyle), and the range of facilities offered is far wider than traditional processes allow. The process is entirely interactive and demonstrates the trend towards the use of personalized multimedia content, characterized by various combinations of images, audio, text, and video through small, personal mobile devices.

Mobile Commerce

Over the past few years consumers have become more familiar and comfortable with paying online for services through their personal computers. The early expectation was that consumers would also be comfortable with Internet-enabled mobile devices to undertake similar transactions. Such *mobile commerce* (or *m-commerce*), refers to the use of wireless devices such as mobile phones for transactional activities, which principally involve monetary exchange for goods and services. M-commerce represents a major change in the way technology can impact marketing communications. Because of the wireless facility, transactions can be undertaken at any place and in real time—a feature referred to as 'ubiquity.' In addition, m-commerce offers reachability, the opportunity to keep in touch, convenience, localization, and personalization. When these facilities are connected to GPS it becomes theoretically possible to track people to particular locations and then deliver personalized and pertinent information, plus inducements and promotional offers in order to encourage specific purchase behavior.

The reality of the situation is that consumer interest in m-commerce, at the time of this writing, has been less than enthusiastic. The blame for the stuttering launch of m-commerce is often leveled at the WAP technology because of its slow speed, unreliability, and user difficulties, such as those associated with using small screens. However, added to this are issues concerning market expectations and overly optimistic predictions about changes in buyer behavior. New and faster technologies, such as General Packet Radio Service (GPRS) and third generation (3G) services enabling sound and image transfers, are expected by many to herald a successful relaunch of m-commerce. If m-commerce is to become a central factor in consumers' lives and, in turn, become a major delivery medium for marketing communications messages, then costs, accessibility, and consumer perceptions will require a fundamental realignment.

There are signs of renewed interest in m-commerce, manifest through the sales growth of color wallpaper (i.e. pictures saved on the display of mobile phones), ring tones, and a move towards richer content through the online purchase of video and games. Mobile services are progressing as technology can now incorporate advanced payment systems. For example, the magazine *Exchange and Mart* offers a mobile service for buyers to search the database of over 140,000 cars and to download the telephone number of selected vendors. This provides increased added value as it enables buyers to search for cars while they are away from their homes. Once again, however, it is questionable whether buyer behavior will change sufficiently to make this type of service profitable for the brand owner.

The demand on marketing communications, should m-commerce become more firmly established, will be to support mobile purchases by providing reasons to buy. The need to stimulate action will be critical as consumers become aware of an array of sites available to them and, with extremely low switching costs, they will need a reason to stay on and return to particular sites. As a result, below-the-line communications are likely to become more central to the mobile market.

Personal Selling

The roots of customer relationship management (CRM) systems can be traced to facilities originally designed to assist the sales force. These have since evolved and developed specific applications, but the automation of many sales-force routines, processes, and procedures has been an important goal for sales-force management. The motivation for many firms is to drive down selling costs, improve the effectiveness of communication activities, and enhance the quality of market and customer information. Widmier et al. (2002) identified sales-force automation as an important aspect of the use of technology within sales-force management. They also argued that technology is used extensively to assist six main sales functions, namely organizing, presenting, reporting, communicating, informing, and supporting transactions. Interestingly, they found that technology is more likely to be used by salespersons in the office (e.g. preparing presentations, proposals, route planning, scheduling, and reporting) rather than in the field with customers.

Although there is no universal agreement about what a sales-force automation (SFA) system is, SFA generally refers to hardware, software, and telecommunication devices used by salespersons in their work-related activities (Morgan and Inks 2001). Not surprisingly, the utilization of various SFA devices varies among organizations and its effectiveness is dependent upon appropriate implementation, proper utilization, and suitable support processes. Morgan and Inks identified SFA failure rates between 25 percent and 60 percent, and attributed these failures to four main elements: (*a*) management commitment, (*b*) training, (*c*) user involvement, and (*d*) accurate expectation setting, with the first of these being a major contributing factor.

It would be dangerous to assume that productivity gains are an automatic outcome of SFA implementation. Organizations can experience high implementation costs, sales-force resistance, and underutilization among other key reasons for the failure to substantially increase productivity in this way (Engle and Barnes 2000).

One additional aspect regarding personal selling concerns the development of video-conferencing facilities. Video conferencing can be used to bring buyer and seller together for negotiations and can save time and travel costs, thereby creating opportunities to close sales. There may be local problems associated with the technology, communicating across time zones, and trying to get people into particular locations at particular times. In addition, there are issues associated with relationship management and related contextual issues, but the video-conferencing market is growing and provides a viable and alternative method for some personal selling activities and situations. With increasing turbulence in world political markets, mounting pressure on environmental resources, greater focus on shareholder value and issues of accountability, it is probable that organizations will make more use of video conferencing, particularly in business-to-business markets.

Sales Promotion

Sales promotion typifies the realm of below-the-line marketing communications and is a tool for which new technology has played a significant role. As mentioned above, sales promotions are normally used to stimulate future sales, to provide a reason to buy or try now. However, for many people, the only reason to use the Internet is to find information and to compare prices. This suggests that the sales promotions approach needs to be reconsidered to be effective in a digital environment. Of the many dimensions associated with sales promotion, three are considered here: reward points, loyalty schemes, and coupons.

New forms of electronic trading points, such as Beenz, Flooz, MyPoints, and iPoints, are all cyber currencies that can be collected at a number of sites and then cashed in for goods at other sites. Beenz and Flooz competed against credit card companies and have since ceased trading, partly because the market they targeted did not offer sufficient volume of trade. More than 100 participating organizations offer iPoints, which can only be accessed at one appointed trader in each sector or participant retail category. These schemes represent early attempts at transferring the off-line sales promotion model across to the online world. However, there is a danger that these currency collection devices might be abused through the development of automated software designed to scan and collect points. Also, there is the likelihood that some people will attempt to cheat the system by 'site grazing' for Web points.

The proliferation of newly developed loyalty programs is mainly a response to the need to retain profitable customers. The terms 'customer retention' and 'customer loyalty' are often used interchangeably, but it should be noted that loyalty is but one of many elements in retaining customers. There is little agreement about the meaning of 'loyalty' in the marketing literature (Egan 2001). The term itself may be misleading because what is sometimes regarded as loyalty may actually be camouflage for convenience or extended utility (Fill and Fill 2005). However, there is general agreement that both loyalty and customer retention can be achieved if the flow of information is reciprocal, emphasizing the importance of dialog between organizations and their customers, rather than monolog-based communications.

Technology has played a significant role in the development of loyalty programs; indeed, their overall viability and functionality is dependent upon the database and associated facilities. An example of a successful loyalty program, the Tesco Clubcard, is described in Chapter 9. Further data analysis allows for better shelf usage and the identification of stores that move particular products (and categories) at different times of the year. The Nectar scheme, recently introduced and run by a consortium of UK retailers, suggests that single company schemes no longer may be the most profitable configuration. Although the Nectar card is a loyalty card, by enabling customers access to earn points at a variety of different stores, it reflects buying behavior and a certain lack of individual store loyalty.

As a means to encourage consumers to seek out and try a specific brand, the use of coupons has been a long-established strategy. Unlike loyalty schemes, which look to reward loyal behavior, coupons encourage brand switching. With an estimated 300 billion coupons printed annually worldwide and only an average 2 percent redemption rate (Slater 2001), the arithmetic is sometimes difficult to understand. However, many experiments to replace coupons with permanently lower prices have failed; one of the most noteworthy of which was undertaken by Procter & Gamble in the mid-1990s. One of the main reasons for the failure of everyday low prices policies is that the vast majority of people prefer coupons simply because they represent added value. Coupons have traditionally been delivered through mass media such as newspapers and free-standing inserts; however, there has been a move towards dispensing them closer to the point of purchase through scanner technologies, frequent flyer programs, the Internet, and direct mail (Slater 2001). There are even websites designed to locate online coupons. Tesco prints coupons through the cash register, not triggered by specific product purchases but as a result of each customer's recent pattern of purchases.

An interesting aspect of online shopping has been a sort of reinvention of the coupon and the subsequent impact on customer behavior (Oliver and Shor 2003). In the offline world, coupon redemption is normally customer-initiated. However, when ordering online, customers are asked to present a promotion code, just before submitting confirmation of their order. If a code is entered, the overall shopping cart price is reduced. The system therefore prompts the customer to use the equivalent of a coupon. The problem appears to be that customers without a code and without the means to get one, tend to exit the website without completing their purchase. This problem, known as 'shopping cart abandonment,' is analogous to shoppers who abandon their full shopping trolleys because the check-out lines are too long (Oliver and Shor 2003). What this also indicates is that online buying behaviors can be different to those understood in the offline world, thereby reinforcing the view that different marketing communication tools may need to be changed or adapted for the online context. In order for this to be undertaken more research and understanding are required.

POSSIBLE FUTURE INFLUENCES OF TECHNOLOGY ON BELOW-THE-LINE COMMUNICATIONS

Technology has rapidly advanced in many different ways and with enormous impact over recent years. Although the Internet lies at the heart of current and future marketing applications, three main thrusts of development can be identified: (*a*) wireless networking, (*b*) smart devices, and (*c*) intelligent communications services (Karnell 2004).

Wireless Networking

The use of wireless technologies is currently in its infancy and many expect that wireless technologies are going to underpin many marketing applications in the coming years. Radio frequency identification (RFID) is an established technology that utilizes a computer chip and an antenna. RFID tags work on the basis that a radio signal, received by the antenna, activates the chip, which in turn transmits a unique code identifying the object that the tag is attached to (Blau 2003). One of the main areas for the development and exploitation of this technology rests in-store and not just from a security aspect. Prada's New York store, Epicentre, is assessing various RFID applications. For example, staff use handheld de-vices to check stock and to assemble orders in the established way, but these tags are also used to trigger screens within changing rooms, enabling customers to view video clips of the merchandise. Using video cameras and plasma screens in place of mirrors, customers are able to see them-selves from behind (Dean 2003).

Bar codes are used everyday in nearly all grocery stores but these need to be scanned manually and read individually. RFID tags do not need line-of-sight reading, which means that hundreds of tags can be read in a second, saving considerable amounts of time. In addition, radio tags are capable of providing not only the universal product codes as used in bar codes but they can also provide a unique identifying code. This means that promo-tions can be based on particular groups of items purchased and changed very quickly as circumstances warrant. A retailer will also have the cap-ability to trace poor quality stock that needs to be removed from the shelves, quickly. This technology can also be used by consumers to sample games and music CDs.

An example of how future technology might influence in-store shopping experiences and drive consumer behavior has been provided by the Metro Future Store in Germany, where an entire building has been covered by a wireless network. This offers the means to interlink a variety of mobile devices, such as personal shopping assistants (PSAs), personal digital assistants (PDAs), and static devices such as electronic shelf labels (ESLs), check-out points, and flat-screen displays for product promotion. PSAs are for the use of shoppers whose shopping trolleys have a touch screen mini-computer linked to the network. The integrated scanner al-lows shoppers to scan their own purchases, with the data then transmitted to the checkout in advance of the shopper. As a result, the payment and associated queuing processes are considerably improved, thereby enhan-cing the customer's shopping experience, and merchandise is handled less. PDAs are also linked to the wireless network and are used by store em-ployees to check inventory by directly accessing Metro's merchandise management system at any time and any point in the store. Using 'voice over Internet protocol' (VoIP) technology, there are plans for the PDAs to receive 'soft phone' functionality, enabling staff to make calls in addition to sending messages or downloading information.

High costs have so far prohibited the widespread adoption of ESL tech-nology. However, these electronic labels are capable of receiving price information directly from the merchandise management system via the radio network, using base stations located in the ceiling. Price infor-mation can be transmitted simultaneously to the shelf and checkout to avoid price differences resulting from erroneous labeling. The price labels are equipped with an easily legible digital display, battery, and radio receiver.

Given these various examples, it is apparent that the potential for RFID applications is enormous. For example, pallets and boxes can be tagged at a distribution center and then recorded as they pass through a gate into a store. This type of application can provide information on warehouse shipments and shop-floor inventory levels, in real time (Blau 2003).

Bar code technology would appear to be at a mature stage, and will gradually be replaced by radio tags as the cost of the embedded chips becomes more affordable. For the moment the cost is too high to prevent a sweeping change, but new plastic chip technologies, once stabilized, will enable costs to be reduced considerably. Also being tested are so-called 'smart shelves,' which have readers embedded in them so that they notify the main system when merchandise is removed, and will then automatically trigger a request for shelf replenishment.

Out-of-store applications of wireless technologies also are expected to grow. Currently, the number of wireless-fidelity (Wi-Fi) access points are limited but this is changing rapidly, to the extent that they will become a regular part of the environment. This means that the Internet will become a ubiquitous information utility whereby corporations, individuals, and governments will access and interact with information anywhere, anytime, and most importantly, with any device. For marketers, this increased access means greater scope for targeted and personalized delivery of timely promotions and increased opportunities for co-branding and marketing alliances.

A current alliance between Starbucks and T-Mobile has made it is possible to download e-mail from a PDA and integrate existing Internet tools when entering into a Starbucks coffee shop (Karnell 2004). The natural development is to open the service so that national and international interactive clients could 'geo-target consumers with timely and actionable offers.' Currently, Starbucks is using wireless-connectivity technology in stores to enhance their customers' experiences. However, as established earlier, the whole aspect of mobile technologies is expanding rapidly such that it is possible to see a strong trend towards visual content and information, perhaps as promotional messages, to be delivered to people wherever and whenever they want it, rather than just in the home or the office.

Smart Devices

Smart (or *information-powered*) *devices* will enable organizations to use Internet and networked information in new and innovative ways. Indeed, these new devices, which will have continuous Internet access and will be embedded into our everyday environment, have the potential to radically change the way consumers interact with brands. For example, products such as watches, chairs, carpets, refrigerators, and clothes may eventually be used for storing these everpresent devices. IBM and Citizen have joined forces to develop the WatchPad. Among other things, this device will use short-range wireless connectivity to enable users to remotely control various devices, such as laptop computers, view e-mail messages and calendar entries, and send and receive text and voice commands to other computers. These devices will be able to receive up-to-date news, traffic, weather, and sports information. In addition to obvious above-the-line communications, this technology opens opportunities for sponsorship and promotional programs.

Intelligent Communication Services

Intelligent communication services represent the next step for integrating smart devices with the Internet. This will enable smart devices to detect changes in their environment and thereby prompt users to act in particular ways. Karnell (2004) suggests that this will enable marketers to track products and consumers and deliver real-time, proximity-specific, and ultrapersonalized information. Thus, as a refrigerator senses that the last carton of jam (previously tagged) has been removed it will prompt, via text, visuals, or vocal communication that a new jar of a particular brand of jam is required. This process may in time be remotely linked through to a specified store that will add the item automatically to the consumer's standing order for home delivery.

Given these developments, consumer decision-making processes and brand choice decisions may be made either in the home, with little consumer intervention, or in the store with smart devices enabling retailers and brand owners to interact with consumers while they are shopping. By creating smart, electronically defined spaces, it is possible to identify which side of an aisle a customer is shopping and, as a result, the customer can receive interactive messages regarding specific products and services. These might highlight lower prices or promotional offers such as time-based coupons, instant free products, and bundles of products, determined by the customer's sales history. Such customization, determined by the shopping profile and preferences of the customer, will likely transform the shopping experience. For example, consumers will be able to access detailed product information and make price and product comparisons at the point of purchase.

Other Developments

At present, applications of biometric technology are at an advanced stage of development (Das 2004). For example, voice recognition technologies have been successfully deployed in back-office and security-related environments. They are currently considered to be best used to gather simple information, such as names and addresses, or supporting applications, such as voice mail account management, through a preset menu of choices. The motivation to further automate customer contact centers is high, as there is a strong drive to reduce costs. However, there are a variety of technical problems with voice recognition applications and, as a result, the use of voice recognition in customer contact centers to date has been limited (see Rockwell 2004). Many of these new technologies are currently used for security-related applications where the principle of using biometric technologies to identify and authenticate individuals is established. What is not yet available is the ability to induce dialog, in real time, with a series of relational databases and intelligent devices in order to communicate personalized product offers and to stimulate cognitive and behavioral responses. These technologies are not yet sufficiently developed to offer commercial advantages. Given that they are in the pipeline, a wide range of privacy and personal freedom issues have yet to be debated, let alone resolved.

CONCLUSION

An increasing proportion of clients' marketing communication budgets is being allocated to below-the-line communications. One of the reasons for this movement of funds is partly associated with an increasing dissatisfaction with the return of capital employed in above-the-line communications, namely advertising. The drive to generate brand values has been gradually diminished in an environment in which it is difficult to establish and sustain distinct and clear points of differentiation. The increasing emphasis on accountability, and the availability of systems that can support appropriate customer relations, has resulted in significant applications of technology in marketing communications.

At times, the influence of technology has been overly accentuated (see Chapter 3). In reality, technology alone is not sufficient to bring about change; rather, it is managerial judgment, propensity to invest, and a willingness to take risks associated with marketing communications that is important. Technology is an enabler, whereas management's ability and willingness to engage with new technology is the key determinant of successful marketing communication efforts.

There have been great advances in technology in recent years and the use of below-the-line communications has increased as a result. Many innovative forms and applications of new technology are being developed, planned, and tested but the degree to which these will be taken up by organizations remains questionable. Customer behavior does not appear to change quickly nor to respond to new forms of technology and delivery mechanisms in sufficient numbers to be profitable, at least in the short term. Investment in below-the-line communications is likely to increase, although it must be remembered that a call to action still requires that brand values be firmly established.

The text-based era is giving way to multimedia formats delivered through wireless and mobile devices. Issues concerning data management, privacy, and overall aspects of social and corporate responsibility will inevitably arise. For example, organizations will need to develop means for controlling spam and fraud, along with security-related issues as they become increasingly immersed in technological applications designed to deliver below-the-line marketing communication messages. Opportunities for the further development of below-the-line communications are inevitable and with moves towards relationship marketing and integrated marketing communications, the influence of technology is likely to grow even stronger.

REFERENCES

Ahmad, R. and Buttle, F. (2001). 'Customer Retention: A Potentially Potent Marketing Management Strategy,' *Journal of Strategic Marketing*, 9 (1), 29–45.

Bartle, J. (1999). 'The Advertising Contribution,' in L. Butterfield (ed.), *Excellence in Advertising*, Oxford: Butterworth-Heinemann, pp. 25–44.

Blau, J. (2003). Supermarket Tunes into Wireless. Available: www.computerweekly.com/articles

Bruhn, M. (2003). *Relationship Marketing: Management of Customer Relationships*. Harlow: FT/Prentice-Hall.

Christopher, M., Payne, A., and Ballantyne, D. (2002). *Relationship Marketing: Creating Stakeholder Value*. Oxford: Butterworth-Heinemann.

Das, R. (2004). The Application of Biometric Technologies: 'The Afghan Girl-Sharbat Gula'. Available: www.technologyexecutivesclub.com

Dean, A. (2003). High Street: The New Technological Battleground. Available: www.raeng.org.uk

Doyle, S. (2003). The Big Advantage of Short Messaging. Available: www.sas.com/news

Egan, J. (2001). *Relationship Marketing : Exploring Relational Strategies in Marketing*. Harlow: Pearson Education.

Ehrenberg, A.S.C. (1974). 'Repetitive Advertising and the Consumer', *Journal of Advertising Research*, 14, 25–34.

Engle, R. L. and Barnes, M. L. (2000). 'Sales Force Automation Usage, Effectiveness and Cost Benefit in Germany, England and the United States', *Journal of Business and Industrial Marketing*, 15 (4), 216–41.

Fill, C. (2002). *Marketing Communications: Contexts, Strategies and Applications*, (3rd edn.). Harlow: Pearson Education.

Fill, C. and Fill, K. (2005). *Business-to-Business Marketing: Relationships, Systems and Communications*. Harlow: Pearson Education.

Gronroos, C. (1994). 'From Marketing Mix to Relationship Marketing', *Management Decision*, 32 (2), 4–20.

Jones, J. P. (1995). 'Advertising Exposure Effects Under a Microscope', *Admap*, (February), 28–31.

—— (1998). 'Is Advertising Still Salesmanship?' in J.P. Jones (ed.), *How Advertising Works*, London: Sage, pp. 82–94.

Karnell, I. (2004). Tech Watch: The Future of One-to-One Marketing. Available: www.the-dma.org

Lloyd, J. (1997). 'Cut your Rep Free', *Pharmaceutical Marketing*, (September), 30–32.

McGuire, W. J. (1978). 'An Information Processing Model of Advertising Effectiveness', in H. L. Davis and A. J. Silk (eds.). *Behavioral and Management Science in Marketing*. New York: Wiley.

Morgan, A. J. and Inks, S. A. (2001). 'Technology and the Sales Force: Increasing Acceptance of Sales Force Automation,' *Industrial Marketing Management*, 30 (5), 463–72.

Oliver, R. L. and Shor, M. (2003). 'Digital Redemption of Coupons: Satisfying, and Dissatisfying Effects of Promotion Codes', *Journal of Product and Brand Management*, 12 (2), 121–34.

Riezebos, R. (2003). *Brand Management: A Theoretical and Practical Approach*. Harlow: Pearson Education.

Rockwell, M. (2004). Can Voice Recognition Answer the Call? Available: www. wirelessweek.com

Said, R. S. (1999). 'Advertising Agency Compensation Systems,' in J. Philip Jones (ed.), *The Advertising Business*. Thousand Oaks, CA: Sage, pp. 111–20.

Short, M. (2004). The Year Ahead. Available: www.mda-mobiledata.org

Slater, J. (2001). 'Is Couponing an Effective Promotional Strategy? An Examination of the Procter and Gamble Zero-Coupon Test,' *Journal of Marketing Communications*, 7, 3–9.

Stone, M. (2003). CRM: The Value of Marketing and Customer Management. Available: www.wnim.com

Strong, E. K. (1925). *The Psychology of Selling*. New York: McGraw-Hill.

Widmier, S. M., Jackson, D. W., Jr., and McCabe, D. B. (2002). 'Infusing Technology into Personal Selling,' *Journal of Personal Selling and Sales Management*, 22 (3), 189–99.

9

Integrated Marketing Communications and the Emerging Role of the Website

Thomas W. Gruen

The emergence and widespread use of the Internet for both consumer and business commerce has fundamentally changed the organization of marketing communications. Historians compare this change with the emergence of other major new media, such as television, which allowed marketing communications to reach a mass audience, thus providing broad-based consistent messages about the features and benefits of a marketplace offering. However, unlike other new media that have provided marketers the ability to utilize the new channel to distribute messages and even conduct commerce (e.g. direct marketing and telemarketing), the world of e-commerce and the emergence of the unparalleled tool we call the Internet, transcends all of the previous media additions. In this chapter, I argue that the central organizing mechanism for communications has—or must become—the organization's website. When one speaks of the notion of Integrated Marketing Communications (IMC), I suggest that the central integrating point—that is, the 'command center' for communications—must migrate to the organization's website.

This chapter begins with a brief background and several examples of firms moving their communications' 'locus of control' to the virtual world. I suggest that this is due to the confluence of two key streams of literature, the first being the notion of the 'marketspace,' and the second the emergence of IMC, both of which are described in greater detail. Following the discussion of how these converging streams create the current fertile conditions that are so ripe for IMC, I then describe a model of how firms can systematically approach building their website to effectively implement the IMC concept. To do so, I utilize the well-established '7-c's' concept of website customer interface, and enhance it with a perspective on how the website becomes the organizing place for IMC. Also discussed are the notion of the 'rider' communication that automatically gets generated when an individual uses a website, and the marketing and ethical ramifications of this unintended, but valuable form of communication. The chapter concludes with a look to the future of the website as the central organizing point for communications, and considers implications as access to the Internet becomes commonplace worldwide, and new technologies allow for broader distribution of websites (such as wireless phones and personal digital assistants (PDAs).

HISTORY AND DRIVING FORCES

During the high-tech boom of the mid to late 1990s, the world of e-commerce received phenomenal attention from the media, financial markets, marketing and communications managers, and top management. Based on the amount of attention the e-commerce businesses received, one might have thought that this focus on the potential of the Internet would have been central to the strategy and thinking of business managers. In reality, most businesses were only acting in a way that was akin to dipping their toes into the water to check the temperature. Many organizations created their websites to provide at the minimum a virtual presence, for fear of being stuck in the 'old economy' (Rayport and Jaworski 1994: 2). Some websites provided actual e-commerce capabilities to capture scattered sales from nontargeted and poorly understood customers, but in many cases these were operated at a financial loss to the organizations. Advertisers and advertising agencies created separate 'Internet advertising' groups with separate budgets in order not to be left behind their competitors and 'new economy' customers in case something really 'big' would take hold (Rayport and Jaworski). Manufacturers made investments in exchanges so as to not be left behind by competitors, finding only residual sales ever took place on the exchange. As hindsight clearly shows, outside of a very few successful business models, most of the attention to e-commerce was devoted to the hype and not to substance, and the 'Internet bubble' crash of April 2000 exposed the vulnerability of the early explorers in this brave new world. The proposed new mechanisms for transferring information and enhancing commerce found many spectators and dabblers, but far too few true followers.

Much like a forest fire creates an environment for new, healthy growth to emerge, the years that have followed the crash of April 2000 have produced a more rational focus on the true role of the Internet and e-commerce in business. From a communications perspective, an organization's center for e-commerce activity is now being seen more and more as the central integrating place for IMC. In essence, e-commerce is beginning to serve, and will continue to do so more and more as the integrating force and place for IMC.

This phenomenon where the website is taking hold as the organization's communications center can be explained by examining the confluence of two streams of thought in marketing and communications. The first was expressed by Duncan and Moriarty (1998) who proposed that communication should become the central integrative process in marketing. The classical communications model (Lasswell 1948) suggests that a *message* first is encoded by a *source*, and then is delivered through a *channel*. Duncan and Moriarty argued that in marketing situations where the relationship with the customer goes beyond the transaction, the communication becomes interactive, and therefore some messages will (and must) transcend the traditional role of persuasion in marketing. Because multiple functions within the organization are responsible for communications with one or more stakeholder groups, communication becomes the integrative element that can drive a consistent message from the organization. Duncan and Moriarty's view suggests that IMC provides the *opportunity* for organizations to integrate their communications at some central point.

The second stream of thought comes from research in the area of e-commerce. Rayport and Sviokla's (1994) classic *Harvard Business Review* article suggested that firms that seek some sort of computer-mediated exchange (CME) activity no longer compete solely in the marketplace, but now must compete in a broader context termed the 'marketspace,' the digital equivalent of the marketplace. Since most organizations today have some sort of digital presence, a marketspace definition of competition describes most organizations. One of the key distinguishing characteristics of the marketspace is that for information, its content, context, and delivery system can be disaggregated; that is, in the marketspace, information is digitized and, as such, the *content* can be separated from and delivered in a number of *contexts*. The delivery then depends on the infrastructure available. Communication in the marketspace can be centralized into a single depository and communications hub for the organization. In essence, the emergence of the marketspace provides the *ability* for organizations to integrate their communications at some central point. From the electronic communications center, the content can be put in multiple contexts depending on the audience. It can be delivered through a common protocol, on-demand, and available whenever and wherever the message receiver wants to obtain the message. Logically, this central location for the organization's communications is the website, where portions can be public, via the World Wide Web, and other portions can be private or only accessed with credentials. But the protocol and gathering point for the communications is centralized.

When the two streams, IMC and Marketspace, intersect, we find that the focal point of electronic commerce for an organization can, and often has, become the integrative function or place for the organization's IMCs.

INTEGRATING IMC INTO THE ORGANIZATION'S WEBSITE

Since the motivation to integrate communications in the organization's website is intriguing, the next step is to understand what should be integrated and how this should occur. To do so requires an understanding of some of the basic concepts of IMC. The premise of IMC is that everything a company does (and sometimes does not do) can send a brand message (Schultz et al. 1993). Duncan and Moriarty (1997: 5) defined IMC as 'a cross-functional process for creating and nourishing profitable relationships with customers and other stakeholders by strategically controlling or influencing all messages sent to these groups and encouraging purposeful dialogue with them.'

According to Duncan and Moriarty, IMC is comprised of three major aspects: (*a*) the concept, (*b*) synergy, and (*c*) process. The *concept* begins with the notion that an organization has a variety of stakeholders who have a variety of contact points with the organization. With each stakeholder contact, a message gets delivered. Generally, responsibility for communication with each stakeholder group has been assigned to a different function of the organization. For example, sales communicates with buyers, customer service with users, public relations with the community, investor relations with investors, human relations with employees, and so on. The nature of this distributed communication responsibility makes it extremely difficult for an organization to obtain communication synergy that can be gained through consistency and coordination of messages. The IMC concept builds integrity for the organization's offerings through message integration. Thus, the natural drive in IMC is to have some sort of centralized control over the many messages that get created and delivered to the many stakeholders. The organization's website offers this centralized location and provides a place where the different functions of the organization can each deliver messages to their stakeholders. Obviously, not every contact will come through the website, nor should it, but the website provides at least one central place where messages can be organized.

The second aspect of IMC, *synergy*, infers that various messages, if coordinated and consistent, have more impact than the individual messages themselves. There are three synergy components: consistency, interactivity, and mission. Consistency is based on the principle that people integrate messages naturally, and do not orient fragments based on the source in order to establish an image. Therefore, it is up to the organization to create a clear, consistent image emanating from its many message sources. Synergy is also gained through interactivity, where there are systems developed for handling questions and providing responses to stakeholder initiated communication. Rayport and Jaworski (2002) note that the Internet affords the opportunity for dialog, which may be in real time or asynchronous, thus providing support that an organization's website is an appropriate place for centralizing IMC. Mission represents the value system that the organization stands for beyond just its product and financial success. In essence, IMC seeks to enhance the meaning of the organization's brand so that it has a distinctive and respected meaning to all stakeholder groups through the organization's messages. Some examples of organizations that have developed a 'mission' include Hallmark (quality), Ben and Jerry's (ecology), and Apple (right-brain computing simplicity).

The third aspect is the IMC *process*, which requires the organization to develop a system for cross-functional planning and execution of all messages. This includes not only all internal functions, but also coordination of any external communication agencies. Like synergy, the process of IMC also leans heavily on a dialog focus, using technology to communicate interactively with stakeholders, as well as being able to individualize and customize contacts through knowledge of individual stakeholders. Rayport and Jaworski (2002) suggested that one of the reasons that the Internet has become so important is the ability to customize the communication experience either through user-initiated personalization (e.g. MyYahoo) or through organization-initiated personalization (e.g. Amazon.com). The IMC process also requires a long-term orientation that, unlike a single specific marketing communication that can deliver an immediate result, delivers long-term value such as enhanced brand image and equity.

In summary, the organization's objective is to have a totally integrated communication program that accounts for all types of messages delivered at every point where a stakeholder comes into contact with the organization. I noted previously that this was very complicated because communication responsibility is delineated to many different functions in the organization. This is further complicated by the fact that there are many message types (Duncan and Moriarty 1997). It is reasonable to think an organization can integrate its planned messages, such as advertising, public relations, sales promotion, signage, stationary, and so on. But it becomes more challenging to integrate messages that are inferred when the organization makes a decision to raise prices, change a distribution channel, or outsource production to a lower cost country. There are also maintenance messages that are delivered constantly through customer service, instruction books, warranty terms, employee handbooks, receptionists, and so on. Other messages are unplanned and for the most part not under the control of the organization. For example, the news media, an advocacy group, or even the user community create messages about an organization at unpredictable times.

This extremely complex system of communication, where messages are created and delivered in so many ways by so many sources, can never be completely controlled and integrated. However, the organization's website provides a place where many types of messages to every stakeholder group can be centralized and integrated. As long as stakeholders have access to the Internet, the organization's website can become a centralized place where IMC can deliver communication effectiveness. Research has shown that organizations can implement IMC effectively using cross-functional teams, without the need for having a 'communications czar' or major restructuring (cf. Duncan and Moriarty 1997). However, successful implementation does require significant commitment to the goals of IMC, and thus a major commitment for all functions to be involved in the organization's website.

INTEGRATING IMC AND THE MARKETSPACE: FIVE EXAMPLES

The following five examples provide illustrations of different ways that the various organizational functions can integrate their communications in the organization's website. While each of these examples takes a different approach to integrating communications over a website, each has the common focus of using the website as a common depository and dispensary of the organization's information.

University Recruiting

In the university, recruiting efforts and related communications used to be the domain of the admissions office, which had the responsibility to produce communications, field phone calls, and arrange campus visits for prospective students who had an interest in enrolling at the university. In what has been a very rapid evolution, today most prospective students begin their search of the university's website, foregoing initial personal contact with admissions officers and the gathering of printed supplementary material.

Even in cases where the school solicits an initial contact via direct marketing, the response mechanism is generally through the website. Once at the website, the prospective student is influenced by communications not only from pages prepared by the admissions office, but also from the overall site itself, plus any other area the prospective student holds of interest, such as financial aid, residence life, curriculum, faculty, facilities, athletics, extra-curricular activities, and so on. Moreover, the website also contains communications aimed at other audiences, such as current students, faculty, staff, prospective donors, the outside community, and alumni. Communications aimed at these targets are now easily accessible and likely to be consumed either deliberately or unintentionally by prospective students as well. Because the website covers all aspects of the university, every communication that is delivered from the website has the potential to influence the prospective student customer. The website has become the place where communications from the various areas of the university come together to represent the university as a whole, and thus the integrating place for IMC.

Interest/Advocacy Group

The next example pertains to an American interest/advocacy group, Life-Ed, that has delivered its messages through late-night television commercials and billboards, providing response mechanisms for interested viewers to contact a local affiliate. Given the nature of the individual likely to respond, the targeted segment is young and college educated, and likely to have frequent Internet usage.

While the organization had their own web-site for donors and other administrative purposes for several years, it recently developed a website, www.proknowledge.org, that contained the complete array of information that the organization wanted to communicate to those responding to their TV commercials or billboards. Further, they recognized that individuals who had not been exposed to one of their advertisements would likely reach them via an Internet search. They recognized that the messages that could be delivered on the website could be much more thorough and effective than traditional nonpersonal media sources (e.g. brochures, direct mail, print advertising) in delivering accurate knowledge as well as evoking attitude change. Individuals would still be encouraged to contact a local affiliated agency via telephone numbers provided by the website. Thus, the addition of the new website has taken over the central role for communication by the advocacy organization, as the junction through which most, if not all, of the organization's communications flow.

The British Grocery Retail Sector

This example is in the area of business-to-business marketing and has become prevalent in contexts where retailers and distributors communicate regularly with suppliers in an ongoing fashion. Grocery retailers in the UK, such as Sainsbury's, Tesco, and Safeway, provide excellent case studies in this area of electronic communications. Specifically, the central communication function is not a public website, but the company's proprietary 'extranet' where suppliers are invited, and often required, to formalize the business activities with the retailer or distributor.

The Web-based nature of the communication provides flexibility for both the retailer and the supplier to exchange information. Additionally, the information can cover and follow all aspects of the relationship. This can include purchase ordering, inquiries, shipping and delivery information, promotions, category planning, invoicing and payables, and score-carding. With *scorecarding*, for example, each party can grade the other on measures of practice and key performance indicators that have been mutually established. The outcomes of these measures can become the mechanism that directs future plans. All of this is done on a Web-based electronic platform that can be accessed at any time and by anyone with permission to access. While the electronic interface does not replace the need for face-to-face meetings, mail, and telephone contact between the retailer and its suppliers, the central organizing place for the communications has become centered on the electronic depository and its Web interface.

UK's leading grocery retailer, Tesco, has also effectively extended its website as the integrating communications center to their consumers. Using the Tesco *Clubcard* loyalty card as a leveraging mechanism, this retailer has developed industry-leading best practices in nonpersonal customized communications with its customers. Tesco mails quarterly mailers and catalogs to its extensive *Clubcard* membership base, but also directs *Clubcard* members to its website where they can view accumulated points, find messages custom-tailored based on their life-stage and recent purchases, and order online (Humby et al. 2003).

Trade Associations

Similar to the advocacy group example is that of trade associations, which function as a place where individuals or organizations convene to enhance the interests of the members. Traditionally, from the members' perspective, associations operate 'virtually,' continuously providing services on the membership's behalf, but only taking on physical form at conventions, in publications, and when the member contacts the home office. The very nature of the association is a model that revolves around a website where members can receive communications from the organization (such as industry studies and research, reports of lobbying activities), communicate with the organization (regarding educational opportunities, membership information, and so on), and communicate with other members as part of a community.

One of an association's primary benefits is for the members to network. In a marketplace environment, networking takes place face-to-face at association meetings. However, in the 'marketspace,' networking can take place in a virtual setting through asynchronous discussion groups (like a message board), or synchronous sessions when members are participating in a discussion on the site at the same time (using live chat or instant messaging). The infrastructure supporting the networking is electronic, and can be part of the association's website. Members can network with each other and provide value to each other without the constraint of specified times and location. In summary, the association's website becomes the central point for communications with members, prospective members, and other constituencies, and it also becomes the central point for communications between members.

Electronic Commerce Business Models

The final general example of the website becoming the communication integrator is that of communication of retailers with the end users (consumers). While there are hundreds of variations of these e-commerce models, three general categories cover most of the variations, and these are hard goods, information-based goods, and service-based offerings. Hard goods electronic retailers have evolved from 'bricks and mortar' retailers and from catalog retailers to provide a separate communications channel (and sometimes even a separate distribution channel) to reach and sell to its customer base. The website operates 24/7 so that customers can shop and obtain information on demand. Additionally, the site provides centralized storage for technical specifications and other information about products that may not be included in direct-mail catalogs, or information that most employees have not committed to memory. As employees, customers, and management becomes more comfortable with the website, they continue to include new applications, and consolidate all of their information in a central repository, including pricing, inventory, sales data, customer data, product data, and so on. Moreover, retail employees can direct customers to the website, and most catalogs generally have the company's Web address prominently displayed. For prospective customers, the site can be designed to provide information and encourage commerce either directly through the website or via other channels. For existing customers, information on product updates can be provided, usage and disposal information delivered, frequently asked questions (FAQs)—information for additional sales—presented, and interactive technical assistance provided.

Examples of information-based goods include software, reference materials, music publishers, magazine publishers, any other information-based product that can be reduced to digital '1s and 0s'. All of these product categories continue to migrate towards Internet-dominant distribution of the product as well as communication surrounding the product. The migration has been slowed by existing legal contracts, technology limitations, and slow-to-change consumer behavior. But as consumers become more comfortable with digitized information, broadband technology allows for faster transfer of large files, and new financial models overcome the status-quo business models, this entire area is rapidly moving towards its communications based around the products' websites. For example, the Britannica website hosts the information from the venerable *Encyclopaedia Britannica, Merriam-Webster's Dictionary, Britannica's World Atlas*, and access to *New York Times* news and information. Information for purchasing all of their products (including the print version *Encyclopaedia Britannica*) has also been consolidated on the site. The efficiencies for the information provider are huge, but so is the convenience for the user.

The third general category is that of traditional services, where the information and often the transaction has been consolidated onto the company's website. There are many service categories such as travel (rental cars, hotels, airlines) and financial services (brokerage houses). The key point is that as the website becomes more used by customers, it also becomes more of the central integrating place for the organization's communications. As an example in services, airline websites provide a centralized place for occasional and frequent flyers to find information, purchase tickets, check in, manage frequent-flyer mileage accounts, make itinerary adjustments, and find information about airports and flights. The airline also can provide information about special promotions designed to sell excess capacity for discounted prices.

SUMMARY OF IMC AND INTEGRATION OF COMMUNICATIONS AT THE WEBSITE

In each of the preceding examples, electronic information distribution, centered on the company's website, has become the dominant centralizing communications depository and delivery mechanism for the organization. The 'always on, 24/7' availability of the information, plus the ability to make continuous updates and changes to the information has placed a heavy burden on management to effectively manage the variety of communications that are to be delivered from the site. Further complicating the process is the fact that multiple individuals in the organization have a stake and interest in the website, thus making IMC difficult to deliver, but all the more a necessity. To extend Duncan and Moriarty's (1998) view that IMC is the integrating marketing function for the firm, it can further be proposed that in the world of electronic communications, the organization's website can become the 'integrator' for IMC. Thus, in the following section, I present a model for integrating communications from a website, including managerial action steps for implementing IMC in the integrated electronic marketspace.

Additionally, in each of the preceding examples, multiple messages from multiple sources within the organization, destined for multiple stake-holders (i.e. message receivers) have been integrated into a single gathering point. The answer to the question of whether this has occurred due to a specific strategy and well executed plan, or has arisen as a byproduct of trying to keep up with technology, is likely to vary depending on the organization. However, my research has revealed that the centralization of communications in an organization's website is more often than not completed on piecemeal basis, and coordination is completed 'after the fact.' As such, most organizations find it difficult to achieve their desired consistency across all their communications sources and thus receive the benefit from the mutual reinforcement of messages (Park and Zaltman 1987).

Regardless of the way the various communications have been pieced together in the organization's website, the motivation for using the organization's website as the integrating point for marketing communications is powerful. As Rayport and Sviokla argue, when offers move from the marketplace to the marketspace, they move from being product based to service based. From a communications' perspective, this has several implications. As a service, the cost to deliver a communication, once it has been created, becomes nearly zero. Using the university example described above, let us assume that the university creates a student recruitment brochure. It can be placed on the website in a PDF form that is available for on-demand download, with the print cost effectively transferred to the prospective student. From a convenience standpoint, the brochure is available whenever the prospective student wants the brochure. Also, the brochure can be ubiquitous; that is, it can be simultaneously available to anyone who can access the website.

IMPLEMENTING INTEGRATED IMC THROUGH THE ORGANIZATION'S WEBSITE: THE 7C'S FRAMEWORK

Assuming that one accepts the notions that (*a*) integration of communication messages from multiple functions within the organization should be an objective and priority for the organization, and (*b*) that the central point for this integration is a digital 'home' most often manifested as the organization's website, then an organizing framework for these messages needs to be available. The '7c's' framework, developed by Rayport and Jaworski (2002) offers such a structure. Based on the design elements of the customer interface, it encompasses the various decisions that must be made regarding how messages will be presented. The seven elements are: context, content, community, customization, communication, connection, and commerce. While these are examined individually below, the impact of IMC will depend on how well all of the 'C's' work together and reinforce each other.

Context

The website's *context* captures its overall look and feel. It includes the colors, graphics, and design features of the website. When designing a website to be the integrating place for IMC, the context is the first and foremost consideration. Rayport and Sviokla (1994) suggest that the context of the website is what captures the loyalty of the consumer. For example, in the competing world of sports information, the content may be similar (i.e. sports news, real-time scores, and sports commentary), but the context provides a place where the user can become comfortable with one format and develop a preference. For example, consider the differences between two sports information websites, ESPN.com and CBS Sportsline. Both sites deliver comprehensive sports reporting, the ESPN site has much more of an entertainment context, while CBS has a more traditional news format.

While organizations can attempt to differentiate on content, that is more easily copied than the context. Amazon.com has developed a context that has been imitated by many organizations that engage in online consumer commerce. Many Internet shoppers have become 'comfortable' with the search and commerce format developed by Amazon.com, and other firms are wise to create a context that also provides a familiar setting when engaging in consumer commerce.

Content

While context focuses on the website's design, *content* refers to what is presented on the website, whether it be text, audio, video, or graphics. The content represents all of the planned messages that the organization wants to deliver. The organization's website can become the centralized depository for all of the organization's planned messages to all of its stakeholders. As websites have developed and users have become more prone to utilize the Internet for their information searches, websites have included an increasingly greater array of content items. The cost to add an item is relatively inexpensive, and the cost to deliver an item to an interested stakeholder also is very low.

Community

The Internet has provided a new means for people to form *community*, and to provide a place for site users to interact is a key decision regarding an organization's website. A community exists because the users find ways to create value for one another. This value creation occurs outside the traditional exchange between the organization and its customers. In general, if there are good reasons that a site's users would want to interact, then it is a good idea to provide that opportunity through the website. Alternatively, there may not be a compelling reason to design community messaging as part of the communications plan for the website. For example, Frontgate.com, a catalog website that sells upscale household products that enhance a luxurious lifestyle for the homeowners, does not provide a place for users to interact. The content and context draw a specific target audience that has (or is aspiring to have) a luxurious lifestyle at home. It is unlikely that these users, even though similar in taste and aspiration, would have any desire or need to interact with other buyers of the product. There is little reason to do so, and providing such a place would feel out of place for such a site. . Thus, as an IMC consideration, Frontgate's lack of community is a consistent message in its own right. Alternatively, many other sites, the overall communications provided by the organization can be greatly enhanced by the customers who eagerly supplement the content provided by the organization, and whose comments are valuable to other website users. For example, at Ricksteves.com, a travel guide site, site users are interested in exchanging travel experiences. Similarly, users of technical products regularly provide user forums that enable consumers to discuss how to use a company's high tech products more efficiently (or how to overcome problems), as with mp3 player sites (Xclef, iRiver).

A user community can be potentially detrimental when community participants provide unplanned messages, such as posting negative reviews about the company's products or criticizing the company's environmental policies. An advocacy group would need to weigh the value of providing an open-access online community where those in opposition to the group could post messages that are in opposition to the organization.

Customization

Customization refers to the website's ability to tailor itself to individual users. Rayport and Jaworski (2002) differentiate between customization by the firm, called tailoring, and customization by the individual, called personalization. Some sites allow both. Amazon.com is a leader in site tailoring, having invested great resources to build algorithms that antici-pate an individual's desires. At the same time, the user can personalize the site, using the 'myAmazon' features. As part of the overall communications strategy, the centralization of all messages at the website allows the user to easily obtain those most useful and targeted messages through tailoring and/or personalization.

Communication

One of the key principles of IMC is the ability to engage in two-way communication with the customer. While nonpersonal marketing media (television, radio, print, direct mail) provide one-way communication (organization to customer), Internet technology provides channels for feedback and thus turn the one-way message on the website into a two-way communication. The ways that an individual can dialog with the site is termed *communication*. There are a variety of technologies that allow for communication, including instant messaging, asynchronous messages, Web chat, and so on. As described above, a key component of IMC is to engage in dialog with the customer; thus, multiple and innovative ways to promote dialog are encouraged by IMC.

Connection

Connection refers to the ways that a site can link to other sites, both to enter and exit the site. For example, many major retail commerce sites have affiliate programs where affiliates can direct their users to the site. The affiliate earns a percentage of the sale made through the users they bring to the retail site. An organization may also have reasons to provide links to other sites where its users may have an interest. From an IMC viewpoint, linking to and from other sites is an important consideration, not only because the decision to have the links creates messages, but the messages from the linked sites can have an impact on the organization's site as well.

Commerce

Commerce capabilities include the ways that the organization can actually engage in transactions with the site users. Along with having an easy means to navigate transactions, concerns about security are also crucial here. Site users must be convinced that the commerce capabilities are secure. The commerce element must also provide clear and accurate information about product availability, shipping time and costs, as well as total cost information.

In summary, those responsible for IMC delivered through the website can and should consider each of the 7c's elements individually and also should take care to review the consistency and fit of the elements as a whole.

PRACTICAL AND ETHICAL CONSIDERATIONS

I recently attended a presentation on a new web-site design and structure for the University of Colorado's business school. After the team had expertly presented their ideas that by all appearances had greatly impressed the audience, they moved to a component of the presentation that, at least for me, completely overshadowed the rest of their ideas. They described the use of the so-called 'Webalyzer,' a commercial tool (among many others) that provides ongoing analysis of utilization and analysis of the website. This tool showed the addresses of site visitors, which site they came from, how they navigated the site, which pages they visited, how long they stayed, what was not ever visited, and so on. I previously was aware that there was considerable information available about website utilization (such as hits, unique vs. repeat visitors, stickiness, and so on), but what surprised me was the ability to match this information with an individual.

In essence, every time someone visits a website, an individual record automatically gets made of that visit. This information can be generated even without the use of more controversial clandestine software, such as cookies or spyware, that are particularly useful for enhancing the personalization experience for repeat visitors. Information generated from basic website analysis tools provides the organization with a whole set of communications that the site visitor has unintentionally provided. Because this information is unintended and 'rides along' the intended communication pattern (getting to the website, browsing and utilizing the website capabilities, and leaving the website), I term this 'Remora communication,' which is named after the Remora fish that attaches to a host fish in a parasitic fashion.

From a practical consideration, the information gained through the use of basic Web analytics is crucial. First, where one has been before entering the website is valuable knowledge to the organization. This tells the organization both where the entry points are, and also where they are not. For example, a firm may spend resources to assure that they have a paid or organically developed high position on a search engine when certain search terms are used. The Web analytics can show the effectiveness of the commitment of these types of resources. Similarly, where the site visitors tend to be exiting is also important information. It may be to a link that was provided in the website, or it could be to a competitor's or a vertical channel member's site. For example, one may search for air travel through an online travel agency such as Travelocity or Orbitz, and then book the ticket directly with the airline. Web analytics would show the pattern of movement out from the agency site to the carrier site. Thus, the organization receives a set of communications from the visitor that likely were not intended by the visitor, but recorded nonetheless. These communications provide valuable market research information.

In addition to understanding where visitors enter and exit the site, the Web analytics provide a set of communications about where the visitors spend time at the website and how they move around the site. Such communications provide the organization with important information for increasing the effectiveness of the website. For example, observing patterns of how visitors get to certain pages may suggest that alternate, more direct routes need to be provided. Some pages may not be getting visited at all, and this may suggest that there are inadequate links to the page. Other pages may be 'termination' pages where visitors end their visit. When a page is not an intended termination page, then additional links from this page can be added. In summary, this unintended freeloaded communication provides the organization valuable information that will help the organization enhance the communication from the website.

From an ethical standpoint, the use of Web analytics continues to fuel the debate between the right of privacy and the utilization of Remora communication knowledge for marketing effectiveness. The key concern seems to arise when the knowledge—which can be examined at the individual level—becomes disaggregated to that level, so that a specific individual's movements are being examined. No one complains when an organization examines aggregate percentages where visitors come from when they reach the site (e.g. from a major search engine such as Google, or from an ISP), or where they go once they leave the site. But when an individual can be tracked, this raises legitimate privacy concerns. For example, when the user is an employee, the organization can trace exiting the website to other sites that may not be business related. While the likelihood of this occurring without prior reason to examine an individual's behavior is small, the ability to do this is disconcerting.

Because Web analytics can be so valuable in making the overall website communicate more effectively, it is important that an organization address the use of Web analytics as part of their stated privacy policy. Privacy policies are now being included in almost every organization's website today. While the content of the privacy policy is important (although few individuals ever take the time to read these), the policy itself is a communication from the organization, and thus must be considered as part of the total IMC. It must have the same elements as any other communication that is to be integrated, including consistency in its look and feel with the other elements, interactivity, and so on. Similarly, an organization can use its website to disseminate privacy information regarding use of customer data that is acquired through other means (such as purchase records, inquiries, etc). Such concerns have been overshadowed by privacy issues surrounding the Internet, but issues regarding the use of customer information for direct mail and telemarketing still exist.

CONCLUSION: THE FUTURE OF COMMUNICATIONS IN AN e-COMMERCE WORLD

The basic premise of this chapter has been that the intersection of the concepts of marketspace and IMC have provided an incredible opportunity to integrate communications in the marketspace, and that the integrating place is currently the organization's website. To adapt the website to become the central depository of the organization's marketing communications requires considerable restructuring of the communications function in the organization, but one that can be carried out through cross-functional communications teams. However, such teams must include those involved with managing and implementing new high technology in the organization, and these should also include consultation with intended audience members.

As a final caveat, even when an organization focuses on providing a website from an IMC perspective, it should not assume that by simply getting a website properly organized that it can be left alone. After all, what the world of technology has given in terms of Internet technology, it will likely also take away. While the website will continue to be the fundamental central point for integrating communications for the foreseeable future, the distribution of communications will continue to change rapidly. From a linear communications model view, the notions of the 'receiver' and 'noise' must be kept in mind. For example, websites are designed for distribution to computer monitor screens that vary in size, but are all within a basic range of sizes. Mobility of technology makes the transport of receiving devices a crucial concern. Even a small laptop computer can be a burden, and wireless telephone sets and PDAs are often becoming the receiving points for Internet delivered communications. The way that an organization delivers its communications in an integrated fashion to smaller interfaces will become a crucial competency in the rapidly approaching future.

REFERENCES

Duncan, T. and Moriarty, S.E. (1997). *Driving Brand Value: Using Integrated Marketing to Drive Stakeholder Relationships*. New York: McGraw-Hill.

—— —— (1998). 'A Communication-Based Marketing Model for Managing Relationships,' *Journal of Marketing*, 62, 1–13.

Humby, C., Hunt, T., and Phillips, T. (2003). *Scoring Points: How Tesco is Winning Customer Loyalty*. London, UK: Kogan Page.

Lasswell, H. D. (1948). 'The Structure and Function of Communication in a Society,' in L. Bryson (ed.), *The Communication of Ideas*. New York: Harper, pp. 37–51.

Park, C. W. and Zaltman, G. (1987). *Marketing Management*. Chicago: Dryden Press.

Rayport, J. F. and Sviokla, J.J. (1994). 'Managing in the Marketspace,' *Harvard Business Review* (November–December), 141–50.

Rayport, J. F. and Jaworski, B.J. (2002). *Introduction to E-commerce*. New York: McGraw-Hill.

Schultz, D., Tannenbaum, S., and Lauterborn, R. (1993). *Integrated Marketing Communications*. New York: Harper & Row.

10

Word of Mouth: The Oldest, Newest Marketing Medium

George R. Silverman

The purpose of this chapter is to identify word of mouth in its various forms, explain why it has such a seemingly disproportionate effect on buying behavior, show why it should be approached proactively as a medium—instead of a serendipitous byproduct of other marketing efforts—and outline a way to think about this very different medium. This chapter describes the conditions and steps necessary for contemporary marketers to harness the power of word of mouth.

DEFINING WORD OF MOUTH

There can be no doubt that the first marketing medium was word of mouth (WOM). By 'word of mouth,' I mean positive or negative communication of products, services, and ideas via personal communication of people who have no commercial vested interest in making that recommendation. It typically takes place among friends, acquaintances, experts, and trusted advisers, although it often occurs among strangers. In fact, WOM paradoxically must have predated speech. Even animals engage in a primitive kind of 'word of mouth' when they demonstrate behaviors for their children and other animals to copy. When a famous basketball star wears a pair of Nike sneakers, he is doing the same thing: recommending nonverbally that the product he is using is the best. Otherwise, most people would think, why would a pro like him use it? I call this 'implied word of mouth.'

Although many authors define WOM narrowly to mean spoken, face-to-face recommendation (Cafferky 1995; Wilson 1994), it is more useful in these modern times to include all forms of communication, in all media, and then make the necessary distinctions when there are differences that really make a difference. WOM may be transmitted via personal face-to-face talk, but also via e-mail, telephone, or any other communication medium. What distinguishes it from other forms of communication is the fact that the communicator has little or no commercial vested interest in the market offering that is the focus of the exchange. Lines can get somewhat blurry, as when the message transmitter obviously benefits from recommending a product, service, or idea, but does not belong to or is not paid by the entity being recommended. Thus, if someone recommends a political candidate, that would correctly be described as WOM. But if they work for a political campaign, that would constitute a sales call.

There are varying degrees of WOM. For instance, I may be part of someone's affiliate program and recommend his or her product on my website. While I may have a small vested interest, it is still WOM communication albeit somewhat suspect, because presumably I would not have put the recommendation on my website unless I was positive toward the product. The commission made by the affiliate program is simply an extra added incentive for me to include something on my website. The reason this is important, as I will explore in greater detail in this chapter, is that the relative independence of WOM is a source of much of its power.

THE POWER OF WORD OF MOUTH

Let me make what might first appear to be a reckless assertion: WOM is more powerful than all of the other marketing methods in this book *put together*. There is currently no scientific, quantitative evidence to back up this claim; rather, the basis of my belief is linked to qualitative, anecdotal support and common sense. Each day, the average consumer is exposed to between several hundred and several thousand commercial communications. The average American, for instance, watches several hours of television per day. The reading of magazines, surfing the Internet, and shopping at a mall will expose people to a minimum of several hundred commercial communications. Nonetheless, people rarely act on these commercial communications. In fact, people are typically exposed to several thousand commercial communications before they take a significant action. Contrast this with WOM. If a friend strongly recommends a movie, book, or other product, there is a much greater likelihood that the recipient will quickly respond to the recommendation.

Further, it is clear that WOM will often override marketing campaigns. When a product gets a bad reputation, it is extremely rare for marketing to reverse the impact of negative WOM. When critics pan a movie, it typically dies. However, this is not always the case because WOM from critics trumps advertising, and WOM from friends trumps WOM from critics. In essence there is a hierarchy of effectiveness among WOM sources.

The important thing to remember is that WOM is many times more powerful than any other kind of conventional marketing. The implications of this are profound. It is important that the marketing professional understands this not only at an intellectual level, but also obtains a visceral feel for the extraordinary power of WOM. For instance, it is more important to cultivate a small number of respected industry experts and see to it that their recommendations are spread, than to have thousands of salespeople running around largely being doubted, if not ignored. It is more important for your product to obtain a favorable review in a print publication than to put numerous advertisements in that publication.

WOM is the nuclear power of marketing. Just as nuclear power is measured in kilotons of conventional explosives, WOM is measured in kilounits of conventional marketing. Anyone who goes up against competitors who do not understand this will have an overwhelming advantage, no matter how large their competitors are. The David who knows how to control word of mouth will win against legions of Goliaths.

Conventional Marketing is Dying, Long Live Marketing

In order to achieve some perspective, it seems safe to assume that ancient WOM must have developed into salesmanship. In fact, it is not a great leap to go from someone enthusiastically recommending a product to rewarding them for recommending the product. As various media became widely accepted, opportunities for the insertion of paid messages arose. Paid messages also started showing up on almost any surface that they could be inserted on, including matchbook covers, hot-air balloons, and even skywriting. Some advertising became long and complex, as is the case with televised infomercials (the typically half-hour paid promotional programs that have an information format, but an obvious sales objective). Others became simple, such as Internet banner ads. But what is common to all the methods is that they are paid intrusions into consumers' daily lives. In fact, advertising professionals use the word 'intrusiveness' to describe the degree to which a message can overcome its surrounding materials and call attention to itself.

There is no disputing the fact that advertising and personal selling can be effective. There also is no disputing the fact that as media have become more pervasive and people are increasingly overloaded and overwhelmed by marketing messages, the effectiveness of conventional advertising and sales is dropping dramatically. Conventional marketing is information-based, so it *contributes to the overload*. That is why it is so often intentionally ignored or filtered out with the assistance of Internet ad blockers, video recorder skip buttons, 'do-not-call lists,' and other screening methods. In general, people do not want more formal marketing information, they want communications that cut through and simplify information and help them apply the information that is useful to them. WOM is rapidly taking the place of commercial marketing communication by satisfying these needs. In the words of dentist Paddi Lund, 'Even those deaf to the bragging cries of the marketplace will listen to a friend' (Lund 2000).

EXPLAINING THE EFFECTIVENESS OF WORD OF MOUTH

The reasons why WOM is so effective may seem obvious, but in fact there is more than meets the eye. A primary explanation for the effectiveness of WOM is that it *gets through* to the intended recipient more dramatically than commercial communications. WOM recommendations are made in the ordinary course of conversations without being intrusive. If that were the only reason for its superior effectiveness, it would be enough for it to be multiple times more powerful than alternatives.

Another obvious reason for the power of WOM is that it is more *credible* than commercial communications (Katz and Lazarsfeld 1964; Rogers 1995). WOM comes from objective sources independent of the manufacturer or seller. People who have no vested interest in the outcome of a communication are less likely to omit, distort, misrepresent, and exaggerate. In other words, they are more likely to tell the truth.

But there is another less obvious reason why WOM is so powerful, and which I believe suggests the source of most of its power. WOM is the best *experience delivery mechanism*. In order for people to adopt a product, they need some experience with it. They need to try it, and they may need a longer-term experience as well. There are only two ways to get experience: directly and indirectly. Initial, direct experience with a product is called 'product trial.' But product trial is often a risky, time-consuming, and expensive way to get to know new products. The trial takes place at a level of proficiency well below that of the regular user. Thus, it often is not the best way to test whether a product is applicable in a particular situation. People tend to realize this, if only on a subconscious level. It is usually much better from the consumer's perspective to try a product vicariously. By observing and hearing about other people's experiences, prospects can often better predict how a product will work out in the real world. In fact, most people will not buy a product without trying it, a fact that is particularly true as the involvement level and expense of the product increases. WOM is the way this experience is delivered quickly and efficiently. It dramatically accelerates the trial phase of the decision process, which is usually the most time-consuming phase. It not only gives people the favorable (or unfavorable) experience of a product that they need in order to make a decision and perhaps move forward, it accelerates that moving forward. In my own professional consultancy experience, I have seen many situations in which a typical several-year adoption process is reduced to just a few days or weeks by the use of teleconferences in which prospects could question users.

Experts vs. Peers

There are basically two sources of WOM: experts and peers. It is very important to understand the function of each. Experts usually tell people about the positive potential of a product or service. Experts are more skilled and have more controlled environments than typical people. For instance, when a medical expert talks about how well a drug performs, that person is usually talking about the controlled environment in a major medical center.

By contrast, peers tell people how things work in everyday experience. As a result, it is sometimes more persuasive to hear from a peer—even a less skilled or less knowledgeable peer—than from an expert. With a peer, the feeling is, 'That person is like me, so if that person can do it or is satisfied with the product, then I can certainly do it or certainly will be satisfied as well.'

HOW TO HARNESS WORD OF MOUTH

In order to get people to talk about your market offerings favorably and in large numbers, the most important thing to remember is that people do not talk about the ordinary, mundane, and boring, unless they are talking about themselves. People tend to talk about the things that they have a considerable amount of energy and emotion for. In short, they will talk about the mundane when they talk about themselves, but not when they talk about other people's products.

The first thing that one has to establish in order to launch a successful WOM campaign is that one has a product that is in some way extraordinary, amazing, unusual, outrageous, or remarkable. It does not have to be better than its competition in a quality sense. In fact, WOM winners rarely win on the quality dimension. That is because even dramatic quality improvements tend to be on the 10 percent to 30 percent level, which typically is not enough to generate positive WOM. Quality in this range is rarely recognized or fully appreciated; that is, one cannot expect to be only a little better and expect everyone to be talking about you. For instance, new drugs are continually being introduced that are marginally better than their competition. Often, physicians regard them as marketing ploys and 'me too' products, and fail to adopt.

It is much more important to be different than to be better. People will not talk about you unless the usual reaction to your product is 'wow,' 'cool,' 'awesome.' A product has to be obviously and dramatically different in a way that gets people to sit up and take notice. There are numerous ways to stand out in the marketplace. The key is to stand out in a way that creates an obvious difference, which is significantly beneficial to the customer, between you and everyone else.

Some of these are surprising ways that logic does not suggest will be effective. Some keys to differentiation have to do with fun, style, and quirkiness. For instance, the reincarnated Volkswagen Beetle looked like a ridiculous idea from a logical standpoint; however, it was just different, quirky (with a built-in bud vase!), and fun enough to attract a certain type of car buyer despite turning off many others. This reflects the reason why so few products are chatworthy. In the course of their development, the committees that have to approve them invariably have members who are tremendously turned off or who quite correctly anticipate that large segments of the marketplace will be alienated. In a reasonable attempt to satisfy these concerns, the product idea is dropped or else its unusual and idiosyncratic nature is toned down. As a result, the marketplace ends up with products that are bland, unimaginative, and boring—products that people do not want to talk about. Idiosyncrasies and other unique characteristics are typically viewed as deviant and deviant is usually viewed as bad. We have been taught that calling attention to ourselves and our products is ego-centered and self-aggrandizing.

So, marketing professionals must get over these tendencies to be 'normal.' They need to realize that most people's lives are filled with mind-numbing sameness, repetition, and blandness. It doesn't take a lot to create things that pleasantly surprise people or to do this continuously, at every turn, and in every way. Apple computer is a wonderful example of this approach. People often have an amazingly strong reaction to the little things and are totally blown away by the big things. These points also hold for products that are not easily changed, such as drugs, medical devices, or other products that are regulated by government edict or something else that has to be standardized. In such cases, there is still a great deal of room for unique innovation in packaging, delivery, service, or other product augmentations that are unexpected and thrilling for their intended target markets.

WORD OF MOUTH AS A MODERN MARKETING MEDIUM

Assume that one has a product that is well differentiated in an obviously beneficial way, so much so that it is outstanding and chatworthy. At one time, even as recently as the 1990s, this is where many marketing managers would stop. A pervasive advertising campaign would have been initiated, highlighting the product's unusual differences in a dramatic way and with the hope that, perhaps as a serendipitous byproduct, people would start talking about it. Instead, an attempt may have been made to get the company's salespeople to go out and sell the product.

These days, even when such an approach works, it works through an intermediary force. People usually do not buy things directly anymore. They check things out with friends, colleagues, and trusted advisors, or they read what people are saying on the Internet. In other words, in this digital age of instantaneous and pervasive communication, there is now almost always a WOM process that goes on between initial interest and purchase. It is just so easy to discuss things first with a knowledgeable friend or colleague, send someone an e-mail, or do a quick Internet search, that people almost always 'check things out' first before making a product purchase decision.

From a marketing perspective, the trick is to have things in place so that prospective customers get the right information that is favorable to your company's offerings, exactly addressing the issues that are key purchase decision barriers. It is important to get satisfied customers participating in websites, to cultivate experts so that they have the right information, and so on. The challenge here is to determine how and where people are going to check out one's product offerings and then to make sure you have the best products and that those places where consumers are most likely to consult have the right information and favorable opinions.

This approach requires a different mentality on the part of marketing managers. If marketers approach prospective customers with a sales persuasion mentality, customers may end up resisting the effort because they feel manipulated. Instead, they must be approached with a collaborative, collegial helpfulness and a demonstrable willingness to tell the full truth. In more cases than not, conventional marketers tend not to employ such a mentality.

To this point, I have focused only on the WOM that takes place when people have found out about and are checking a company and its offerings. Although this is reactive, the new marketplace allows for a much more proactive approach to WOM. In fact, it requires a paradigm shift. Instead of thinking about WOM as a serendipitous byproduct of good marketing, WOM should now be thought of as 'media' in and of itself. Rather than thinking of WOM as an uncontrollable force in the marketplace, we need to realize that it is much more controllable than marketers previously may have thought. In other words, one can cause WOM to happen in a coordinated campaign, even if its results are fairly unpredictable, like other media.

CONSTRUCTING A WORD-OF-MOUTH CAMPAIGN

Before outlining the steps involved in developing a successful WOM campaign, it is essential to assume that one has an outstandingly differentiated product. If not, there is simply no way to get people to talk about you positively with great frequency. Traditionally, in order to determine the media through which to communicate the product, one must determine which medium will reach the largest number of qualified prospects in the most persuasive and cost-efficient way. The same criteria apply with WOM except that the message will be transmitted through live people who are not in the company's employ. Obviously, marketers will want to approach people who will reach the maximum number of other people, in the most credible way. Such people are called by various terms: mavens, gurus, network hubs, sneezers (Godin and Gladwell 2001), evangelists (McConnell 2002), and influentials. I prefer to call them 'leveraged influencers.' As previously described, they may be peers or experts. The important point here is that in most situations the aim is not to get people talking with one or two other people; rather, the aim is to get people to talk to the largest number of other people possible. For instance, if twenty-five people communicate with twenty-five other people (in face-to-face contact, by telephone or e-mail, and so on) this only has to be repeated six times to reach the entire population of the USA or seven times to reach the entire population of the world. Not that this would happen, but it is rather dramatic to realize that it does not take many repetitions for an explosive spread of information.

Contrary to much popular writing on the subject (e.g. Cafferky 1995; Gladwell 2002; Godin and Gladwell 2001), I believe that ideas do not spread like viruses. Viruses tend to spread with relatively low rates of contact, though pervasive contact, in a slow but very steady manner. Ideas tend to spread explosively, in a chain reaction that is more like a nuclear explosion, rather than the slow and relentless spreading of something that requires an incubation period. Either one gets the job done, but the explosion model obviously gets it done faster. Nevertheless, WOM sometimes does spread slowly. But in such cases, the slow spread reflects the likelihood that the idea is not exciting enough for it to keep going, and it usually fizzles once it gets beyond the initial enthusiasts. Successful WOM has the characteristic that no one has heard of the product, and then suddenly, often within hours or days, everyone seems to be talking about it.

The next two considerations involve (*a*) how it is possible to find the right people, the leveraged influencers, and (*b*) how it is possible to motivate them to talk about your product. Because they are not in the company's employ, you must somehow motivate the influencers to talk about the product(s). There are basically two key ways to accomplish this task: directly or through 'embedded talk.'

When people are talking about a product directly, they are doing so because the product is so unusual that they want to share that information with others. By contrast, embedded talk is where people talk about a company's offerings as part of something else that is interesting. For instance, even if the product is not wildly different, it may be marginally better, or more reliable, or more available, or has some other edge over current offerings. People might talk about it embedded into the context of some other useful information. As a rather mundane and common example, consider the following: Let's say you have an excellent olive oil. It is high quality and offered at a good value. But it cannot be claimed to be the best, and even if it were, most people cannot really tell the difference between a very good brand and the best one in such a product category. So what are you to do? You can get people talking about you directly, perhaps by charging three times more than any other, or putting it in a very fancy package, thereby capturing the part of the market who want to get only outrageously scarce and expensive products, so that they can brag, or feel special, or celebrate the fact that they have earned the right to this kind of extravagance. Such an approach would constitute direct WOM.

Now let us consider the olive oil example from the perspective of embedded talk. For example, you can embed the brand recommendation into a terrific recipe for salad dressing or a whole family of heart-healthy gourmet recipes that people will pass around to each other, or they will buy the bottle because you have a little recipe book hanging from it that has great-looking recipes. In each recipe you put a little asterisk and explain at the bottom that olive oils vary wildly in quality, consistency, and price. You can add that the recipe will be ruined by an inferior olive oil, which is the major taste ingredient. You have been named 'most consistently excellent and best value' by three famous Italian chefs and a famous Italian cooking institute. By taking such an approach, you will have embedded your good product into an excellent context, one that people will pass around, even if your product in itself is not chatworthy.

This approach has been used for many pharmaceutical products, which are not in and of themselves dramatically superior. They are recommended, in company-sponsored seminars, for instance, as part of a medication regimen explained by a well-respected expert who asserted that this is the drug he or she is comfortable with, that it's a brand name that will not be substituted for in the pharmacy, that this is the drug whose efficacy is supported by research studies, and so on. If it is a three-drug regimen, with three different drug classes, each having 10 choices, you have 1000 combinations, not counting dosage variations. It is infinitely easier to just go with what the expert recommends, in the order recommended.

As another example, in the early 1970s, I developed the telephone focus group, a marketing research tool that is in many ways superior to face-to-face groups, because people feel safer and open up more. At first, I tried to sell their superiority, but such claims went contrary to common sense. After all, it is easier to read people who you can see, and potential clients thought that participants were being as open as they could be in traditional face-to-face groups. So, my claims were rejected. I then started writing articles in business newsletters and similar outlets about how to research hard-to-get people (such as experts, mavens, and other types of leveraged influencers), as well as people up the distribution chain (such as dealers, distributors, and professional buyers). I clarified how to get to deeper psychological levels in focus groups and also described some research designs that can really only be effectively utilized with telephone groups.

These articles were passed around among researchers in agencies and companies with high-level, difficult-to-reach customers, such as pharmaceutical firms. The articles created a strong demand without ever convincing people that telephone focus groups were better in any traditional sense. In fact, many initial customers were convinced that the telephone was an *inferior* way to get people into groups, but when it was the, *only* way, they were willing to try it. Because the articles were noncommercial and contained useful tips, suggestions, and methods, people were eager to pass them along, or even reprint them in other publications, until they would eventually reach someone who wanted to run groups consisting of, for instance, the heads of the leading alcoholism clinics in major cities, or the heads of ophthalmology in the major medical centers. These first users likely did not realize that they were the recipients of a very deliberate WOM campaign—one that, as it turns out, did not even focus on the superiority of a product, but on the usefulness of doing something that was not being done before, even if suboptimally. Once they obtained direct experience and heard how interactive and open the groups were, they became evangelists who had to get their colleagues to try the method. (Some of these articles can be found reprinted on *www.mnav.com*.)

Another example of embedded talk was circulating around the Internet via e-mail at the time of this writing. The content of the message was written by author Joey Green in his best-selling book, *Polish Your Furniture with Panty Hose*. It involves a product called Bounce, which is a sheet of fabric softener that goes into a clothes dryer:

- *Repel mosquitoes.* Tie a sheet of Bounce through a belt loop when outdoors during mosquito season.

- *Eliminate static electricity from your television screen.* Since Bounce is designed to help eliminate static cling, wipe your television screen with a used sheet of Bounce to keep dust from resettling.
- *Dissolve soap scum from shower doors.* Clean with a used sheet of Bounce.
- *Freshen the air in your home.* Place an individual sheet of Bounce in a drawer or hang one in the closet.
- *Prevent thread from tangling.* Run a threaded needle through a sheet of Bounce to eliminate the static cling on the thread before sewing.
- *Eliminate static cling from pantyhose.* Rub a damp, used sheet of Bounce over the hose.
- *Prevent musty suitcases.* Place an individual sheet of Bounce inside empty luggage before storing.
- *Freshen the air in your car.* Place a sheet of Bounce under the front seat.
- *Clean baked-on food from a cooking pan.* Put a sheet in the pan, fill with water, let sit overnight, and sponge clean. The antistatic agents apparently weaken the bond between the food and the pan while the fabric softening agents soften the baked-on food.
- *Eliminate odors in wastebaskets.* Place a sheet of Bounce at the bottom of the wastebasket.
- *Collect cat hair.* Rubbing the area with a sheet of Bounce will magnetically attract all the loose hairs.
- *Eliminate static electricity from venetian blinds.* Wipe the blinds with a sheet of Bounce to prevent dust from resettling.
- *Wipe up sawdust from drilling or sandpapering.* A used sheet of Bounce will collect sawdust like a tack cloth.
- *Eliminate odors in dirty laundry.* Place an individual sheet of Bounce at the bottom of a laundry bag or hamper.
- *Deodorize shoes or sneakers.* Place a sheet of Bounce in your shoes or sneakers overnight so they'll smell great in the morning. (Copyright © 1995 by Joey Green, www.wackyuses.com. Reprinted with permission.)

Such a message on the Internet gets people talking about Bounce, increases product awareness and 'buzz,' and even gets Bounce mentioned in marketing books.

The Identification, Care and Nurturing of Leveraged Influencers

In order to identify and locate leveraged influencers (often called 'evangelists,' which implies an extreme level of enthusiasm that is not always necessary), the most straightforward approach is simply to ask people to play that role. If you want the most influential endocrinologists or clinicians, for instance, to spread the word about a product, you could ask internists who they would most want to consult with if they had a difficult patient or if there were a new drug that they were not sure how to use. Alternatively, you could ask them who they would send a loved one to for treatment. If you want to know which women in each city or community influence the most other women in choice of hair care, you have to do a wider sociological study of the personal influence network in the area. This can be costly, but very effective, and it would usually involve written or telephone surveys. There are increasing efforts to identify and enlist teenagers, trendy drinkers, fashion mavens, gadget nerds, and the like into networks of people who can influence others. These people can be so leveraged that it pays to give them all kinds of free products to influence their opinions and to give them things to demonstrate to their friends. Once identified, you have to cater to them and enlist their aid, for example, in product development—in a word, involve them.

It is critical to supply leveraged influencers with valuable materials to give to their friends or colleagues, including tools such as electronic presentations, talking points summaries where they insert their personal experiences, useful how-to articles, and special reports. In other words, it should not be assumed that they will have the words with which to spread the word. To them, a product can be seen as a tool, a gift, a happening, a way of reinforcing their expertise, and a fun interlude in a routine stretch of repetitive activity. Help them look good to their colleagues and friends and you will have an important collaborator over the long term. Microsoft is a master of this technique: For everyone of their important products, they provide information managers with presentations and other materials that help justify the upgrade expenses to their often less technologically comfortable bosses. Once management realizes that WOM is a medium that can be influenced directly and treated proactively, a whole new world opens up.

Leveraged influencers and evangelists are easy to identify. Their names can be captured from their positive communications with a company, from feedback forms, and from comments to salespeople. If necessary, survey teams can be sent out to the places where the mavens hang out. This can be expensive, but well worth the effort.

WHY WORD-OF-MOUTH MARKETING REQUIRES A DIFFERENT WAY OF THINKING

The contemporary world involves a whole new approach to marketing. Instead of thinking about marketing as something that is done *to* the customer, we must now think about marketing as something that is done *for* the customer. A central role of contemporary marketing is to help people buy and to help them move forward in their decision process, rather than to push products at them. Imagine what would happen if companies did not engage in marketing. People would find out about market offerings much more slowly, if at all. This would deny them the benefits of products and services that could satisfy their needs. In essence, companies are doing consumers a *service* by marketing and a disservice by not marketing. In this light, it is essential that marketers engage in real interactive marketing, instead of the superficial customer response mechanisms that they have been calling interactive marketing. Giving people a comment form on a website is not interactive marketing. Marketers must engage people in their relationship through people they already have relationships with, including friends, colleagues, family members, neighbors, and trusted advisors. This can be accomplished by implementing the following steps:

1. Differentiate your product in a meaningful way that people want to talk about, or embed your product in something they want.
2. Determine where your customers are in the adoption cycle and what kind of adopter types they are. For instance, they may be early adopters in the trial phase of the decision process. (Rogers 1995; Moore 1999, 2002)
3. Determine specifically what customers need to hear from their friends, colleagues, and trusted advisors, particularly the things that they will not believe when they hear it from marketers. Use the Decision Matrix™ (see below) to figure out exactly what the various adopter types need to hear in the various stages of the decision process.
4. Identify, design, and create the sources and delivery mechanisms of WOM that will be most persuasive and motivating. These can be everything from expert endorsements, public relations media coverage, WOM incentive programs, expert round tables, speaker programs, teleconference seminars, testimonials on Web pages, and other methods for delivering WOM proactively.

THE DECISION MATRIX

The idea behind the decision matrix (see Table 10.1) is to move customers to the next stages of the decision process, using the messages below in the right order, from the right sources. For example, if early adopters are to be targeted, read across the early adopter row in order to determine the best approach for generating WOM (see Silverman 2001, for greater detail).

Table 10.1. The decision matrix (what the customer wants to hear in nonitalicized type; examples in italics)

Adopter category (from earliest to latest adopters)	Deciding to decide	Weighing information	Trial	Implementing	Expanding commitment
Innovator: wants to be outstanding	Wants to hear how 'far out' the product is.	There is little information to gather. Customer will have to investigate the product first hand.	Wants to be among the first to try.	Wants to be the pioneer who will lead the way for other people.	Wants to push the envelope to the limits.
	It's so new and unusual, no one's even heard of it or tried it. It works on a totally new principle. Most people wouldn't even understand it.	*It's so far out that there is nothing to compare it to. It's in a different class.*	*It is so new that no one has tried it yet. You would be the first.*	*Now that you've tried it successfully, you can help others learn about it.*	*Have you tried the wild new things it might be used for?*
Early adopter: driven by excellence	Concerned more about possibilities than actualities.	Looking not as much for 'hard' information than for a vision of what might be.	Does not care that it has not been used in one's situation, just that it may be applicable.	Knows there will be problems, wants to know what they are and how they can be handled.	Wants a major advantage for being at the beginning of the curve.
	Think of the possibilities. If this product really worked in your situation, it would change your life or give you a competitive edge.	*Here's how I envision using the product. The other products are more ordinary. This one has possibilities.*	*This product doesn't work all the time. But when it does, wow!*	*Here is how to get the most out of it and minimize the problems.*	*Here are the additional possibilities that will give you a competitive edge.*
Middle majority (in the marketing literature, this is usually referred to as 'early majority'): wants to be competent	Concerned with practicalities.	Wants comparisons about how it is working out in situations similar to one's own.	Wants to verify that it will work in one's situation without investing too much time and trouble.	Wants to know that there is an easy way out if it does not work out.	Wants to know usage is getting pretty standard.

	This has been tried and really works in situations like yours, in your industry, etc.	*Here is the practical information about how this is working out in the real world.*	*The bugs have been worked out and it is highly predictable.*	*Training, support, and guarantees are in place and reliable.*	*It is rapidly becoming the standard in our industry.*
Late adopter (in the marketing literature, this adopter category is usually referred to as 'late majority'): wants to reduce risk	Promise a good deal on a tried and true product.	Wants to 'shop around' and get the proven product with the best deal.	Trial tends not for product excellence but centers on the support system.	Wants complete support for rolling out full usage of the product.	Wants to use what everyone else is using, in the way that they are using it.
	It has become virtually a commodity and this product can get you better price, delivery, service, training, etc.	I've checked out the pricing, service, etc., and it seems to be the best product.	Check out how wonderful they are to deal with, everyone can fix your problems, etc.	They'll come in and do it all for you.	Everybody is using it for everything.
Laggard: wants to be completely safe	Wants reassurance that it is a safe product where nothing will go wrong.	Wants to find the loopholes, problems, negatives, etc. If none are found, will keep looking.	Basically will not try anything new. Needs reassurance that the product is the standard product used in one's situation, etc.	Implements only when one has to.	Wants reassurance that one is using it in the standard way.
	You'll get in trouble if you aren't using this.	Here are the risks and how to render them harmless.	Try it, everyone else has and likes it.	Adopt this product, or else.	That's the way we all use it.

CONCLUSION: CHALLENGES FOR THE TWENTY-FIRST CENTURY

We are now at the beginning of an information revolution. This means that exponentially increasing numbers of people in the industrialized world have instant access to almost any kind of information they want. Marketers no longer control the information flow and so it is more difficult than ever before for them to influence consumers by omission, distortion, hyperbole, or any of the other 'persuasive' techniques that have been used in the past. Product disadvantages are quickly known. For many professionals, business people, and consumers, it is possible to learn about customers' experiences with products simply by consulting a relevant Internet site. At the same time that people have instant access to almost any information they want, they are increasingly encountering information overload. One of the basic ways they can cut through this information overload is to rely on experts, rating services, and other variants of WOM.

It is interesting to point out that in an age of overload, people have a different set of standards. Truth is no longer of paramount importance for many customers—relevance is. It does not matter if I overwhelm you with fifty scientific studies showing that my product is better; you probably want only two or three useful tips from experts that you can use today. The increase in information overload in the contemporary marketing context is presenting marketers with different challenges than those faced in the past, when the key was to find ways to cut through the marketing noise. In the past, there was a cacophony of competing messages and the challenge was to stand out from that distracting *static*. Now, the challenge is that there is too much *signal* (potentially useful information), not too much noise. This is a much more serious problem because so much of the signal seems to be valuable, but the information often is conflicting, distracting, or difficult to evaluate and apply. A serious challenge for marketers is how to provide genuinely useful information that consumers will pay attention to and which will offer them guidance instead of confusion.

The most difficult challenge of all is how to assess both the quantity and quality of WOM that is going on at any given time and to assess the WOM that originates from different strategies and delivery mechanisms. It is not possible to simply measure the effects on people who have been exposed to WOM efforts compared with people who have not, because the very point of WOM is that people talk to other people, and the second order of WOM effects can be even more powerful as the circles of influence expand. Thus, because the whole point of a WOM marketing campaign is to contaminate the control group, exact measurement is likely to be impossible. As of the time of this writing, I am unaware of any research design for measuring WOM that can withstand careful scientific scrutiny. A huge amount of measurement is being attempted with invalid designs because the people doing the measurement do not take into account the contamination of the control group Achilles heel.

WOM is by far the most powerful force in the marketplace. Like Galileo, we must make a paradigm shift and realize that WOM is the sun, the center of a marketing solar system, not some outlying planet. It shines thousands of times more brightly than anything else. These days, it is the source of much marketing effectiveness, either directly or in its reflection. It can be harnessed proactively by setting up mechanisms to use its power. In fact, in the future, nearly everything in marketing may be designed in terms of the potential impact on WOM.

REFERENCES

Cafferky, W. E. (1995). *Let your Customers do the Talking: 301+ Word-Of-Mouth Marketing Tactics Guaranteed to Boost Profits.* Chicago, IL: Upstart Publishing Company.

Gladwell, M. (2002). *The Tipping Point: How Little Things can Make a Big Difference.* New York: Little, Brown.

Godin, S. and Gladwell, M. (2001). *Unleashing the Ideavirus.* New York: Hyperion.

Katz, E. and Lazarsfeld, P. (1964) *Personal Influence: The Part Played by People in the Flow of Mass Communications.* New York: Free Press.

Lund, P. (2000). *Building the Happiness Centred Business.* Capalaba, Queensland, Australia: Solutions Press.

McConnell, B. (2002). *Creating Customer Evangelists: How Loyal Customers Become a Volunteer Sales Force.* Chicago, IL: Dearborn Trade.

Moore, G. A. (1999). *Inside the Tornado: Marketing Strategies from Silicon Valley's Cutting Edge.* New York: HarperBusiness.

Moore, G. A. (2002). *Crossing the Chasm.* New York: HarperBusiness.

Rogers, E. M. (1995). *Diffusion of Innovations.* New York: Free Press.

Silverman, G. (2001). *The Secrets of Word-Of-Mouth Marketing: How to Trigger Exponential Sales Through Runaway Word Of Mouth.* New York: AMACOM.

Wilson, J. (1994). *Word-of-Mouth Marketing.* Wiley: New York.

III

RETHINKING MARKETING COMMUNICATION STYLES

In recent years, a growing chorus of critics has lamented the fact that despite changes in consumers, companies, societies, and technologies, the language and ideology of marketing to a great extent has remained rooted in an increasingly dated marketing concept, which focuses on the satisfaction of consumer needs through the creation and exchange of products and value. In the realm of marketing communications, researchers have gained great insight into how consumer targets 'read' the words and images they encounter in marketing message and have long understood that the nature of the message style results in differential responding from recipients. This recognition was perhaps most clearly pointed out by the communications guru Marshall McLuhen in his famous aphorism, 'the medium is the message.'

However much McLuhen's proclamation remains true today, the nature of people's reactions to marketing communication has changed, perhaps even more quickly than the content of the marketing messages audiences are being asked to respond to. Marketing communicators must keep pace with their audiences or run the risk of becoming ineffective, if not completely irrelevant. As consumers become more discerning with regard to marketing efforts in general, they also have become more demanding in terms of the information they receive from marketers. As British marketing lecturer Tony Yeshin (*Integrated Marketing Communications: The Holistic Approach*, Oxford, UK: Butterworth-Heinemann, 1998: 70) recently observed:

Marketing communications propositions developed in the 1950s and 1960s would be treated with disdain by today's more aware consumers. Specious technical claims and pseudo-scientific jargon which were at the heart of many product claims are no longer given quite the same credence. Consumers have changed from being deferential and generalised to personal and selective.

Indeed, we also have seen that consumers have become more proactive in their response to marketing messages that conflict with their values, beliefs, or moral precepts. This has become progressively more apparent in recent years with the emergence of so-called 'culture jammers' or 'media hackers' who deliberately disrupt, distort, or subvert the content of mainstream marketing messages, typically by altering the intended meaning of the messages through vandalism or other acts of sabotage (e.g. by defacing the photographic images of attractive models in outdoor billboards). In one such movement during the late 1990s, a collective known as 'Hocus Focus' vandalized outdoor billboards promoting Apple's 'Think Different' campaign by adding slogans (e.g. 'no product is a hero') in an attempt to undermine the profit-oriented objectives of the corporation and as a means of critiquing the company's use of historical personalities in ads in order to promote a consumer product.

In an ironic twist, marketers have begun to respond to such antimarketing campaigns by subverting their own messages, in the sense of developing ads that are self-deprecating or respectful of their increasingly cynical audiences (e.g. a print ad prominently displaying the advertised running shoe followed by the text 'Advertisement. Blah, blah, blah.'). To a large extent, these trends reflect back to the long-standing questions pertaining to how advertising works, and also have implications for broader issues, such as the extent to which marketing communication alters life experience or the very essence of the modern world.

This third and final section of the book is comprised of four chapters that tackle a range of challenging questions pertaining to marketing communication style and discourse. In Chapter 11, Fırat and Christensen focus on the much-discussed philosophical movement of postmodernism and its prevailing set of doctrines, such as those which question the modernistic notion that there can be consensus regarding a single best mode of living or being. Whereas the postmodernism debate has made significant incursions into the marketing literature during recent years, as Fırat and Christensen point out, little has been said about the implications of this movement with respect to marketing communication phenomena. The authors attempt to rectify this omission by first clarifying the often confused notions about what constitutes the idea of 'postmodernism,' and then by applying a postmodernistic framework to demonstrate how current marketing communication perspectives are 'incompatible with contemporary practices of consumption and communication.' In Fırat and Christensen's assessment, the postmodern tendencies of contemporary consumers and the transformations in marketing communications require and foster each other.

In Chapter 12, Arnould and Tissier-Desbordes also wrestle with some of the basic tenets of modernism and postmodernism and their implications for marketing communication through the application of another newly emerging perspective, hypermodernism. According to proponents of the hypermodernity view, certain aspects of the modernistic project continue to have utility for understanding the ways that consumers relate to the meaning of marketing messages. At the center of the hypermodern view is the recognition that certain key features of the modern world have begun to undergo exaggeration in recent years, such as the speed by which things change. We see this evidenced in the way new technologies that have dramatically facilitated the communication process, such as the fax machine and the videocassette recorder, are already becoming obsolete less than thirty years after their introduction into the consumer marketplace.

Arnould and Tissier-Desbordes discuss the potential value of hypermodernism in the realm of marketing communication by focusing on the role of scientific discourse in message development. Through an analysis of the ways the human body is depicted in the marketing of body care products, they demonstrate that scientific discourse is alive and well in the development of contemporary marketing communications. Additionally, rather than rejecting modernistic notions related to the utility of the methodology of the physical sciences as a means for achieving knowledge, the authors reframe them within the context of a contemporary preoccupation with individualistic concerns.

In Chapter 13, Borgerson and Schroeder bring the discussion of emerging developments in marketing communication squarely into the realm of ethics by questioning the legitimacy of the representational conventions that underlie the depiction in marketing messages of products, individuals, and group identities. Academics and practitioners have long debated the ethicality of a wide range of questionable marketing communication practices, in terms of their consequences for individual consumers (e.g. the argument that the high cost of advertising drives up prices or that deceptive promotions overstate product features) and society as a whole (e.g. the charge that marketing creates false wants and the encouragement of materialistic lifestyles or that excessive marketing and advertising clutter lead to cultural pollution). Borgerson and Schroeder point out, however, that debates concerning marketing ethics rarely address the more subtle consequences of the creation of meaning for consumer audiences outside the context of the focal product or service that lies at the center of a promotional message. With this in mind, the authors evaluate the contemporary status and potential impact of marketing communications through an analysis of common visual representations and conventions, and conclude by offering principles for a more ethical approach to the development of marketing messages.

In the final chapter, Brownlie and Saren provide an appropriate concluding focus by considering issues related to the way that marketing is communicated, in terms of how the subject is written about and represented by various writers and actors in the marketing process. Starting from a broad definition of 'marketing communications,' the authors argue that a complete examination of its subject matter requires a consideration not only of the content of what is communicated about marketing practice, but also 'what we say it is, how we package or represent those statements through communicative practice, and how that practice actively mediates or frames what we can and cannot say.' In their assessment of marketing discourse, Brownlie and Saren shed light on the way that communication functions as a social process within the realm of marketing and, in so doing, reveal certain problems within the marketing academy that will have to be overcome in order to further enable the future possibilities and promise of the marketing enterprise.

11

Marketing Communications in a Postmodern World

*A. Fuat Firat and Lars Thøger Christensen**

Although relatively new, the subject of postmodernism has evoked considerable debate and discussion in the field of marketing (Brown 1993*b*; Firat and Dholakia 1998; Firat and Venkatesh 1995; Firat et al. 1993/1994; Holbrook 1993; Ogilvy 1990; Sherry 1991). With few exceptions (Christensen, Torp and Firat 2005; Proctor and Kitchen 2002), however, only little of this debate is reflected in the subfield of marketing communications. The aim of this chapter is to apply insights and perspectives from discussions of postmodernity to marketing communication phenomena so as to demonstrate that the conditions for communication in today's world are radically different from what they used to be.

Following an introduction to postmodernity, we discuss how prevailing perspectives of marketing communications are based on a notion of sender control that is incompatible with contemporary practices of consumption and communication. We also argue that the classical marketing concept, and its notion of consumer sovereignty, presumes an interest and involvement in corporate messages that is out of tune with today's communication environment. Together, these trends suggest important implications for the future of marketing communications.

POSTMODERNITY: AN INTRODUCTION

Postmodernity designates a social condition of profound doubt in what is often called 'the grand project of modernity' (Lyotard 1984). Modernity

* Lars Thøger Christensen's contribution to this chapter was made possible by a grant from The Danish Social Science Research Council.

is referred to as a *grand* project because its goals and values—progress, rationality, development, individuality, emancipation, etc.—have been regarded, since the Enlightenment, as universal; that is, valid and relevant across the globe and in all contexts and circumstances. Further, it is a project because modernity is the period, beginning with the Enlightenment, when human beings considered it possible to take their destiny into their own hands by controlling nature in order to build a society of great ideal qualities (Angus 1989). Future-oriented projects like liberalism and Marxism are—although in different ways—manifestations of modernity's grand project. While modern thinkers (e.g. Habermas 1983) still consider modernity an unfinished project, postmodern writers contend that developments in history, science, politics, literature, and art are seriously shaking the project's foundation (Lyotard 1984). Modern science itself has also contributed, especially through developments in twentieth-century physics, to an erosion of a universal and privileged point of reference (Greene 2000). At the same time that the natural sciences demonstrated the universe to have no center and that observations are always relative to the observer, philosophers began questioning the foundation of our knowledge (e.g. Prigogine and Stengers 1984). Traces of this questioning can be found in a variety of disciplines and social practices, including philosophy, art, architecture, literature, literary criticism, history, and social theory (Rosenau 1992). In these different disciplines, the erosion of an authoritative point of reference stimulates new modes of expression that at once challenge our notion of a single reality and suggest alternative ways of combining styles, genres, and worldviews.

Postmodernism is a call to recognize the problematic nature of the single-minded grand project of modernity—what Lyotard (1984) termed modernity's *metanarrative*—and to remove this metanarrative of progress from the lofty, privileged pedestal it inhabited for the last few centuries. In postmodernity there is a clarion call for appreciation of difference and against framing difference in terms of superiority versus inferiority. Without eliminating preference, postmodern writers advocate tolerance, appreciation, and respect for difference (Best and Kellner 1991; Featherstone 1991; Gottdiener 1995; Harvey 1990; Kellner 1989). Rather than converging towards a single mode of being or living that is deemed to be the *best*, as envisioned by the project of modernity, postmodernity allows for the recognition that various communities will have preferences for different ways of being and living, and that these preferences most likely will be shaped by a multiplicity of goals and values (Fırat and Dholakia 1998).

The postmodern sensibility, in other words, does not envision the possibility of consensus on any foundational or fundamental essentials representing 'a universal.' Instead, a multiplicity of perspectives, truths, and life experiences are sought and expected. In the postmodern, what is valued is the ability to navigate, to become immersed in, and to experience different orders or cultures, through which meaning and substance in the present moments of life are enriched. This folding-in of the past and the future into the here-and-now is a necessary concomitant of an era that lacks grand, singular projects and narratives.

Postmodern culture calls for engagement with numerous conditions created or reinforced, at the same time that they are denied, by modernity. Some oft-discussed conditions include hyperreality, fragmentation, decentering of the subject, paradoxical juxtapositions of opposites, and tolerance for difference and multiplicity (Baudrillard 1993; Best and Kellner 1991; Caputo 1997; Featherstone 1991; Foster 1983; Jameson 1991; Lyotard 1984; Jencks 1987). *Hyperreality,* which is the focus of Chapter 12, is defined as the becoming real of that which was or is hype or simulation; that is, when a substantive and powerful segment in society believe certain conditions that are forcefully represented to be the case, these conditions then become their reality. A simple example may be that when a group of young people believe that wearing athletic shoes of a certain brand will bring them popularity, it indeed becomes the case.

Fragmentation is the condition that life in modern society and, thus, people's experiences are disconnected or disjointed. Home life, work life, recreation time, time with television, time with pets, and the like, are all separate experiences and lack a center or unity, except perhaps in the minds of some people who feel that they have to find a center or unity to their lives. *Decentering of the subject* is the condition in modern life that the subject (the human agent), who was considered to be the center of all reason, has lost her/his agency, and has to share the capability to act upon things with objects (of desire), or is often acted upon by objects. An obvious example is the influence of objects such as television and the automobile on human beings. *Paradoxical juxtaposition of opposites* is the condition that many so-called 'proper' ensembles are no longer exercised. This is a condition that is especially recognized in architecture, where architectural elements from different systems considered to be incompatible are combined (Jencks 1987), but is also found in everyday clothing and lifestyles, for example, in the combined use of punk hairdos with high-fashion clothing. Finally, *tolerance for difference and multiplicity* is a condition that results from all of the above as well as the loss of commitment to the monolithic project of modernity. There is a tacit understanding among peoples of the world who realize the futility of seeking a consensus among all different perspectives, values, and worldviews, and instead accept an openness toward a multicultural existence.

Together, these conditions represent a blurring of distinctions that were fundamental to the constitution of modernity: the distinctions between reality and fantasy, mind and body, subject and object, material and symbolic, production and consumption, order and chaos, material and symbolic. Through these distinctions, modernity attempted to construct a normative order for the realization of the modern project (Steuerman 1992). In the postmodern sensibility, these bipolar or oppositional dichotomies that determine what is proper and improper, what is a privileged norm or unworthy, are diffused, offering instead multiplicity and complexity. Under these conditions, to expect a single meaning or interpretation to be derived from one's communication is neither possible nor fruitful. Instead, one must be ready and open for playful yet critical engagement in the collaborative production of multiple, deconstructive, fluid, imaginative, and inventive creations of meaning constellations. *Playfulness* indicates the impulse to not completely commit to any single way of understanding, being or living, but instead to realize the inexorable paradoxes of good and bad in all ways, and to experience each with a degree of caution, creativity, and diversionary fun.

COMMUNICATION AND THE MARKETING CONCEPT

Although marketing, as a number of scholars have pointed out (e.g. Brown 1993*a*, 1999*b*; Fırat and Venkatesh 1993; Ogilvy 1990), has a postmodern impetus, its theoretical and practical orientation is fundamentally modern. Since the articulation of modern marketing, which many agree began in the 1950s with the work of Wroe Alderson (Bagozzi 1975; Kotler 1972), the marketing orientation has increasingly become the mode of relations in all spheres of Western society. Whether we are in the sphere of politics, religion, or education, it is now common practice to consider the constituencies—voters, worshippers, or students—as 'customers,' and to employ a marketing orientation in relating to them. There are almost two distinct interests guiding this orientation, one of which is the business interest. By relating to consumers/customers in a way that better understands and responds to their desires and behaviors, it is presumed that business success will be improved. The other interest is a more social and, in a sense, idealistic one. The marketing orientation, or as modern marketing academics call it, the *marketing concept*, enables the institutions of society to better serve the needs of their constituencies or markets. Rather than push what companies can produce on to consumers, the marketing concept allows them to deliver what consumers want and assures consumer sovereignty.

Communication is fundamental to this modern conception of marketing. Indeed, it may be argued that communication is the sine qua non of the marketing concept. Since the 1950s, marketing has established itself as the managerial norm for how organizations must deal with their market(s). As a creative response to the growing critique of business corporations since World War II, marketing introduced a new business orientation that

committed public and private organizations to focus their activities primarily on the satisfaction of their relevant publics (e.g. Keith 1960; Kotler
and Levy 1969). Central to this orientation is the notion of marketing as an
ongoing *dialog* between organizations and their markets (Stidsen and
Schutte 1972; Levy 1978). According to Stidsen and Schutte (1972: 27), 'The
marketing task is that of creating and maintaining a fully functioning
producer-consumer communication system ... The ideal marketing process is the functioning dialogue involving a communication system which
enables consumers and producers to significantly influence each others'
goal attainment.'

The dialog organized by marketing is designed to stimulate organizational openness and responsiveness and to set the marketing approach
apart from the often criticized production, product, and sales orientations
of the past (e.g. Kotler 1991). In contrast to these orientations, marketing
prides itself in being obsessively preoccupied with its external world and,
in particular, the consumer. As a consequence, communication becomes
the *raison d'être* of the marketing discipline and an indispensable activity
for the marketing organization. Through a well-functioning communication system, the marketing-oriented organization is expected to stay in
close contact with the market and thereby remain sensitive to changes in
the needs and wants of present and prospective customers. Although the
scope of contemporary marketing practice reaches far beyond the acts of
sending and receiving messages, its basic function is to link, by means
of communication, the organization with the market it claims to serve.

COMMUNICATION AS CONTROL

Although the communication ideal of modern marketing is founded on the
marketing concept and its notion of dialog and sensitivity to the needs of
the consumer, it simultaneously exhibits a desire to strategically manage
the communication process. By applying strategic principles to the communication process, the author (e.g. the marketing organization), attempts
to assure the delivery of the right message and, thus, provide predictability
to the sender organization. An effective, modern marketing communicator,
then, is one who controls the meaning of the communicated message and
strategically manages the way it is relayed to the audience (i.e. the target
market). The mode of communication is one of delivering or providing
meaning to the receiver.

This delivery or provision mode of marketing communication is also a
representational mode of communication. That is, the meaning of the
message to be communicated is known or determined before its encoding
by the marketing organization that serves as author. The organization

knows what it wants to relay to the target market and the message is then composed in an attempt to *represent* this meaning in a most accurate and persuasive way. The message is composed of words and other signs (visual images, sounds, etc.) that together best represent the meaning sought to be relayed. That is, this representation must be true to the meaning it attempts to get across. The words and other signs do not construct or determine the meaning or propose a meaning; in principle, they should simply reflect the meaning. In this mode of communication, it is understood that without such a representational relationship between the meaning and the signs, there would be more confusion than communication. This principle in modern (marketing) communication follows modern scientific principles, where constructs, theories, and models must represent reality, not construct or propose it (Bhaskar 1986).

In addition to message delivery, marketing communication must be persuasive to achieve its goals. In fact, we might argue that all modern marketing communication is persuasive communication. The most benign intent of modern marketing communication, when it is truthful, is to persuade consumers that the product offered is indeed the one most fitting the consumer's needs and desires. The necessity to reach the targeted consumers above the clutter and noise from all other communicators is often emphasized in marketing textbooks. To achieve this goal, the author of the message must design and transmit the message with an understanding of all the elements of the communication process in order to assure that it indeed 'gets through' as intended.

Modern communication principles follow from the system of modern thought mentioned above. In concordance with the modern construction of the human being as the subject, these principles indicate the primary responsibility of the communicator in making the message understood and persuasive. In effect, the author assumes ownership of communication, and with that responsibility comes the authority to decide what is to be communicated. If the message is not understood as intended, the presumption is that it is the author's fault, as a function of having poorly composed the message or having failed to recognize the interactions between message content or composition and other elements of the communication process (such as the media, audience, context, and noise). What was communicated was the result of the communicator's decision, whereas the audience (i.e. the receivers) merely was exposed to the message and expected to decode it. Following this logic, one can argue that if the members of the audience misunderstand, or if they are not persuaded, it is because the author did not sufficiently take into consideration the targets' language, literacy, psychology, culture, and the like (Eckhouse 1999; Baguley 1994). Again, while some marketing communicators may fail, the emphasis is on communication management, predictability, and control.

Curiously, this view of marketing communications is not restricted to the era of the classical, modern marketing concept. Today, we find the control perspective reintroduced under headings like 'corporate communications' and 'integrated marketing communications' (Christensen et al. 2005). Although these subfields of marketing claim to take their point of departure from the notion that contemporary consumers and other audiences of marketing communication messages are empowered to decide which messages to attend to and which to ignore, they simultaneously operate under the assumption that messages and interpretations can be managed by controlling the many 'contact points' between organizations and their customers (e.g. Schultz et al. 1994). Amidst a market of increased fragmentation and complexity, the promise of these disciplines is to provide managers with a tool to coordinate and synchronize all corporate messages so that their organizations are perceived as monoliths that speak consistently or with one voice.

THEORETICAL IMPLICATIONS

This modern notion of communication has a number of important implications for marketing communication theory and practice. In the modern context, communication is not considered an active and constitutive force in itself, a process through which we create the world, but is seen as a mere carrier of messages between producers and consumers. Communication, in other words, is regarded as a conduit through which messages are transmitted in a more or less linear fashion. As a consequence, the environment of the organization—the needs and wants of consumers—is treated as something separate from the organization, something external or pregiven to which the organization needs to adapt. Likewise, the organization is regarded as a separate and independent body with a clear identity and distinct boundaries. Just as the market is seen as separate from the flow of messages between producers and consumers, the organization is similarly regarded as an entity that exists 'outside' its own communication. As such, the role of the modern marketing organization is to facilitate and monitor the exchange of messages and to ensure that the flow of communication continues as unrestrained as possible. To be marketing-oriented, in other words, implies the need to create and maintain the most effective and efficient way to get messages across without bias or misinterpretation.

Consequently, the modern marketing communication literature concentrates on the elements of communication that facilitate or hinder the ability of the communicator to get across a message in a way that would be completely and accurately understood by the receiver(s). These are elements such as the characteristics of the message itself (content, form, and structure), the context of the message, the media used for transmitting the message, the characteristics of the communicator (also referred to as the 'sender' or 'source' of the message), the element of noise, and the characteristics of the receiver. The purpose of knowing about all of these elements is to understand how to minimize miscommunication while maximizing message effectiveness and communication goals. Thus, the objective in modern marketing communication is to minimize the difference between the meaning of the intended message that is encoded by the sender (the author of the message) and the meaning of the message as decoded and understood by the receiver. Accordingly, *the ideal situation for the communication process would occur when the two meanings are exactly alike.*

Within this perspective, 'noise' is defined as anything that blocks, delays, or otherwise hinders a smooth transmission of messages through the conduit. Just as communication is seen as separate from the organization, so too is noise regarded as an externality that *can* be reduced, under favorable circumstances, but is produced by forces detached from the sender and the message. Whereas consumers and their divergent interpretations represent one source of noise, another stems from the competitive messages of other players in the marketplace. In the mindset of the modern marketing communicator, the emphasis is on how to reduce such noise; that is, how to manage and control the context and the meaning of the message.

CHALLENGES TO MODERNITY

Recent developments in other fields, such as semiotics (the study of signs in society) and sociology, are forcing us to rethink the principles of modern marketing communication. In particular, two developments along theoretical dimensions indicate the necessity to rethink the modernist position. One development is the growth of postmodernist insights regarding transformations in culture and, accordingly, changes in values and attitudes. As explained below, these transformations render the modern marketing communication orientations ineffective. The second development is the growing recognition of the complex systems of meaning constitution in human communication, aided by perspectives such as deconstructionism, reader response theory, and reception theory. Further, we argue that the increasing influence of multimedia technologies in everyday life requires a rethinking of literacy and meaning construction.

Today, the modern project of taking control of nature and, thus, the destiny of humanity, is faced with serious doubts (Angus 1989). Among these doubts are questions about progress, goals, means, science, and limitations to our knowledge: Will human beings be able to agree on and judge the progress that is taking place? Is the way we have chosen to arrive at the destiny that we seek the correct one and how can we know? Has not modernity, having largely dominated Western societies for the last 400 years, produced as many problems and much misery as it has created progress?

Consequently, cultural tendencies that abandon the single-minded commitment to one project for humanity are increasingly observed (Featherstone 1991). A major aspect of this loss of commitment is the turn to multiple possibilities and experiences for finding meaning and substance in life, in the present moments that life is lived. This leads to a growing acceptance of different orders rather than compliance to a single order that is, scientifically or otherwise, deemed most rational or 'best.' This cultural sensibility contradicts the modern impulse to orient all matters of life toward one rationale or one form of reason. Instead, it highlights the interest within newly forming communities in pursuing different modes of interpretation of life's conditions and existence (Fish 1980; Maffesoli 1996). Thus, there is a rise in demand for a so-called 'deconstructive engagement' (Derrida 1982) involving all forms of communication and 'multivalent readings' (Stern 1998). That is, rather than 'reading' messages as they are intended by the author, the call is to discover the contradictions, historical silences, and assumed axioms in the 'writings' of the author, thus insisting that the meanings produced by the 'reading' are different from the meanings intended in the 'writing.' Now the assumption is that in whatever the author wrote, there are unspoken or hidden agendas, historical baggage, and political imperatives that the author may or may not be aware of. Therefore, from each reader's point of view, era, and culture, there can and should be different, critical readings, which effectively reconstitute what is written.

THE RECEIVER AS COCREATOR

From a marketing communication perspective, one of the most important implications of postmodernity is the loss of control, consistency, and predictability that the modern perspective on communication took for granted. According to Ogilvy (1990: 15), the postmodern consumer is 'a semiotic field of mixed messages, conflicting meanings, and inconsistent impulses.' Thus, whereas modern marketing is founded on the principles of analysis, planning, implementation, and control (e.g. Kotler 2003), contemporary marketers need to realize that they no longer are masters of meaning, that their products and messages are creations with a life of their own, and that their intended receivers are not passive targets but creative partners in the production of experiences and identities. Thus, brand communities (discussed in Chapter 4), the members of which creatively coconstruct brand meanings, are increasingly recognized.

More specifically, the presumption of control is being challenged by the realization that consumers and other audiences, rather than simply receiving corporate messages and images in a passive and receptive mode, actively participate in the construction of meaning in their surroundings. As Duranti (1986) has pointed out, interpretation is not a passive activity through which an audience is trying to figure out what the author meant to convey. Rather, it is a way of making sense of a piece of communication by linking it to the context that is familiar or meaningful to the audience. Faced with numerous corporate messages each day, consumers rarely read an advertisement in order to understand the intention of the sender. Rather, they make sense of the advertisement by relating it to their own structure of relevance and experience. Again, brand communities, such as the Harley Davidson 'gangs,' constitute a good example of this phenomenon (Schouten and Alexander 1995).

Inspired by phenomenology and reception theory (Iser 1974; Jauss 1982; Duranti 1986), marketing scholars have called for more in-depth studies of what corporate symbols, such as advertisements and brands, mean to receivers (e.g. Buhl 1991; Mick and Buhl 1992). As Buhl (1991) has demonstrated, consumers are involved in advertising messages to the extent that these messages allow them to confirm or augment their own personal projects—for example, their project of identity. When consumers find an advertisement relevant, they are cocreating this relevance themselves 'through self-organizing activities in which the ad is a resource of information rather than instruction' (Buhl 1991: 120). Thus, for example, Buhl found that readers of ads ascribed meaning to nonexplicit information in the ad as in empty slots (e.g., the story behind the depicted scene). Many readings of ads, he found, were not tied directly to the concrete ad, but involved instead the reader's own situation and experiences. The reception of advertising messages thus can be described as self-referential in the sense that receivers read meaning into the message by importing relevant information from their own world (cf. Eco 1979; Iser 1974). According to Buhl (1991: 119), 'Advertising, then, is not so much what the sender says but what the receiver understands. This understanding is greatly influenced by the contexts (personal, economical, social, cultural, and national) in which the recipient lives, integrates, and disintegrates meanings.'

Following this idea, Buhl (1991) suggested that the question of what advertising does to the consumer should be replaced with the question of what the consumer does with advertising. The assumption is that consumers read ads primarily by referring to their own subjective worlds of experience. In Buhl's view, making sense of advertising is a specific method of self-creation—a constantly evolving process of reality construction.

While this observation, and the implied insight that follows from it, is tremendously important to the field of marketing communication, it still has not significantly affected marketing practice. This is so primarily because the notion of self-referential reception introduces a level of complexity into marketing communications that can be difficult to deal with in practice. If consumers receive and interpret corporate messages individually and according to their own subjective worlds of experience, how can senders construct their messages consistently and how can responses be predicted? Even if sophisticated market research techniques enable us to record the differences in message reception, the question remains as how to organize such differences within one coherent campaign. The notion of active and creative receivers, in other words, conflicts with the modern desire to secure order and predictability in the marketing communication process.

The authority of the creators of marketing messages is further challenged by arguments derived from so-called 'reader-response theory.' Here, what is brought into contention is the notion that an author could ever have authority in inscribing a fixed meaning to a text or, put differently, that 'authoring' could be a single-source act. In marketing communication terms, the idea that the marketing organization responsible for encoding the message is the single determinant of its meaning is questioned. Instead, all meaning is determined by a triad consisting of the author, the text, and the reader, and thus the engendering (or 'writing') of a message can be seen as evolving from a relationship involving these three elements. As a result, the modern impulse to control or manage communication is also challenged. Rather than an act of determining, encoding, and relaying meaning, communication is regarded as a collaborative act, requiring a complete reorientation toward its practice. Below, we have attempted to provide some preliminary insights as to what the principles of this new orientation may be; however, a full articulation is not yet possible because we are only just beginning to observe and understand the necessity of this reorientation—a reorientation reinforced by the advent of new communication technologies (Dholakia et al. 1996).

Beginning with photography and film, advancing with television, and now with computers and the Internet, the word—especially the written word—has largely lost its primacy and dominance. Visual images and sounds have begun to overpower the (written) word in communications transmitted via the new technologies (Firat 1996; Poster 1990).

It is readily realized that images or sounds can be interpreted (or 'read') to provide multiple meanings. A sky-blue, sporty automobile racing along a coastal road or a Rolling Stones tune, for example, will evoke many different associations and meanings, even among members of the same culture. And, with new technologies, the possibility of determination or control of meaning by a single agent is waning (e.g. Vattimo 1992).

The recognition that such signs are quite independent of any one determined meaning has reflected on and put to doubt our modern assumption that even within a language a word represents a meaning that is completely agreed upon by all participants in the communication process. In effect, we realize that words are, as are all signs, 'free-floating' signifiers, despite the fact that they may indicate at times more or less precise meanings within a language and a culture. Therefore, communication increasingly comes to be understood as an interplay rather than a unilateral delivery or transmission of meaning.

To be fair, it should be noted that while these receiver-oriented perspectives on communication seriously challenge modern notions of communication management and control, these perspectives are not without problems themselves. With their emphasis on the individual receiver they tend to forget that reception always takes place within a cultural context that shapes the range of possible interpretations. As a field of shared significations that we lean on and take for granted when we communicate with each other, culture helps us understand and interpret messages of others and create meaning in any specific situation (Castoriadis 1987). While culture does not determine or control the exact content of a message or series of messages, it 'supports' the process of meaning construction by providing and highlighting certain frames for interpretation and excluding others. Because we exist in a social world, we are dependent upon meaning and are often willing, as Merleau-Ponty (1989) pointed out, to sacrifice a great deal of individuality to the institutions that provide it. Although this willingness seems to be dwindling in today's postmodern world, the interpretations of receivers are not arbitrary and isolated phenomena, but creative processes that acquire their individuality through their interplay with the sanctioned set of interpretations provided by culture. In spite of these shortcomings, the notion of an active, constructive, and, to some extent, self-referential receiver poses an important challenge to modern marketing communicators.

CHANGING MARKETING PRACTICES?

Although many marketing organizations still hold on to a modern approach that seeks to completely control meaning, marketing communicators are beginning to take heed of the cultural trends that create a growing desire among consumers to become active participants in the marketing process, as evidenced by research on Internet behavior, brand communities, and sites such as Las Vegas (Firat 2001; Muñiz and O'Guinn 2001). Also recognized is the development of consumers in mature markets, in terms of becoming savvier about marketing and business. An increasing number of consumers not only understand and have begun to grow wary of marketing strategies, but they are beginning to become small-scale marketers themselves (Brown 1993*a*, 1993*b*). As managers of fashion magazines have long been aware, consumers are 'customizing themselves' through varied wardrobes and styles to present different images that fit different situations (Condé Nast Editors 1989). While consumers may not be able to match the knowledge, skills, and resources of marketing organizations, and are still heavily influenced by them, they are becoming less receptive to marketing that is unidirectional and that does not take into consideration their desire to be involved (Miller 1989).

In this context, some marketing organizations are already changing their forms or styles of marketing communication, if not their underlying philosophies. For example, television advertising, in particular, has increasingly become transformational rather than informational (Puto and Wells 1984). Rather than directly informing consumers about products and product benefits, many TV ads have incorporated suggestions from which consumers can derive ideas about the experiences they might have with products or how their lives may be enhanced by the products. 'Just do it!' *Nike* advertisements, or *Levi's* 501 Jeans advertisements where the models are seen in situations that illustrate or express the experience or the feelings one would have when using these brands—without providing any direct information about the products other than the brand name—are examples of this trend.

Table 11.1 depicts some of the major changes that are occurring in the forms of communication with the erosion of modernity's influence. Related to the increase in the use of transformational messages in marketing communication is the move away from material content that describes or exhibits the actual ingredients, forms, or benefits towards greater use of the symbolic, and from overt messages to more subtle ones. Again, these are largely responses to cultural trends and the resulting reactions of consumers to communication from organizations.

More symbolic and subtle messages allow for playfulness and better fit the consumer desire to engage. An ad for Long John Whiskey, for example, shows two women, perhaps twins, sitting on a couch. The women have the same type of hair and wear almost identical dresses. A closer look, however,

Table 11.1. Changes in the forms of communication

Informational	$\longrightarrow$	Transformational
Material	$\longrightarrow$	Symbolic
Overt	$\longrightarrow$	Subtle
Verbal	$\longrightarrow$	Multisensory

reveals that while the one dress has a rectangular neck-opening, the other is rounded. The perceptive reader will observe that the two bottles of Long John standing on the floor next to the couch differ in a similar manner: while the label on the one bottle is rectangular, the other is rounded. The ad reads: 'We could never improve the contents. So we've redesigned the label.' While the straightforward message obviously is that the whiskey is so good that it doesn't need to change, there is a more sophisticated reading available. Indirectly, what the advertisement says is that the brand's communicators are aware that the consumer is savvy enough to know that it is all communication. So instead of pretending something else, Long John invites us to participate in the esthetic game of discovering and playing with shapes, colors, and forms. Something similar is apparent in the well-known campaigns from Absolut Vodka and Silk Cut cigarettes. While Absolut Vodka incites us to look for the shape of the bottle—the only common denominator in the campaign—in numerous contexts and situations, Silk Cut invites us into an almost endless universe of purple silk that is cut. Through their use of sophisticated *intratextuality*, these campaigns tend to close in on themselves to become what Perniola (1980) and Baudrillard (1994) call *simulacra*; that is, 'autonomized' images without reference to anything but themselves. At the same time, however, they open an infinite field of signifiers in which receivers can play out their favorite interpretations.

New communication technologies provide the possibility for the use of multisensory means of communicating, which allow for multivalent readings. Indeed, modern discourse has preferred *the word*—especially the written word—partially because of the belief that it has overt and clear meaning that does not, when used correctly, allow varied readings. This belief is now under great doubt, but it is widely accepted that signs other than the word, such as visual and sonic signs, provide much greater latitude for multiple readings (Fish 1980; Postman 1985). The possibilities of multiple readings will become more pronounced as communication technologies, such as film, television, the Internet, and possibly future virtual reality technologies, allow for a greater integration of signs that impact on multiple senses.

POSTMODERN IMPLICATIONS FOR MARKETING COMMUNICATIONS

With growing emphasis on reception and the notion that consumers are active participants in the communication process, the modernist approach to marketing communications is seriously challenged. However, we believe that this challenge is not articulated radically enough. In postmodernity, neither the control orientation of the marketing concept nor the subjectivist perspective of reception theory are able to account for significant dimensions of the marketing communication process. While the former—as we have discussed—privileges the text and the intentions of the sender, the latter tends to privilege receivers and *their* account of their own market behavior. However, as a number of studies have demonstrated, consumers are not always consciously aware of what they are doing in the marketplace and why they are doing it, and often they are not able to account correctly for their behavior (e.g. Brown 2003). Rather, consumers have a tendency to rationalize their behavior in terms that they believe is socially acceptable or would please the interrogator. Thus, the notion of communicating with consumers in order to discover their wants, needs, and interpretations becomes a tricky undertaking and, perhaps, an elusive goal.

We need at least to recognize that consumers themselves—although active and creative participants in the communication process—may not be the most suitable source of knowledge about how marketing communications work. Whereas marketing and other kinds of persuasive communication have often been seen, both by critics and practitioners, as systems of one-way seduction, the tendency to emphasize the consumer's own voice may well reverse the process and seduce corporate communicators to believe that they in fact communicate with the market. By focusing on how consumers read and interpret corporate messages, the question of what behavioral effects the messages set in motion is replaced by the question of how consumers understand the messages. And while this latter question is always relevant and interesting, it may not have much to do with actual marketplace behavior. Consumers' affective reactions to advertisements, for example, often have little or nothing to do with their shopping behavior. Moreover, by assuming a primacy of deep meanings (typically uncovered through long, in-depth interviews) over consumer actions, the reception approach tends to reproduce the notion that consumers are deeply involved in the corporate messages. In an interesting and ironic twist, such allegedly receiver-oriented perspectives may end up confirming the sender perspectives they set out to refute.

In order to arrive at a more sophisticated conception of marketing communications in today's world, we need to understand more profoundly the postmodern conditions for communication. Postmodernity is often described as a social space saturated with images primarily referencing themselves (e.g. Baudrillard 1981, 1988; Ewen 1988). This is evident in advertising, which increasingly employs sophisticated forms of *intertextuality*, whereby messages refer to other messages across product categories—often without mentioning the product (e.g. Allen 2000). For example, in a witty reference to the famous Nike slogan, Sisley Underwear suggests, 'Just *Un*do It.' Likewise, Apples' 'Think Different' campaign built on IBM's classic slogan 'Think.' Before Apple's campaign, ICL Computers challenged the market leader with its 'Think ICL,' Burroughs (later Unisys) asked consumers to 'Think Twice,' and Hewlett-Packard suggested 'Think Again.' Also, as we described, some brands like Absolut Vodka and Silk Cut cigarettes engage in *self-referential advertising*, acting with 'autonomized' images without reference to anything but themselves.

Within this communication arena, the notion of 'noise' needs to be reconceptualized. In contrast to the modern understanding of noise as something external to the communication process, the condition of message clutter and self-referentiality has made us aware of the need to think of noise as something intrinsic to the process of crafting and sending messages. Thus, in postmodernity, marketing communications have become a double-edged sword: where media consultants seek to convince organizations to communicate more in order to gain a larger 'share of voice,' many decision makers have come to realize that what they gain is primarily a larger share of noise.

At the same time, organizations are increasingly facing an audience that is neither interested nor receptive to corporate messages. As advertising consultant Morgan (1999) pointed out, the consumer is content or bored, but not interested. According to Morgan, most people think of advertising as 'a nuisance business,' a type of communication they would rather be without. To consider the market as comprised of 'audiences' presupposes that people are actively paying attention, which is rarely the case. Similarly, others have argued that attention and interest are among the scarcest resources in the current marketplace (e.g. Schudson 1993). While some expressions of popular culture may attract much attention, advertising rarely is one of them. As some marketing consultants have pointed out, consumers are growing more indifferent, cynical, and apathetic (e.g. Bond and Kirschenbaum 1998).

These trends do not imply that nobody is interested in marketing communications. As Schudson (1993) has argued, the people who make the ads, pay for them, or are otherwise dependent on them are usually highly interested in corporate messages. While sales personnel, for example, work harder for products that are well advertised, retailers often reorganize the shopping environment based on the expectation that well-executed ads will attract more customers. Advertising, then, may help producers sell more products without convincing the consumer about anything.

Following this line of thought, Christensen (1997) has argued that marketing is a sophisticated form of *auto-communication* (cf. Broms and Gahmberg 1983; Lotman 1990). That is, in contrast to conventional notions of communication, auto-communication is not primarily a matter of sending and receiving messages. It is a ritual through which a sender confirms his or her own perspective. In this sense, auto-communication is an integral aspect of culture. According to leading anthropologists, all cultures communicate with themselves through rituals that help their members share and reinforce their most fundamental values (e.g. Geertz 1973). Thus, through the process of auto-communication, cultures not only maintain but also construct or develop themselves (cf. Sherry 1987). While auto-communication may be a rather self-centered enterprise, its logic does not rule out the possibility that the messages in question *also* communicate to external audiences (Christensen and Cheney 2000). However, in a cluttered communication environment saturated with messages asserting importance and uniqueness, it is highly unlikely that corporate messages will be able to stimulate more than a passing interest, let alone engagement, outside the organization's formal boundaries. Thus, under the postmodern condition it becomes increasingly difficult to maintain clear distinctions between senders and receivers.

Together these trends—message clutter, self-referentiality, indifference, auto-communication, and reversed seduction—suggest that postmodern marketing communication differs radically from the conditions and assumptions that previously informed and shaped the discipline. As postmodern cultural trends prevail, a different philosophy of marketing communication will be required. First, communication will have to be defined not as delivery or transmission of predetermined messages (i.e. a set of symbols) but as a means to open the possibilities for coproduction of meanings in 'conversation' among marketing organizations and consumers. Second, marketing communicators may need to look for alternative—and more involved—audiences both outside and within the sender organization. As attention and interest increasingly become scarce resources, the challenge for contemporary marketing communicators is to abandon the linear notion of communication—from producer to consumer—in favor of more sophisticated approaches that include many types of influence and persuasion.

Table 11.2 illustrates the changes that are required in thinking about communication given postmodern challenges. Communication is in every act, and thus communicators have to consider the communicative effect of every act they perform. Further, they have to realize that each and every communicative act is coproduced, not only in terms of the multiple influences in the construction of the communicative act, but also in its continual reinterpretation by self and others.

Maturing consumers may be likened to maturing children or emancipated people who, rather than looking for caretakers and father

Table 11.2 Changes in meaning of communication

Signs transmitted	⟶	Symbols coproduced
(Predetermined set of symbols sent through predetermined media)		(Symbolic meanings constructed together with customizers)
Communication as a separate act	⟶	Communication as inseparable from other acts

figures, begin to seek partners, playmates, and collaborators. Marketing organizations that are fearful of letting go of their conventional roles in the modern marketplace and their previous ways of relating to their consumers, and that fail to adapt to a new paradigm, may survive for some time thanks to their initial success, but will have little if any chance of surviving over the long term.

REFERENCES

Allen, G. (2000). *Intertextuality*. London: Routledge.

Angus, I. (1989). 'Circumscribing Postmodern Culture,' in I. Angus and S. Jhally (eds.), *Cultural Politics in Contemporary America*. New York: Routledge.

Bagozzi, R. P. (1975). 'Marketing as Exchange,' *Journal of Marketing*, 39, 32–9.

Baguley, P. (1994). *Effective Communication for Modern Business*. New York: McGraw-Hill.

Baudrillard, J. (1981). *For a Critique of the Political Economy of the Sign*. St. Louis, MO: Telos Press.

—— (1988). *The Ecstasy of Communication*. New York: Semiotext(e).

—— (1993). The *Transparency of Evil: Essays on Extreme Phenomena*. New York: Verso.

—— (1994). *Simulacra and Simulation*. Ann Arbor, MI: The University of Michigan Press.

Best, S. and Kellner, D. (1991). *Postmodern Theory: Critical Interrogations*. New York: Guilford Press.

Bhaskar, R. (1986). *Scientific Realism & Human Emancipation*. London: Verso.

Bond, J. and Kirshenbaum, R. (1998). *Under the Radar: Talking to Today's Cynical Consumer*. New York: Adweek Books.

Broms, H. and Gahmberg, H. (1983). 'Communication to Self in Organizations and Cultures,' *Administrative Science Quarterly*, 28, 482–95.

Brown, S. (1993a). 'Postmodern Marketing?,' *European Journal of Marketing*, 27, 19–34.

—— (1993b). 'Postmodern Marketing: Principles, Practice and Panaceas,' *Irish Marketing Review*, 6, 91–100.

—— (2003). *Free Gift Inside!!: Forget the Customer. Develop Marketease*. Oxford: Capstone.

Buhl, C. (1991). 'The Consumer's Ad: The Art of Making Sense of Advertising,' in H.H. Larsen, D.G. Mick, and C. Alsted (eds.), *Marketing and Semiotics. Selected Papers from the Copenhagen Symposium*. København: Handelshøjskolens Forlag.

Caputo, J. D. (ed) (1997). *Deconstruction in a Nutshell: A Conversation with Derrida*. New York: Fordham University Press.

Castoriadis, C. (1987). *The Imaginary Institution of Society*. Cambridge, MA: MIT.

Christensen, L. T. (1997). 'Marketing as Auto-Communication,' *Consumption, Markets & Culture*, 1, 197–227.

—— and Cheney, G. (2000). 'Self-absorption and Self-seduction in the Corporate Identity Game,' in M. Schultz, M. J. Hatch, and M. H. Larsen (eds.), *The Expressive Organization*. Oxford: Oxford University Press.

—— Torp, S., and Fırat, A. F. (2005). 'IMC and Postmodernity: An Odd Couple?,' *Corporate Communication: An International Journal*, 10, in press.

Condé Nast (eds.), (1989, November). Interviews with Magazine Editors in 'Image and Reality in America: Consuming Images'. *The Public Mind* (television program), hosted by B. Moyers, Part 1, Public Broadcasting Service.

Derrida, J. (1982). *Margins of Philosophy.* Chicago: University of Chicago Press.

Dholakia, R. R., Mundorf, N., and Dholakia, N. (eds.) (1996). *New Infotainment Technologies in the Home: Demand-side Perspectives.* Mahwah, NJ: Lawrence Erlbaum Associates.

Duranti, A. (1986). 'The Audience as Co-author: An Introduction,' *Text*, 6, 239–47.

Eckhouse, B. (1999). *Competitive Communication: A Rhetoric for Modern Business.* Oxford: Oxford University Press.

Eco, U. (1979). *The Role of the Reader: Explorations in the Semiotics of Texts.* Bloomington: Indiana University Press.

Ewen, S. (1988). *All Consuming Images: The Politics of Style in Contemporary Culture.* New York: Basic Books.

Featherstone, M. (1991). *Consumer Culture and Postmodernism.* London: Sage.

Fırat, A. F. (1996). 'Literacy in the Age of New Information Technologies,' in R. R. Dholakia, N. Mundorf, and N. Dholakia (eds.), *New Infotainment Technologies in the Home: Demand-side Perspectives.* Mahwah, NJ: Lawrence Erlbaum Associates.

—— (2001). 'The Meanings and Messages of Las Vegas: The Present of Our Future,' *M@n@gement*, 4, 101–20.

—— Venkatesh, A., and J.F. Sherry, Jr. (eds.) (1993/1994). 'Special Issues on Postmodernism, Marketing and the Consumer,' *International Journal of Research in Marketing*, 10, 11.

—— and —— (1993). 'Postmodernity: the Age of Marketing,' *International Journal of Research in Marketing*, 10, 227–49.

—— and —— (1995). 'Liberatory Postmodernism and the Reenchantment of Consumption,' *Journal of Consumer Research*, 22, 239–67.

—— and Dholakia, N. (1998). *Consuming People: from Political Economy to Theaters of Consumption.* London: Routledge.

Fish, S. (1980). *Is There a Text in this Class? The Authority of Interpretive Communities.* Cambridge, MA: Harvard University Press.

Foster, H. (1983). *The Anti-aesthetic: Essays on Postmodern Culture.* Port Townsend, WA: Bay Press.

Geertz, C. (1973). *The Interpretation of Cultures.* New York: Basic Books.

Gottdiener, M. (1995). *Postmodern Semiotics: Material Culture and the Forms of Postmodern Life.* Oxford: Blackwell.

Greene, B. (2000). *The Elegant Universe: Superstrings, Hidden Dimensions, and the Quest for the Ultimate Theory.* New York: Vintage.

Habermas, J. (1983). 'Modernity—an Incomplete Project,' in H. Foster (ed.), *The Anti-aesthetic.* Seattle, WA: Bay Press.

Harvey, D. (1990). *The Condition of Postmodernity: An Enquiry Into the Origins of Cultural Change.* Oxford and Cambridge: Blackwell.

Holbrook, M.B. (1993). 'Postmodernism and Social Theory,' *Journal of Macromarketing*, 3(Fall), 69–75.

Iser, W. (1974). *The Implied Reader.* Baltimore, MD: Johns Hopkins University Press.

Jameson, F. (1991). *Postmodernism, or, the Cultural Logic of Late Capitalism*. Durham, NC: Duke University Press.

Jauss, H. R. (1982). *Toward an Aesthetic of Reception*. Minneapolis, MN: University of Minneapolis Press.

Jencks, C. (1987). *What is Postmodernism?* New York: St Martin's Press.

Keith, R. J. (1960). 'The Marketing Revolution,' *Journal of Marketing*, 24, 35–8.

Kellner, D. (1989). *Jean Baudrillard: From Marxism to Postmodernism and Beyond*. Stanford, CA: Stanford University Press.

Kotler, P. (1972). 'A Generic Concept of Marketing,' *Journal of Marketing*, 36, 46–54.

—— (1991). *Marketing Management: Analysis, Planning, Implementation, and Control*, (7th edn.), Englewood Cliffs, NJ: Prentice-Hall.

—— (2003). *Marketing Management. International Edition*, 11th edn. Englewood Cliffs, NJ: Prentice-Hall.

—— and Levy, S. J. (1969). 'Broadening the Concept of Marketing,' *Journal of Marketing*, 33, 10–15.

Levy, S. J. (1978). *Marketplace Behavior—Its Meaning for Management*. New York: Amacom.

Lotman, Y. M. (1990). *Universe of the Mind: A Semiotic Theory of Culture*. London: I.B. Tauris.

Lyotard, J. F. (1984). *The Postmodern Condition*. Minneapolis, MN: University of Minnesota Press.

Maffesoli, M. (1996). *The Time of the Tribes: The Decline of Individualism in Mass Society*. London: Sage.

Merleau-Ponty, M. (1989). *Phenomenology of Perception*. London: Routledge.

Mick, D. G. and Buhl, C. (1992). 'A Meaning-based Model of Advertising Experiences,' *Journal of Consumer Research*, 19, 317–38.

Miller, M. C. (1989, November). Interview in 'Image and Reality in America: Consuming Images'. *The Public Mind* (television program), hosted by B. Moyers, Part 1, Public Broadcasting Service.

Morgan, A. (1999). *Eating the Big Fish: How Challenger Brands can Compete Against Brand Leaders*. New York: Wiley.

Muñiz, A. M., Jr. and O'Guinn, T. C. (2001). 'Brand community,' *Journal of Consumer Research*, 27, 412–32.

Ogilvy, J. (1990). 'This Postmodern Business,' *Marketing and Research Today*, (February), 4–20.

Perniola, M. (1980). *La Societê dei Simulacri*. Bologna: Capelli.

Poster, M. (1990). *The Mode of Information: Poststructuralism and Social Context*. Chicago: University of Chicago Press.

Postman, N. (1985). *Amusing Ourselves to Death: Public Discourse in the Age of Show Business*. New York: Penguin.

Prigogine, I. and Stengers, I. (1984). *Order Out of Chaos: Man's New Dialogue with Nature*. London: Heinemann.

Proctor, T. and Kitchen, P. J. (2002). 'Communication in Postmodern Integrated Marketing,' *Corporate Communication: An International Journal*, 7, 144–54.

Puto, C. and Wells, W. D. (1984). 'Informational and Transformational Advertising: The Differential Effects of Time,' in T. C. Kinnear (ed.), *Advances in Consumer Research*, 11, Ann Arbor, MI: Association for Consumer Research, pp. 638–43.

Rosenau, P. M. (1992). *Post-Modernism and the Social Sciences: Insights, Inroads, and Intrusions*. Princeton, NJ: Princeton University Press.

Schouten, J. W. and Alexander, J.H. (1995). 'Subcultures of Consumption: An Ethnography of the New Bikers,' *Journal of Consumer Research*, 22, 43–61.

Schudson, M. (1993). *Advertising, the Uneasy Persuasion. Its Dubious Impact on American Society*. New York: Basic Books.

Schultz, D. E., Tannebaum, S. I., and Lauterborn, R. F. (1994). *The New Marketing Paradigm. Integrated Marketing Communications*. Chicago: NTC Business Books.

Sherry, J. F., Jr. (1987). 'Advertising as a Cultural System,' in J. Umiker-Sebeok (ed.), *Marketing and Semiotics. New Directions in the Study of Signs for Sale*. Berlin: Mouton de Gruyter.

—— (1991). 'Postmodern Alternatives: The Interpretive Turn in Consumer Research,' in H. H. Kassarjian and T. Robertson (eds.), *Handbook of Consumer Research*. Englewood Cliffs, NJ: Prentice-Hall.

Stern, B. (1998). 'Deconstructing Consumption Text: A Strategy for Reading the (Re)Constructed Consumer,' *Consumption, Markets & Culture*, 1, 361–92.

Steuerman, E. (1992). 'Habermas vs. Lyotard: Modernity vs. Postmodernity?' in A. E. Benjamin (ed.), *Judging Lyotard*. New York: Routledge.

Stidsen, B. and Schutte, T. F. (1972). 'Marketing as a Communication System: The Marketing Concept Revisited,' *Journal of Marketing*, 36, 22–7.

Vattimo, G. (1992). *The Transparent Society*. Cambridge: Polity Press.

12

Hypermodernity and the New Millennium: Scientific Language as a Tool for Marketing Communications

Eric J. Arnould and Elisabeth Tissier-Desbordes

Twenty years of scholarship exploring the illuminating potential of the idea of postmodernity has left its mark on sociological thinking about marketing and consumption (Brown 1995; Cova 1996; Fırat et al. 1995; Fırat and Venkatesh 1995). But now a new concept—hypermodernity—may help us explicate some apparently contrary trends in the practice of marketing communications. Proponents of postmodernism in marketing focus on the conditions of postmodernity, and especially of marketing and consumption that constitute a rejection of the tenets of modernity (see Chapter 11). In opposition, the proponents of hypermodernity assert that key aspects of the modernist social project continue, while some tenets of modernity retain their sign value for consumers even if their commitment to and understanding of their substance has eroded. For example, an understanding of hypermodernity requires a consideration of its relationship to science and scientific discourse, which modernists, postmodernists, and hypermodernists alike agree had been central to the projects of the modern era.

The primary objective of this chapter is to show the extent to which marketing communication specialists have taken to using elements of scientific discourse in message development, and to place this discussion within the context of the newly emergent hypermodern perspective. The first part focuses on the hypermodernity concept and distinguishes it from modernity and postmodernity. Next, it considers the role of scientific discourse in contemporary marketing communications, specifically through a focus on the depiction of the human body in the marketing of body-care products.

DEFINING HYPERMODERNITY

Because the marketing literature has devoted little discussion to the notion of hypermodernity, a good starting point is to consider how this concept is defined and how it can be distinguished from related notions. To do so, however, first requires familiarity with the postmodern movement in marketing scholarship. Postmodernity is discussed in greater detail in Chapter 11, so we will not revisit this discussion here.

Since postmodernity has started coming under criticism, notably for its inattention to enduring structures of power and inequality and the lack of empirical referents for the hypothesized postmodern consumer (Harvey 1990; Hannerz 1992), new terms have arisen to characterize the current era. Lipovetsky (1983) originally chose to adopt the term 'postmodernity' because he felt that it correctly reflected the loss of ideological benchmarks and the late twentieth century advent of an era of personal emptiness (Cushman 1990). However, he now considers that modern society is characterized by hyperconsumption, hypernarcissism, and hypermodernity—that is, that we are entering a 'hyper' era (Lipovetsky 2003). According to Lipovetsky, the prefix 'post' in the word 'postmodern' has kept our attention focused on a dead past. Instead, he argued:

A climate of epilogue has been followed by the awareness of a flight into the future, unbridled modernization generated by increasingly widespread commercialism, economic deregulations and techno-scientific frenzies whose effects convey as much promise as they do peril (Lipovetsky 2004: 72).

Tellingly, for our subsequent analysis, Lipovetsky singled out techno-science and commercialism as hallmarks of the hypermodern age.

An increasing number of authors have put forth the idea that a new phase of modernity has dawned. For example, Ascher (2000) suggested three phases of modernity: an initial modern phase characterized by market-oriented capitalism; a second modern phase driven by Fordist industrial capitalism; and a third phase called hypermodernity. The first two phases of modernity were characterized by a larger-scale integration of formerly isolated local communities and a departure from tradition and religion. These phases included a movement toward individualism, rational or scientific organization of society, egalitarianism, and the separation of production from consumption (the former of which is institutionally controlled and public, whereas the latter is domestic and private). The most defining events in the modern period include a faith in humanity's ability to understand, control, and manipulate human experience. This is manifested in a forward-looking commitment to science and knowledge, particularly with regard to the convergence of technology and biology. The emphasis on the value of science and technology to overcome natural limitations lends itself to a diminution of the role of the past in society (Firat and Venkatesh 1995).

In Ascher's third stage, more than the end of modernity, we now are witnessing the exaggeration of some of the key features of modernity's early phases (Lash and Urry 1994). A simple definition of hypermodernity is elusive, but we can characterize some elements that other scholars have posited. Giddens (1994) has opposed the postmodern vision of a 'discontinuous' modern history in terms of three aspects: speed of change; scope of change; and the intrinsic nature of modern institutions. In his view, modernity's current dynamism is explained by the separation of time and space, the development of delocalizing mechanisms, and the reflexive appropriation of knowledge, to such an extent that the modern world 'seems more like racing full speed on the back of a tractor-trailer than a quiet car trip' (Giddens 1994: 59). Thus a dizzying pace of social change characterizes hypermodernity.

Hypermodernity also differs from earlier eras of modernity in that it involves an even greater commitment to reason and to an ability to improve individual choice and freedom. Modernity merely held out the hope of reasonable change while continuing to deal with a historical set of issues and concerns; hypermodernity posits that things are changing so quickly that history is not a reliable guide. The positive changes of hypermodernity supposedly include rapidly expanding wealth, better living standards, medical advances, and so forth. Individuals and cultures that benefit directly from these things can feel that they are pulling away from the natural limits that have constrained human life. But the negative effects also can be seen as tending toward a soulless, commercially driven sameness, as well as toward exaggerated cleavages in quality of life between different classes, groups, and world regions.

Hypermodernity also refers to trends in advanced market economies in which the power and the pervasiveness of digital code expands and the acceleration of communications becomes dizzying. Rifkin (2000) spoke of a golden age of access, and Toffler (1991) emphasized the importance of intangibility and information. Hypermodernity is also characterized by an uncontrolled exploitation of the natural environment that threatens the biosphere; biotechnology that begins to unravel the laws of nature; scientific, industrial, and material knowledge that surpasses our knowledge of how to live peacefully and happily; a world in which neoliberal economics is globally ascendant, and in which ideological and religious fragmentation and polarization create multiple rifts across societies. Society, in short, is increasingly unable to assimilate its technical advances and the profusion of information it produces (Barus-Michel 2004; Botting 2003; Wegierski 1995).

In hypermodernity, consumers have become the center of reference for society—but also for themselves. They are lost in an unresolved identity quest (Arnould and Price 2000). Modern ideals imagined a person driven by principle; hypermodernity produces a person as mere image and representation. Modern ideals advance the idea of the person who strives to realize certain universal ideals. In hypermodernity, consumers strive for a posthuman fabrication of a narcissistic self through the techniques of science, bioscience, or communications media; hence, the popularity of 'idols' type television programs, utopian 'reality' programming, plastic surgery, quests for personal sponsorship in new extreme sports, and the like (Barus-Michel 2004; Botting 2003).

Although Giddens questioned the continuing benefits of contemporary progress, he insisted on the continuity of the social mechanisms of trust, 'a fundamental concept for the institutions of modernity' (Giddens 1994: 34). Significantly we argue that the existence of social trust can be found in consumers' acceptance of the discourse of marketing communications. Like all communications, marketing communications take the form of discourse (see Chapter 14). In the social sciences, *discourse* is considered to be an institutionalized way of thinking, a social boundary defining what can and cannot be said about a specific topic. Discourse analysis studies language use by members of speech communities, such as consumers of nature, health, and fashion products (Thompson 2003; Thompson and Haytko 1997), or the producers of marketing communications (Kover 1995; Proctor et al. 2002). It examines both language form and language function, including the study of spoken interaction and written texts. It identifies linguistic features that characterize different genres as well as social and cultural factors that aid in our interpretation and understanding of different texts and types of talk. The chosen discourse delivers the vocabulary, expressions, and also the style needed to communicate. Discourses, as taken-for-granted modes of communication, affect our views of all things; in other words, it is not possible to escape discourse. For example, consistent with North American cultural understandings, words and images in television commercials for coffee in the USA stress its role as a social lubricant typically between dyads, consumed in restaurants, offices, and the more public spaces of homes. However, it is never presented as an appropriate social lubricant for children, nor is it ever shown served in bathrooms, bedrooms, or around the swimming pool (Hirschman et al. 1998). According to Giddens, consumers have faith in brands because they trust and accept the discourse that brands put forth through marketing communications. The brand and the firm that promotes it through artful marketing communications and as conforming to implicit discursive norms are cultural intermediaries (McCracken 1986), which thereby become 'system experts' (Giddens 1994).

It has been suggested that postmodernity implies an 'abandonment of metanarratives,' meaning a rejection of the belief that knowledge is based on solid foundations; a renunciation of faith in scientific progress; the coexistence of a plurality of different types of knowledge; and the loss of commitment to grand projects (Lyotard 1979). However, one criticism of postmodern theory is that consumers continue to trust scientific discourse. Indeed, scientific knowledge is transmitted in most modern educational systems in such a way that it is presented as certain and not to be questioned (Giddens 1994; Haraway 1997: 106–113). While emphasizing the ambivalent nature of individuals' trust in scientific knowledge, Giddens asserted that 'by operating thusly, science has long preserved an image of reliable knowledge. From this derives an ingrained attitude of respect for most forms of technical specialization' (Giddens 1994: 95). This claim is certainly bolstered by our enduring infatuation with technology in management and its spillover into other domains (Long 1993).

If people's attitudes toward science are ambivalent, hypermodernist theory explains that this is because its current possibilities seem so immense. For example, medical science is thought capable of controlling and metamorphosing the body, reshaping the human figure, and correcting natural flaws (Foucault 1975; Frank 1998; Illich 1976; Turner 1987, 1992). It offers the promise of ending age-old scourges such as polio, and finding rapid solutions, such as vaccinations, for terrifying new global plagues (e.g. SARS, avian flu). Moreover, medical science is part of our market-oriented environment. Branded products, such as medicine, body-care products, and sun cream use scientific discourse to promise people progress. The link between consumers' taken-for-granted beliefs in science and consumer behavior in the marketplace is further developed below in our discussion of a particular discursive aspect of marketing communications.

HYPERMODERNITY, MARKETING COMMUNICATIONS, AND SCIENTIFIC DISCOURSE

Hypermodernity can be found in marketing communications in the same way that it can be found in other aspects of the modern world. The consumption (or, to be more precise, hyperconsumption) society is an integral part of hypermodernity, what with all of the marketing tools that are available to firms to help them support and enhance consumption. Within the framework of hypermodernity, the focus of study is on the greater customization of communication tools that increasingly target individuals as opposed to the masses, the use of new technologies (e.g. Internet, Instant Message Services), and an advertising language that uses the signs of hypermodernity, such as the language of science and technology. In the remainder of this chapter we concentrate specifically on how scientific language is used in advertising discourse. In order to develop this scientific discourse notion within the context of marketing, the discussion below focuses on contemporary developments in advertising for body products.

Scientific Communications and the Human Body

The human body and body product advertising have become special topics of interest for research into the signs of hypermodernity. For example, Baudrillard (1980: 155) argued that the body is part of a capitalist political economy that organizes social relationships around the management of signs. In his view, the body has become a 'graveyard for signs.' Not only must it be cared for and maintained, but it also has to be exposed, as witnessed by the rise of topless sunbathing on European beaches (Kaufmann 1998). The increasing exhibition of the body has been accompanied by a growing interest in fashion and in all other products that allow people to put their bodies on display.

The concept of the body has been developed in a variety of ways by modern thinkers; for example, it has been considered as a tool of social interaction (Goffman 1974); a historical idea in the sense of being a simple product of a society's cultural construction (Foucault 1993); a contested cultural marker (Bordo 1993; Godelier and Panoff 1998; Joy and Venkatesh 1994); and a place to register one's habitus (Bourdieu 1979). In poststructuralist thought, 'habitus' refers to a person's total ideational environment. It includes beliefs and dispositions, and prefigures everything that that person may choose to do.

In the West, the twentieth century has transformed the body into a consumer good. The contemporary focus on the body mainly takes shape in the three domains of health, beauty, and sexuality. In these three areas, the body must satisfy the demands of a capitalist world in the sense of performance (Ehrenberg 1991), pleasure and well-being (Bruckner 2000), and youthful esthetics. In each of these areas, the power of biotechnology makes its mark.

The body supplies the contours of one's identity and the sense of being oneself (Le Breton 2002). According to Merleau-Ponty (1964: 180), 'the body intrinsically belongs to two orders: the order of the object and the order of the subject.' By describing the body in this way, he argued for a distinction between the body 'in oneself' and the body 'for oneself.' In other words, the body is simultaneously an object that one can act upon (e.g. by putting on makeup, getting a tattoo, or subjecting it to various therapeutic regimes), but is also a constituent of one's identity (Thompson 2003; Velliquette et al. 1998). Importantly, the operation of the Western tradition of mind-body dualism as a practical cultural blueprint for action is reflected in the ubiquitous images of observable, objectified bodies and body parts in advertisements, the ideology of 'mind over body' in weight-loss and self-help programs, and the multitude of products and medical procedures promoted as enhancing appearance. This dualism underlies a pervasive cultural ideology of control in which the rational, masculinized self (mind) uses its knowledge of technology to manage and control the other side of the duality (body). This desire to control nature through technological intervention is central to Western conceptions of medical science (Thompson and Hirschman 1995). In their desire to have control over various aspects of their environments, individuals often seek first to control their bodies.

Contemporary medical discourse constantly reinforces this notion of the necessary and desirable control of the body. According to Parisoli (2002: 48):

For medicine, the body can be understood through highly sophisticated medico-scientific analyses whose psychophysical standards are often derived from an ideological definition of normality, and where differences from the normative models on offer are almost always interpreted as imperfections to be corrected and as deviations to be judged.

Often enough, normalizing medical discourse has been shown to stigmatize and exert disciplinary control over even marginally deviant behaviors (e.g. Talbot 2004). Medical discourse about the benefits of a balanced diet and daily physical exercise pervades the media. It is amplified by advertising discourse and by the omnipresence of images of normative models, who are generally young, thin, and toned. The consumer body has been denounced by authors (Bordo 1993) who view it as evidence of a masculinist ideology or who feel that the consumer culture places too much value on the body and not enough on the mind (Joy and Venkatesh 1994). But these authors rather miss the point that ideologies of self-control, bodily control, and scientific progress are deeply rooted in our Enlightenment past.

The body has always been an object for a host of care products, finery, embellishments, and staging practices. In fact, in consumer society, where there is a persistent tendency to commercialize anything that has not yet been commercialized, a number of markets have developed that focus on the body. Within these markets, numerous products and services, as well as related marketing communications, are oriented to the importance of keeping the body in good health and to the desire to beautify it; or more precisely, to help it to conform to the esthetic canons of the moment. Thus, sales of over-the-counter beauty products grew by 5 percent a year between 1995 and 2000, becoming a combined $3.2 billion market in France, Germany, Italy, Spain, the UK, and the USA (Gardyn 2001). In China, plastic surgery is on the increase, with an estimated $2.4 billion spent during 2003 (BBC-News 2004). In 2001, French household consumption of beauty-care and body-maintenance products had become a €1.2 billion market that had grown by 60 percent in seven years (Briard 2003). At least 15 percent of Americans have a tattoo and 2 percent are pierced (Whalen 2001). The desire to transform one's body in order to transform one's life has become increasingly widespread: in 2003, 8.8 million Americans underwent cosmetic surgical procedures, a rise of 33 percent over the preceding year (www.plasticsurgery.org). In 2002, 6 percent of French women had plastic surgery (www.ifop.com). Numerous magazines devote long articles to the body, and many books on this topic have become best sellers. Paradoxically, however, the bodies shown in magazines correspond less and less to the reality of consumers' own bodies, in large part due to increased obesity in a growing number of Western societies.

Why do we devote so much importance to, and invest so much money in, the maintenance of our bodies? Many consumer behavior researchers have broached this topic, but often through a postmodern approach focused on such ideas as the liberation of the body, the search for pleasure, the refusal of modernity, the quest for authenticity, and a quest for the natural. In the remainder of this chapter, we argue that this vision does not correspond to the advertising trends currently found in the field of body-care products. Although some body-care brands have adopted a positioning based on natural ingredients and the quest for nature, authenticity, or regional embeddedness, it appears that marketing communications for the more successful brands support the thesis that we inhabit a hypermodern moment, inasmuch as they are promising to reshape people's bodies via the benefits of science. By so doing, they paradoxically signal a retrenchment of one of the basic principles of modernity, faith in scientific progress.

Scientific Discourse and Brands

What discourse do brand managers use for body products? What promises are they making? These are the questions that are important in attempts to understand the nature of this discourse, and to distinguish its elements of modernity, postmodernity, or hypermodernity.

Advertising analysis seems useful in this regard because it comprises one element of cultural meaning transfer. According to McCracken (1986), three places of signification exist in the consumer marketplace: the cultural world, consumer goods, and consumers' habitus. There are also two kinds of transfer: one from the cultural world to goods and the other from goods to consumers. Institutions such as the fashion and advertising industries transfer the cultural world's meanings to products through the discourse of marketing communication, while through ritualized exchange, possession, or grooming practices consumers' appropriate products' meanings.

We examined fifty-five body-product advertisements published in the French women's press appearing in June 2003. The first observation about these advertisements that needs to be made relates to the omnipresence of a form of scientific discourse. The various forms this scientific or para-scientific discourse assumes are described below, but at the outset it should be noted that all of the advertisements used some form of scientific discourse. Even products positioned according to traditionalism or authenticity used scientific discourse, at least to some degree. One interesting example is the retail beauty products chain L'Occitane, which has experienced rapid international growth. It uses retro packaging, affirming that, 'Since ancient times, the immortal is known as an eternal flower. She carries within her the extraordinary secret of youth.' The container is a deep-blue flask with a sepia-colored base and the image of a bouquet of flowers stuck on to remind people of the product's natural ingredients. Here we are close to the trends that postmodernism's proponents have described as the return to one's origins and to magic, mystery, secrets, and nature. However, along with this discourse we find written in small print: 'efficiency tested over six weeks: 38% reduction in total wrinkling area, 89% of all women experience a regenerated and restructured skin, 91% a fresher and younger skin, and 95% a smoother skin.' In other words, statistics are used to bolster the natural claim. The magical natural aspect ('Elixir 100% vegetal in origin') is supplemented by a dose of vitamin E. By including the company's website address in the ad, modernity also is conveyed.

Another general observation pertains to the frequent absence of body images in marketing communication messages for body products. Such images were only apparent in half of the advertisements sampled. Often, only a part of the body is shown, such as the face, hair, or bust. Body images were entirely absent from the other advertisements, suggesting that bodies are no longer needed for communicating about body products. Apparently, its objectification is such that it no longer has to be represented.

THE SIGNS OF HYPERMODERNITY

Among the various signs of hypermodernity that are evident in advertisements for body-care products, five are directly related to science: (1) use of scientific terms, (2) use of technical terms, (3) presence of scientific accessories, (4) depiction of people in scientific professions, and (5) use of statistical terminology. Two other elements that are less directly related to science are (6) use of English terminology in French-language ads; and (7) showing only parts of the body. These signs of hypermodernity are discussed in greater detail below with examples taken from our sample of analyzed body-care product advertisements.

Scientific Terms

The first thing one notices when assessing body-care advertisements is the scientific jargon that is employed. Each product is based on one or several elements that include a number of scientific, chemical, or medical connotations. For example, L'Oréal's 'Visible Lift' is promoted as the first revitalizing foundation with 'Proretinol A+ X-Tensium'. The 'ol' ending evokes chemical products (e.g. alcohols like ethynol, glycol, methanol), whereas 'A+' is a blood category and thus may connote something that seems more 'scientific.' 'X-tensium' evokes both a metal with its 'ium' ending (as in 'uranium') as well as a physical effect, a tightening in one's skin. The trivialization of this term is avoided, however, due to its 'X-' prefix. This is no longer a simple 'tensium' but an 'X-Tensium,' the 'X' making it seem at once more scientifically sophisticated than the simpler variant and more mysterious (as in 'The X-files'). Clarins has a cream proposing a unique 'Multi-Lamellins' technique. 'Lamellins' is a term nowhere to be found in a French dictionary, but it does evoke the word '*lamelles* (small strips),' thus suggestive of layers of skin. Some advertisers apparently have no hesitation in positioning themselves in describing their product as the 'first truly scientific revolution in cosmetics' ('Body Déclic' by Phytomer).

Advertising discourse coopts and sometimes creates linguistic fashions. Some unknown scientific terms have acquired rapid notoriety, occasionally offering a great deal of evocative potential. For instance, although the product arrived in France only in 2003 (Normand 2003), most French consumers are now aware of what 'Botox' is—a purified protein produced by the *Clostridium botulinum* bacterium, according to the official US website (www.botox.com), which reduces the activity of the muscles that causes frown lines to form, and dramatically reduces superficial wrinkling. The same website claims that over one million persons worldwide have been helped by Botox.

Technical Terms and Body as Machine

Most of the body-product advertisements studied used technical language and approaches, referring for instance to processes and formulae (e.g. 'with its active concentrate of cocoa, the Celluli-Choc formula is designed in such a way as to trigger the thinning process'; Lancaster's 'cellular recharger'). Products are promoted as having come from patented scientific research studies (e.g. 'our secret Bio-energetic complex—a registered patent'). Specific scientific words also tend to appear in the ads (e.g. 'Pro-retinol A is encapsulated in nanosomes').

There also is the tendency for science to be mystified in advertisements for body-care products, with a hint of religiosity and magic. Brands have their secrets or magical aspects: 'the magic of X-Tensium, with its unique active tensor.' Mention also is sometimes made of therapy, such as Clinique's active 'water therapy.'

The implication in these sorts of advertisements is that the consumer is supposed to integrate these practices into a rigorous self-caring approach. Caring for one's skin is no longer depicted as an isolated act, but as an entire program. Clarins' lotion is promoted as the 'second stage of the 3-part Basic beauty program.' This is the case even for toothpaste, for which consumers' usage behavior is supposed to fit into long-term programs. Thus, the toothpaste brand Rembrant markets 'an out-patient whitening program.' The parascientific vocabulary can appear to create a scientific feel yet be quite mundane. For instance, Onagrine offers a product featuring active enzymes with a so-called 'double chamber system.'

Body-care products are not the only ones to use scientific or parascientific terms. Cosmetics, which in fact affect appearance much more than skin care, also seek to guarantee their products in scientific terms. For example, Nivea markets a 'Skin-like eye color' eye shadow, an innovation by Nivea Beauty that is 'the first eye shadow with biomimetic ingredients.' Scientific terms can help to reinforce the product's positioning (e.g. portraying it as an innovative product 'that marries your eyelids all day long (biomimetism)'). L'Oréal offers 'Glam Shine,' a moisturizing lipstick with 'a unique crystal micro-particles technology' that is supposed to amplify the 'glamour' and shininess effect.

Body-care products are sometimes depicted as professionally manufactured laboratory preparations (e.g. Wella's 'Système Professionnel'). Natural science terminology can also be used. Liérac markets a product that includes 'Collagen II accelerating vectors.' We also find mention of enzymes, 'bio-active products,' or terms highly evocative of modernity's embrace of technology (e.g. a 'very powerful high-tech filter'; an 'exceptional technology for exceptional care').

Consistent with modernity's embrace of technological progress and scientific management, body-care products often employ the metaphor of the body-as-a-machine. Some products supposedly help to reorganize the body: Vichy's 'Normaderm', which 'reorganizes cells into healthy skin within 4 weeks,' can treat 'a major disorganization of the epidermis.' The time involved, when quantified in this way, reassures people as to the product's efficiency while indicating that the body-as-a-machine can be repaired relatively quickly, and that it is possible to change the course of time and 'resorb imperfections'; that is, to get the body back to normal, as intimated by the product's name ('Normaderm'). The product's density and concentration in active principles are also supposed to guarantee its efficiency: Biotherm's 'Source Therapie' features a 'pure thermal concentrate skin protector' plus 'exceptional concentration in Pure Extract of Thermal Plankton with power to sooth.' Note that capital letters make relatively trivial components seems somehow nobler. Like a machine, the body is meant to use the products on offer to undertake certain tasks. For instance, with Adi-Pill the body will be able to engage in a 'combustion of fat.' With Clarins, the body can eliminate dead cells.

Scientific Accessories

Science is manifest in many accessory objects in body-care advertisements, such as white smocks, stethoscopes, and injections. In Neutrogena's 'Visibly Young' advertisements, for example, the injection symbolizes the strength of a cream that is allegedly just as powerful as a collagen injection. It is interesting to note that although what is being promised is 'visibly younger skin without the need for collagen injections,' a barely visible footnote reads, 'this anti-age care agent is no substitute for the efficiency of a collagen injection.' The product's packaging can also serve to remind people of the realm of the scientific through mimicry—a medicine bottle (Adi-Pill) or mini-doses of serum (Liérac).

Statistical Terminology

Numbers in advertisements often provide linguistic signs of scientific proof and, in fact, we find statistical language is frequently used in brand promotions. For instance, Biotherm claims to possess 'a proven efficiency, as many women agree: 73% say their cellulite is gone, 90% that their capillaries are smoother and 87% that their skin is more beautiful (out of a total 60 women tested over 4 weeks).' Similarly, with Mixa's Intensif Peau Sèche dry skin treatment, 'tests prove its great efficiency: +95% remoisturization, −67% dryness, +87% suppleness.' In the Mixa ad, a footnote refers to the 'findings of a cosmeto-clinical study.' Specific information concerning how many persons were questioned, what was being measured, whether the moisturizing effect was real or simply a perception is not provided. Mixa's claims also provide evidence of the typical consumer's satisfaction with the brand's promised actions. These uses of statistics also show implicit knowledge of framing effects. Thus, Maxi's claim of a −67% dryness reduction, or Phytomer's claim that Body Déclic 'blocks 75% of all fat formation' reminds us of classic research in prospect theory (Tversky and Kahneman 1974).

The Presence of People in Science

As has long been the case in television advertising, a person dressed in a white smock or otherwise surrounded by scientific-looking paraphernalia symbolizes scientific knowledge. Actors appear as doctors on studio sets that look like doctors' offices or labs. This practice is found in print advertising as well. For example, an advertisement for the biscuit brand, Gerblé's, depicts a person in a white smock who could be a medical student, and who the ad implies has survived his difficult studies by eating biscuits 'with choco-magnesium, rich in magnesium, vitamin B and wheat germ.'

The body-care advertisements described here did not overtly feature characters dressed as doctors or scientists, but they did refer to persons in science—be they doctors, nutritional experts, or dermatologists. Products are described as having been designed by doctors (e.g. Clarin's 'designed by dermatologists'clearing lotion) or 'formulated under medical control' (e.g. Mixa Intensif Peau Sèche dry skin treatment). Members of the medical profession also recommend (e.g. Onagrine is 'recommended by dermatologists') and message recipients are encouraged to seek the advice of scientific professionals (e.g. 'Consult your pharmacist today').

English Language

Science cannot remain bound by national borders; in fact, the rhetoric of modern science makes claims to international significance. The use of international languages alone is often a sign of globalism, as is apparent in other advertising contexts (Sherry and Comargo 1987). Many French advertisements use English language terminology, most often in the product's name (e.g. Estée Lauder's Day Wear Plus, Phytomer's Body Déclic, Clinique's Water Therapy, Guerlain's 'Happylogy'), but also in slogans (e.g. Wella's 'Beautiful hair needs an expert') and in representations of the product's possible effects (e.g. Liérac 'Self-lifting'). This usage of the English language in European advertisements is partially explained by the products' international distribution. In addition, use of English may reflect North America's assertion of high technology as a 'national symbol of progress' (Nelkin 1997: 33; Thompson and Hirschman 1995). Given the other signs of science in the ads, the implicit claim to scientific universalism cannot be discounted.

The Absent Body or The Body-As-An-Object

The images that appear in advertisements are often offered as proof of perfection. For example, an advertisement for the L'Oreal line of body-care products, Biotherm, claims that the product can provide the consumer with a 'bottom with not one gram of cellulite.' For this advertisement, only the lower part of the model's body is depicted. The subject disappears to create room for the 'body-as-an-object' that is broken down into parts and thus objectified. It can be said that the absent woman is a foundational element of scientific discourse, a taken-for-granted constituent of this discourse since the seventeenth century (e.g. Haraway 1997).

Transfiguration

Through partial depiction in advertisements, bodies appear to be transfigured. *Transfiguration* refers to attempting to live and consume in ways that will lead toward acceptance according to the conventional canons of society. For consumers whose gaze is directed to these objectified, normalized, and perfected body parts, the problem becomes how to transform oneself from a condition of failure to conform to cultural standards to an ultimate state of meeting the standards for normality. In many cases, the route toward such a transformation lies in consumption aimed at physical beautification via the products promoted in the ads. Through consumption of 'scientific' body-care products, consumers are expected to reflect acquired perfection, in line with dominant ideals (Holbrook et al. 1998; Thompson and Hirschman 1995).

EXPLAINING THE USE OF SCIENCE AS A MARKETING COMMUNICATION TOOL

Scientific and technological discourse in the communications environment is ubiquitous. Its ubiquity is reflected in the large number of popular science vehicles, including magazines like *Popular Mechanics*, *Discover*, *National Geographic*, and, *Scientific American* and television programs such as 'Nova' and cable channels (Discovery, Animal Planet, National Geographic). Journalistic representations of scientific arguments swirl about important policy debates over atmospheric ozone, the effects of chemical residues in the environment, biotechnology, and global warming (Gross 1990; Nelkin 1997). Perhaps then it is not surprising that marketing communication also turns to the language of science.

Many advertisements (like those for the body-care products described above) and other types of marketing communications make frequent and recurring allusions to science. Promotional appeals based on medical scientific claims can be traced to the late nineteenth century (Gusfield 1992). Yet few studies have focused directly on the efficiency of scientific discourse when used to promote products or services, although Ippolito and Mathios (1990) did demonstrate its persuasive strength in their studies of cereal consumption. Our study suggests no abatement in the deployment of the signs of science in advertisements, as one might expect if the alleged postmodern retreat from modernist master narratives prevailed.

But can the discourse apparent in marketing communications really be described as a scientific one? Most consumers are not familiar with the way the products discussed above have been manufactured or with the research methods used to develop them. Thus, we may be 'impregnated with scientific thinking' as Granger (1993: 14) claimed, but this is a science that is distant from the experience of most of us, revealing its secrets scientists and scientific journalists are quick to assert only to select initiates (Nelkin 1997; Shapin and Schaffer 1985).

We argue that what are proposed to the consumer through the scientific discourse in marketing communications are really instrumentalist technological solutions. Instrumentalist technology involves using artifices to extend human capabilities (Borgmann 1987), and it reverts back to the pervasive cultural ideology of control in which rational selves use knowledge and technology to manage and control the body (Thompson and Hirschman 1995).

Currently, advertisements like those described in the section 'The Signs of Hypermodernity' above imply that consumers need no longer make active efforts to control the body. The omnipresence of instrumental technological solutions including all types of creams, lotions, dietary supplements, pills, plastic surgery, and silicone implants is the solution. In addition to their scientific tone, magic and hedonism color these ads, as evidenced by messages like 'lose weight effortlessly' and 'a diet you'll love,' respectively. And, consistent with our claim that the present age is more hypermodern than postmodern is evidence that shows how little the overall ideology of bodily control has changed. Thus, dieting has never been more fashionable and has an increasingly significant impact on the nature of offerings in the consumer marketplace, such as the recent fad for high protein, low carbohydrate offerings (e.g. the Atkins diet). From the starved androgynes of the 1960s, to the aerobicized bodies of the 1980s, and the dieted, plastic-surgically enhanced bodies of today, panopticism and internalization of a norming medical-technological discourse is evident.

For metaphysical realists (Gross 1990), science and reason continue to go hand-in-hand, but the popular belief in science is not entirely grounded in reason. During the later 1800s, Broca (1989: 51) wrote:

Science should refer to itself and to nothing else. It must not capitulate to demands expressed by any parties. It is an august goddess that reigns o'er humanity, to lead us but not to follow. Only of science can it ever be said that she was made to command without ever having obeyed.

Contrary to his likely intent, Broca's words tellingly deify science, placing it above reason. Chalmers (1987: 13) similarly suggested that 'the modern era holds science in high esteem.' This is consistent with the idea that science is assimilated to a sort of mythic belief in the popular mind; an ideology implanted and progressively extended since the Enlightenment (Fayera-bend 1979; Shapin and Schaffer 1985). But a belief in what? Haraway (1997: 41) argued that for most of us, the 'principle social weight of technoscience' is and has been its promise of miraculous solutions to come. And in this way, technoscience in the popular mind is really not very different from marketing in which the transformative promise of the brand is central.

In short, advertising claims offered in terms of the signs of scientific research, real or ostensible, are customarily viewed as guidelines to which rational individuals should adhere (Thompson and Hirschman 1995). But a significant aspect of their persuasive force is provided by 'technoscientific salvation stories' of perfection that lie 'at the heart of Enlightenment humanism' (Haraway 1997: 8–9).

CONCLUSION

Lasch (1977: 46) lamented the contemporary preoccupation with mental and physical well-being:

With the world assuming an increasingly threatening tone, life has become an endless quest for health and well-being through exercise, diet, medicine, all sorts of spiritual regimes, psychic assistance for oneself and psychiatry. People preoccupied with their own state of health are people who are no longer interested in the outside world, except insofar as it remains a source of gratification or frustration.

More recently, Lipovetsky (1983) affirmed that the growing significance attributed to the body is a reflection of rising individualism that has led to 'advanced narcissism.' Individuals are interested in themselves, hence the concentration on their own bodies with a view towards controlling (and even reshaping) them. Narcissism is fertile terrain for the cultivation of a kind of cyborg esthetics to which contemporary advertisements respond.

As previously discussed, proponents of postmodernism view the modern era as one marked by an abandonment of metanarratives, by mistrust of science, and by renunciation of faith in technoscientific progress (Lyotard 1979). Yet what the foregoing has revealed is the use being made of the signs of scientific discourse in contemporary marketing communications, as well as the existence of a presumptive belief in the possibilities of science as something capable of metamorphosing our bodies. Real and make-believe scientific terms are being used everywhere, giving an illusion of science and, hence, new potentialities. The impression this gives the user of the products involved is one of omnipotence, a belief apparently cultivated by the huge biotechnology industry (Haraway 1997: 63–66).

In our view, advertising specialists' use of scientific discourse demonstrates the ongoing strength of metanarratives such as progress in science and the predominance of the singular; that is, of the individual as opposed to the masses. Thus, in marketing communications in the hypermodern period can be seen an intensification of two of the founding signs of modernity—individualism and science.

REFERENCES

Arnould, E. J. and Price, L. L. (2000). 'Authenticating Acts and Authoritative Performances: Questing for Self and Community,' in S. Ratneshwar, D. G. Mick, and C. Huffman (eds.), *The Why of Consumption: Contemporary Perspectives on Consumers' Motives, Goals, and Desires*. New York: Routledge, pp. 140–63.

Ascher, F. (2000). *Ces Évènements qui nous Dépassent, Feignons d'en être les Organisateurs*. Paris: Editions de l'Aube.

Barus-Michel, J. (2004). 'L'hypermodernité, Dépasssement ou Perversion de la Modernité,' in N. Aubert (ed.), *L'individu Hypermoderne*, Ramonville Saint-Agne, France: Érès, pp. 239–48.

Baudrillard, J. (1980). *L'échange Symbolique et la Mort*. Paris: NRF.

BBC-News (2004, August 4). China to Hold Fake Beauty Contest. Available http://news.bbc.co.uk

Bordo, S. (1993). *Unbearable Weight, Feminism, Western Culture and the Body*. Berkeley, CA: University of California Press.

—— (1998). 'Bringing Body to Theory,' in D. Welton (ed.), *Body and Flesh*. Oxford, UK: Blackwell.

Borgman, A. (1987). *Technology and the Character of Contemporary Life*. Chicago: University of Chicago Press.

Botting, F. (2003). 'Metaphors and Monsters,' *Journal for Cultural Research*, 7, 339–66.

Bourdieu, P. (1979). *La Distinction : Critique Sociale du Jugement*. Paris: Editions de Minuit.

Briard, C. (2003). Le « Spa », Marché en Plein Bouillonnement. *Les Echos*, (February 25), 47.

Broca, P. (1869/1989). *Mémoires d'anthropologie*, Paris: J.M. Place.

Brown, S. (1995). *Postmodern Marketing*. London: Thomson Learning Europe.

Bruckner, P. (2000). *L'euphorie Perpétuelle. Essai sur le Devoir de Bonheur*. Paris: Grasset.

Chalmers, A. (1987). *Qu'est-ce que la Science?*. Paris: La Découverte.

Cova, B. (1996). 'The Postmodern Explained to Managers: Implications for Marketing,' *Business Horizons*, 39, 15–24.

Cushman, P. (1990). 'Why the Self is Empty: Towards a Historically Situated Psychology,' *American Psychologist*, 45, 599–611.

Ehrenberg, A. (1991). *Le Culte de la Performance*. Paris: Calmann-Lévy.

Fayerabend, P. K. (1979). *Contre la Méthode*. Paris: Seuil.

Firat, A. F., Dholakia, N., and Venkatesh, A. (1995). 'Marketing in a Postmodern World,' *European Journal of Marketing*, 29, 40–56.

—— and Venkatesh, A. (1995). 'Liberatory Postmodernism and the Reenchantment of Consumption,' *Journal of Consumer Research*, 22, 239–67.

Foucault, M. (1975). *The Birth of the Clinic: An Archaeology of Medical Perception*. New York: Vintage.

—— (1993). *Surveiller et Punir*. Paris: Gallimard.

Frank, A. W. (1998). 'Foucault or not Foucault? Commonwealth and American Perspectives on Health in the Neo-liberal State,' *Health*, 2, 329–48.

Gardyn, R. (2001, February). The Mane Event. *American Demographics*, pp. 12–13.

Giddens, A. (1994). *Les Conséquences de la Modernité*. Paris: L'Harmattan.

Godelier, M. and Panoff, M. (1998). *La Production du Corps*. Paris: Archives Contemporaines.

Goffman, E. (1974). *Les Rites d'interaction*. Paris: Minuit.

Granger, G.-G. (1993). *La Science et les Sciences. Que sais-je?*. Paris: PUF.

Gross, A. G. (1990). *The Rhetoric of Science*. Cambridge, MA: Harvard University Press.

Gusfield, J. R. (1992). 'Nature's Body and the Metaphors of Food,' in M. Lamont and M. Fournier (eds.), *Cultivating Differences,*. Chicago: University of Chicago, pp. 75–103.

Hannerz, U. (1992). *Cultural Complexity: Studies in the Social Organization of Meaning*. New York: Columbia University Press.

Haraway, D. J (1997). *Modest_Witness@Second Millennium. FemaleMan©_Meets_OncoMouse™*. New York: Routledge.

Harvey, D. (1990). 'Between Space and Time: Reflections on the Geographical Imagination,' *Annals, Association of American Geographers*, 80, 38–47.

Hirschman, E. C., Scott, L., and Wells, W. B. (1998). 'A Model of Product Discourse: Linking Consumer Practice to Cultural Texts,' *Journal of Advertising*, 27, 33–51.

Holbrook, M. B., Block, L. G, and Fitzsimons, G. J. (1998). 'Personal Appearance and Consumption in Popular Culture: A Framework for Descriptive Analysis,' *Consumption, Markets and Culture*, 2, 1–56.

Ippolito, P. M. and Mathios, A. D. (1990). 'The Regulation of Science-based Claims in Advertising,' *Journal of Consumer Policy*, 13, 413–45.

Illich, I. (1976). *Medical Nemesis: The Expropriation of Health*. New York: Pantheon.

Joy, A. and Venkatesh, A. (1994). 'Postmodernism, Feminism and the Body: The Visible and the Invisible in Consumer Research,' *International Journal of Research in Marketing*, 11, 333–57.

Kaufmann, J.-C. (1998). *Corps de Femmes, Regards d'homme, Sociologie des Seins nus*. Paris: Nathan.

Kover, A. J. (1995). 'Copywriters' Implicit Theories of Communication: An Exploration,' *Journal of Consumer Research*, 21, 596–612.

Lasch, C. (1977). *Haven in a Heartless World*. New York: Basic.

Lash, S. and Urry J. (1994) *Economies of Signs and Space*. London: Sage.

Le Breton, D. (2002). *Signes d'identité*. Paris: Editions Métailié.

Lipovetsky, G. (1983). *L'ère du Vide*. Paris: Gallimard.

—— (2003, March-April). La Société d'hyperconsommation. *Le débat*, 124, 74–98.

—— (2004). *Les Temps Hypermodernes*. Paris: Grasset.

Long, T. L. (1993). *A Postmodern Critique of Business and Education Partnerships in the Technical Community College*. Paper presented at the Southern Humanities Council Annual Conference, University of Alabama at Huntsville, February 13, 1993.

Lyotard, J.-F. (1979). *La Condition Postmoderne*. Paris: Minuit.

Marzano Parisoli, M. M. (2002). *Penser le Corps*. Paris: PUF.

McCracken, G. (1986). 'Culture and Consumption: A Theoretical Account of the Structure and Movement of the Cultural Meaning of Consumer Goods,' *Journal of Consumer Research*, 13, 71–84.

Merleau-Ponty, M. (1964). *Phénoménologie de la Perception*. Gallimard: Paris.

Nelkin, D. (1997). *Selling Science: How the Press Covers Science and Technology*, (2nd edn.), New York: W. H. Freeman.

Normand, J.-M. (2003). Botox, l'antirides qui fait des Vagues. *Le Monde*, (March 26), 33.

Proctor, S., Proctor, T., and Papasolomou-Doukakis, I. (2002), 'A Post-Modern Perspective on Advertisements and Their Analysis,' *Journal of Marketing Communications*, 8, 31–45.

Rifkin, J. (2000). *The Age of Access, the New Culture of Hypercapitalism, Where All Life is a Paid-for Experience*. New York: G.P. Putnam's.

Shapin, S. and Schaffer, S. (1985). *Leviathan and the Air-pump: Bobbes, Boyle, and the Experimental life*. Princeton, NJ: Princeton University Press.

Sherry, J. F., Jr. and Camargo, E. G. (1987). 'May Your Life be Marvelous: English Language Labelling and the Semiotics of Japanese Promotion,' *Journal of Consumer Research*, 14, 174–88.

Talbot, M. (2004). The Bad Mother. *The New Yorker* (August 9), 62–5.

Thompson, C. J. (2003). 'Natural Health Discourses and the Therapeutic Production of Consumer Resistance,' *Sociological Quarterly*, 44, 81–103.

—— and Haytko, D. L. (1997). 'Speaking of Fashion: Consumers' Uses of Fashion Discourses and the Appropriation of Countervailing Cultural Meanings,' *Journal of Consumer Research*, 24, 15–43.

—— and Hirschman, E. C. (1995). 'Understanding the Socialized Body: A Poststructuralist Analysis of Consumers' Self-conceptions, Body Images, and Self-care Practices,' *Journal of Consumer Research*, 22, 139–53.

Toffler, A. (1991). *Powershift: Knowledge, Wealth, and Violence at the Edge of the 21st Century*. New York: Bantam.

Turner, B. S. (1987). *Medical Power and Social Knowledge*. London: Sage.

—— (1992). *Regulating Bodies: Essays in Medical Sociology*. London: Routledge.

Tversky, A. and Kahneman, D. (1974). 'Judgment Under Uncertainty: Heuristics and Biases,' *Science*, 185, 1124–31.

Velliquette, A. M., Murray, J. B., and Creyer, E.H. (1998). 'The Tattoo Renaissance: An Ethnographic Account of Symbolic Consumer Behavior,' in J. W. Alba and

W. Hutchinson (eds.), *Advances in Consumer Research*, Provo, UT: Association for Consumer Research, 25, 461–67.

Wegierski, M. (1995). 'The Dilemma of Hypermodernity: Hypermodernity vs. Post-modernity,' *Journal of Religion and Psychical Research*, 18, 21–5.

Whalen, D. (2001). 'Ink me, Stud,' *American Demographics* (December), 9–11.

13

Identity in Marketing Communications: An Ethics of Visual Representation

Janet L. Borgerson and Jonathan E. Schroeder

In contemporary marketing communications, images claim center stage. The focus on image—over and above function—challenges basic notions of marketing practice, shifts appropriate topics of analysis, and reinforces the visual domain's centrality. Serving as stimuli, signs, or representations that drive cognition, interpretation, and preference, images influence what we know and believe (cf. Zaltman 2002). Not surprisingly, images consti-tute much corporate communication about products and services, economic performance, and organizational identity. Pictures of people—models, celebrity endorsers, spokespersons, 'average' consumers, man-agers, and employees—make up a large part of marketing imagery. More-over, images provide resources for, and, hence, shape, our understandings of the world, including the identities of its people and places. If marketing communications depend upon images, including brand images, corporate images, product images, and images of identity, then ethical tools meant to provide guidance in marketing communications must be capable of ad-dressing the concerns that such depictions evoke.

In this chapter, we investigate marketing communication's role in 'the taken-for-granted political and ethical practices of envisioning others' (Hey-wood and Sandywell 1999: x). Discussions of marketing ethics rarely include visual issues, apart from largely atheoretical concerns over shock advertis-ing, sexual appeals, or stereotyping; rather, they typically revolve around deception, the questionable accuracy of product claims, and the targeting of vulnerable consumers, such as children (e.g. Smith and Quelch 1993). These approaches to marketing ethics generally adopt an information-based model of marketing communication, emphasizing marketing's role as a strategic conduit of information for consumers, rather than fully acknowledging how marketing also acts as a representational system that produces meaning outside the realm of the promoted product or service (see Schroeder and Salzer-Mörling 2005; Scott and Batra 2003). This situation emerges in part because of a failure to confront the ethical concerns that arise in the wake of the prominence of the image—including advertising images, corporate images, and images of identity—within today's image economy.

Ethically motivated criticisms of marketing communications are often simplistically understood as generalized critiques of capitalism and related excessive consumption (e.g. Crane and Matten 2004; Thompson 2004). Our work in marketing communication ethics does not include criticism of consumption per se, nor do we take a moralistic stance against material- ism or marketing's possible role in promoting materialistic desires—valid as those criticisms may be. Rather, we focus on ethical issues pertaining to representations of identity, in that represented identities profess to express something true or essential about those represented. Just as personnel policies have had to accommodate changing norms about hiring and promotion when it comes to women and minorities, marketing managers must be aware of representational practices that may cause harm. Our analysis concerns not only the ethical implications or consequences of *representational conventions*—customary ways of depicting products, people, and identities—within marketing communications, but empha- sizes the ethical context from which such representational conventions emerge.

Whereas discussions of marketing communication ethics often encour- age appropriate use of images, most lack a conceptual framework for recognizing and understanding ethical issues in visual representation. Typical guidelines for marketing communication ethics list categories such as legal matters—false claims, misleading statements, and improper labeling—deceptive pricing, and image appropriateness as relevant for ethical review (Armstrong 2004; Crane and Matten 2004). However, ethical checklists provide few criteria by which to judge whether ads contain, for example, 'sexual innuendos which are considered inappropri- ate for audience,' or 'no ethnic stereotyping.' We introduce an ethics of visual representation that provides such criteria and sheds light on the appropriateness dimension of marketing communications. Evalu- ations of ad appropriateness must be informed by an awareness of the ethical relationship between marketing representations and identity. We conclude by discussing the implications arising from an ethics of visual representation as a vital issue for marketing communication practice and research.

VISUAL REPRESENTATION WITHIN THE
IMAGE ECONOMY

Visual images exist within a distinctive sociolegal environment—unlike textual or verbal statements, such as product claims or political promises, pictures cannot be held to be true or false. Thus, images provide an efficient means by which marketing strategists can avoid being held accountable for false or misleading claims; images elude empirical verification. For example, cigarette manufacturers have learned not to make text-based claims about their products, relying instead on visual imagery such as the lone cowboy roaming the American West.

Concerns about the persuasive power and rhetorical influence of marketing images have been countered by references to so-called 'postmodern' notions of resistance and rising advertising literacy (cf. Elliott and Wattanasuwan 1998; O'Donohoe and Tynan 1998; Pettigrew 2001). That is, continued criticisms of marketing communication's power to exert influence and reinforce ethically irresponsible representations of identity—such as a beer company's sexist and long-running, imaginary 'Swedish bikini team'—have been met with claims that consumers knowingly interpret visual or text-based advertising messages, selectively choose meanings, and resist rhetorical persuasion. For example, a recent business ethics textbook downplays concerns about advertising's perpetuation of harmful stereotypes by claiming that many 'social commentators ... contend that, as a society, we have never been so informed and educated about the role of advertising, promotion, and branding as we are today' (Crane and Matten 2004: 276). On the contrary, we argue that, outside of university courses in communication and cultural studies, there is relatively little education about marketing communication's social, cultural, and pedagogical roles, nor about the production, history, and theory of visual representation.

Marketing communication's ubiquity does not necessarily improve one's capacity to *see*—to actively engage one's senses in reflective analysis (Schroeder 2002). Further, it is unclear how each new generation of consumers might benefit from such so-called advertising literacy; that is, children are not born with the innate ability to understand the underlying context of cultural meanings at work in marketing communications, no matter how many times parents tell them that an advertised toy will only be fun for a few minutes, although it looks great in the ads, or that a pair of athletic shoes cannot really make you run faster, or that models really do not look like that in real life.

Even when consumers realize an image or image-based scenario is not 'real,' the image may influence how they perceive and respond to their world. Whereas decades of women realize that the bloody shower scene in Alfred Hitchcock's harrowing film, *Psycho,* is not 'real,' images from that scene, and others like it, no doubt have discouraged many from enjoying a shower. Similarly, images of the 'exotic other'—from Augustus Earle's sketches of early 1800s Pacific islanders and Edward S. Curtis's twentieth century photographs of Native Americans to the iconic native island girl in tropical holiday promotions, suntan lotion ads, and fashion shoots—give us a sense that we know places, times, and peoples that we have never directly experienced. Given such wide-ranging influence, recent work in marketing scholarship urges us to consider marketing images as cultural texts, and not merely as accurate or true strategic pictures that transparently record faces, families, or familiar products, services, and sights (Mick et al. 2004; Schroeder 2002; Scott 1994).

Images in marketing communication frequently stand in for experience, especially when other sources have less prominence, and serve as a foundation for future attempts to comprehend and construct the world around us. As a result, images have attracted attention from marketing strategists, advertising practitioners, and consumer researchers, and have increasingly evoked criticism from cultural theorists and policy makers. Moreover, although researchers increasingly acknowledge consumer response as fundamental to ad interpretation, the power of images is not well understood. Ours is not a naive claim that consumers believe artificial, stereotypical, or idealized realms can or do exist, or that consumers consume advertising images from a single, unitary, or predetermined (so-called 'structuralist') perspective. Rather, marketing images contribute to the 'reality' into which contemporary consumers are socialized and often evade notions of creative interpretation and critical resistance.

According to some critics, pictures themselves contain such potent rhetorical authority that they require drastic action to curb their persuasive appeal (see McQuarrie and Mick 1999; Schroeder 2002; Scott 1994). For example, Dan Romer, from the Annenberg Public Policy Center, has argued that 'banning pictures from ads would help end the image that smoking is fun and give marketing campaigns about tobacco dangers a chance to work' ('Cigarette Ads' 2001: 6). Images of beautiful people exhibiting no signs of nicotine addiction or its debilitating effects help maintain a positive vision of smoking. This persuasive power of marketing images depends largely upon the rhetorical representational conventions of photographic reproduction; that is, advertising, corporate reports, packaging, product catalogs, promotional materials, and Web graphics rely heavily upon photographic information technology to produce meaning within a circuit of production and consumption.

Photographic images—including digital pictures, film, video, and Internet graphics—perform so often and so fluidly for marketing, scientific, legal, and political purposes that it can be difficult to keep in mind that photographs are selectively edited and culturally produced images that exist within shifting planes of meaning and significance. Photographs often appear as if they are merely visual records of what has happened, how people look, or where events took place at a particular moment. Marketing communication researchers must acknowledge the subjectivity of visual representation in studying the commercial landscape that everyday consumers encounter, keeping in mind that art directors, photographers, advertising executives, and corporate strategists choose from a range of images and juxtapose these with product and text in order to create 'ordinary advertisements.'

Viewers make sense of visual images in a number of ways, many of which are automatic or without awareness (cf. Bargh 2002). Many perceptual processes fluctuate between conscious and unconscious control. For example, cognitive as well as physiological processes govern eye movement, attention, and awareness. Perceptual codes influence visual information processing—Westerners generally read from left to right, and from top to bottom. Further, perceptual cues, such as relative size, shape, color, and symmetry contribute to consumer cognition at a level at which most are only dimly aware (cf. Arnheim 1974). Objects or people that appear larger in the visual frame are generally ascribed more perceptual and symbolic importance than those that appear small. Representational conventions—or common patterns of portraying objects, people, or identities—work in conjunction with these perceptual and cultural processes that often elude marketing communication research.

ETHICAL FOUNDATIONS

An image economy requires approaches to ethics and marketing communication that move beyond codes of conduct, individual manager's actions, or particular campaigns. The ethics of visual representation that we propose focuses on representational practices and their ethical implications, and emphasizes the ethical context from which representational conventions emerge. Along these lines, philosopher Margaret Urban Walker (1998: 178) contended that the assumption that people are a *kind* or *type* is propagated and created by representational conventions, which 'are among those that construct socially salient identities for people.' She further argued that if representational practices 'affect some people's morally significant perceptions of and interactions with other people, and if they can contribute to those perceptions or interactions going seriously wrong, these activities have bearing on fundamental ethical questions' (Walker 1998: 179). One of the most serious outcomes of representational practices is that people's perceptions, even 'misinformed perceptions,' often have 'the weight of established facts' (Gordon 1995: 203).

Contemporary ethical theorists have written extensively on the relation between representation and identity, calling attention to ontological status—understood as semiotically constructed rather than 'natural' (e.g. Bartky 1991; Borgerson 2001; Butler 1987/1999; Gordon 1995; Walker 1998). *Ontology* centers on notions of being or identity—including human identity—who one is and who one is not, including how relationships form and function. Ethics and ontology are linked by a concern about how visual markers such as skin color, embodiment, and gendered attributes represent or determine the status of human beings, particularly in the context of racism and sexism. Thus, what we think we know about others from representations of identity—including those within marketing communications—can affect how we see, treat, and understand them. Although alternative or resistant ways of looking at marketing images are possible (e.g. reading mainstream ads as 'gay' or interpreting sexist ads as 'camp,' 'ironic,' or 'parody'), this often simply reflects responses to or reconfigurations of the dominant system (Bourdieu and Passeron 1990; Kates 1999). Representations of subordinate groups, such as the poor (Kay and Jost 2003), the elderly (Carrigan and Szmigin 2000), and ethnic minorities (O'Barr 1994) rarely contradict and typically reproduce versions of subordination. For example, a comprehensive study of gender roles in television advertisements around the world found that, despite some recent changes, ads 'typically show men as authoritative and knowledgeable, whereas women are confined at home' (Furnham 1999: 434). In this way, the global commercial environment reproduces stereotypes that tend to limit women's opportunities and potential.

Basic communicative building blocks revolve around identity and difference (cf. Woodward 1997). Ontological assumptions related to representations of identity, or assumptions about who and what the represented ones are, intersect with culturally defined hierarchies and dominant semiotics used in marketing communications. *Dominant semiotics*—grounding what categories, characteristics, or individual signs can mean within the dominant culture—prescribe and structure the elements of identity and difference that will be readily rendered as culturally intelligible. Semiotic meaning draws upon dualistic notions of being, identity and difference—such as self/other, male/female, White/Black, rational/emotional, culture/nature, and normal/exotic—the opposed elements of which stabilize various positive and negative cultural associations and values. These semiotic associations are taken seriously, and often purport to express something natural and true. Setting one element against the other (e.g. White vs. Black) has perpetuated and reinforced the dualistic hierarchical orderings that historically have favored the male, the White, and the rational (cf. Goldberg 1993). Representational conventions in marketing communications draw upon these meaning systems, which may reinforce and reproduce damaging images of identity. In such a context, those associated with the privileged elements—the male, the rational, and the normal—stand in the position to claim knowledge of and denigrate all that is important to know about those associated with the subordinated elements—the female, the emotional, and the exotic (Borgerson 2001).

This type of semiotically dualistic relation engages with the potential for *epistemic closure*, an ethical concept calling attention to the danger of typified representations of identity that increase the probability of human subjects interpreting what they experience or have represented to them as typically true. Typified representations, especially those that are racist or sexist, may undermine a group's dignity and historical integrity and cast a demeaning light upon their physical and intellectual habits and ontological status as human beings. A worldview informed by epistemic closure abstracts and condenses characteristics that create familiar group associations, identities, and types. Epistemic closure leads people to believe that they know the other's being completely, undermining the other's status as human being and limiting possibilities for human relationships (Gordon 1997). We contend that marketing images are never appropriate if they create epistemic closure without reasonable justification.

In sum, marketing representations have the power to lead us to believe that we know something we have no experience of and to influence the experiences we have in the future. The way that such representations stand in when experience is lacking, or function in conjunction with experience, is of particular concern in marketing strategy and ethical analyses of marketing communications. How does one recognize ethically problematic representations? In the following sections we argue that marketing requires a semiotic understanding of the cultural context in which images and representation circulate.

THE CONTEMPORARY STATUS OF MARKETING COMMUNICATIONS

Although marketing communication remains first and foremost a strategic tool, our analysis attempts to locate marketing images within a complex visual signifying arena that includes the interrelated domains of the esthetic and the ethical (cf. Hall 1997). Therefore, we situate marketing communications within a system of visual representation that creates meaning within the circuit of culture—often beyond the managerial control of any one organization or strategic vision. This circuit assumes that marketing messages both create and contribute to culture, largely via representational conventions (see Hall 1997; Schroeder and Zwick 2004; Stern and Schroeder 1994; Thompson 1995). A simple representational convention occurs in wristwatch ads, where most watches show the time as ten minutes past ten o'clock. Another familiar convention appears in the so-called 'portrait' format—the vertical orientation of celebrity 'head shots,' executive portraits, pictures of satisfied consumers, and most magazines and newspapers. Other, more complicated conventions include the way fashion models pose in highly stylized manners, taught by modeling agencies and expected by photographers and designers.

Conventional views of representation hold that categories, such as objects, products, or consumers, exist in the material and natural world, and that their material characteristics define them in perfectly clear terms; representation, according to this view, is of secondary importance in the construction of meaning. In our view, meaning is produced or constructed by social and cultural forces; thus, representation assumes primary importance. The process of representing objects, ideas, and identities shapes how we think of them; in this way, representation enters into the very constitution of things and categories. Because representation refers to meaning production through language systems, how language—including visual representation—functions is central to creating meaning. Using representation as an analytic tool, researchers have emphasized how cultural practices, such as laws, rituals, norms, art, and advertising, contribute to meaning production within marketing (e.g. Andersson et al. 2004; Floch 2001; Hall 1997; Schroeder 2002; Schroeder and Salzer-Mörling 2005).

As part of a long line of visual expression, marketing representations remain embedded within a myriad of historical, cultural, and social situations, contexts, and discourses. At times this image creation draws upon and reinforces simplified, even subordinating, representations of cultural difference, group identity, and geographic specificity. According to cultural theorists Hall and Sealy (2001: 4), within visual representations:

profound differences of history, culture and experience have often been reduced to a handful of stereotypical features, which are 'read' as if they represent a truth of nature, somehow indelibly described on the body. They are assumed to be 'real' because they can be *seen*—difference, visible to the naked eye.

Such epistemically closed representations of identity, harnessed in the attempt to create brand images or corporate identity, potentially undermine the full human status of represented groups and individuals (e.g. Dávila 2001; Goffman 1979; O'Barr 1994; Schroeder and Borgerson 1998; Stern 1993).

Identities that are exoticized, sexist, or racist damage the reputation of represented groups and associated group members, and manipulate their being for consumption by others. Further, some identities are systematically excluded from marketing images, while others are represented in ethically problematic ways. The claim is not that some advertising, as well as other forms of marketing communications, might offend the concerned group and its members, but that certain forms of representation may limit their opportunities for the future by undermining or sabotaging their reputation. For example, Native American groups have protested professional sports teams such as the Atlanta Braves, the Cleveland Indians, and the Washington Redskins' use of stereotyped, red-faced Indian figures in their promotional imagery, claiming that these representations have little to do with their identity, the oppressive history that they have endured, and their ongoing struggles to become valued American citizens (cf. Whitt 1995).

REPRESENTATIONAL CONVENTIONS

Visual theorists have raised important points regarding the production of media representations and the potential repercussions for individuals, groups, and societies (e.g. Gross 1988; Lutz and Collins 1993; van Leeuwen 2000). Many studies have documented and criticized how ads often portray women and racial minorities in stereotyped and often negative ways (e.g. Bristor et al. 1995; Cortese 1999; Gandy 1998; Giroux 1994; Goldman and Papson 1996; Schroeder 2000; Stern 1993). In a groundbreaking discussion of 'image ethics,' media researcher Larry Gross (1988) began to articulate an ethics of representation pertaining to the media. He proposed two fundamental principles: (*a*) groups should be allowed to speak for themselves, and (*b*) media practices, including advertising, should be used to equalize the unequal distribution of power in society, or at least not to perpetuate inequality. These proposals have far-reaching implications for making subordinated voices heard and for promoting human equality. Consistent with Gross's image ethics, we would hope that an ethics of representation could convince those in marketing communications, as Hippocrates suggested, to 'first do no harm.'

Visual communication theorist Theo van Leeuwen (2000, 2001) identified two basic questions regarding the conventions of visual representation: (*a*) how are people depicted in relation to each other or their surroundings?, and (*b*) how are people depicted in relation to the viewer? He focused on pictorial representations of people and asked 'what choices does "the language of images" give us to depict people?' (van Leeuwen 2000: 341). For van Leeuwen, representational choices revolve around issues of exclusion of certain identity groups, portrayed social roles, stereotypical depictions, and categorization into types. These representational variables often combine to produce epistemically closed portrayals; for example, creating a category of 'third world poor' to juxtapose with images of affluence from the developed world.

Van Leeuwen identified several strategies (or representational conventions) of visual racism in an in-depth study of how people are represented in images. Visual racism involves issues of 'othering,' exclusion, and stereo-typing—where stereotyping involves not just negative cultural depictions but also showing certain groups as homogeneous without distinguishing individual characteristics and differences. For example, typical *National Geographic* magazine photographs often portray 'natives' as different from the assumed reader—*other* to the reader's self (Lutz and Collins 1993). Van Leeuwen's analysis of the relationship between the viewer and depictions of people identified three pictorial dimensions: (*a*) the *social distance*—assumptions about how the social status of one differs from the status of another, (*b*) the *social relation*—power differences, including how involved or detached the figures appear, and (*c*) the *social interaction*—the gaze of the depicted figure (outward, downward, and so forth) and its implications for interpersonal connection.

Visual representations express social psychological relations, such as closeness, involvement, and status (Larsen et al. 2004; Nederveen Pieterse 1992). Some images invite interaction; whether the pictured person looks at, or gazes at, the viewer is critical in determining the potential (implied) relationships. Although these interactions or relations are imagined, viewers often perceive depicted individuals or groups as though they were strangers or friends, and, in terms of the camera angle, physically or socially above or below them. Camera angles also structure social relations (e.g. whether the viewer sees depicted subjects from above, eye level, or below) and can allude to symbolic involvement or detachment (e.g. coming face-to-face with someone, confronting them, or sidling up to them) (van Leeuwen 2000). A woman lying down can be generally said to exhibit less status, as an object of the male gaze (Goffman 1979; Schroeder and Borgerson 1998). In a television advertisement, a 'long shot' (one taken from far away, often with a telephoto lens), may indicate a distant relationship between characters or between a character and the viewer, whereas a close-up is likely to connote intimacy.

These pictorial dimensions—social distance, social relation, and social interaction—indicate a larger ethics of power and representation articulated within the *gaze*. To 'gaze' implies more than to look at—it signifies a psychological relationship of power, in which the gazer is superior to the object of the gaze. Royalty gaze upon their subjects, viewed as property in the kingdom. Explorers gaze upon newly 'discovered' land as colonial resources. Although recent theoretical treatments of the gaze acknowledge the myriad forms it may take, including a female gaze, advertising has been called an extreme expression of the male gaze, producing stereotyped and typified representations of men and women, the good life, and sexual fantasy (cf. Jacobson and Mazur 1995; Schroeder and Borgerson 2003; Schroeder and McDonagh 2005; Stern 1993).

Marketing communications often depend upon the gaze to build relationships between consumers and fashion models, products, or companies. Shields and Heinecken's (2002: 83) research suggested how the gaze interacts with marketing communications: 'while both men and women discussed the pleasure of looking at attractive females, men tended to make their comments within the larger context of the way they look at women in general, not confining their comments to the advertisements in front of them.' For example, one male respondent reported that ads please him as a 'visual stimuli kind of thing. I find women attractive and it makes me feel good to look at them ...I guess I equated that with having a lot of fun. You know, being at a party...kind of like being on a beer commercial' (Shields and Heinecken 2002: 84). Here the male consumer's gaze expresses social distance, social relation, and social interaction; he apparently believes that he is in a position to judge and appreciate attractive women, that he is welcome to party with them. In this way, marketing communications help and compel him to define his identity and his potential relationship with women.

The representational choices described by van Leeuwen, in conjunction with such pictorial variables as distance, angle, and gaze, animate images of identity. They also help point to marketing practices, such as drawing unreflectively upon semiotic meanings and representing people as 'others,' that can produce unethical imagery (Borgerson and Schroeder 2002; O'Barr 1994; van Leeuwen 2000). Further, these choices may lead to subtle racist, sexist, and or epistemically closed representations that could undermine marketing communication, particularly global campaigns aimed at diverse consumers. Whereas van Leeuwen proposed a rather deterministic model of pictorial meaning, we argue for an approach that considers the cultural and ethical context in which meaning arises, which we believe can supply the necessary theoretical underpinning for an ethics of visual representation.

In the next section, we present several representational conventions to ground analysis and enhance understanding of the ethical implications of images in marketing communication. We discuss how the language of images presents marketers with choices about how to depict people, among other subjects, and how these choices coalesce into certain representational conventions.

A FRAMEWORK FOR IMAGE ANALYSIS

In order to articulate an ethics of representation for marketing communication, we focus here on four representational conventions to provide a broader context for recognizing and understanding ethical issues in marketing representation:

- face-ism
- idealization
- exoticization
- exclusion

Face-ism describes how mass media systematically show men with more prominent faces than women and how women are negatively affected by this representational convention.

Idealization concerns how marketing communications routinely depict ideal types—young, thin models, unrealistic scenarios, or unattainable goals—and the negative effects these often have, beginning in childhood (e.g. Belk and Pollay 1985; Martin and Gentry 1997; Richins 1991; Shields and Heinecken 2002).

Exoticization refers to the process of making someone seem exotic, strange, or different in ways that call attention to certain identity characteristics, such as skin color, dress, or appearance.

Exclusion indicates how certain types of people (e.g. poor, marginalized, or underrepresented individuals and groups) have traditionally been left out of the marketing communication pantheon.

These analytic categories, discussed in greater detail below, together with the aforementioned pictorial dimensions, can be useful in generating ethical insights and investigating how marketing communications represent and construct identities. However, it must be kept in mind that they do not comprise an exhaustive list and may at times overlap. We believe that they illuminate the key representational tensions and ethical issues within contemporary marketing communications.

Face-ism

In their classic study on the forms and consequences of stereotyping, sociologist Dane Archer and his colleagues identified a pervasive form of representational bias that they call face-ism. Five studies involving various media were conducted to investigate the facial prominence of men and women and subsequent social psychological consequences. The researchers' interest in facial prominence stemmed from their belief that, 'because the face and head are the centers of mental life—intellect, personality, identity, and character—the relative prominence of this part of the anatomy may be symbolically consequential' (Archer et al. 1983: 726). The phenomenon of face-ism refers to the prominence or significance of the face in photographs or images, and can be indexed through a consideration of a ratio based on two linear measurements—the distance between the top of the subject's head and chin divided by the distance between the top of the head and the lowest visible part of the subject's body. Thus a 'mug shot,' which shows only the head of a recently arrested person, has more facial prominence than a full-body picture of a runway model. Because it is a ratio, the face-ism index can be applied to any human image, including people depicted in advertisements and other marketing communications.

Archer and his colleagues found that males were portrayed with more prominent faces than females in news photographs appearing in American periodicals, in newspapers from various countries, and in art portraits dating from the past 600 years. When asked to draw human figures, both male and female research participants drew women with less prominent faces and more prominent bodies. The researchers also demonstrated the possible negative consequences of face-ism. In rating people portrayed in manipulated photographs, participants consistently rated those with less prominent faces as less intelligent, less ambitious, and less attractive, regardless of the sex of either the rater or the person in the photograph (Archer et al. 1983).

In other words, when *either* men or women appear in images that show more of their body, viewers tended to attribute fewer positive attributes to them, suggesting 'that perceived intellectual (and other) qualities may be significantly and favorably affected by something as simple as the relative prominence of the person's face (in a photograph)' (Archer et al. 1983: 732). Interestingly, these results suggest that both men and women could potentially suffer the effects of face-ism from being shown with less relative facial prominence. However, despite the feminist movement, increased attention to the women's market, and the growing number of women in roles of power, face-ism remains a well-substantiated yet little known representational convention that continues to favor men (King 2002; Levesque and Lowe 1999).

Idealization

A growing body of consumer research has revealed specific links between glamorized images in television ads and dissatisfaction with the self (e.g. Peck and Loken 2004; Richins 1991). Photographic techniques, such as digitization, cropping, and image manipulation can accelerate the extent to which marketing messages negatively affect self-image. In a recent analysis of the effects of idealized imagery in marketing communications, Shields and Heinecken (2002: xv) argued that:

There is profound evidence suggesting that girls and young women (in Western cultures) are particularly vulnerable to particular kinds of mass media messages: those pertaining to body images, size, and appearance. They are not more vulnerable than boys or men because they are somehow weaker against the power of these messages. They are more vulnerable because the culture they are born into subscribes to the notion that women should be the objects of vision. Female bodies are held up to inspection to a much greater degree than are men's in this culture. Women's worth is judged generally by appearance first and abilities second.

Idealized bodies, in particular, help construct notions about female identity, attractiveness, and normality in ways that can damage identity. Critically, images influence how we think about the ideal or good life, what is sexy, and what will be seen as attractive by desired others (cf. Belk and Pollay 1985; Crocker and Linden 1998; Pollay 1986). These points were reflected in some of the comments of young women interviewed by Shields and Heinecken (2002: 82); for example: 'they are unattainable, these thin bodies, perfect hair, fine clothes. This is the cause of so much distress and poor self-images of women today.' Such comments illuminate ethical problems with contemporary imagery as they point to the negative role of marketing communication's identity constructions.

Exoticization

A particularly virulent form of stereotyping that combines several problematic representational conventions, exoticization affects many identity categories appearing in marketing communications, including Africans, Asians, Blacks, Native Americans, and indigenous peoples (Desmond 1999; O'Barr 1994; Williamson 1986; Woodward 1997). For example, marketing representations of Hawaiians, Polynesians, and other Pacific Islanders, reflect a dominant cultural view of the exotic other (Costa 1998). In other words, 'Hawaiians are repeatedly presented as people whose lives are less complex and less valuable than the lives of Euroamericans' (Wood 1999: 113). Research on marketing representations from advertising, tourist brochures, record albums, Hollywood films, and kitsch Hawaiiana has revealed that exoticized depictions of 'natives' are commonly used to portray the image of Hawaii (Borgerson and Schroeder 2002). This vision of an exotic vacation paradise currently informs tourism campaigns for such destinations as Ibiza, Jamaica and Bali in a kind of representational pattern that may undermine unique identities and geographies (cf. Borgerson and Schroeder 2003).

Visions of 'exotic' peoples do not just exist 'out there' but must be created and recreated. Much of the ideological power of the representations lies in their almost infinite repetition—similar images are presented over and over, in a wide variety of marketing contexts and epochs. Unfortunately absent from most marketing communications about Hawaii, island resorts, and paradisal escapes is the reminder that exoticization always functions within a context of unequal power and epistemic closure. The indigenous peoples of Hawaii have a rich, largely unrepresented culture, yet the image of Hawaii that dominates many people's imagination comes from marketing communications, travel brochures, promotional cookbooks, record albums, musicals, and films. These representations are instrumental in constructing the image of Hawaii as an exotic, primitive paradise within colonial, patriarchal, and racist discourses, placing Polynesia within an 'orientalist' discourse of the other (e.g. Said 1978).

Exclusion

Exclusion indicates the likelihood of not representing particular people in marketing communications. In other words, it marks an absence. Although this seems unlikely in an era of increasingly focused target marketing, some people, such as minorities, the poor, or otherwise 'different' individuals, have been traditionally underrepresented (or excluded entirely) from marketing images. For example, companies such as BMW, Timberland, Tommy Hilfiger, and Abercrombie & Fitch have come under fire from minority groups for excluding them from the brand's identity by not including diversity within advertising, catalog imagery, and websites (cf. Berger 2001). By excluding to varying degrees certain representations, possible meanings, interpretations, and understandings are limited in ways that may negatively influence certain individuals, groups, scenarios, and even geographic locations.

Some may argue that increasing representation of the formerly excluded in marketing images is an improvement over earlier periods, when many marginalized groups were not represented at all. One might think that simply including images of underrepresented or marginalized cultural groups in marketing communications would reduce exclusion's ethical impact, but this strategy often leads to images informed by exoticization, typicality and 'token' images. For example, Benetton's approach to cultural 'inclusion' has been widely criticized as perpetuating stereotypes of difference—an ironic result that illustrates the complex intersection of identity, representation, and marketing within the global economy.

CONSUMER INTERPRETATION AND REPRESENTATIONAL CONVENTIONS

Representational conventions and related pictorial dimensions may operate within marketing communications to systematically and unconsciously influence consumer perception at a fundamental cognitive level, via a process that we call *tacit interpretation* (Schroeder and Borgerson 2004). Relatively few people realize how face-ism, idealization, exoticization, and exclusion pervade marketing representations, or how they influence perceptual processes. We are not implying that consumers or marketers are unaware of representational conventions; nevertheless, consumers may remain unable to resist or deconstruct them (cf. Kates 1999; Thompson and Haytko 1997). Representational conventions such as face-ism are especially significant because they establish a link between visual representation and ontological attributions, illuminating the central role visual representations and semiotic dualisms have in social stereotyping. Moreover, representational conventions point to potential blind spots in consumer's responses to images of identity, alerting marketers to gaps between strategic conceptions about brand identity and consumer perceptions of brand image.

MARKETING RESEARCH IMPLICATIONS

Representational conventions can be seen as part of a class of tacit interpretation effects that lead people to judge others on the basis of subtle visual cues, social categories, and cognitive schemas. Moreover, they generally serve to psychologically justify the status quo, operating as identifiable, stable, and often unconscious, interpretive conventions (cf. Bargh 2002; Schroeder and Borgerson 2004). Additionally, representational conventions point to potential blind spots in consumers' responses to images of identity, alerting researchers to methodological implications. That is, conventions such as face-ism, idealization, exoticization, and exclusion should be considered within research design, particularly experiments that manipulate pictures of people. Any study that employs depictions of people may be affected by these kind of representational conventions.

For example, in their research on how cropped photographs affect product evaluations, Peracchio and Myers-Levy (1994: 192) showed some participants an ad with an 'exotic-looking woman who appeared to be consuming the product.' It is unclear from their brief description what was 'exotic' about the woman, how this was visually represented, and how her appearance might have affected viewer's perceptions about her and the product—or why the researchers used this particular image at all. Further, 'exotic' is not a neutral descriptive term—it invokes a long history of Orientalism that undermines and undervalues the intellectual capacities and human qualities of those labeled 'exotic' (e.g. Said 1978). Thus, by depicting an 'exotic-looking woman' in their study, they may have inadvertently confounded their experimental design, as research participants may have responded to the representational ramifications of exoticism. In this way, representational conventions have the potential to compromise research validity. Thus, each study that utilizes images of people needs to assess the potential for representational bias, including exoticization and face-ism.

CONCLUSION

Marketing communication commodifies human beings, employing bodies and body images to promote products and services, thus associating identity with consumption and existence with market processes. How can marketing prevent related problems in visual representation? Linking marketing communication to ontological dilemmas in identity representation enables marketers to recognize a global communication system based on visual images. An awareness of the theoretical, methodological, and strategic implications of face-ism, idealization, exoticization, and exclusion can contribute to a deeper understanding of the ethical implications of marketing communication.

We propose two principles for an ethics of representation: (a) marketers must become culturally, ethically, and visually literate in representational conventions and semiotics if they are to recognize and understand ethical problems, and (b) judgments of image appropriateness should be informed by an awareness of potential epistemic closures. We insist that an ethics of representation must emphasize issues that arise when brand identity, corporate communication, and visual strategy rely upon representations of identity. We further argue that ethical analyses must offer accounts for how marketing images represent identity. Table 13.1 provides a list of Websites devoted to image analysis, a necessary first step in addressing ethics in marketing communication.

When marketing campaigns represent identities of groups or individuals so that the representations themselves purport to express something true or essential about those represented, esthetic and ethical questions intersect and allow certain ontological assumptions to emerge. In addition to

Table 13.1. Recommended websites for ethical analysis of marketing communication

Website	Contents
J. Scott Armstrong's advertising principles http://fourps.wharton.upenn.edu/advertising/	Provides worksheet for ethical evaluation of advertisements
Daniel Chandler's analysis of advertisements http://www.aber.ac.uk/media/Modules/MAinTV/analad.html	Excellent introduction to semiotic communication analysis
The gender ads project http://www.genderads.com/	Includes many examples of advertising images deemed sexist, racist, and exoticized
The commercial closet http://www.commercialcloset.com/cgi-bin/iowa/themes.html	Comprehensive resource about gay advertising themes, including positive and negative evaluations

damaging the reputation of members of represented groups, some forms of representation that are exoticized, stereotypical, sexist, or racist actually manipulate these groups for consumption by others. Given extant power inequalities and lack of access to mass media forms of representation, subordinated or oppressed individuals and groups often do not have much control over how they are represented, particularly within the discourse of marketing communication. We do not suggest marketing communication causes these cultural prejudices, but that a close ethical analysis of marketing communication reveals problematic representational conventions that might be avoided.

REFERENCES

Andersson, S., Hedelin, A., Nilsson, A., and Welander, C. (2004). 'Violent Advertising in Fashion Marketing,' *Journal of Fashion Marketing and Management*, 8, 96–112.

Archer, D., Iritani, B., Kimes, D., and Barrios, M. (1983). 'Face-ism: Five Studies of Sex Differences in Facial Prominence,' *Journal of Personality and Social Psychology*, 45, 725–35.

Armstrong, J. S. (2004). Evaluating Ads. Available: www.advertisingprinciples.com

Arnheim, R. (1974). *Art and Visual Perception*. Berkeley, CA.: University of California Press.

Bargh, J. A. (2002). 'Losing Consciousness: Automatic Influences on Consumer Judgment, Behavior, and Motivation,' *Journal of Consumer Research*, 29, 280–85.

Bartky, S. (1991). *Femininity and Domination*. New York: Routledge.

Belk, R. W. and Pollay, R. W. (1985). 'Images of Ourselves: The Good Life in Twentieth Century Advertising,' *Journal of Consumer Research*, 11, 887–97.

Berger, W. (2001). *Advertising Today*. London: Phaidon.

Borgerson, J. (2001). 'Feminist Ethical Ontology: Contesting "the Bare Givenness of Intersubjectivity," ' *Feminist Theory*, 2, 173–87.

Borgerson, J. L. and Schroeder, J. E. (2002). 'Ethical Issues of Global Marketing: Avoiding Bad Faith in Visual Representation,' *European Journal of Marketing*, 36, 570–94.

—— and —— (2003). 'The Lure of Paradise: Marketing the Retro-escape of Hawaii,' in S. Brown and J.F. Sherry, Jr. (eds.), *Time, Space and the Market: Retroscapes Rising*, New York: M.E. Sharpe, pp. 219–37.

Bourdieu, P. and Passeron, J. C. (1990). *Reproduction*. London: Sage.

Bristor, J., Lee, R. G., and Hunt, M. (1995). 'Race and Ideology: African American Images in Television Advertising,' *Journal of Public Policy and Marketing*, 14, 1–24.

Butler, J. (1999/1987). *Subjects of Desire: Hegelian Reflections in Twentieth-Century France*. New York: Columbia University Press.

Carrigan, M. and Szmigin, I. (2000). 'The Ethical Advertising Covenant: Regulating Ageism in UK Advertising,' *International Journal of Advertising*, 19 (4), 509–28.

Cigarette Ads Still Enticing Teens to Smoke, Study Shows. (2001, June 12). *The Providence Journal-Bulletin*, p. 6.

Cortese, A. J. (1999). *Provocateur: Images of Women and Minorities in Advertising*. Lanham, MD: Rowman and Littlefield.

Costa, J. A. (1998). 'Paradisal Discourse: A Critical Analysis of Marketing and Consuming Hawaii,' *Consumption Markets and Culture*, 1, 303–46.

Crane, A. and Matten, D. (2004). *Business Ethics: A European Perspective*. Oxford: Oxford University Press.

Crocker, D. A. and Linden, T. (eds.). (1998). *Ethics of Consumption: The Good Life, Justice and Global Stewardship*. Lanham, MD: Rowman and Littlefield.

Dávila, A. (2001). *Latinos, Inc.: The Marketing and Making of a People*. Berkeley, CA: University of California Press.

Desmond, J. (2003). *Consuming Behavior*. New York: Palgrave.

Desmond, J. C. (1999). *Staging Tourism: Bodies on Display from Waikiki to Sea World*. Chicago: University of Chicago Press.

Elliott, R. and Wattanasuwan, K. (1998). 'Brands as Symbolic Resources for the Construction of Identity,' *International Journal of Advertising*, 17, 131–44.

Floch, J.-M. (2001). *Semiotics, Marketing and Communication: Beneath the Signs, the Strategies*. Hampshire: Palgrave.

Furnham, A. (1999). 'Sex Role Stereotyping in Television Commercials: A Review and Comparison of Fourteen Studies Done in Five Continents Over 25 Years,' *Sex Roles*, 41 (September), 413–437.

Gandy, O. H. (1998). *Communication and Race: A Structural Perspective*. London: Arnold.

Giroux, H. A. (1994). *Disturbing Pleasures: Learning Popular Culture*. New York: Routledge.

Goffman, E. (1979). *Gender Advertisements*. New York: Harper and Row.

Goldberg, D. T. (1993). *Racist Culture: Philosophy and the Politics of Meaning*. Oxford: Blackwell.

Goldman, R. and Papson, S. (1996). *Sign Wars: The Cluttered Landscape of Advertising*. New York: Guilford Press.

Gordon, L. R. (1995). *Bad Faith and Antiblack Racism*. Atlantic Highlands, NJ: Humanities Press.

—— (1997). *Her Majesty's Other Children: Sketches of Racism from a Neocolonial Age*. Lanham, MD: Rowman and Littlefield.

Gross, L. (1988). 'The Ethics of (Mis) Representation,' in L. Gross, J.S. Katz and J. Ruby (eds.), *Image Ethics*, New York: Oxford University Press, pp. 188–202.

Hall, S. (ed.) (1997). *Representation: Cultural Representations and Signifying Practices*. London: Open University Press/Sage.

—— and Sealy, M. (2001). *Different: Contemporary Photographers and Black Identity*. London: Phaidon.

Heywood, I. and Sandywell, B. (1999). 'Introduction: Explorations in the Hermeneutics of the Visual,' in I. Heywood and B. Sandywell (eds.), *Interpreting Visual Culture: Explorations in the Hermeneutics of the Visual*, London: Routledge, pp. ix–xviii.

Jacobson, M. F. and Mazur, L. A. (1995). *Marketing Madness: A Survival Guide to Consumer Society*. Boulder, CO.: Westview Press

Kates, S. M. (1999). 'Making the Ad Perfectly Queer: Marketing "Normality" to the Gay Men's Community,' *Journal of Advertising*, 28, 25–37.

Kay, A. C. and Jost, J. T. (2003). 'Complementary Justice: Effects of "poor but happy" and "poor but honest" Stereotype Exemplars on System Justification and Implicit Activation of the Justice Motive,' *Journal of Personality and Social Psychology*, 85 (5), 823–37.

King, J. M. (2002). 'Photographic Images of Gender and Race in *Fortune* 500 Company Web Sites in the United States,' *Business Research Yearbook* 7, 852–56.

Larson, V., Luna, D., and Peracchio, L. A. (2004). 'Points of View and Pieces of Time: A Taxonomy of Image Attributes,' *Journal of Consumer Research*, 31 (1), 102–11.

Levesque, M. J. and Lowe, C. A. (1999). 'Face-ism as a Determinant of Interpersonal Perceptions: The Influence of Context on Facial Prominence Effects,' *Sex Roles*, 41 (3/4), 241–59.

Lutz, C. A. and Collins, J. L. (1993). *Reading National Geographic.* Chicago: University of Chicago Press.

Martin, M. C. and Gentry, J. W. (1997). 'Stuck in the Model Trap: The Effects of Beautiful Models in Ads on Female Pre-adolescents and Adolescents,' *Journal of Advertising*, 26, 19–33.

McQuarrie, E. F. and Mick, D. G. (1999). 'Visual Rhetoric in Advertising: Text-interpretive, Experimental, and Reader-response Analyses,' *Journal of Consumer Research*, 26, 37–54.

Mick, D. G., Burroughs, J. E., Hetzel, P., and Brannen, M. Y. (2004). 'Pursuing the Meaning of Meaning in the Commercial World: An International Review of Marketing and Consumer Research Founded on Semiotics,' *Semiotica*, 152, 1–74.

Natanson, M. (1986). *Anonymity: A Study in the Philosophy of Alfred Schutz.* Bloomington: Indiana University Press.

Nederveen Pieterse, J. (1992). *White on Black: Images of Africa and Blacks in Western Popular Culture.* New Haven, CT: Yale University Press.

O'Barr, W. M. (1994). *Culture and the Ad: Exploring Otherness in the World of Advertising.* Boulder, CO: Westview Press.

O'Donohoe, S. and Tynan, C. (1998). 'Beyond Sophistication: Dimensions of Advertising Literacy,' *International Journal of Advertising*, 17, 467–82.

Peck, J. and Loken, B. (2004). 'When Will Larger-sized Female Models in Advertisements be Viewed Positively? The Moderating Effects of Instructional Frame, Gender, and Need for Cognition,' *Psychology and Marketing*, 21 (6), 425–42.

Peracchio, L. and Myers-Levy, J. (1994). 'How Ambiguous Cropped Objects in Ad Photos Can Affect Product Evaluations,' *Journal of Consumer Research*, 21, 190–204.

Pettigrew, S. (2001). 'King or Pawn? The Role of the Australian Beer Drinker,' *Journal of Research for Consumers*, 2. Available: www.jrconsumers.com.

Pollay, R. (1986). 'The Distorted Mirror: Reflections on the Unintended Consequences of Advertising,' *Journal of Marketing*, 50, 18–36.

Richins, M. L. (1991). 'Social Comparison and the Idealized Images of Advertising,' *Journal of Consumer Research*, 18, 71–83.

Said, E. (1978). *Orientalism.* New York: Vantage Press.

Schroeder, J. E. (1998). 'Consuming Representation: A Visual Approach to Consumer Research,' in B. B. Stern (ed.), *Representing Consumers: Voices, Views and Visions*, London: Routledge, pp. 193–230.

Schroeder, J. E. (2000). 'Édouard Manet, Calvin Klein and the Strategic Use of Scandal,' in S. Brown and A. Patterson (eds.), *Imagining Marketing: Art, Aesthetics, and the Avant-garde*, London: Routledge, pp. 36–51.

—— (2002). *Visual Consumption*. London: Routledge.

—— and Borgerson, J. L. (1998). 'Marketing Images of Gender: A Visual Analysis,' *Consumption Markets and Culture*, 2, 161–201.

—— —— (2003). 'Dark Desires: Fetishism, Ontology and Representation in Contemporary Advertising,' in T. Reichert and J. Lambiase (eds.), *Sex in Advertising: Perspectives on the Erotic Appeal*, Mahwah, NJ: Lawrence Erlbaum Associates, pp. 65–87.

—— —— (2004). 'Tacit Processes in Consumer Interpretation,' in S. Brown and D. Turley (eds.), *European Advances in Consumer Research*. vol. 7. Valdosta, GA: Association for Consumer Research, pp. 70–2.

—— and McDonagh, P. (2005). 'The Logic of Pornography in Digital Camera Promotion,' in J. Lambiase and T. Reichert (eds.), *Sex in Consumer Culture: The Erotic Content of Media and Marketing*, Mahwah, NJ: Lawrence Erlbaum Associates.

—— and Salzer-Mörling, M. (2005). *Brand Culture*. London: Routledge.

—— and Zwick, D. (2004). 'Mirrors of Masculinity: Representation and Identity in Advertising Images,' *Consumption Markets and Culture*, 7, 21–52.

Scott, L. A. (1994). 'Images of Advertising: The Need for a Theory of Visual Rhetoric,' *Journal of Consumer Research*, 21, 252–73.

—— and Batra, R. (eds.) (2003). *Persuasive Imagery: A Consumer Response Perspective*. Mahwah, NJ.: Lawrence Erlbaum Associates.

Shields, V. R. and Heinecken, D. (2002). *Measuring Up: How Advertising Affects Self-image*. Philadelphia, PA: University of Pennsylvania Press.

Smith, N. C. and Quelch, J.A. (1993). *Ethics in Marketing*. Homewood, IL: Irwin.

Stern, B. B. (1993). 'Feminist Literary Criticism and the Deconstruction of Ads: A Postmodern View of Advertising and Consumer Research,' *Journal of Consumer Research*, 19, 556–66.

—— and Schroeder, J. E. (1994). 'Interpretive Methodology from Art and Literary Criticism: a Humanistic Approach to Advertising Imagery,' *European Journal of Marketing*, 28, 114–32.

Thompson, C. J. (1995). 'A Contextualist Proposal for the Conceptualization and Study of Marketing Ethics,' *Journal of Public Policy and Marketing*, 14, 177–91.

—— (2004). 'Dreams of Eden: A Critical Reader-response Analysis of the Mytho-ideologies Encoded in Natural Health Advertisements,' in K. Ekström and H. Brembeck (eds.), *Elusive Consumption*, Oxford: Berg, pp. 175–204.

—— and Haytko, D. L. (1997). 'Speaking of Fashion: Consumers' Uses of Fashion Discourses and the Appropriation of Countervailing Cultural Meanings,' *Journal of Consumer Research*, 24, 15–42.

van Leeuwen, T. (2000). 'Visual Racism,' in M. Reisigl and R. Wodak (eds.), *The Semiotics of Racism: Approaches in Critical Discourse Analysis*, Vienna: Passagen Verlag, pp. 333–50.

—— (2001). 'Semiotics and Iconography,' in T. van Leeuwen and C. Jewitt (eds.), *Handbook of Visual Analysis*, London: Sage, pp. 92–118.

Walker, M. U. (1998). *Moral Understandings: Feminist Studies in Ethics*. New York: Routledge.

Whitt, L. A. (1995). 'Cultural Imperialism and the Marketing of Native American Culture,' *American Indian Culture and Research Journal*, 19, 1–31.

Williamson, J. (1986). 'Woman is an Island: Femininity and Colonization,' in T. Modleski (ed.), *Studies in Entertainment: Critical Approaches to Mass Culture*, Bloomington: Indiana University Press, pp. 99–118.

Wood, H. (1999). *Displacing Natives: The Rhetorical Production of Hawai'i*. Lanham, MD: Rowman and Littlefield.

Woodward, K. (ed.). (1997). *Identity and Difference*. London: Sage/Open University Press.

Zaltman, G. (2002). *How Customers Think*. Boston, MA: Harvard Business School Press.

14

The Communication of Marketing: A Critical Analysis of Discursive Practice

Douglas Brownlie and Michael Saren

In this chapter we have taken the opportunity to interpret the phrase 'marketing communications' in a broad fashion. In doing so we raise a number of fundamental issues that inform our understanding of communications as a social process, and what follows reveals why our arguments are a relevant addition to this book's coverage.

All marketing communications can be said to function by virtue of discourse—a discourse of Marketing. This immodest tautology is itself an interesting phenomenon to study. In this chapter we hope to explain what it means and to explore some of the important issues arising from an analysis that attempts to situate the possibility of marketing communications within wider social considerations. In taking this perspective on the 'communications' of marketing, we effectively turn a penetrating gaze upon ourselves, as Shroeder (2003) urged, in order to critically evaluate the communicative practices of marketing—as a subject, a body of knowledge, and as a discipline.

In recent years there has been much published work and theoretical development in the area referred to as 'critical marketing.' It is within this school of thought that our analysis of marketing communications is positioned. In many respects critical marketing studies do not comprise a discrete, easily labeled 'school' at all. A variety of critical approaches can be found, for example, in the literature on advertising ideology (Wernick 1991; Williamson 1978), advertising and consumption (Nava et al. 1997), environmental sustainability (Fuller 1999), ethics (Crane 1997), social marketing (Hastings and Saren 2003), feminism (Catterall et al. 1999), constructivism (Hackley 2001), discourse analysis (Brownlie and Saren 1997; Svensson 2003), postmodernism (Fırat and Venkatesh 1993) and multiculturalism (Burton 2002). They share the goal of critically questioning marketing knowledge, from its declared theoretical underpinnings to its mooted practical outcomes, including the following:

- ideological premises and underlying assumptions of marketing theory and practice;
- specific marketing activities and practices (e.g. customer databases, product labeling, advertising, and loyalty schemes);
- effects of the marketing system (e.g. social exclusion, material and social waste, creation of false needs, and identities and commodity fetishism);
- ethics, morality, and 'values' of marketing;
- understanding and knowledge of marketing (e.g. academic models and methods, market research, consulting, and marketers' 'know-how'); and
- validity of marketing ideas and concepts.

In this chapter, we aim to critically evaluate these various considerations, which collectively are encompassed within the area of the communication of marketing, its discourse, language and linguistic practices.

Several authors have argued that marketing should not simply be regarded as a managerial business function, but should be viewed within a wider context of social practice (Brown 1995; Brownlie et al. 1999; DuGay and Salaman 1992; Hirschman and Holbrook 1992; Morgan 1992). Some see the subject of marketing as inseparable from the linguistic practices that mediate our efforts to communicate about marketing in a meaningful way, as evidenced by the following comments:

- 'I think marketing studies become viable when the field is seen as a discourse inseparable from mediated communications' (Hackley 2001: 102).
- 'Marketing communications is communication and communication is marketing' (Schultz et al. 1994: 46).
- 'It is difficult to imagine how any marketing activity could be performed without language, whether it be related to delivering customer service, writing advertising copy, building long term customer relationships, writing training manuals, composing academic papers, conducting research projects, completing questionnaires: those activities and more involve people spending a lot of time talking to each other, reading reports, watching advertisements, writing marketing plans, listening to other people' (Brownlie and Saren 1997: 153).

We use the word *discourse* as an umbrella term for linguistic and communicative practices, covering all forms of spoken and written interaction, formal and informal (Potter and Wetherell 1987). Our concern for marketing is that communicative practices can themselves become embedded islands of habit, myopia, and inflexibility. We seek to explore ways of raising awareness of the dangers of this, especially because marketing language, like the English language from which it springs, is in a continual state of flux. Further, our broad concerns with marketing discourse throw into high relief the privileged and privileging forms of linguistic interaction and communicative practice currently operating within the marketing academy. In this light we first consider the representation of marketing and its practice. We then turn our attention to the constitutive character of the language of marketing, which we argue frames our view of marketing phenomena.

THE REPRESENTATION OF MARKETING PRACTICE

In order to examine marketing communication, the chapter asks the reader to consider two levels of marketing practice: (*a*) the marketing practice we write and talk about, including the sales analysis and planning, client presentations, in-store merchandising checks, pricing and promotional activities, etc.; (*b*) the communicative practices by means of which we communicate ideas about the first. So, at one level this chapter is indeed about marketing practice, whereas on another level it reflects how marketing practice is represented through our marketing communications. That is, the object of inquiry is not simply what marketing communication is (as the chapters of this book show)—there is a plethora of texts that can do this—but what we say it is, how we package or represent those statements through communicative practice, and how that practice actively mediates or frames what we can and cannot say.

Entering into any debate about discursive processes in marketing is typically avoided in the marketing literature through (often unconsciously) recognizing a method or a concept as constituting the subject of marketing research and communications itself—in other words, that what we see as the object of inquiry and what we set out to measure about its behavior is determined by our research design, especially data generation. If we encounter measurement problems that perhaps undermine the validity of our results, we tend to focus with forensic intensity on identifying weaknesses in our methodology. Thus, research methods and the operationalization of constructs and concepts can then become the de facto objects of inquiry in studies of marketing practice, especially those based on cross-sectional survey designs. The problem of representation manifests itself differently in qualitative designs. This is especially so where interviews form the basis of data generation, for in this case we are bound to search for pathways between the raw textual data and the body of theory that frames our study, in order to chunk strings of text together into meaningful categories, typically under a suitably symbolic word or phrase that has its origins in our transcriptions of the lived experience related by our interviewees. In this sense we can think of knowledge-making in marketing as the appropriation of signs circulating between expert marketing discourse and the negotiated narrative of the lived experience of those who practice 'marketing,' so that the signs produced by way of marketing knowledge tend to be 'reified images of social relations,' as Goldman and Papson (1996: 13) observed. Table 14.1 illustrates an example of this process.

To follow this example, starting at the top, 'consumers' are categorized as a 'market,' which itself becomes an object of study that is further recategorized into 'segments.' Details of these segments are stored in a database (e.g. customer information), which can be further categorized and stored as 'coded data.' This process continues on to higher levels of abstraction towards the construction of a causal model to explain significant relationships in the data. In some contexts, particularly within the marketing academy, this process can continue to even higher levels of abstraction, perhaps towards the construction of a detailed causal model to explain significant relationships in the data. Along the way there are chains of signifiers symbolizing, or standing-in for some concept. Those pathways or chains are typically embedded within the conventions and norms of discursive practice within the marketing discipline.

It is through webs of such linguistic chains and crisscrossing circuits of communication that the constitutive character of language brings marketing into being, rendering marketing ideas communicable. This notion is drawn from the social constructionist ideas of Burger and Luckman (1966), who showed how objects assume a socially constructed reality through their linguistic representation. For example, one may reasonably assume that the ontology of the fictional character Harry Potter is such that he does not exist in the 'real' world. However, countless books, movies, stories, and 'imaginary friends' of Harry Potter do exist through linguistic interaction everyday. Despite having no corresponding presence in the physical world the character of Harry Potter in this sense does exist as a feature of discourse.

We argue that to understand what knowledge production practices mean within the field of marketing communications, we must find out

Table 14.1. Example of the process of signification and reification in marketing discourse

Representation	Object
Market	Consumers
Segments	Market
Database	Segments
Coded data	Database
Significant statistical relationships	Coded data
Causal model	Significant [statistical/conceptual?] relationships

how they mean, which requires us to consider the way in which they work communicatively. It is necessary to investigate the linguistic representation of marketing concepts in order to begin to understand how marketing topics can be made communicable and how such communicative processes and their content or messages are mediated by discourse. Others have called for and taken a similar linguistic turn in marketing's cognate areas, such as advertising (Williamson 1978), economics (McCloskey 1985), strategic management (Rouleau and Seguin 1995), enterprise studies (Du Gay and Salaman 1992), corporate culture (Swales and Rogers 1995), advertising (Elliot and Wattanasuwan 1998), organization studies (Gergen 1992; Jeffcutt 1993) and marketing itself (Hackley 2001).

THE NATURE OF DISCOURSE

The term 'discourse' has been distinguished on the basis of whether it is consistent with an Anglo-Saxon or European perspective (Potter and Wetherell 1987). The Anglo-Saxon view considers the term narrowly as involving predominantly language-based vocal interactions at the level of individuals. By contrast, the European perspective, typified by Foucault (1981), is concerned with discourse as a much wider system of social relations or 'field' of interlinked communicative events, embracing the possibility of strategic choice within the encompassing effects of history and culture.

According to Fairclough (1995), the constitutive effects of discourse are comprised of three functions: (*a*) an identity function (how discourse affects the construction of social identities), (*b*) a relational function (the social relationships formed through discourse), and (*c*) an ideational function (the beliefs and systems of knowledge that discourse creates and communicates). In light of these distinctions, we view the term 'marketing' less as a shorthand for one particular all-encompassing discourse, than as a particular set of constitutive effects within a range of discursive practices.

We do not believe that marketing discourse can be seen as an invariable and taken-for-granted structure of predetermined categories. On the contrary, we take our inspiration from the work of Foucault (1981), who viewed discourse as a recursive form of 'strategic' arranging—putting in place a territory of strategic possibilities—that evolved through historically developing linguistic practices. In essence, we treat discourse as a set of embedded patterns or structures that reproduce themselves, and that can be imputed to networks of social relations within a specific cultural location. And so it is that marketers could be said to live their lives as marketers through acts of discourse (Steiner 1961). In seeking to achieve meaningful communications through using strings of marketing vocabulary and terminology in an appropriate way—that is, through placing words in particular contexts, while following conventions of placement and usage—not only do marketers adhere to those conventions, but they also sustain and reproduce them. Those conventions are then written into marketing communications rather as the medium is within the message.

Marketing practice is called into being through processes of linguistic interaction in social settings; that is, we talk and write it into life, then act collectively 'as if' it were real, 'as if' it was 'out there' as a concrete social fact, staring us in the face. The 'out there' is thus constructed by our discursive conceptions of it and those conceptions are collectively sustained and continually renegotiated in the process of 'making' sense. The role of language in constituting 'reality' is therefore central to our understanding of the knowledge practices of the academy; and all of our attempts to discover and communicate 'truth' should be seen for what they are—forms of discourse (Parker 2002). Discourse constitutes our sense of the world. It throws us into our world and makes it available to us in order for us to imagine ways of exercising power over it. The key character of discourse regarding communicative practice is its *performative effects*, for language not only says things, it does things (Goffman 1971), and it is through the 'illocutionary force' of speech acts (discursive practice) that social relations can be seen as accomplishments.

THE LANGUAGE OF MARKETING

If the world is seen as being constituted by shared language, then people can only know the world through the particular forms of discourse that their culture and language create and allow them access to. This line of thought is common to the works of such thinkers as Kristeva (1969), Derrida (1978), and Rorty (1979), who have described how language has multiple layers and meanings; how it orders our perceptions; how it gives shape to our understandings of social practice (such as writing and talking about marketing communications); and how language makes things happen through its use to construct, channel, and preempt social interaction. Recent examples of this are to be found in press accusations that major British firms are engaging heavily in 'spin' to cover up or otherwise (mis)-represent the damage to the local environment caused by their operations. The aim of these firms is not merely to divert attention from environmental consequences of those operations, but to preempt criticism so to exercise control over the basis and manner of discussion. And thus it may be that a marketing staff may have to say one thing in public, while lobbying for another behind the scenes, reminding us of the subtle ways in which communicative practice must be sensitive to context.

We urge that 'reality,' or the world 'out there' does not give us language—marketing language included—so that words are not neutral reflections of the world or 'mere messengers from the kingdom of reality' (Gergen 1992: 213). Rather, we argue that there are no sharp distinctions between subjective and objective worlds and that our shared language, and the images and ideas it gives shape to, is the means through which we make our reality and come to constitute the world. This focus on language helps to reveal how we construct (or invent) our marketing realities—even if we say that we have discovered them—and how our shared language of marketing speaks us, as much as we speak it.

As mentioned above, several authors have demonstrated the value of considering the use and effects of language as subjects of inquiry in various fields. Building on the work of Potter and Wetherell (1987), who applied this approach in the field of social psychology, we argue that there are good reasons why students of marketing should similarly be interested in those topics. The familiarity of language may make it transparent to those who use it, but, as Potter and Wetherell argued, it is the most basic and pervasive form of interaction between people. Social interactions are performed through language, in the sense that writing, talk, and gesture are not merely conceptual devices, but channels for action, as language is inseparably involved with processes of thinking and reasoning.

McCloskey (1985, 1990) developed a similar line of argument about the constitutive effects of communicative practice in economics, suggesting that what is taken for knowledge in economics is mediated by convention and linguistic practice. She argued that economists, like all scientists, must use language to give expression to their ideas, and that the use of language is a social act that serves many purposes other than merely making a literal statement of apparent scientific character. She urged economists to study the language and communicative practices used to persuade others of the legitimacy of their interpretation of rules of evidence governing the admissibility of data, and the legitimacy of hypotheses, models, and conclusions. In McCloskey's view, only through studying rhetorical practice and linguistic norms could economists obtain a deeper understanding of how unspoken and unnoticed conventions and values frame what can be said within the domain of economics.

McCloskey understands rhetoric as a form of persuasive discourse, encompassing the use of reliably attested facts and logic (so beloved of marketing scientists), as well as the rational use of metaphors (models to marketing scientists; images to advertising creatives) and other figures of speech. Rhetoric is not simply a matter of communicating ideas persuasively, it is central to processes of human thought: for when we think, it could be said that we are debating with ourselves, turning ideas over in our heads, and pitting one argument against another through the use of images and silent rhetoric. Billing (1987: 111) neatly captured this perspective when he said that 'humans do not converse because they have inner thoughts to express, but they have thoughts because they were able to converse'—which is reminiscent of Weick's (1979) famous aphorism, *how do I know what I think, until I hear what I say?*

Boylan and O'Gorman (1995) described how McCloskey's ideas draw attention to the potential of literary criticism to reveal how economic texts accomplished their results. Stern (1989, 1990) has applied devices of literary criticism to marketing texts in an effort to raise awareness of how marketing language and communicative practice frame our perspective. And we argue that to push marketing toward new ways of understanding itself as a discipline and a body of communicative conventions and practices, we must move beyond the extant and largely taken-for-granted metanarratives of marketing, such as the infallible marketing concept, through which we currently give shape to the world of marketing and ourselves within it. It follows that we must find ways of calling into question the typically uncontested normative patterns of communication, such as those embedded in the form of journal articles that not only define what is sayable, but constrain it as well, in order to reveal the contradictions contained within the ways we typically manage language in our accounts of marketing. For example, when we write of the 'organization' in marketing we must see it as a verb and a process, not merely as a noun describing the imputed content of an occupational category. Of course, 'organization' is also a metaphor. Writing and formalizing our accounts of marketing practice therefore are ways of managing language: we invoke marketing practice through the language that we have access to and through seeking to stage the language effects that are admissible to the marketing academy. We then can understand the many studies of marketing practice that have effectively rediscovered the canons of normative marketing thought (e.g. the more marketing, the better) as examples of the self-justifying effects of marketing discourse.

As Hirschman and Holbrook (1992) suggested, we cannot afford to lose sight of the social and cultural practices that inform and guide the linguistic constructions by means of which we make marketing reality 'real.' If we are to find a way to temporarily evade the unwitting foreclosure of our ideas, then the communicative aspects of generating and disseminating marketing knowledge through communicative performances should be subjected to scrutiny in a way that they currently are not, unlike other structural features of the practice of generating marketing knowledge, particularly research design and related issues such as rules of evidence.

Given the issues we have now discussed, it follows that legitimate areas for inquiry include our assumptions about acceptable compositional forms and textual organization, assumptions about acceptable styles of written expression and representation in journals and books, and embedded norms regarding presentational practices at conferences, seminars, in the boardroom, and in the classroom, or other venues where we are required to perform our marketing knowledge and to manage those performances. Thus, as Williamson (1978) argued for advertising, we should begin to explore how texts, both written and verbal, textual and visual, formal and informal, are used symbolically in particular social and cultural contexts to achieve particular effects, rather than focusing on the supposed literal or technical meaning of words (Phillips and McQuarrie 2004).

The crux of the matter resides in the reflexive nature of marketing communications. In marketing research about marketing communications we cannot escape the problem of language and discourse. Nor can we go beyond language and discourse in order to look at an issue from an objective and distant perspective, for we end up having to use the medium of language to construct this objectivity through presupposing objects and distance. As the famed communication guru Marshall McLuhan once observed, 'the personal and social consequences of any medium—that is, of any extension of ourselves—result from the new scale that is introduced into our affairs by each extension of ourselves' (1964: 7). Thus, researchers are not only part of what they study; additionally, they influence it in the very process of studying it, transforming it through the researcher's gaze that envelopes it within the conventions of particular media. One way of dealing with this issue, as Hammersley and Atkinson (1983) suggested, is not to engage in futile attempts to eliminate the effects of the researcher, but rather to write our research accounts in a more reflexive way; in a way that lets the reader follow the operation of the writer's hand in the act of crafting the text. In other words, authors must put enough of themselves in the text so that readers can recognize that the author is an actor in the text, too (Watson 1995). The active reader perspective is also very popular among contemporary understanding of how advertising is consumed, where readers of advertising texts are seen as the final authors of such texts, actively involved in the construction and negotiation of advertising meanings (O'Donohoe 2000).

RHETORIC AS PERSUASIVE DISCOURSE

Drawing inspiration from the work of Williamson (1978), Bauman (1986), and Clifford (1994), we suggest that the persuasiveness and coherence of marketing science relies not only on conventions governing the logic of evidence, proposition, and reason, but also on such literary devices as metaphor, analogy, and allegory. As Seidman (1994) and Watson (1995) observed, it is through the strategic use of such devices in our compositions that we can bring coherence and meaning to our spoken and written statements. Rhetoric and figures of speech therefore play an integral part in the research process, by virtue of their power to conjure up images that lend authority, legitimacy, and persuasiveness to lines of argument (Whyte 1981). The craft of the effective marketing communicator resides not only in the careful presentation of information, but in the creative art of weaving narratives, visuals, and commentary together, supported with appropriate imagery, into what will inevitably be a highly designed product, composed deliberately in anticipation of achieving desired effects among a target audience. Just think of the great care and effort involved in writing a report for a client: circulating drafts for comment and input; strategically melding structure, style, evidence, text, and image to deliver the desired points; editing the text carefully word by word, phrase by phrase, to ensure the end product strikes the right note before it is released for publication and circulation.

Writers not only cast a narrative beam on the activities of research participants or the expectations of a target audience, they also play an active role in shaping those activities and expectations through the rhetorical devices they employ in putting words together, and weighing up the pros and cons of arguments, propositions, and admissible interpretations of data. All of these activities are cast in language, ranging from the terse nomothetic modes of expression of mathematics and statistics, to more textual-based content. Thus, we argue that accounts of marketing science also exhibit a rhetorical character, even if a limited repertoire of literary devices is currently admissible to the academy.

As an example of the literary character of marketing communications, consider the boldly speculative paper by Peter and Olsen (1983), 'Is Science Marketing?,' published in the *Journal of Marketing*. In this intriguing paper the authors made metaphorical use of the 4 'Ps' of the marketing mix and target marketing to build a simple syllogistic line of argument crudely capable of answering the question of whether science is marketing, without a trace of irony. Elsewhere, Brown (1995) provided an illuminating example of how it is possible to deconstruct the notion that the marketing discipline is in crisis through the creative use of marketing rhetoric, where the crisis being referred to is that surrounding the declared scientific character of marketing research and knowledge making. He concluded that some marketing scholars may be claiming that the field is in crisis, or attempt to engineer it into a crisis, as a rhetorical device to pursue their own publishing interests. After all, cries of scientific crises emanating from fully paid-up members of the marketing establishment do tend to generate interest among editors and publishers, encouraging them to free up space for measured debate and discussion before, of course, returning to business as usual. In essence, Brown provided a timely example of the staging of contemporary truth effects by those attempting to 'talk up' the crisis. He also highlighted the recursive nature of marketing discourse in action, given that he could not write about the staging of the crisis in marketing without there being the effects of a staged crisis to discuss—otherwise known as the *performative contradiction*; that is, an anticrisis view cannot exist without there already being in place a crisis view.

CRITIQUING MARKETING DISCOURSE

One means of analyzing marketing discourse is provided by critical discourse analysis (Fairclough 1995). Set within the context of wider social relations, structures, and processes, this method focuses on the practices involved in the production, communication, and consumption of a text; that is, the linguistic outcome of a discursive event such as a meeting, a conversation, or a report. This approach involves three levels of analysis: (*a*) close reading of the text in terms of vocabulary, structure, grammar, syntax, etc.; (*b*) the processes of production, dissemination, and interpretation in terms of the text's relationship to genres, voices, the author, the reader, and other texts; and (*c*) the wider context in which the discursive practices are embedded, including power relations and ideology as revealed through the situational, institutional, sociocultural, and political structures (Althusser 1966).

A topical example of the way in which particular marketing texts can be analyzed is reflected by written works that emphasize (and in some cases, attempt to quantify) the impact of marketing on shareholder value (e.g. Doyle 2000). On one level, this trend in the literature can be understood as an attempt to reassert or merely remind readers of the 'relevance' of marketing tools and techniques (developed in the 1970s and 1980s) to the pursuit of corporate financial goals, through updating and reorienting them to the dynamics of the contemporary competitive environment. Another interpretation is that this is all part of a perceived publishing opportunity driven by the wider professional struggle to improve the relative positioning of marketing practitioners vis-à-vis accounting and finance, human resources, engineering, procurement, and the like. At another level, the selection of this literature's terminology and topic suggests that its 'target audience' includes not only business managers, but also analysts and shareholders. This implies that such writing not only seeks to demonstrate marketing's value to such shareholders, but also is posited in the 'language' of shareholder value.

Taking a broader view of the wider circumstances in which these texts were conceived, written, and published as responses to perceived business opportunities involves a consideration of the interests of persons (such as authors, readers, shareholders, employees, and distributors) who could be said to gain from such a course of action.

It can be argued that the struggle for influence between the managerial professions is in terms of capturing or defining the 'interests' of capital. Armstrong (1984) demonstrated that such interests represent highly contested strategic territory, not merely an objective, predefined investment heuristic. And as organizations continue to downsize and dismantle functionally based organizational structures, competition between managerial disciplines will continue to intensify. A similar contextual analysis may account for the newly improved 'shareholder value-orientated' marketing texts. The marketing profession is competing (for survival, some would argue) by defining and demonstrating marketing's function in achieving not simply 'profitability' or contribution to 'the bottom line,' but in terms of being able to put forward a persuasive case for laying claim to *the central role* in defining the dominant contemporary measure of business performance, the creation of shareholder value. Today, 'competitive success' sounds rather tame by comparison.

In marketing's early days, during the 1950s and 1960s, much marketing discourse utilized the techniques, tools, and language of psychology in order to demonstrate that it possessed the means to understand 'customer' behavior, with the customer serving as the presumed central focus of business. Psychology's behavioristic view regarded the consumer as a conditioned organism, open to reconditioning. Even contemporary advertising textbooks frequently position the consumer audience as a noncognitive 'behaving machine,' automatically reacting within a landscape filled with signifying stimuli from the promotional mix (Shankar and Horton 1999).

A more contemporary view of marketing is based on a dominant technical-rational view of knowledge from which it 'naturally' follows that consumers are knowable entities with characteristics that can be identified and measured like natural phenomena (Morgan 1992). Thus, historically, marketing has strategically generated so-called 'technologies of governance' through securing its control of market research and extending this through new information technology (IT) driven discourses, such as customer relationship management (CRM). Such discursive developments ensure the never-ending need for marketing because of its dual 'dialectical' role in generating knowledge about customers, as well as acting on this knowledge through marketing mixes targeted at specific customer groups. In addition, some argue that perpetuating the interests of marketing in this way also perpetuates, not the sovereignty of consumers, but their subservience to technorational discourse and apparatus of the 'free' market and the interests of various marketing experts. According to Horkheimer (1967: 345) 'the majesty of the customer... hardly plays any part any longer for the individual in relation to the advertising apparatus, the standardization of commodities and other economic realities.'

EMERGING MARKETING TRENDS AND DISCOURSE ANALYSIS

Looking ahead as we move further into the twenty-first century, the dominance of marketing's technocontrol language and techniques may be expected to decline with the continuing advance of relationship marketing and its central focus on individual customers, their satisfaction, and the relational antecedents of commitment and trust. It certainly is true that relational thinking has had a fundamental impact on marketing over the last two decades. The discipline has moved from a single dominant approach characterized by transactions, tool-boxes, and military metaphors, to include alternative practices informed by the nature of human relationships, the importance of social networks, and customer (not simply shareholder) value. However, this does not necessarily mean that a total 'paradigm shift' has occurred. Marketing can be viewed today as a set of pluralistic approaches from transactional to relational (Brodie et al. 1997). Advances in information technology have facilitated the deployment of these new approaches way *beyond* their origin in business-to-business marketing, and into the provision of customized services and mass consumer goods retailing.

The move towards more relational practices and thinking recently has been subject to criticism, and some even argue that there is nothing new about it. The 'new' concepts and language are simply reinventions of the same old marketing methods—'the emperor's new clothes,' as Gummesson (1997) has described it. Certainly, marketing has always been concerned with the influence, if not manipulation, of consumer demand. However, we suggest that the ethos of 'relationship' marketing is different in the following regards: (*a*) the objective has shifted from sale closure to customer retention and loyalty; (*b*) marketing communications, information, and delivery are customized for the individual consumer, rather than mass segmentation; and (*c*) IT-enabled techniques are employed not only to stimulate desires and needs, but more fundamentally to develop identity with the brand, psychological (as opposed to behavioral) loyalty, and customer 'lock-in.'

DOMESTICATING MARKETING ACADEMICS

In order to map the contours of marketing discourse, we must first look at the forms and styles of communicative practices admissible within the marketing academy. One could speculate that the knowledge base and expertise that marketing managers bring to their judgments, decisions, and activities are likely to be wider than that captured by normative marketing prescriptions and related techniques. Such prescriptions will achieve expression through a conceptual vocabulary and rhetorical effects embedded within a repertoire of communicative practice that is accessible to socialized (i.e. domesticated) members of the marketing academy.

The use of concepts and rhetoric by marketing practitioners to articulate and explain their professional 'practice' may be further influenced by two important considerations. First, the conceptual vocabulary of marketing is increasingly accessible to both marketing researchers and managers. Both constituencies appropriate it strategically in pursuit of their own interests—typically to accomplish persuasive effects in their communicative practice, whether writing for a journal or making a pitch for business to potential clients. This shared vocabulary not only informs the way researchers formulate and ask research questions, it also informs the thinking of managers and so forms the basis by which managers can construct their answers when they feel it is in their interest to do so. Many marketing managers are now fluent in the 'techno-speak' of marketing academia and can easily talk to researchers using this vocabulary when they think it appropriate to do so. Second, while it is hardly surprising to find that the tales that marketing practitioners tell researchers are prepackaged for academic consumption, those representations need careful scrutiny because the effect is to legitimize the point being made, and potentially to distort it.

At one level the researcher may take some solace from the notion that informants are able to articulate and communicate views in a way that the marketer can understand. But, this does not mean that what goes on within the organization is made any more transparent. At another level, one could say that managers are strategically deploying the 'expert speak' language of marketing in order to rationalize and protect the judgments and thinking lurking in the shadows of the tales they tell. Whether they do so deliberately or unintentionally is not at issue here. Rather, it is the value of the effect on researchers of being aware of the need to bring different readings or interpretations to the local context under study; of being able to place themselves as actors in the construction of those readings; and of understanding the provisionality of any accounts that are derived from those readings.

There is an interesting symbolism operating in situations where the practitioner and the academic exchange opinions: managers tell academics a few stories, laced with the virtuous details of real-world events, which may then be related with great gusto and elan by the academics to their students; in return, the managers acquire the organizational kudos of successfully manipulating inquiring academics. Whatever view is taken, it is difficult to escape the conclusion that managers, as well as academics, are implicated in the representations that circulate in marketing discourse.

Although both parties are inscribers of marketing practice, academics have to move beyond naive literal interpretations of interview transcripts as an analytical strategy, just as their management informants often have done.

The danger of not understanding the dynamics of research as communicative practice is that survey respondents may have important insights that can become distorted when they try to use 'normal' marketing terminology and rhetoric; that is, they are forced 'to wear the wrong clothes.' This typically is the case with survey designs employing self-completion instruments, especially where pretesting is poor and questions are expressed in terms that, although consistent with the literature, do not necessarily render the issues in ways that resonate with the lived experience of respondents.

Research into the communicative practice of marketing management should also look at these other 'dimensions' of experience, especially judgment and creativity, which are in danger of being hidden by the limitations of the normative marketing discourse. Practitioners may have imminent and insistent experience and knowledge of these other dimensions that cannot be given expression through the received concepts and language of marketing.

CONCLUSION: TALKING THE TALK

We have argued that the problem of understanding marketing practice lies less with marketing practitioners than with the marketing academy and its understanding of itself as it is manifest in its communicative practices. We have sought to show how it is possible to deny that there is any single, inevitable or deep language that is determinative of marketing management. We have also argued that it is no longer sufficient to try to continue to evade this problem through ignoring language and discourse as legitimate areas of inquiry in marketing. It is necessary to look for ways of problematizing marketing discourse through a disruption of the normative patterns of representation if marketers are to better understand themselves as a community, with their own rather curious, and perhaps stifling, rituals, conventions, images, and systems of representation.

We also argue that the poverty of much marketing rhetoric resides in its effect, in the sense that it projects one view of marketing practice onto the research base itself and delineates that which can be talked about and thus 'known.' Our research should permit marketing practitioners to talk of sensations, judgments, impressions, emotions, and visions, which arguably comprise the ways in which the customer is creatively 'understood.' However, before we can expect marketing practitioners to engage in non-literal discussions, marketing scholars and students must open their eyes to these issues. What is it about marketing practice that we do not notice, that we cannot see, and of which we dare not speak, or that we can see, but turn a blind eye to because our domesticated research imperatives will not admit discussion of it as acceptable practice or evidence? We believe that marketing scholars must broach such issues in their journals and conferences or else their research practice will continue to mine and represent a very narrow vein of human experience and endeavor.

We argue that it is in the marketing academy's interest to better understand the tensions within the discourse and to influence their character, but not to resolve them through diktat. On the contrary, in order to enrich current discourse we should seek to expand the existing repertoire of accounts of the practices that define the conditions of possibility of marketing processes. The challenge for opening up marketing discourse requires that we reflect upon ideas that we often take for granted about what can and cannot be said about marketing, especially given that markets, consumers, marketing management, marketing managers and marketing academics are all called into being through the language we employ.

Finally, we suggest that marketing communicators should be guided by the insights of Law (1994) in their attempts to analyze marketing discourse. That is, marketing communicators must try to achieve reflexivity and focus more attention on marketing discourse as a set of patterns that might be imputed to the networks of the marketing academy; they should encourage discourses in the plural, not discourse in the singular; they should treat those discourses as ordering attempts, not orders; they should explore how the discourses are performed, embodied, and related in different textual materials and discursive practices; and they should consider the ways in which those materials and practices interact with wider circumstance and cultural change.

REFERENCES

Althusser, L. (1966). *For Marx*. London: Verso.

Armstrong, P. (1984). 'Competition Between the Organised Professions and the Evolution of Management Control Strategies', in K. Thompson (ed.), *Work, Employment and Unemployment*. Milton Keynes, UK: Oxford University Press.

Baker, M., Hart, S., Black, C., and Abdel-Mohsen, T. (1986). 'The Contribution of Marketing to Competitive Success: A Literature Review', *Journal of Marketing Management*, 2, 39–61.

Baudrillard, J. (1981). *For a Critique of the Political Economy of the Sign*. St Louis, MO: Telos Press.

Bauman, Z. (1986). 'Is There a Postmodern Sociology?,' *Theory, Culture and Society*, 5, 217–37.

Billing, M. (1987). *Arguing and Thinking: A Rhetorical Approach to Social Psychology*. Cambridge: Cambridge University Press.

Bloom, M. (1973). *The Anxiety of Influence: A Theory of Poetry*. New York: Oxford University Press.

Bourdieu, P. (1994). *Distinction: A Social Critique of the Judgement of Taste*. London: Routledge.

Boylan, T. and O'Gorman, P. (1995). *Beyond Rhetoric and Realism in Economics: Towards a Reformulation of Economic Methodology*. London: Routledge.

Brodie, R., Coviello, N., Brooks, R., and Little, V. (1997). 'Towards a Paradigm Shift in Marketing? An Examination of Current Marketing Practices', *Journal of Marketing Management*, 13, 383–406.

Brown, S. (1995). 'Life Begins at 40? Further Thoughts on Marketing's "mid-life crisis" ', *Marketing Intelligence and Planning*, 13, 4–17.

Brownlie, D. and Saren, M. (1997). 'Beyond the One-dimensional Marketing Manager: The Discourse of Theory, Practice and Relevance', *International Journal of Research in Marketing*, 14, 147–61.

—— , —— , Wensley, R., and Whittington, R. (eds.). (1999). *Rethinking Marketing: Towards Critical Marketing Accountings*. London: Sage.

Burger, P. and Luckman, T. (1966). *The Social Construction of Reality: A Treatise in the Sociology of Knowledge*. Garden City, NY: Doubleday.

Burton, D (2002). 'Towards a Critical Multicultural Theory', *Marketing Theory*, 2 (2), 207–36.

Clifford, J. (1994). 'On Ethnographic Allegory', in S. Seidman, (ed.), *The Postmodern Turn*, Cambridge, UK: Cambridge University Press, pp. 205–28.

Catterall, M., Maclaren, P., and Stevens, L. (1999). Marketing and Feminism: Past, Present and Future. Available: www.mngt.waikato.ac.nz

Crane, A. (1997). 'The Dynamics of Marketing Ethical Products', *Journal of Marketing Management*, 13, 561–77.

Derrida, J. (1978). *Writing and Difference*. Chicago: University of Chicago Press.

Doyle, P. (1985). 'Marketing and the Competitive Performance of British Industry', *Journal of Marketing Management*, 1, 87–98.

—— (2000). *Value-based Marketing: Marketing Strategies for Corporate Growth and Shareholder Value*. Chichester, UK: Wiley.

DuGay, P. and Salaman, G. (1992). 'The Cult(ure) of the Customer', *Journal of Management Studies*, 29, 615–33.

Eagleton, T. (1991). *Ideology: An Introduction*. London: Verso.

Elliott, R. and Wattanasuwan, K. (1998). 'Brands as Resources for the Symbolic Construction of Identity', *International Journal of Advertising*, 17, 131-144.

Fairclough, N. (1995). *Critical Discourse Analysis: The Critical Study of Language*. London: Longmans.

Firat, A.F. and Venkatesh, A. (1993). 'Postmodernity: The Age of Marketing', *International Journal of Research in Marketing*, 10, 227–49.

Foucault, M. (1981). *The History of Sexuality*, Vol. 1: *An introduction*. Harmondsworth, UK: Penguin.

Fuller, D.A. (1999). *Sustainable Marketing: Managerial-ecological Issues*. London: Sage.

Gergen, K. (1992). 'Organization Theory in the Postmodern Era', in M. Reed and M. Hughes (eds.), *Rethinking Organization: New Directions in Organizational Theory and Analysis*, London: Sage, pp. 207–26.

Goffman, E. (1971). *The Presentation of Self in Everyday Life*. London: Penguin.

Goldman, R. and Papson, S. (1996). *Sign Wars: The Cluttered Landscape of Advertising*. New York: Guilford Press.

Gummesson, E. (1997). 'Relationship Marketing as a Paradigm Shift: Some Conclusions from the 30R Approach', *Management Decision*, 35, 267–73.

Hackley, C. (2001). *Marketing and Social Construction*. London: Routledge.

Hammersley, M. and Atkinson, P. (1983). *Ethnography: Principles in Practice*. London: Routledge.

Hastings, G. and Saren, M. (2003). 'The Critical Contribution of Social Marketing', *Marketing Theory*, 3, 305–22.

Hirschman, E. and Holbrook, M. (1992). *Postmodern Consumer Research: The Study of Consumption as Text*. London: Sage.

Horkheimer, M. (1967). *Zur Kritik der Instrumentellen Vernunft*. [Towards a Critique of Instrumental Reason]. Frankfurt am Meine: Europäische Verlagsanstalt.

Hunt, S. (1993). 'On Rethinking Marketing: Our Discipline, our Practice, our Methods', *European Journal of Marketing*, 28, 13–25.

Jeffcutt, P. (1994). 'The Interpretation of Organization: A Contemporary Analysis and Critique', *Journal of Management Studies*, 31, 225–50.

Jeffcutt, P. (1994). 'From Interpretation to Representation', in J. Hassard and M. Parker (eds.), *Postmodernism and Organizations*, London: Sage, pp. 25–48.

Kristeva, J. (1969). *Semeiotike: Researches for a Semioanalysis*. Paris: Editions du Seuil.

Law, J. (1994). *Organising Modernity*. Oxford: Blackwell.

McCloskey, D. (1990). 'Reply to Munz', *Journal of the History of Ideas*, 51, 143–47.

—— . (1985). 'The Rhetoric of Economics', *The Journal of Economic Literature*, 21, 481–517.

McLuhan, M. (1964). *Understanding Media*. New York: Routledge & Kegan Paul.

Marcuse, H. (1964). *One-dimensional Man: Studies in the Ideology of Advanced Industrial Society*. London: Routledge and Kegan Paul.

Morgan, G. (1992). 'Marketing Discourse and Practice: Towards a Critical Analysis', in M. Alvesson and H. Willmott (eds.), *Critical Management Studies*, London: Sage, pp. 136–58.

Munz, P. (1990). 'The Rhetoric of Rhetoric', *Journal of the History of Ideas*, 51, 121–42.

Myerson, G. (1994). *Rhetoric, Reason & Society: Rationality as Dialogue*. London: Sage.

Nava, M., Blake, A., MacRury, I., and Richards, B. (1997). *Buy this Book: Studies in Advertising and Consumption*. London: Routledge.

O'Donohoe, S. (2000). 'Reading Advertising Texts: Understanding Advertising Consumption', in S. Beckmann and R. Elliot (eds.), *Interpretive Consumer Research: Paradigms, Methodologies and Applications*, Copenhagen: Copenhagen University Press, pp. 151–75.

Parker, M. (2002). *Against Management: Organisation in the Age of Managerialism*. Cambridge: Polity Press.

Peter, J. and Olsen, J. (1983). 'Is Science Marketing?', *Journal of Marketing*, 47, 11–125.

Potter, J. and Wetherell, M. (1987). *Discourse and Social Psychology: Beyond Attitudes and Behaviour.* London: Sage.

Phillips, B. and McQuarrie, E. (2004). 'Beyond Visual Metaphor: A New Typology of Visual Rhetoric in Advertising', *Marketing Theory*, 4, 113–36.

Rorty, R. (1979). *Philosophy and the Mirror of Nature.* Princeton, NJ: Princeton University.

Rouleau, L. and Seguin, F. (1995). 'Strategy and Organization Theories : Common Forms of Discourse', *Journal of Management Studies*, 32, 1, 1–17.

Seidman, S. (1994). *The Postmodern Turn: New Perspectives on Social Theory.* Cambridge, UK: Cambridge University Press.

Schipper, F. (2002). 'The Relevance of Horkheimer's View of the Customer', *European Journal of Marketing*, 36, 23–35.

Schultz, D., Tannenbaum, S., and Lauterborn, R. (1994). *Integrated Marketing Communications.* Chicago: NTC Business Books.

Shankar, A. and Horton, B. (1999). 'Ambient Media: Advertising's New Media Opportunity?', *International Journal of Advertising*, 18, 305–21.

Schroeder, J. (2003). *Visual Consumption.* London: Routledge.

Steiner, G. (1961). *The Retreat from the Word.* London: Faber & Faber.

Stern, B. (1989). 'Literary Criticism and Consumer Research: Overview and Illustrative Analysis', *Journal of Consumer Research*, 16, 322–34.

—— (1990). 'Literary Criticism and the History of Marketing Thought: A New Perspective on "reading" Marketing Theory', *Journal of the Academy of Marketing Science*, 18, 329–36.

Svensson, P. (2003). *Setting the Marketing Scene: Reality Production in Everyday Marketing Work.* Lund, Sweden: Lund Business Press.

Swales, J. and Rogers, P. (1995). 'Discourse and the Projection of Corporate Culture: The Mission Statement', *Discourse and Society*, 6, 223–42.

Watson, T. (1995). Shaping the Story: Rhetoric and Creative Writing in Organizational Ethnography. *Studies in Organizations and Societies*, 1, 301–11.

Weick, K. (1979). *The Social Psychology of Organising.* Reading, MA: Addison-Wesley.

Wernick, A. (1991). *Promotional Culture: Advertising Ideology and Symbolic Expression.* London: Sage.

Whyte, W. (1981). *Street Corner Society: The Social Structure of an Italian Slum.* Chicago: University of Chicago Press.

Williamson, J. (1978). *Decoding Advertisements: Ideology and Meaning in Advertising.* London: Marion Boyars.

Index